The Impact of Incomplete Contracts on Economics

The Impact
of Incomplete Contracts
on Economics

EDITED BY PHILIPPE AGHION
MATHIAS DEWATRIPONT
PATRICK LEGROS
and
LUIGI ZINGALES

OXFORD
UNIVERSITY PRESS

OXFORD
UNIVERSITY PRESS

Oxford University Press is a department of the University of Oxford. It furthers the University's objective of excellence in research, scholarship, and education by publishing worldwide. Oxford is a registered trade mark of Oxford University Press in the UK and in certain other countries

Published in the United States of America by Oxford University Press
198 Madison Avenue, New York, NY 10016, United States of America

Library of Congress Cataloging-in-Publication Data
Names: Aghion, Philippe, editor.
Title: The impact of incomplete contracts on economics / edited by Philippe
Aghion, Mathias Dewatripont, Patrick Legros, Luigi Zingales.
Description: New York : Oxford University Press, 2016. | Includes bibliographical references and index.
Identifiers: LCCN 2015034912 | ISBN 9780199826216 (paperback)
Subjects: LCSH: Incomplete contracts—United States. | BISAC: BUSINESS & ECONOMICS /
Economics / Theory. | LAW / Contracts. | BUSINESS & ECONOMICS / Business Law.
Classification: LCC KF817 .I47 2016 | DDC 346.7302/2—dc23 LC record available at
http://lccn.loc.gov/2015034912

1 3 5 7 9 8 6 4 2

Printed by Sheridan Books, USA.

CONTENTS

FOREWORD

PHILIPPE AGHION, MATHIAS DEWATRIPONT, PATRICK LEGROS,
AND LUIGI ZINGALES

The book collects the presentations and discussions made at the conference celebrating the 25th anniversary of the publication of "Grossman and Hart (1986).[1] The conference brought together scholars who, in different fields, have used and explored Grossman and Hart's key insights. The collection of these essays represents a unique up-to-date analysis of the broad set of applications of the incomplete contract framework.

The GH framework was developed to answer a somewhat naive but fundamental question, raised by Ronald Coase in 1932 during his undergraduate studies: if the market is an efficient method of resource allocation, then why do so many transactions take place within firms? There was no model at the time to address this question. Coase (1937) relied on informal arguments for the existence of firms, particularly emphasizing haggling problems in decentralized market transactions, which he thought authority within firms could partly overcome. In other words, firms exist because there are costs to using the price mechanism: prices must become known, bargains must be made, contracts must be written.

These ideas were not formalized, and until the 1970s all we could find in a formal textbook was the neoclassical theory of the firm: namely, there are economies of scale (or scope) which justify that production activities up to some efficient scale (or up to efficient variety) be concentrated within one firm rather

---

[1] The conference took place at the Université Libre de Bruxelles in June 2011 and had benefited from the financial support of the Communauté Française de Belgique, ECARES, the Initiative on Global Markets (Chicago Booth), and Cornerstone Research and Analysis Group. Part of this introduction as well as the five survey papers in chapters 6, 9, 12, 18 and 21 have been published as part of a special issue of the *Journal of Law, Economics and Organization* which has graciously granted the right to reproduce them in this book. We thank Pablo Spiller and the editors of the journal for their help during the editorial process and for having been supportive of this project.

than being scattered across multiple producers. This approach, however, raised the question: why can't one get around the diseconomies of scale or scope by just creating new plants within a same firm?

The 1970s witnessed the emergence of so-called agency theories. According to the agency view of the firm (in fashion in the late 1970s and early 1980s), firms help solve agency problems, whether these emanate from moral hazard (the agent's action or effort is unobservable by the principal) or from adverse selection (the agent's type is unobserved by the principal). In other words, it is easier for a firm owner (principal) to monitor an employee than an independent subcontractor. The problem is that the theory does not explain why agency problems are different within and across firms, nor can it explain what the notion of "merging" even means in a world of optimal complete contracting.

An important precursor to incomplete contract theory and the modern theory of the firm is Williamson (1971, 1975, 1979): his basic insight is that market transactions can become very costly when agents have to make relationship-specific investments. For example, suppose an electricity generator has to locate near a coal mine (this example obviously predates the debates on global warming). Building a new generator involves a sunk investment. However, once this investment is sunk, the generator firm finds itself in a bilateral monopoly situation vis-à-vis the coal mine, and the coal mine will typically take advantage of this situation when bargaining ex post with the generator firm. This ex post "hold-up" situation may then result in the generator firm getting too little of the ex post revenues to cover its initial sunk investment. Then, anticipating this, the generator may simply decide not to make the investment altogether.

Now, why don't the two parties simply write a contingent contract ex ante, whereby the generator firm is entitled to a minimum revenue share if it makes the sunk investment. Williamson's answer is that ex post asymmetric information or moral hazard problems may be unavoidable. In that case, vertical integration between the generator firm and the coal mine is one way to ensure that the investment will be sunk, as integration simply eliminates the scope for ex post opportunism. However, Williamson's theory leaves the following question unanswered: aren't there costs (not just benefits) to vertical integration, which could explain why firms have boundaries and why not all transactions are taking place within a single firm?

With their path-breaking paper on the costs and benefits of vertical integration Grossman and Hart (1986) develop a powerful answer to these questions. The basic idea is that contracts cannot specify all states of natures or all actions in advance (for example, because agents are boundedly rational); or there are states of nature or actions which cannot be verified by third parties ex post and therefore are not ex ante contractible either. The best evidence we have that contracts are incomplete in practice is that we observe renegotiation, whereas a complete optimal contract is never renegotiated in equilibrium. Now if we admit that contracts are incomplete, then one immediately obtains a theory of ownership and vertical integration. In a nutshell, when contracts are incomplete, and consequently not all uses of an asset can be specified in advance, the contract negotiated ex ante inevitably leaves some discretion over the use of the assets. Who decides in these contractual holes? Grossman and Hart (1986) define the "owner" of the firm as the party who has the right to decide in all the contractual holes, that is, the party with the residual rights of control. These residual rights give the owner the ability to hold up the other party involved. The hold-up power does not affect the efficiency of the ex post outcome: in Grossman and Hart (1986), bargaining is frictionless. But it does determine the division of the surplus. In the ex post bargaining the owner is able to capture a larger share of the benefits of his investment. The benefit of integration, thus, is that the owner has more incentive to invest in the relationship. The cost is that the other party will tend to underinvest in the relationship.

Grossman and Hart go on to argue that the optimal governance structure is the one that maximizes the ex ante surplus, given that contractual relations between parties are typically incomplete. For instance, the contracting parties may have a common understanding of the quality of a good to be traded, but this might not be understood by a third party such as a court of law. Hence, certain contracts may be unenforceable, and the parties may have to rely on ex post bargaining. When costly private investments in the production process need to be made ex ante, this contractual incompleteness can lead to efficiency losses. When there are no constraints on the trading of ownership rights, for example, when the parties have access to nondistortionary finance, optimal governance structures are those that provide the incentives that best minimize the efficiency losses.

In the next chapters, John Moore, Bengt Holmström, and Jean Tirole reminisce about the genesis of the incomplete contract approach and why it has proven so influential, then Steve Tadelis and Thomas Hubbard highlight the need to make the theory operational for applied economists. The following chapters illustrate how incredibly helpful the GH paradigm has been to improve our understanding of firms' organizations, markets, and institutions and how applied economists have been able to develop strategies to identify some of the GH effects.

Sections 1 to 8 illustrate the wealth of fields and questions that have benefited from the incomplete contract (IC) approach. IC helped apprehend the determinants of firm size and firm's decisions whether or when to vertically integrate (chapter 1); shed light on the determinants of firms' internal organization (chapter 2); and has been used to analyze firms' financial decisions (chapter 3), business alliances, or the performance of small firms (chapter 4). It has also led to new questions and answers to old questions on the interplay between firm organization and market performance (chapter 5); on the relationship between trade flows, intrafirm trade patterns, and the international organization of production (chapter 6); the role of public ownership (chapter 7); or the design of institutions in a political context (chapter 8). This suggests that IC "works in practice." The papers in section 9 tell us whether IC also "works in theory," that is, whether there are theoretical foundations for the paradigm. This chapter is also a way to go back on the active controversy that took place following Grossman and Hart (1986) about the possibility for clever mechanisms to undo the incompleteness of contracts. The papers in section 10 suggest that behavioral approaches, for example, the idea that contracts may serve as a reference point, may make IC "work in experiments" also.

All together, the papers in this book document the broad applications of the GH framework. They also suggest that time has come to make operational the basic qualitative insights of incomplete contract theory. This step forward requires linking ownership or integration decisions to variables that can be quantified and also providing a framework for identification. This book is therefore not only a way to celebrate the anniversary of the Grossman and Hart (1986) contribution but also a way to highlight a path forward and the importance for the incomplete contracting ideas to permeate empirical and experimental work.

References

Coase, Ronald H. (1937). The Nature of the Firm. Economica, 4(16), 386–405.

Grossman, S., and O. Hart 1986. "The Costs and Benefits of Ownership: A Theory of Vertical and Lateral Integration." *Journal of Political Economy* 94: 691–719.

Williamson, Oliver (1971), "The Vertical Integration of Production: Market Failure Considerations," American Economic Review, 61, 112–23.

Williamson, Oliver (1975), Markets and Hierarchies: Analysis and Antitrust Implications, The Free Press, New York.

Williamson, Oliver (1979), "Transaction Cost Economics: The Governance of Contractual Relations," Journal of Law and Economics, 22, 233–261.

The Impact of Incomplete Contracts on Economics

PART 1

PERSPECTIVES ON GROSSMAN AND HART (1986)

Introductory Remarks on Grossman and Hart (1986)

JOHN MOORE

You may be wondering who would have the temerity to make remarks about a masterpiece from the annals of economic thought? (Evidently, this piece started life as a speech, opening the conference to celebrate the twenty-fifth anniversary of the publication of Sandy and Oliver's article, and it hasn't managed to shake off its rhetorical roots.)

Let me explain. Back in 1986, the editors of the *Journal of Political Economy* in their wisdom published "The Costs and Benefits of Ownership: A Theory of Vertical and Lateral Integration" by Sanford Grossman and Oliver Hart. The same august journal subsequently published, in 1990, another article by Oliver Hart, "Property Rights and the Nature of the Firm", this time coauthored with John Moore. Taken together, the two articles make up what is known as the GHM Property Rights Theory. I am M. In recent Bond movies I've been played by Judi Dench, then Ralph Fiennes.

How did I get on to the GHM ticket? When I was a graduate student at the London School of Economics (LSE), Oliver phoned me quite out of the blue and asked if I would like to work with him. Me! I wasn't even his student. He wasn't even at the LSE. It was my Kate Middleton moment. Picked from a bevy of beauties by the Handsome Prince himself. Well, the parallels aren't exact. But I would like to take this opportunity to put on record that the moment Oliver chose to work with me was the turning point of my intellectual life, and I thank him.

I first met Sandy when he was visiting Oliver at the LSE. His reputation went before him: completed a Chicago PhD at the age of $12^3/_4$, rapidly followed by tenure as an Ivy League Full Professor. When I knocked on Oliver's door, I couldn't believe it when Sandy sprang to his feet and warmly shook me by the hand, saying what a pleasure it was for him to meet me. I think he mistook me for Jim Mirrlees.

The GHM moniker is so flattering (to me) that it's incumbent on me to propose a small modification. At the twenty-fifth anniversary celebrations, our drinks were laced with a drug having this molecular formula:

$$
\begin{array}{ccc}
 & \text{H} & \text{H} \\
 & | & | \\
\text{H} - & \text{C} - \text{C} & - \text{O} - \text{H} \\
 & | & | \\
 & \text{H} & \text{H}
\end{array}
$$

Ethyl alcohol: C_2H_6O (or, more properly, ethanol: CH_3CH_2OH). No one would ever write it as CHO, because that wouldn't give any sense of the respective contributions of the three elements that make up the molecule. And I think that by the same logic, no one should write GHM. So I'd like to propose a citations based way of writing the various multiletter theories we have in our profession. I'm going to use a Google citation based weighting:

$$G_{5600}H_{9100}M_{3500}$$

That is one heck of a molecule. I should explain that the Grossman-Hart paper had just under 5,600 Google citations at the time of the celebrations. And the Hart-Moore paper I'm afraid had only 3,500. (The passage of time has been kind. At the time of writing [2014], these figures have risen to 8,850 and 5,110 respectively.)

If you divide by 700, you get something a little more manageable. So I propose that our theory is called the

$G_8H_{13}M_5$ Property Rights Theory

to reflect the respective contributions of Grossman, Hart, and Moore. Thank our good fortune it isn't known as "Grossman et al.'s Property Rights Theory," because I'd be Al and Oliver would be E.T.

On the subject of citations, which as you know is the only thing we are judged by, my second contribution here is to introduce what might be called the Average Moore Score (AMS) of any group of economists $\{i = 1, \ldots, I\}$. The idea is to average over their highest number of Google citations:

average maximum [number of Google citations for an article by i]
$\{over\ i\}$ $\{articles\ by\ i\}$

To make it plain, take someone like me, and ask what is my best article in terms of Google citations—no surprise it's the 1990 paper with Oliver, which, at the time of the twenty-fifth anniversary celebrations, had 3,500. Hence my contribution is 3,500. Repeat the question for everyone in the group. Averaging then arrives at the group's AMS.

I did that for all the thirty-seven Nobel Laureates in Economics since 1990, and at the time of the celebrations their AMS was 5,533. Luckily, Grossman-Hart (1986) had 5,576 Google citations, a bigger number. Just. Whew.

But note. That illustrious group's AMS, 5,533, was dominated by the likes of Ronald Coase and people who are cited by psychologists or statisticians. So on reflection, I don't think averaging is necessarily the best way to calculate a Score. It may be better to look at the Median Moore Score (MMS):

median maximum [number of Google citations for an article by *i*]
{*over i*}   {*articles by i*}

The MMS for the same group of thirty-seven Laureates was 2,767. In that context, Grossman and Hart's 5,576 looks good.

The *Journal of Political Economy* used to publish a Hall of Fame—sadly, no longer—which made up a formidable list of papers. For example: Hotelling (1931) on exhaustible resources; Tiebout (1956) on local expenditures; Conrad and Meyer (1958) on slavery; Stigler (1961) on the economics of information; Becker (1968) on crime and punishment; Barro (1974) on Ricardian equivalence; Kydland and Prescott (1977) on rules over discretion; Hall (1978) on the life cycle; Jovanovic (1979) on job matching; Fama (1980) on agency; Diamond and Dybvig (1983) on bank runs; Shleifer and Vishny (1986) on large shareholders; Romer (1986, 1990) on endogenous growth; Krugman (1991) on economic geography. These and many other *JPE* papers make up an astonishing group. And yet, according to the last *JPE* Hall of Fame ranking, which paper beat the lot? Grossman and Hart (1986)! I don't know how the ranking was arrived at, but the only *JPE* article that outranked Grossman-Hart (1986)—rhetorically, I could have done without this—is the Black and Scholes (1973) paper on options pricing (presumably the financial community added considerable heft).

Finally on the matter of statistics, we should always take into account Oliver's 1995 book. (I should say that the Moore Score, average or median, relates only to articles, not books.) Oh, that book. The Good Book. After W.Shakespeare there came O.Hart. *Firms, Contracts and Financial Structure*, a book for the masses: it just flies off the shelves of British bookstores. One can but feel for A.Smith and his *Wealth of Nations*.

Frank Hahn, on one of his royal visits down from Cambridge (England) to give a seminar to the peasants at the LSE, famously pronounced—and I remember this—"Grossman and Hart are now together in Cambridge working on the theory of the firm, but are very depressed about how hard it is." Since, according to Hahn, "Grossman and Hart have IQs unbounded above," it struck us graduate students that the theory of the firm must be very hard indeed.

I understand that the breakthrough in Sandy and Oliver's research came when Sandy acted as an expert witness in an antitrust case. Naturally, Sandy was working pro bono for a little guy (AT&T) defending itself against an oppressive state. Sandy and Oliver found themselves bumping up against the most basic question of all: what is a firm? Indeed, that is the first sentence of their 1986 article. Four years later, Oliver and I began our paper with the same opening line. We obviously must have felt that he and Sandy and hadn't fully figured out the answer.

I would like to tell you about the answer they gave. This is Grossman and Hart (1986) viewed through the lens of Hart-Moore (1990). See Figure 1.1.

There is pair of agents, managers M_1 and M_2—say, me and you, respectively—and a pair of assets a_1 and a_2. There are three dates. At the earliest date 0, ex ante, the parties contract over asset ownership A_1 and A_2. At an interim date $\frac{1}{2}$, a noncooperative game is played of investments x_1 and x_2, which are private and noncontractible. At date 1, ex post, we may or may not trade (in equilibrium we will). If we trade, then our combined utility is $u_1(x_1)$ plus $u_2(x_2)$. Note that these utilities are functions of our respective date $\frac{1}{2}$ investments. If we can't agree terms of trade (off the equilibrium path), then we go our separate ways, and I get $v_1(x_1|A_1)$. Notice that v_1 is a function both of my investment x_1 and, crucially, of the set of assets A_1 that I was given control over back at date 0 when we wrote our contract. And, in the event of breakdown in ex post bargaining, you get $v_2(x_2|A_2)$—where A_2 is the set of assets over which you were given control.

I've already committed a serious crime by saying that the only thing we can contract over at date 0 is who gets to own—to have control over—which assets.

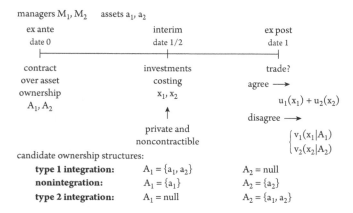

Figure 1.1 Grossman and Hart (1986) viewed through the lens of Hart and Moore (1990)

The crime, of course, is not to justify why we don't write a contract at date 0 to govern the terms of trade at date 1. That is how classical mechanism design would think about it. Even though I'm a criminal, let me plough on.

Since there are just the two of us and just two assets, there is only a small set of simple ownership structures. Three candidates spring to mind. The first is *type 1 integration* where I own both assets and you don't own either. Next, *nonintegration* where I own my asset, a_1, and you own yours, a_2. Finally, *type 2 integration* where you own both assets and I own nothing. (I believe Grossman and Hart [1986] was the first time anyone had formally made the point that there could be a difference between your acquiring my assets—type 2 integration—and my buying yours—type 1.)

A few assumptions, the main one at the end: Define ex post surplus as the sum of the u's minus the sum of the v's—that's what we're bargaining over at date 1—and assume it is positive. Given the way I've set up the algebra, our private investments affect only our own utilities (on or off the equilibrium path), so there are no direct externalities. Another point to bear in mind, slightly more smuggled under the rug of algebra, is that the investments are in human capital only. Why? Because in the algebraic formulation, if the ex post bargaining breaks down, and you, for example, go off with your assets A_2, then those assets aren't affected by your (or my) investment. Let the u's and v's satisfy all the usual assumptions (smooth, strictly increasing, and concave in investment).

Now for the main assumption: for $i = 1$ and 2,

$$\frac{\partial u_i(x_i)}{\partial x_i} > \frac{\partial v_i\left(x_i \mid \{a_1, a_2\}\right)}{\partial x_i} \geq \frac{\partial v_i\left(x_i \mid \{a_i\}\right)}{\partial x_i} \geq \frac{\partial v_i\left(x_i \mid \text{null}\right)}{\partial x_i} \geq 0$$

This line-up of inequalities says that the marginal product of investment by agent M_i within the relationship (u_i) strictly exceeds all M_i's marginal products of investment outside the relationship (the v_i's). The second term in the line-up is the marginal product of investment if M_i owns both assets. From the second inequality we learn that this is larger than if M_i owns only asset a_i. The third inequality says the marginal product is least if M_i owns nothing. In other words, there are complementarities between access to physical assets and returns to investment in human capital. Think of this as an assumption over the sign of the second-order cross-partial derivative of returns with respect to physical and human capital.

We can view the v's as the managers' status quo payoffs in an ex post bargain. Figure 1.2 illustrates.

The 135-degree line is the date 1 utility frontier. The v's, the coordinates of the blob southwest of the utility frontier, is what happens if we don't reach

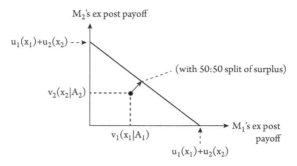

Figure 1.2 The date 1 bargain

agreement, the status quo. We are assumed to divide the surplus equally, taking us from the blob due northeast to hit the frontier.

Now the crucial question is: bearing in mind this 50:50 division of surplus (we have rational expectations about how the bargaining is going to work out at date 1), how will we choose, noncooperatively, to invest at date $\frac{1}{2}$? Here is the answer: for $i = 1$ and 2,

M_i chooses x_i to maximize

$$v_i\left(x_i|A_i\right) + \tfrac{1}{2}\left\{\text{ex post surplus}\right\} - x_i$$

First-order conditions:

$$\tfrac{1}{2}\frac{\partial u_1\left(x_1\right)}{\partial x_1} + \tfrac{1}{2}\frac{\partial v_1\left(x_1|A_1\right)}{\partial x_1} = 1$$

$$\tfrac{1}{2}\frac{\partial u_2\left(x_2\right)}{\partial x_2} + \tfrac{1}{2}\frac{\partial v_2\left(x_2|A_2\right)}{\partial x_2} = 1$$

As agent M_1, I look ahead at my status quo payoff $v_1(x_1|A_1)$ plus my 50% share of the ex post surplus, minus my investment cost x_1 which I've assumed to be one-for-one.

From our respective first-order conditions (FOCs) for our investments emerges the conclusion that both of us are underinvesting relative to first-best. In first-best we would equate the marginal product of investment to the marginal cost of investment (unity); and along the equilibrium path, the products of investment come wholly through the u's—the v's are irrelevant.

When we examine the private optimization problem, however, we discover that the weight we put on the first term on the left-hand side of our FOCs is only $\frac{1}{2}$, because of hold-up. Each of us anticipates that of every dollar we contribute to the joint surplus, fifty cents are going to be stolen by the other party in the bargaining. Little wonder, then, that we have diluted incentives to invest. But there is an offsetting incentive: to feather our own nests. This is what the less obvious second term is all about.

I've got one eye looking toward what will happen on the equilibrium path (here the 50% dilution factor kicks in), and the other eye looking toward making sure I'll have a good outside option from where to start the bargaining. It turns out that I put a 50% weight on that, too. The same applies to you.

So, instead of putting a weight of 100% on the social return, the u's, and nothing on the v's, we each put a weight of 50% on both. This ameliorates the dilution but doesn't offset it entirely because, from the line-up of inequalities, the second term on the left-hand side of our FOCs is smaller than the first term, for each of us. Hence it doesn't add up to what a social planner would want: there is under-investment relative to first-best:

$$x_i < x_i^* \quad \text{where} \quad \frac{\partial u_i\,(x_i^*)}{\partial x_i} = 1$$

After all this ground clearing, we at last arrive at Grossman and Hart's insight: giving control of an asset to one agent improves his or her incentive to invest, but it reduces the other agent's incentive. See Figure 1.3.

Imagine moving up a hierarchy, let's say from one extreme, type 2 integration, through nonintegration, to the other extreme, type 1 integration. As we go up, I (agent 1) have ever greater incentive to invest. But you (agent 2) have ever smaller incentive. The proof comes from examining the pair of FOCs that constitute our Nash equilibrium at date $\frac{1}{2}$. As the set of assets A_1 that I control expands, it pushes up the left-hand side of the top equation. But it's a hard fact of life—of physics—that we can't both control the same assets. So though I'm getting an expanded set A_1 as we progress up the hierarchy, your set A_2 is shrinking. And that pushes down the left-hand side of the bottom equation. There's a trade-off.

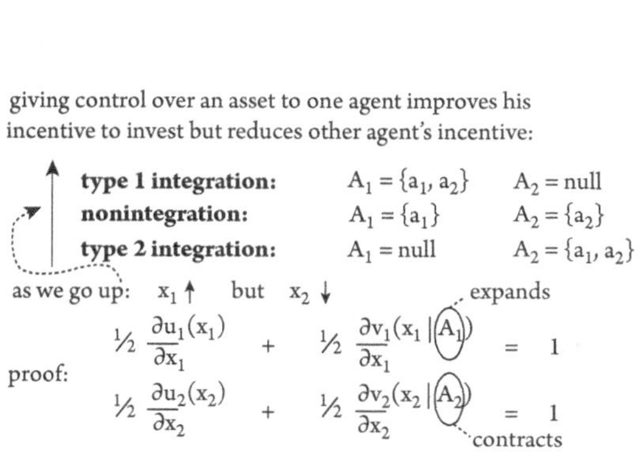

giving control over an asset to one agent improves his incentive to invest but reduces other agent's incentive:

	type 1 integration:	$A_1 = \{a_1, a_2\}$	$A_2 = $ null
	nonintegration:	$A_1 = \{a_1\}$	$A_2 = \{a_2\}$
	type 2 integration:	$A_1 = $ null	$A_2 = \{a_1, a_2\}$

as we go up: $x_1 \uparrow$ but $x_2 \downarrow$ expands

proof:
$$\frac{1}{2}\,\frac{\partial u_1(x_1)}{\partial x_1} + \frac{1}{2}\,\frac{\partial v_1(x_1\,|\,A_1)}{\partial x_1} = 1$$
$$\frac{1}{2}\,\frac{\partial u_2(x_2)}{\partial x_2} + \frac{1}{2}\,\frac{\partial v_2(x_2\,|\,A_2)}{\partial x_2} = 1$$
contracts

Figure 1.3 The effects on incentives of transferring control over an asset

A gloss that you might put on this theory, due I believe to Bengt Holmström, is that assets correspond to bargaining chips. Bargaining power emanates from control over assets. And bargaining power is a scarce commodity. Of course it would be wonderful if we could both have control over both assets. But that's infeasible, and we must allocate the chips judiciously.

Let me make a few remarks about the strengths and weaknesses of the Grossman and Hart model. Its strength is that it delivers a great insight. That insight is also a simple insight. Of course it is, because all great insights are simple. (Dispiritingly, not all simple insights are great.)

Grossman-Hart (1986) introduces into the formal literature the notions of power and control. It's obvious, isn't it, that we need to have power and control in our understanding of society—we need to have those as ingredients in our modeling? Yet the economist's bedrock, the Arrow-Debreu framework—and even an embellished Arrow-Debreu framework encompassing all of agency theory and information economics—does not admit power and control, a rather naked force that seems extremely important.

Within a world of incomplete contracts, Grossman and Hart proposed equating power with control over *nonhuman* assets. In so doing, they decisively moved away from the earlier literature dating back to Coase (1937) that had arguably gotten mired in a discussion of human capital and an idea that Coase had put on the table: that if I work for you, I must do what you tell me to do; whereas if I am an arm's-length contractor, I needn't. That loose idea sat in the literature until 1986 when Grossman and Hart shifted it entirely. They argued that we shouldn't think in terms of someone having direct control over other people, because a person's human capital is inalienably his or her own (I've got mine, you've got yours, and that's all there is to it). Simply relabeling someone an employee cannot solve agency problems. Instead, Grossman and Hart argued, we should think about control over nonhuman assets. Only *indirectly* might that form of control give someone control over other people.

It's clear that in practice, control over nonhuman assets matters a great deal. In the absence of any specific agreement about how a particular asset is to be used, the party who owns the asset has control over it: the right to decide how to use it, who to give access. But such power is a scarce commodity and needs to be allocated across society, asset by asset. This allocation is done by means of contracts. Although Grossman and Hart's is a model of power in society, their society is legally structured. Their equating of ownership with control conforms well with the views of lawyers.

Rather unusually, the model has only one force at work. It happens to cut two ways. If you've got control, then I haven't; and vice versa. In other words, the cost of integration is simply the dark side of the benefit. That elegant idea wasn't in the earlier literature on the firm. In the earlier literature, because there was a strong sense that integration, the creation of a single firm, reduces agency problems, there were many apparent benefits. Costs were of another variety altogether, perhaps something to do with limited managerial span. As a general rule of research, it's a pity to write down a model in which benefits and costs are distant cousins. Such a model can seem too kitchen sink. An ideal theory has a single force working in two ways, so that the costs and benefits are two sides of the same coin. The Grossman-Hart (1986) paper has exactly this feature. Their model is beautiful in its simplicity; and from the simplicity comes a broad set of applications.

(This insight—that the cost of integration is the obverse of the benefit—is unique to Grossman and Hart (1986). It would be a mistake to think that all Grossman and Hart did was to put into math what was already in the literature. This is not a matter of math versus no math; it's a matter of clear thinking versus less-than-clear thinking. A precise contribution of Grossman and Hart's 1986 article was to show that the costs and the benefits of integration stem from the same force.)

Not only is the model beautiful, it also makes very sensible predictions, such as: (1) Important people should be bosses, i.e. should be owners. (2) Complementary assets should be owned together. (3) Assets that have nothing to do with each other shouldn't be owned together. If (2) and (3) are combined, we arrive at Dennis Robertson's analogy, quoted by Coase (1937), of "lumps of butter coagulating in a pail of buttermilk": firms are the lumps of butter in the market economy, the buttermilk. Or, to put it less poetically, the optimum size of the firm is interior: it's not zero, but it's not the whole economy either.

When teaching this paper, I find this last point strikes home the most. Grossman and Hart (1986) is as much a theory of the market, of the benefits of decentralization, as it is a theory of the firm. Although these are equivalent ways of looking at the paper, the interpretative stress is different. Earlier in Figure 1.3, when moving up the hierarchy of ownership structures from type 2 integration through to type 1, it was easy to skip over the middle option: nonintegration. (In *A Fish Called Wanda*, Kevin Kline stole the show—and won an Oscar—playing nasty-but-dim Otto. The running gag had Otto replying to any triplet of choices, "What was the middle one?") The fact that nonintegration is typically superior to the other two ownership structures is a terrific argument in favor of the market economy and decentralization.

The theory has profoundly influenced many fields. I'm particularly keen on the application to corporate finance, with Aghion and Bolton (1992) the starting point. And Grossman-Hart (1986) will find ever more application to political economy: how can we model government without modeling power and control, and how can we understand power and control without their idea?

Weaknesses. Etiquette perhaps demands that I not write about these in a celebratory volume, but one weakness of the model just presented is that, in order to yield most of the sensible predictions, we need to make assumptions signing second-order cross-partial derivatives. It seems a pity that an idea so apparently clear-cut and intuitive descends—should that be ascends?—into a discussion about second derivatives. Somehow, I fear we've climbed a derivative unnecessarily. One ought to be able to tell this story about power and control at the level of first derivatives (or below) and not have to worry about the signs of second-order cross-partials.

Another worrying sign—thanks here to de Meza and Lockwood (1998)—is that the predictions are vulnerable to putting a different bargaining game into the model. Instead of having a 50:50 division of surplus from a status quo pair of payoffs, if an outside option game of bargaining is used then de Meza and Lockwood show that the predictions of the model can change radically. I think this may be connected to my first point: we're too many derivatives up for comfort.

The Grossman-Hart model perhaps puts too great an emphasis on interim inefficiency. Hold-up is important, but looking around the world, it seems that ex post inefficiencies are even more important. Coase (1960) is acting as a straitjacket to ensure that ex post bargaining is fully efficient. Although a world of frictionless trading at date 1 is a sensible place to begin, I'd prefer to get away from full ex post efficiency. Also, it would be good to jettison that middle date $\frac{1}{2}$ and investments: they snarl up the analysis and force us to think about second derivatives. I'm not the first to say these things. Oliver and I have worked on the matter more recently, making use of the idea that contracts may act as reference points (Hart and Moore, 2007, 2008); and he's taken this on further in his own work (Hart, 2008, 2009, 2013).

Finally by way of criticism, the elephant in the room: why are contracts incomplete? I don't see this as a fatal criticism of the Grossman and Hart paper. In 1986 they took the bold step: Let's *assume* contracts are incomplete—there are some wonderful footnotes in the paper wrestling with ideas to justify this assumption—and let's put power and control into the picture. But haven't they had a hard time from some pure theorists! I don't think it's Grossman and Hart's fault. It's our fault. Mea culpa. We've had 25 years to come up with a watertight theory of contractual incompleteness and we haven't succeeded yet. Eventually someone will.

The model I first heard Oliver give at the LSE wasn't the one I've described above. It was another, very different, model—published later in a book edited by Razin and Sadka. I'd love to have been a fly on the wall when Sandy and Oliver were doing their research. My hunch is that they began by writing down this other model. Then, to deal with the constraints imposed by Coase (1960), the model had to be embellished with investments and hold-up to generate inefficiencies. Let me describe the other model (see Grossman and Hart 1987).

Take a buyer and a seller, and dispense with date $1/2$ and investments. The buyer's value v and the seller's cost c are independently and uniformly distributed ex ante. First-best has ex post trade if and only if v exceeds c. But, crucially, there is no ex post renegotiation. Contracts, written at date 0, are assumed to be wildly incomplete, with no attempt at building in mechanisms to make the trading price contingent on revelations of the state of nature. Simply assume that a contract specifies a trade price p_1 and a no-trade price p_0. (The paper has some interesting early rationalizations for why this may not be such a bad assumption.)

The contract also specifies which party, if either, has control. In a situation of nonintegration, trade has to be voluntary, so the gap between the prices, $p_1 - p_0$, has to be less than v and more than c in order to induce both parties to trade. Or the buyer might be given control, and then he'll have the ability to force trade through even if the seller doesn't want to: there will be trade whenever v is greater than $p_1 - p_0$. Or the seller might be given control and there will be trade whenever c is less than $p_1 - p_0$.

In sum, the design of a contract involves: first, deciding which party, if either, has control; and, second, choosing the values of p_1 and p_0. The analysis boils down to studying diagrams like those in Figure 1.4.

Remember the distributions of v and c are uniform and therefore lie in a rectangular box in v–c space. In first-best, we want trade if and only if we are north west of the 45-degree line, where $v > c$. But we're limited by the crudeness of the contracts that we have at our disposal. Under nonintegration, there is trade if and only if $v > p_1 - p_0 > c$; see the top diagram. Trade happens in the shaded area.

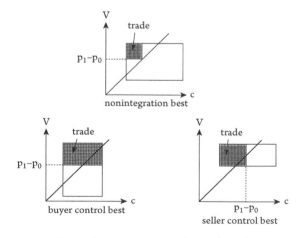

Figure 1.4 Grossman and Hart (1987)

There is undertrading—too little trading relative to first-best. However, given the position of the box, it turns out that both of the other two control structures (buyer control, seller control) are worse.

If the box is in a different place, as in the bottom left diagram, it turns out that nonintegration and seller control are both beaten by buyer control. With buyer control, there is trade if and only if $v > p_1 - p_0$. Notice that we've got a lot more trading here, but some of it is inefficient: we have overtrading as well as undertrading.

In the bottom right diagram, we have a yet differently placed box (the dimensions and positions of these boxes are worth thinking about), and now it turns out that seller control is the optimal contractual arrangement.

What I really like about this simple model is that it has nothing to do with second derivatives or even first-order conditions. The model has a naked ex post inefficiency—of course we should be anxious about Coase (1960)—but it distills the essence of the matter. Contracts are incomplete. Someone has to make a decision. Inevitably, the other party may find that decision costly, and thus there is trade-off between costs and benefits. The three diagrams capture that idea beautifully. I believe this may be the right line for future research: the role of a contract is to steer parties close to their ex post efficient frontier. Yes, they may be able to rely on renegotiation at date 1 to take them even closer to that frontier, but there are sensible reasons why they may have difficulty reaching it. I think this much cruder way of capturing the effects of allocating control power has a lot to recommend it compared with the rather subtle business of trying to induce interim investments.

Sandy and Oliver thought up their theory in a week, working on it together in Chicago, provoked by the AT&T case. (I'm not sure how much of this is true; but it is the way I remember it.) The next bit I do remember well. Oliver flew directly from Chicago to Penn for a summer workshop I was also attending. He was palpably excited, saying he'd just had the best week of his life with Sandy, and that they had perhaps come up with something important. As he told me, he was trembling in a rather un-Oliver way, even in the sweltering heat as we devoured hoagies from the vans that park just off Locust Walk. Oliver said that he thought their idea was their best thing yet: he felt that nothing they had written before came close. This was hot off the press, the day he'd just left Sandy. I thought, wow, this from two guys who had, as sole authors, already revolutionized asset price theory (in the case of Sandy) and general equilibrium theory (in the case of Oliver). I was caught up in Oliver's excitement and I told my friends on the quiet that they were on to Something Big. Of course, I didn't know what it was.

It's worth saying that when the paper finally emerged, not everyone fell about declaring it a masterpiece. One LSE professor, who will remain nameless, said:

"The theory is not very interesting. It'll never go anywhere. But the application to the insurance industry in the last section—that might be worked up a little. That's the only part that will be remembered."

When real business cycle (RBC) theory was first presented, it fell to Ken Rogoff to act as discussant. Rogoff pointed out that there were two tests of a true scientific revolution. At first the idea must seem mad. Then it must seem obvious. And he felt that the RBC theory certainly passed the first test. Now Grossman and Hart's 1986 paper was also a scientific revolution—to my mind just as important to microeconomics as RBC theory is to macro—because, as I've emphasized, their theory puts the idea of power and control into mainstream economics, and without these we can have little handle on many important economic phenomena. Ironically, maybe the greatest legacy of Grossman and Hart (1986) will be outside the relatively narrow confines of organizational theory. But arguably Grossman and Hart's theory fails Rogoff's first test, because it has never seemed mad. Their theory seems almost self-evident, which is perhaps the greatest of compliments.

Although the property rights theory has become an indispensable tool for many applied economists, among pure theorists it has proved harder to win friends, largely because we still lack a theory of contractual incompleteness. Martin Hellwig, hearing of the title to Jean Tirole's 1994 Walras-Bowley Lecture (published in *Econometrica*, 1999), ribbed "Incomplete Contracts: Where Do We Swim?"

As has been said of the decentralized competitive system, it works in practice, but does it work in theory? Well, the authors in this book will be discussing these and many other fascinating matters, all because 25 years ago these two gentlemen had a stroke of genius.

References

Aghion, P., and P. Bolton. 1992. "An Incomplete Contracts Approach to Financial Contracting." *Review of Economic Studies* 59: 473–94.

Coase, R. 1937. "The Nature of the Firm." *Economica* 4: 386–405.

Coase, R. 1960. "The Problem of Social Cost." *Journal of Law and Economics* 3: 1–44.

de Meza, D. and B. Lockwood. 1998. "Does Asset Ownership Always Motivate Managers? Outside Options and the Property Rights Theory of the Firm." *Quarterly Journal of Economics* 113: 361–86.

Grossman, S., and O. Hart 1986. "The Costs and Benefits of Ownership: A Theory of Vertical and Lateral Integration." *Journal of Political Economy* 94: 691–719.

Grossman, S., and O. Hart 1987. "Vertical Integration and the Distribution of Property Rights." In A. Razin and E. Sadka (eds.) *Economic Policy in Theory and Practice*. London: Macmillan, pp. 504–46.

Hart, O. 1995. *Firms, Contracts, and Financial Structure*. Oxford: Oxford University Press.

Hart, O. 2008. "Reference Points and the Theory of the Firm." *Economica* 75: 404–11.

Hart, O. 2009. "Hold-Up, Asset Ownership, and Reference Points." *Quarterly Journal of Economics* 124: 267–300.

Hart, O. 2013. "Noncontractible Investments and Reference Points." *Games* 4: 437–56.

Hart, O., and J. Moore 1990. "Property Rights and the Nature of the Firm." *Journal of Political Economy* 98: 1119–58.

Hart, O., and J. Moore 2007. "Incomplete Contracts and Ownership: Some New Thoughts." *American Economic Review* 97: 182–86.

Hart, O., and J. Moore 2008. "Contracts as Reference Points." *Quarterly Journal of Economics* 123: 1–48.

Tirole, J. 1999. "Incomplete Contracts: Where Do We Stand?" *Econometrica* 67: 741–81.

2

Grossman-Hart (1986) as a Theory of Markets

BENGT HOLMSTRÖM

It's a great pleasure to be celebrating Sandy and Oliver's landmark paper. I would like to do so by describing briefly how the paper has influenced my thinking about the firm since its publication 25 years ago. My perspective, or at least my emphasis, is not quite the same as the original paper's, and it has evolved over time. That is the way it should be. Great papers tend to metamorphose, as one goes back to them over and over. But let me start with a brief rehearsal.

The paper opens with the question "What is a firm?" and proceeds to answer it in a way that at once seems obvious and yet is profoundly novel. Instead of focusing on the transaction as the unit of analysis, as Williamson famously put it, the paper suggests that the essence of the firm is in the decision rights that ownership of its assets confers. In a world of incomplete contracting, decision rights play a key role in determining the incentives of the owner—in the paper, the only role, really. When firm A buys firm B, the incentives of the owner of firm A become stronger, while the incentives of the owner of firm B (now a worker of firm A) become weaker. When the firms stay independent, the incentives are more balanced. It has been noted already that the theory has the desirable feature that one instrument—asset ownership—generates both benefits and costs of integration and a trade-off between integration and nonintegration. Actually, I just misspoke. The theory makes the further prediction that it generally matters whether A buys B or B buys A. I remember thinking at the time that this was a bit odd, because we were so used to the dichotomous choice between integration and nonintegration. Today I see the asymmetry as quite supportive of the theory. The identity of the buyer in corporate transactions clearly matters. I believe more could be made of this empirically.

With this prelude, my next observation will sound strange. Over time I have come to see the paper as saying more about markets than about firms. I mean this as a compliment. The Grossman-Hart property rights theory is the first theory that explains in a straightforward way why markets are so critical in the context of organizational choice. The virtue of markets (nonintegration) is that owner-entrepreneurs can exercise their hold-up power. They can refuse to trade and go elsewhere. This right is a powerful driver of entrepreneurial incentives both in the model and in reality. Of course choice plays a critical role also in neoclassical models, but choice and hold-ups are never the drivers of organization.

This explanation should be contrasted with Williamson's analysis. Williamson takes as the starting point the idealized competitive market that would achieve the socially optimal outcome. But market outcomes, especially after asset specific investments have been made, can be expected to lead to hold-up attempts and costly haggling. This pushes some transactions out of the market and into integrated firms. On the other hand, firms face a variety of costs such as bureaucracy and low-powered incentives, which push in the opposite direction.

The weakness with this line of reasoning is that it does not provide a direct explanation of the virtue of the market, because the idealized, first-best market is taken as the default. A comparison of relative weaknesses rather than relative strengths determines whether the transaction ends up in the market or inside a firm. This may seem like semantics—looking at the same coin from two sides. But, as all of us who have worked on the theory of the firm know, it has always been easier to find reasons for integration than it has been to find reasons for market outcomes. Indeed, Williamson correctly identified "selective intervention" as the key puzzle to explain why a single firm cannot replicate the market when that is optimal and improve on the market by intervening when the market is suboptimal (e.g., because of hold-ups). But I think the multifaceted forces he identified as explanations, although relevant, failed to put the finger on the key point: the virtue of market transactions stems from the hold-up power conferred by ownership. The essence of the Grossman-Hart model (especially as extended in the Hart-Moore model of 1990) concerns the optimal distribution of that hold-up power.

One could go as far as to say that the property rights model in the Grossman-Hart paper is about the distribution of assets among individuals (the entrepreneurs) rather than firms. Indeed, this is what Hart and Moore explicitly assume in their 1990 property rights theory. One can always interpret the individuals as firms, but of course this leaves entirely open the question of how firms organize themselves internally. Also, it does not directly address one of the central questions for a theory of the firm, namely, why firms rather than the workers tend to own most if not all the nonhuman assets used in the production of goods and services. One explanation for this is suggested by a key result in Hart-Moore: complementary assets should be owned by a single individual.

Doing otherwise would only lead to wasteful hold-ups. In my paper on the firm as a subeconomy, I offered another reason, also related to power. By putting all the nonhuman assets in the hands of the firm, those in charge of the firm will have maximal power to decide how the firm is organized and run.

Marx would have agreed with this characterization of the firm. But unlike Marx, who thought the primary purpose of the firm's concentrated power was to exploit the workers, in the logic of the (extended) property rights theory the purpose is to allow the firm to design more efficient organizational structures, in situations where markets function poorly, because of externalities (such as excessive hold-ups). Firms are far from democratic, but they are kept in check by the fact that workers, who own their human capital, can go elsewhere if they are unhappy—another illustration of the effectiveness of property rights.

The property rights theory has set us on a path to study formally the central role of power through decision rights in the organization of economic activity. I have tried to argue that the main contribution of the initial property rights publications has been in providing a simple, elegant, and compelling explanation of a decentralized entrepreneurial market economy. Where we formerly had to resort to explanations of disintegration based on myriad dysfunctional firm features, we now have a single, clean decision rights structure to build on.

One of the most successful applications of the property rights theory has been in corporate finance, where the control theoretic view has become influential. The theory has also been helpful in thinking about strategic alliances and competitive strategy. Where the paradigm remains underutilized, paradoxically, is in the study of the internal organization of firms. There are some important contributions, such as Aghion and Tirole's study of formal versus real authority, the paper by Baker, Gibbons, and Murphy that incorporate relational contracts, and the paper by Rajan and Zingales on power within the firm. But much more can be done. Power can be and is distributed within the firm in complex ways to implement strategic objectives. Firms frequently restructure themselves, not just by moving people around but also by changing reporting structures, job descriptions, and remarkably the whole internal architecture of the firm. In all cases, decision rights are at the center: they are being regrouped and reallocated to gain more effective incentive and communication structures, much like an army regroups its troops in response to changing objectives. This ongoing dynamic, which can be done without procuring new decision rights, and therefore done more quickly, is something that seems to me ripe for serious empirical and theoretical studies.

The story I have told says that markets are good because of hold-ups and firms are good because of low-powered incentives that make it easier to control people and get them to cooperate. If this sounds like Williamson's work put on its head, it is so, because I wanted to emphasize how the decision rights perspective aptly brings out two different sides of the same organizational coin.

References

Aghion P., and J. Tirole. 1997. "Formal and Real Authority in Organizations." *Journal of Political Economy* 105: 1–29.

Baker, G., R. Gibbons, and K. Murphy. 2002. "Relational Contracts and the Theory of the Firm." *Quarterly Journal of Economics* 117: 39–84.

Holmstrom B. 1999. "The Firm as a Subeconomy." *Journal of Law, Economics and Organization* 14: 74–102.

Rajan, R., and L. Zingales. 1998. "Power in the Theory of the Firm," *Quarterly Journal of Economics* 113: 39–84

3

Remarks on Incomplete Contracting

JEAN TIROLE

Let me first thank the organizers for making this event happen. "GH at 25" brings back a lot of memories to me. I moved to MIT's economics department in September 1984. Oliver arrived the same month, and we were placed next door to each other. As you might imagine, Oliver was all excited about incomplete contracts and ownership; I was fascinated by his ideas and insights around the concept of ownership and more circumspect about foundations of contract incompleteness. We immediately engaged in exciting and endless discussions in his office or mine; I would ask, "Why don't you consider an option to buy or to sell?" and Oliver had a clear answer: "Sure, but it's not a robust contracting feature because of X." I would come back with another way of making contracts more efficient and Oliver would say, "Oh no, that doesn't work because of Y." After seven or eight times, I understood that Oliver had thought deep down the tree; our conversations resembled the *Mad* magazine comic strip "Spy versus Spy"; he had all the answers and characteristically was thinking deeply about what he was doing, much beyond the simple model he was elaborating with Sandy Grossman. While we did not converge on the methodological front, there was much agreement on the ideas. We then went on to work together on other topics and became good friends. It was quite a privilege to have one's office next to Oliver's. I should add that two offices away sat Eric Maskin, so that was really an exciting environment for discussing incomplete contracts.

The only thing that bothered me about Oliver was his accent, a bit hard to fathom for someone like me, who partly learned English by going for a PhD in the United States. While I am talking about Oliver's accent, since the beginning of this conference, we have had Oliver stories; we have had Philippe [Aghion] stories. I cannot resist telling an Oliver–Philippe story. This story took place in a train from London to Oxford, around 1993–1994; we were at the time working with Philippe on real versus formal authority. Philippe was discovering the cell phone. He was working at Oxford but living in London, and he was always on the phone in the train from London to Oxford and back. Philippe, being a good son, was calling not only his many coauthors and friends but also his mother and his father. But one day, a tad overworked, he fainted while talking to his father in the train from London to Oxford; he told his Dad "I am not feeling well. . ." and then went blank. He was taken to a hospital at the next train stop between London and Oxford; coincidentally, Michael Kremer happened to be in the same train and took him to the hospital. Then followed two intense days in the hospital where he sent me a record number of faxes concerning our project. When Philippe got to the hospital and, having recouped his spirits, he recalled that his father could not hear what had happened and must have been concerned. For a reason I can't recall, Philippe could not reach his father and asked Oliver, "Could you please call my father, I stopped talking to him and he must be very, very worried." And so Oliver calls Philippe's father, whom he had met, and said, "Hi, it's Oliver," but thanks to Oliver's accent, Philippe's father understood "Hi, it's all over. . ."

Lots of nice things have already been said in this conference about the GH 1986 paper, and I share everything which has been said. John [Moore] raised the question of what drives the incompleteness of contracts, and there have indeed been several lines of research relevant to this question. One voluminous line of research takes the view that we should keep using mechanism design techniques and find structured environments in which optimal contracts are actually very simple and look incomplete. Two lines here; the first one, pioneered by Kathryn Spier's 1992 paper, builds on adverse selection; in that paper, one informed party to the contract basically tells the other party: "I don't propose that the contract's be made coningent on some state of nature—say, in which the relationship would go sour—because that would look very suspicious to you. Indeed I'm not demanding to index the contract on that state of nature in order to 'prove' to you that this state is unlikely." Such an informed principal approach is related to some work on short-term contracting performed earlier by Philippe Aghion and Patrick Bolton in an industrial organization context (1987), by Doug Diamond in a corporate finance context (1993), and by Ben Hermalin in a labor context (1988). By signing a short-term contract, the informed party tries to signal that he or she is not afraid of entry or of going back to the capital or labor market. A short-term contract is a form of incomplete contract.

But there are many other forms of simple, apparently incomplete contracts: no contract at all, an authority relationship, a property right, or many of the familiar governance structures (committee or collegial decision making, gatekeeping power). Another line of research thus looks at structured environments without adverse selection at the contract design stage but with enough structure (often contract renegotiation and limited liability). Classic works along these lines include Che and Hausch (1999)'s model of "cooperative investments" (roughly, an investment is cooperative if it affects the trading partner's surplus more than the investing party's surplus), and Segal's (1999) and Hart-Moore's (1999) results on "selfish investments" (namely, investments that mainly affect the investing party's surplus).[1]

A standard motivation for contract incompleteness is the presence of unforeseen contingencies; intuitively, if the parties cannot describe the state of nature or figure out the actions to be taken, they cannot write them down explicitly in the contract. Alas, as long as these are ex post observable (which is assumed in this literature), indescribability per se does not provide a foundation for incomplete contracts. The revelation mechanisms that Eric Maskin and later John Moore and Rafael Repullo worked on are extremely powerful. My work with Eric Maskin (1999) unveiled a tension between two standard assumptions: that of rationality and the impossibility to write complete contracts. Under common knowledge of von Neumann-Morgenstern utilities (which we usually assume), parties can in general write contracts that will make efficient use of contingencies and actions once their identity have been learned;[2] put differently, our standard assumption that parties to a contract are aware they are unaware implies that under assumptions that are usually satisfied in the literature, the parties ex ante can take the necessary steps to let the contract adjust properly once the information about state of nature and actions accrues.

Nash implementation mechanisms à la Maskin or Moore-Repullo use complex and unrealistic mechanisms because they are designed to apply to completely general environments, but simpler and more palatable mechanisms (options, auctions, valuation through financial market trading, and so on) can be used in simpler ones. The paper of Aghion et al (2012) makes an important point about the robustness of such Nash implementation mechanisms to asymmetric information. One would want to impose some lower hemi continuity property on the equilibria of such mechanisms. But here I would apply the standard mechanism design point that a horse race must be conducted between simple mechanisms (ex-post bargaining or property rights, etc.) and more complex mechanisms; that is, the robustness test must be applied to both the Maskin approach and the simpler contracts posited in the literature.

---

[1] See also Aghion-Dewatripont-Rey (1994), Edlin-Reichelstein (1996), and Noldeke-Schmidt (1995).

[2] Except when the ratio of marginal utilities of money is state independent (so indescribable income shocks impacting von Neurmann-Morgenstern utilities cannot be elicited ex post, and so insurance against such shocks cannot be provided ex post) or when no information can be inferred about investments from knowing exactly which of payoff-equivalent states ω and ω' occurred (the impossibility to distinguish between ω and ω' under indescribable contingencies does not affect the parties' ability to provide incentives.)

Despite recent progress on robust mechanism design, this avenue of research is still underexplored and has not yet provided conclusive foundations to incomplete contracting.

Most of us at this conference have at some point made a side comment at the end of a paper on incomplete contracts that it would be nice to have a bounded rationality theory. Unfortunately there is still no accepted framework that could lay some foundation. Starting with their 2008 piece, Oliver and John have written some very interesting papers in which the wording of the contract affects preferences, providing some foundations. But this is more a behavioral approach (which I sympathize with) than a bounded rationality one.

In my 2009 paper,[3] I have been interested in a different take on incomplete contracts, emphasizing cognitive costs. Writing a contract or a charter can consume a great deal of the time of people who are already terribly busy. It may also involve substantial costs linked to the participation of engineering, legal, or other experts. (If we want to consider related behavioral aspects, one can add that the cost of writing contracts is affected by cognitive loads, frames, limited attention, etc.) Intuitively, under scarce cognitive capacities, parties will try to identify bad news for themselves and good news for the other party; and they will rarely acquire all relevant information, as the cost of doing so, in money and in delay, would be prohibitive.

Incompleteness can then be measured by the frequency with which the contract must be revised ex post to make up for its ex ante shortcomings. More cognition makes for fewer incomplete contracts.

Costly cognition has several implications. First, it gives rise to endogenous adverse selection. If I contract with some party, I should wonder how much that party has thought about the matter before dealing with me. Second, there can be too little (free-riding) or too much (rent-seeking) cognition. Third, simple contracts ("no-brainers") are attractive provided that they require little cognition and give rise to limited adverse selection.

The attractiveness of no-brainers can help explain why short-term contracts may be selected over longer term ones or why contract completeness can be dispensed with through repeated interactions or vertical integration. Short-term contracts are no-brainers, whereas for a contract to work well in the long run, parties have to engage in a fair amount of cognition and will still worry about facing strong adverse selection. Ownership limits costly cognition because the owner knows can adjust imprecise contracts without being exposed to a hold-up.

---

[3] This theory is connected with Xavier Gabaix and David Laibson's theory of shrouded attributes (2006)—there is actually a formal analogy—and with Patrick Bolton and Antoine Faure-Grimaud's (2010) work on "satisficing contracts."

These various approaches of course only cover a small and biased fraction of the voluminous research on incomplete contracting. The impetus for this research owes much to the GH 1986 piece and subsequent work by Hart and Moore. Celebrating this paper is therefore most appropriate!

References

Aghion, Philippe and Patrick Bolton. 1987. "Contracts as a Barrier to Entry." *The American Economic Review*, 77, 388–401.

Aghion, Philippe, Drew Fudenberg, Richard Holden, Takashi Kunimoto and Olivier Tercieux. 2012. "Subgame Perfect Implementation Under Information Perturbations." *The Quarterly Journal of Economics*, 127 (4), 1843–1881.

Aghion, Philippe, Mathias Dewatripont and Patrick Rey. 1994. "Renegotiation Design with Unverifiable Information." *Econometrica*, 62(2), 257–282.

Bolton, Patrick, and Antoine Faure-Grimaud. 2010. "Satisficing Contracts," The Review of Economic Studies, 77(3), 937–971.

Che, Yeon-Koo and Donald Hausch. 1999. "Cooperative investments and the value of contracting." *American Economic Review*, 89(1), 125–147.

Diamond, Doug. 1993. "Seniority and Maturity of Debt Contracts", *Journal of Financial Economics*, 33(3), pp. 341–68.

Edlin, Aaron and Stephan Reichelstein. 1996. "Holdups, standard breach remedies, and optimal investment." *American Economic Review*, 86(3), 478–501.

Gabaix, Xavier and David Laibson. 2006. "Shrouded Attributes, Consumer Myopia, and Information Suppression in Competitive Markets." *The Quarterly Journal of Economics*, 121(2), 505–540.

Hart, Oliver and John Moore. 1999. "Foundations of Incomplete Contracts." *The Review of Economic Studies*, 66(1), 115–138.

Hart, Oliver and John Moore. 2008. "Contracts as Reference Points" *Quarterly Journal of Economics*, 123 (1): 1–48.

Hermalin, Ben. 1988. Three Essays on the Theory of Contracts, Ph.D. dissertation, M.I.T.

Nöldeke, Georg and Klaus M. Schmidt. 1995. "Option Contracts and Renegotiation: A Solution to the Hold-up Problem." *The RAND Journal of Economics*, 26(2), 163–179.

Segal, Ilya. (1999). "Complexity and Renegotiation: A Foundation for Incomplete Contracts." *The Review of Economic Studies*, 66(1), 57–82.

Spier, Kathryn E. 1992. "Incomplete Contracts and Signalling." *The RAND Journal of Economics*, 23(3), 432–443.

Tirole, Jean. 2009. "Cognition and Incomplete Contracts." *American Economic Review*, 99(1), 265–294

4

Property Rights and Transaction Costs Theories

STEVE TADELIS

I will describe how I view the Grossman and Hart (1986) paper as it fits into a very long history of thought vis-à-vis boundaries of the firm and vertical integration in organizational design. The article that we are celebrating today starts with a question, as does the important follow-up paper that Oliver and John Moore (1990) wrote, "what is a firm?"

I want to take you back to 1937. When Coase wrote his paper, he didn't start it with a question, but very soon we come to the question he tries to answer, which is, why are there firms, and what would determine the boundary of these firms? What I think is a nice similarity between these two papers is that first, neither of them answers the question they pose, and second, they offer deep and important methodological contributions to help us answer these questions, which we are still struggling to answer today. In short, I think there are a lot of parallels between these two papers.

What I am going to argue, therefore, is that the Grossman and Hart paper, and the Grossman-Hart-Moore property rights theory more generally, is really a methodological contribution, rather than what I believe many people think of these—namely, as applied theory contributions. This distinction has been important for me to understand the literature and make sense of it.

Often we tend to judge papers for their contributions and not necessarily for what they complain about or what they critique in the previous literature. Still, let me start with three critiques that the Grossman and Hart paper highlights, and say a word or two about how the paper deals with each of these critiques. Then I will describe what I believe the important contributions of Grossman and Hart are in light of these critiques.

First, the Grossman-Hart paper claims that the transaction cost literature developed by Williamson, inspired by Coase before him, doesn't really explain how integration solves the scope of opportunistic behavior. On one hand, there is definitely some truth to this critique in the sense that a tradeoff between market-based and firm-based transactions is not parsimoniously modeled. On the other hand, the critique is too harsh because Williamson does introduce the notion that there are important institutional differences between hierarchy and markets. Disputes within firms are settled and controlled by fiat, whereas market transactions rely on the legal support of contracts, and these are fundamentally different ways to deal with problems of coordination and adaptation. In turn, these different institutions change the way people behave because each gives them different instruments for control. That said, the precise working of the institutional details described in the less formal transactions cost literature are still somewhat vague. I believe that one of the most important contributions of Grossman and Hart is to offer a clean and clear modeling framework of institutional choice. In particular what they do, in hindsight, is that they take cost and benefit functions, which we all love and use all the time, and inject into them institutional variables in a simple and coherent way. The question, then, is how do those institutional variables affect the cost and benefit functions, and in turn, how do these affect the behaviors of the agents in the transaction? The methodological approach allows us to model the way in which institutional choice affects behavior, and how this behavior affects efficiency. Until the Grossman and Hart paper was written, we did not have an apparatus for this kind of analysis, and that is a fundamental contribution. Indeed, in Tadelis and Williamson (2012) I use this modeling apparatus to put together a simple model that illustrates the central concepts of transaction cost economics as they relate to vertical integration. In many ways, I see the Grossman and and Hart paper paralleling Coase's paper, in the sense that before Coase we did not even think of applying the notion of cost-benefit analysis at the margin to the question of why firms exist.

A second critique that Grossman and Hart present is that the transaction cost literature does not acknowledge the cost of integration: "how can integration ever be strictly worse than nonintegration; that is, what limits the size of the firm?" (p. 693). This is another fundamental question, and this critique is definitely in place, though maybe it too is a bit harsh. If you go back to many of Williamson's publications, e.g., Williamson (1975, 1985), there is a lot of discussion that Jean described nicely. Namely, the benefits of integration come from control but the costs take on too many forms to concisely describe in a parsimonious model: bureaucratic costs, limits to managerial span of control, and many other forces seem to be at work. In my view, therefore, an important contribution of Grossman and Hart is to move the ball forward by formalizing the notion of *control* and offering a simple yet rigorous apparatus to model it. The idea of control was central to Williamson's work, but the description of control was too vague to be modeled precisely. In particular, Williamson's important notion of the *impossibility of selective intervention* was hard to capture precisely. This idea goes to the heart of Grossman and Hart's second critique: I can create one huge firm; whenever centralization is important, I will utilize control, but whenever it isn't, I will just let the market work and not intervene. Grossman and Hart contribute to this important puzzle with their definition of residual control rights: "Moreover, the owner cannot commit himself to intervene selectively in his subsidiary's operations since by their very definition residual rights refer to *powers that cannot be specified in advance*" (p. 693, emphasis added). This clear and crisp way of thinking about ownership as residual control rights is a fundamental leap forward that gives us an apparatus to model the puzzle of selective intervention.

The third critique raised by Grossman and Hart is, "what does it mean for one firm to be more integrated than another?" For example, is a firm that calls its retail force "employees" more integrated than one that calls its retail force "independent but exclusive sales agents?" I think this really resonates with what Francine Lafontaine writes in chapter 7 as an empirical scholar who wants to study real-world applications: what *is* vertical integration? This vague definition is very frustrating for applied researchers. I think that a big part of the blame actually goes back to Coase's original 1937 paper. I am assuming that most of you haven't looked at that paper for a while because we think we know the synopsis of it. However, if you go back and read it carefully, after Coase describes what a firm is—the number of transactions under control of an entrepreneur—he presents a long-winded section on the employment relationship that, in my view, just goes off on a tangent. I believe that this discussion of the employment relationship together with the discussion of the boundaries of firms muddled these two concepts together. But these are different issues that are unrelated, and Grossman and Hart focus on integration in a crisp way: "We define integration in terms of the ownership of assets and develop a model to explain when one firm will desire to acquire the assets of another firm" (p. 693). It is not that clear, however, what defines one firm as more integrated than another.

This crisp definition relates to something that John Moore emphasized earlier. What the literature has picked up in this definition of residual rights and ownership from Grossman and Hart is not the ownership of assets per se, as that definition is too narrow. Several fundamental and important papers follow from Grossman and Hart, like Aghion and Tirole (1997), Aghion and Bolton (1992), and Rajan and Zingales (1998). What these papers do is take the notion of residual control rights and expand the application of the Grossman and Hart apparatus to issues of access, control, and exclusivity. In other words, the formalism of Grossman and Hart offers a way of modeling issues that had previously been hard to model, such as power and control, in a formal and clear way through which we can employ cost-benefit analysis.

A short remark is warranted about the way in which many papers that followed the original Grossman and Hart model had departed from it. In particular, I think that the way many papers have used (or abused) the Grossman and Hart set-up is a bit unfortunate. If you go back to the original Grossman-Hart paper, the notion of ex post decisions, the "q's," play a very prominent role. Later in the Hart and Moore paper, and much of the follow-up work (most notably in Oliver Hart's book), these have been suppressed altogether. I think this is a shame because in my view ex post decisions—and you know of course that I am biased by my own work on this topic—are fundamentally important to understand the boundaries of firms and the meaning of integration and control. This resulted in a rather clear distinction between most of the early property rights literature, which focused on providing ex ante incentives, and the transaction cost literature, which focused mostly on accommodating ex post adaptation.

I want to comment about what John Moore said: another important contribution of the Grossman and Hart paper is the single dimension of costs and benefits. Not only is the property rights theory very clear about cost and benefits, but also, a lot of people see the contribution of the approach as putting these on the same dimension. When I take assets (or decisions) away from you, I have stronger incentives while you have weaker incentives, and vice versa. This differs from transaction costs economics where, as John noted, there are many sources that come together as the costs of integration, not all of which are clearly spelled out. But let me share something I have recently learned: *in theory there is no difference between theory and practice, but in practice there is.* The fact that both costs and benefits are on a level playing field is a beautiful and elegant contribution of the Grossman and Hart theory. I think, however, that in practice, all of these other costs like bureaucratic control, influence costs, politics and power, are real. We are still struggling, as modelers, to find ways to put these all together.

The contribution of Grossman and Hart, which I claim is methodological, offers a way of modeling control and ownership and was fundamental in helping many scholars write many important papers, some of which I have mentioned. But there are several critiques of the property rights approach. Despite its expressed objective to explain the boundaries of firms, the Grossman and Hart paper, in my view, fails to do so. This critique is made forcefully in Bengt Holmström's "subeconomy" paper (1999). Still, when Bengt continues to describe a firm, he uses the notion that the firm *owning* these assets gives the firm the ability to contract. So, as much as the critique of Grossman and Hart is valid, in many ways the notion of ownership as a vehicle of control, which is fundamental in Grossman and Hart, is still used. So the question we should be exploring in this regard is when and how we are using this notion of ownership.

Another critique that we have heard about the property rights theory is the empirical challenges that it poses. I would argue is that as long as we view the Grossman and Hart paper as a *methodological* paper, this critique is vacuous. Once we try, however, to take the Grossman and Hart paper seriously as an applied theory paper, with empirical predictions, then we get into trouble. For example, Acemoglu et al. (2010) have to take many leaps of faith in applying the theory to measureable variables in existing data, and I do not view that exercise as convincing. In the same way, Coase (1937) says that we can use the simple economic tool of costs and benefits at the margin to explain the existence of firms, but there are no empirical implications that can be taken to data. Only after Williamson (1971) introduced the important ideas of specificity, complexity, and adaptation were applied scholars able to take the ideas of transaction costs to data. It is incumbent on us applied folks to do the same for the property rights theory.

To summarize, the contribution of Grossman and Hart is fundamental as a methodological paper, without which many important papers would not have been written. I think that the role of the applied economist (and I view myself as one) is to use the approach rigorously with good institutional knowledge. The objective, in my view, should be to derive refutable implications from marrying the formalities of the property rights theory with the institutional details that the applied scholar possesses about the problem being studied.

References

Acemoglu, Daron, Rachel Griffith, Philippe Aghion, and Fabrizio Zilibotti. 2010. "Vertical Integration and Technology: Theory and Evidence." *Journal of the European Economic Association* 8(5): 989–1033.

Aghion, Philippe, and Patrick Bolton. 1992. "An Incomplete Contracts Approach to Financial Contracting." *Review of Economic Studies* 59(3): 473–94.

Aghion, Philippe, and Jean Tirole. 1997. "Formal and Real Authority in Organizations." *Journal of Political Economy* 105(1): 1–29.

Coase, Ronald. 1937. "The Nature of the Firm." *Economica*, 4(16): 386–405.

Grossman, Sanford, and Oliver D. Hart. 1986. "The Costs and Benefits of Ownership: A Theory of Vertical and Lateral Integration." *Journal of Political Economy* 94(4): 691–719.

Hart, Oliver D. 1995. Firms, Contracts, and Financial Structure. Oxford, UK: Oxford Unibersity Press.

Hart, Oliver D., and John Moore. 1990. "Property Rights and the Nature of the Firm." *Journal of Political Economy* 98(6): 1119–58.

Holmström, Bengt. 1999. "The Firm as a Subeconomy." *Journal of Law, Economics, and Organization* 15(1): 74–102.

Rajan, Raghuram G., and Luigi Zingales. 1998. "Power in a Theory of the Firm." *Quarterly Journal of Economics* 113(2): 387–432.

Tadelis, Steven and Oliver E. Williamson. 2012. "Transaction Cost Economics," in Robert Gibbons and John Roberts (Eds.) *Handbook of Organizational Economics*. New Jersey: Princeton University Press.

Williamson, Oliver E. 1971. "The Vertical Integration of Production: Market Failure Considerations," *American Economic Review* 61(2): 112–123.

Williamson, Oliver E. 1975. *Markets and Hierarchies, Analysis and Antitrust Implications.* New York: Free Press.

Williamson, Oliver E. 1985. *The Economic Institutions of Capitalism.* New York: Free Press.

5

GH and Applied Theory

THOMAS HUBBARD

Usually I find myself agreeing with Steve Tadelis and disagreeing with him, sometimes even in the same sentence.

I do think of the Grossman and Hart article as applied theory. Their work is not just a way of modeling the world; it has profoundly informed the way I think about the world itself. The idea that the allocation of control rights—particularly residual control rights—strengthens some incentives and weakens others, and that strong incentives could be both good and bad at the same time, means that trade-offs emerge. Their work wraps up into this wonderful idea of how and why the allocation of control and power within relationships matters, and how this introduces trade-offs that were not really in the foreground before the paper's publication.

As far as the empirical application goes, there have been various threads in the literature. My own approach to empirics and theory in general is twofold, and these are the first two points I would like to make about Grossman-Hart as an applied theory.

First, one should test propositions that are motivated by theory but not necessarily the models themselves. I doubt very much that the *model* that Grossman and Hart write down in section 3 of their famous paper maps directly to the real world all that frequently. I interpret this and other theoretical models as examples of how the theory can play out in practice. But how one models the central theoretical idea would differ depending on the particular context; this more detailed applied modeling captures exactly what the marginal returns are, what the bargaining positions are, and what the contracting environment looks like in the context at hand. The insights from Grossman-Hart, the theory, are far broader than the model. And the empirical work is about taking the theory—the central insights—to the world. This perspective makes it much more reasonable to treat Grossman-Hart as an applied theory.

Second, with respect to empirical work, it is often useful to exploit what happens when one changes a theory's maintained assumptions rather than the assumptions or parameters that theorists vary in their model. Particularly with Grossman and Hart, changing the maintained assumptions about the contracting environment gives you a whole new set of implications. The original article does not explicitly examine the effect of changes in the contracting environment on optimal ownership. But understanding how the contractual environment might change over time or differ in the cross section, and applying this in the context of their theory, can let researchers use the Grossman-Hart theory to develop testable propositions about the organization of industries beyond those that follow from their specific model.

My third point about Grossman-Hart as an applied theory is that its power is actually significantly underutilized. Researchers have too long ignored the word *lateral* in the title, especially researchers in the field I am often associated with, industrial organization. The question of industry structure and the question of the boundary of the firm are the same question. You can't have one without the other. Of course, the usual industry structure analysis in industrial organization completely abstracts from control or incentive issues. Oliver and Sandy put their fingers on this. Vertical relationships are important, but so are horizontal relationships. I use a framework that's motivated by Grossman and Hart to teach my MBA students how to think about how contractual problems shape industry structure. Although some other researchers have done this in the specific context of franchising, these issues and how they bear on industry structure, as Grossman and Hart imply with the title of their article, are broader.

Grossman and Hart's theory allows you to cut through some difficult horizontal issues that standard theories cannot. Franchises are complicated, because as you know, the control rights are often unclear. Sometimes they are shared. For example, is McDonald's one firm or many firms? I have been thinking about that for 10 years, and I still don't know the answer. With McDonald's, franchises do not have control rights over an awful lot of assets that are essential for production, including the land. Why is this the case, and what would lead this to change? These are the types of questions that you can get at when you are looking at control rights issues in horizontal contexts. Another concerns "roll-up strategies": one firm in an industry will sometimes "roll up" a lot of other small firms in the same industry through buy-outs to create a large chain. When are such strategies likely to succeed? Well, Grossman-Hart can tell you how and why changes in management jobs at individual outlets and in the contracting environment can make a roll-up suddenly advantageous whereas before it was not. Their ideas can and do inform business decisions; they can affect researchers' understanding of industry structure and how it changes for reasons that traditional industrial organization–style industry structure analysis just does not accommodate.

So I think Grossman-Hart is underutilized with respect to that issue in particular. An injection of the cost and benefits of control into traditional industrial organization–style analysis will tend to bear a lot of fruit.

PART 2

INCOMPLETE CONTRACTS AND FIRM BOUNDARIES

6

Incomplete Contracts and Firm Boundaries: New Directions

WOUTER DESSEIN

In the last 25 years, a formal literature has developed which analyzes firm boundaries and institutional choice, building on the incomplete contracting framework proposed by Grossman and Hart (1986) (GH). In this paper, I discuss some new directions that the literature has taken since. As a central challenge for the literature, I identify the need to provide a theory of the firm in which management and bureaucratic decision making play an important role in coordinating economic activity. Merging a number of existing incomplete contracting models, I propose two ways to integrate managerial direction in a theory of the firm.

A major contribution of GH has been to provide scholars with the tools necessary to study the boundaries of the firm in a clear and consistent way. GH provides a parsimonious and formally tractable definition of what constitutes a firm and how it differs from the market or "nonintegration."[1] Firms are identified with asset ownership and residual control rights, and integration with joint ownership. Firm boundaries matter because contracts are incomplete, and ownership provides residual decision rights over the use of the firm's nonhuman assets, that is, the rights to use assets in whatever way the owner likes unless otherwise prohibited in a contract.

Unlike the preceding informal theories (Coase 1937; Williamson 1971), GH and the property rights theory of the firm (see also Hart and Moore 1990;

I would like to thank Patrick Bolton, Bengt Holmstrom, Navin Kartik, Tano Santos and Steve Tadelis for very useful discussions on this topic and Rob Gertner, Bob Gibbons, and Niko Matouschek for comments on a earlier draft. This paper grew out of a presentation prepared for the "Grossman and Hart at 25" conference held in Brussels on June 24-26, 2011.

[1] See Aghion and Holden (2011) for an excellent nontechnical exposition of the Grossman and Hart model, and Holmström (1999) for a more detailed critical assessment.

Hart 1995) provide a clear identification of the benefits of nonintegration.[2] In the theory, ownership of an asset increases the bargaining power of a player. In most versions of GH, an independent supplier is therefore more motivated—has higher-powered incentives to make noncontractible relation-specific investments—than an integrated supplier.[3] As noted by Holmstrom and Roberts (1998), however, firms are rather poorly defined in the property rights model. There is no management or headquarters in the theory, just a buyer and a seller who trade in a decentralized way. It is further not clear how one can scale up the model to make it relevant to large organizations where residual control over all assets involved in production are exercised by a central office on behalf of the firm, and employees simply contribute human capital (Holmström 1999; Williamson 2002).

In this paper, I discuss two modeling approaches which introduce managerial direction and authoritative decision making in a formal theory of the firm. In the proposed models, managers are different from production workers in that they are not strictly needed for production. Rather their role is to coordinate and direct production by other agents.[4] Importantly, this ability of managers to coordinate is compromised under nonintegration. In particular, in the proposed models, asset ownership allows owners or their designated managers to direct the actions or decisions of employees in a way they would be unable to do so, say, with an independent supplier.

Both modeling approaches draw largely on existing incomplete contracting models but differ substantially in their contractual assumptions. The common feature is that both assume that actions are ex post noncontractible and, hence, the ability to direct and control behavior of agents is fundamentally different under integration and nonintegration. In contrast, in traditional property rights models, residual control rights do not affect ex post decision making

---

[2] More recent contributions to the property rights theory have broadened the concept of ownership to that of access (Rajan and Zingales 1998) and extended the theory to incorporate dynamic considerations and relational contracting (Baker, Gibbons, and Murphy 2002). Whinston and Segal (2010) provide a comprehensive overview and analysis of property rights models.

[3] Empirical support for this can be found in Woodruff (2002), Baker and Hubbard (2003), Acemoglu et al. (2010), as well as in the literature on franchising and manufacturer-retailer relationships, as surveyed by Lafontaine and Slade (2007). More generally, it is optimal to assign asset ownership to the party who must make the most important noncontractible relationship-specific investments. As has been noted by other authors, however, the latter prediction may depend on often subtle details of the model (see, e.g., Holmström and Roberts 1998; Whinston 2003). The only general insight is that asset ownership affects investments.

[4] I do not emphasize the difference between management and the owners of the firm. Managers could be the owners of the firm, or temporarily delegated (loaned) the residual control rights over the assets of the firm. As such, I also ignore any of the incentive problems between owners and managers that have been the subject of much research in corporate finance.

as they simply affect threat points under friction-less Coasian bargaining.[5] Conceptually, the proposed models are therefore closer to the informal theories proposed by Coase (1937) and Williamson (1971, 1975, 1985), who identified firms with decision making by command. Both approaches, however, follow GH in proposing theories that provide a unified account of both the cost and benefits of integration. Moreover, as in GH, firms remain defined in terms of residual control rights over nonhuman assets.

The remainder of the paper goes as follows. In Section 1, I discuss what I refer to as "moral hazard theories" of the firm. In those theories, the relevant actions are controlled by the agents or "implementers" of the firms (as opposed to the owners of the firm, or their designated managers). Since actions are non-contractible, they are formally equivalent to "effort" in standard moral hazard models. Owners or management of the firm can influence those actions only indirectly by giving directions which agents (or suppliers) must be willing to follow. In contrast, in Section 2, I discuss "control theories" of the firm, where asset ownership is assumed to provide direct control over the relevant actions. Since those actions are again noncontractible, residual control rights do not serve as a bargaining tool as in GH, but they are exercised in equilibrium. Section 3 summarizes and concludes.

1. Moral Hazard Theories of the Firm

A direct implication of contractual incompleteness is that contracting on cost and revenue streams is likely to be imperfect. As Holmstrom and Tirole (1989) argue

> Ownership provides residual return rights to all kind of assets, physical as well as financial. The right of a residual return stream is after all nothing more than a right to decide how to spend the firm's money, which has not been explicitly contracted for.

Moral hazard theories of the firm focus on this aspect of incomplete contracts.[6] Other ways in which residual control rights might matter, such as direct control over actions, are minimized by assuming that all actions are both inalienable and noncontractible. That is, actions are like effort in standard moral hazard models. Asset ownership then matters only to the extent it provides

---

[5] The property rights literature, instead, focuses on the impact of asset ownership on ex ante noncontractible investments, for example in relation-specific human capital.

[6] In their book *Economics of Property Rights*, Furubotn and Pejovich (1974, 4) argue that the rights of ownership of an asset include (1) the right to use the asset, (2) the right to appropriate returns from the assets, and (3) the right to change the form and/or substance of an asset.

parties with income streams—or makes them responsible for financial outlays—that otherwise cannot be contractually assigned. Residual control right, for example, may allow owners to appropriate part of the returns of the assets under their control, as in Hart (1988), Stein (1997), or Hart and Holmstrom (2010). Noncontractible effort may further affect the future profitability or resale value of assets, as in Holmstrom and Milgrom (1991, 1994) and Baker and Hubbard (2003, 2004), and it may be difficult to contract on this resale value.

In its simplest incarnation, where actions are modeled as one-dimensional effort, this approach transforms the asset ownership problem into a moral hazard in teams problem with budget balance. Just as there are only so much bargaining chips to go around in the standard property rights model, there are now only so many residual income rights to be allocated. Allocating more assets to one party increases the latter's incentives, but unavoidably reduces the incentives of another party. As in the traditional property rights theory (PRT) models, assets should then be allocated to the party whose effort is most important.[7] This simple model, therefore, does not break much new ground relative to PRT.[8] To develop a theory of the firm in which managerial direction plays a meaningful role, the remainder of this section considers a model in which actions or effort are multi-dimensional, as in Holmstrom and Milgrom (1991, 1994). I first provide an informal discussion of the model and the related literature, with the formal model being presented later.

1.1 Managerial Direction in a Theory of the Firm

Consider a firm which manufactures, markets, and sells a product, and where production requires the firm to make or buy a specialized input. Making this specialized input requires both human capital and the use of some dedicated assets. Under nonintegration, asset ownership by an independent supplier increases the latter's incentives for cost minimization—as the supplier must provide, maintain, and manage all the necessary assets for production (machines,

[7] While theoretically less interesting, this model is more tractable than the classic PRT model and its implications are less susceptible to particular assumptions about bargaining protocols or outside options (De Meza and Lockwood 1998). Moreover, the interpretation of noncontractible relationship-specific investments can be broadened to include effort more broadly. This increases the applicability of the model, and makes it more applicable to, say, franchising contracts (Bhattacharyya and Lafontaine 1995; Lafontaine and Slade 2007).

[8] An important exception is the famous paper by Alchian and Demsetz (1972) who proposed the concentration of profits shares in the hands of a specialized monitor as a solution to the moral hazard in teams problem. As they argued, such a monitor could overcome the noncontractibility problem by effectively measuring inputs of individual workers and mete out the appropriate rewards. As the focus of this paper is on formal theories, I refer to Holmström and Tirole (1988) for a discussion of Alchian and Demsetz and its shortcomings as a workable theory of the firm.

materials, real estate, working capital) and incurs all the associated financial out-lays. In contrast, under integration, the firm provides all the necessary assets and incurs the associated financial outlays. The supplier is then an employee who provides only human capital. While the firm and the supplier may con-tract on cost measures, those measures are very noisy. At the optimum, the wage paid to a supplier-employee—or the price paid for the input to an independent supplier—is therefore not very sensitive to the actual production costs of the input.

Drawing on Holmstrom and Milgrom (1991, 1994), a theory of the firm can then be obtained in which asset ownership by a firm increases the ability of firm owners or their designated managers to steer, direct, and coordinate the efforts of employees in a way it cannot steer the effort of an independent sup-plier. In particular, in addition to cost-reducing effort, I assume the supplier can also undertake some actions which improve coordination and the compatibility of the input, but also increase the cost of that input. [9] The role of management is to identify which coordinating actions are worthwhile and direct the supplier to undertake those. Since actions are noncontractible, however, directions take the form of orders—modeled as cheap talk—which employees must be willing to follow. Following the logic of multitask models, nonintegration reduces the ability of management to direct the supplier who may balk when efficient, but cost-increasing actions are requested. Indeed, nonintegration results in high-powered incentives for cost reduction by an independently operated supplier. In contrast, under integration, the employee-operated supplier has a limited stake in cost reductions. While the employee-supplier is then less entrepreneur-ial, diligent, and motivated to reduce costs, management will find it much easier to direct and steer the actions of this supplier-employee toward coordination and compatibility.

The model, formally developed later, shows how incomplete contracting models can provide a foundation for the idea, central to transaction cost eco-nomics and Coase (1937), that firms distinguish themselves from markets by their ability to coordinate economic activity through bureaucratic decision making. It further provides a number of testable predictions for integration deci-sions. First, the model delivers the insight, prominently featured in Roberts (2004), that the choice between firms and markets involves a trade-off between motivation and coordination. I show that integration is more likely to be optimal when coordination is more important or noncontractible effort is less impor-tant. Second, the model allows us to analyze how optimal integration decisions are affected by the contractibility of input measures, such as costs, and output

---

[9] I follow the approach in Dessein, Garicano, and Gertner (2010) to model such coordinating actions.

measures, such as gross profits or revenues. Perhaps counterintuitively, the impact of a better contractibility of input costs on firm boundaries is shown to be ambiguous. On the one hand, a better contractibility of costs allows for more efficient cost-plus contracting with an independent supplier. Such cost-plus contracting facilitates coordination with an independent supplier who is then more willing to follow orders. On the other hand, a better contractibility of costs also allows the firm to provide higher powered incentives for cost-reduction to an employee and, hence, duplicate the benefits from asset ownership within its boundaries. It follows that an improved contractibility of input costs mitigates agency problems both inside firms and between firms. Later I provide exact conditions for when it favors (non-)integration. In contrast, I show that a better contractibility of gross profits/outputs tends to favor nonintegration/outsourcing as contracting on output measures only serves to improve coordination decisions by the agent.

The theory of firm boundaries draws heavily on on the insights and models by Holmström and Milgrom whose focus was on in-house versus independent sales agents.[10] In addition, the trade-off between coordination and motivation also plays a central role in the models by Athey and Roberts (2001), Dessein, Garicano, and Gertner (2010), and Friebel and Raith (2010). A similar trade-off further arises in the choice between fixed price and cost-plus incentive contracting, as studied in Bajari and Tadelis (2001). The low-powered incentives associated with cost-plus incentive contracting allow for more flexible renegotiation when ex post adaptation is required, but it also creates limited incentives for cost reduction through privately costly effort. Put differently, a buyer has more control over a seller when the latter is motivated by a cost-plus contract than by a fixed price contract. Building on this paper, Tadelis (2002) provides reduced form foundations for transaction cost economics. Finally, obedience or the willingness to follow others has previously been studied by Van den Steen (2007, 2010) and Marino, Matsusaka, and Zabjonik (2010). Van den Steen (2010) follows GH in that asset ownership affects the outside the options of the players. Moving asset ownership from the agent to the principal then lowers the outside option of the agent and raises that of the principal. It therefore makes it more costly for the agent to get fired and easier for the principal to commit to firing a disobeying agent. Van den Steen (2007) does not study firm boundaries, but emphasizes that high-powered incentives come at the expense of disobedience.

---

[10] Baker, Gibbons, and Murphy (2002) provide a dynamic version of Holmström and Milgrom where the principal offers a relational rather than a formal contract to the supplier. As in Holmström and Milgrom, integration results in lower-powered but more balanced incentives than nonintegration. Their model, however, is much closer to the original PRT model in that they explicit model trading decisions, bargaining, and hold-up.

1.2 A Model of Managerial Direction

I now formally develop a simple moral hazard theory of the firm, based on Holmstrom and Milgrom (1991, 1994) and Dessein, Garicano, and Gertner (2010). A firm manufactures, markets, and sells a product. I take it as a given that the firm owns all the assets necessary for manufacturing, marketing, and selling the product. Production, however, also requires that the firm makes or buys a specialized input.[11] Making this specialized input requires both human capital and the use of some dedicated assets. Under integration, the firm provides and owns the dedicated assets, and an employee of the firm provides human capital. Under nonintegration, the provider of human capital also provides and owns the dedicated assets. I will refer to both the employee (under integration) and the owner-operator (under nonintegration) as the agent, unless it is necessary to distinguish the two.

Input Cost: The cost of the input depends on some effort e provided by the Agent at a private cost $e^2/2$. In addition, the Agent takes a continuum of non-contractible actions $i \in [0, 1]$, each of which may increase the gross profits of the firm. For example, such actions may improve the coordination with other business units or make the input more compatible. Each of these actions, however, also increases the cost of the input. Formally, the production cost of the input, gross of any effort costs, equals

$$C = \mathbb{C} - ve + \int_0^1 I_i k_i di, \qquad (1)$$

where v is the marginal value of effort,

$$I_i = \begin{cases} 1 & \text{if the coordinating action } i \text{ is undertaken} \\ 0 & \text{if the coordinating action } i \text{ is not undertaken.} \end{cases}$$

and k_i is an i.i.d random variable, uniformly distributed on $[0, 1]$.

Gross Profits: Profits of the firm, gross of the cost of the input and any transfer to the agent equal

$$R = \Psi + \int_0^1 I_i \Delta_i di, \qquad (2)$$

where $\Delta_i \in \{0, 1\}$ is an i.i.d random variable with $E(\Delta_i) = p$. The parameter p can be interpreted as the value or importance of coordination.

Firm Boundaries: Under nonintegration, the owner-operator provides all the machines, real estate, materials, and working capital necessary for production of

---

[11] The only role that asset specificity plays in the model is conceptual: there is no competitive input market from which the firm can buy this input, or to whom the supplier can sell his input.

the input. As a result, the owner-operator incurs the cost C in addition to his private effort cost $e^2/2$. Under integration, this cost C is incurred by the firm, who then provides and controls all assets necessary for production. Similarly, since the firm controls all the other production activities (manufacturing, marketing, and selling) and provides the necessary assets, the firm is always residual claimant of the gross profit stream R. The model envisions a setting in which the firm is much larger than the supplier, and where the firm's owners are necessarily passive investors. Hence, unlike in GH, there is no difference between forward and backward integration.[12]

Management and Managerial Direction: The residual control rights over the assets of the firm are delegated to a manager (or central office) who is not engaged in production but maximizes expected firm profits, for example because she can divert part of the profits of the firm (Hart 1988; Stein 1997; Hart and Holmström 2010).[13] While not essential for the results, I assume that only management of the firm observes $\Delta_i \in \{0, 1\}$, but she can make a cheap talk statement regarding Δ_i to the Agent. Without loss of generality, I restrict cheap talk to a continuum of messages $m_i \in \{0, 1\}$, for $i \in [0, 1]$, where m_i can be interpreted as an order or request by management of the firm to the Agent to choose $I_i = m_i$. One role for management is thus to coordinate and direct the activities of the Agent so that externalities with other activities of the firm are taken into account. In particular, since k_i is uniformly distributed on $[0, 1]$, the Agent should take the coordinating action i whenever $\Delta_i = 1$.

Contracting: While R and C are not contractible, there exists a correlated cost stream $P_c = C + c + \varepsilon_c$ and a correlated gross profit stream $P_r = R + r + \varepsilon_r$, where ε_c and ε_r are random variables with $\varepsilon_c \backsim N(0, \sigma_c^2)$ and $\varepsilon_r \backsim N(0, \sigma_r^2)$. The constants c and r reflect predictable differences between real and measurable cost and revenues.[14] Without loss of generality, I set $r = c = 0$. At the optimum, any transfer t from the firm to the agent will be contingent on the realization of P_c and P_r. I follow Holmström and Milgrom by considering only transfers that are a linear function of P_c and P_r, that is

$$t^g = b_0^g + b_r^g P_r - b_c^g P_c, \qquad g = I, NI.[15]$$

---

[12] See also note 13.

[13] In particular, managing the firm is not compatible with providing the human capital and effort e required for the specialized input

[14] For example, $r < 0$ represents a case where contractible gross profits substantially understate the true profitability of a product, for example, because management can manipulate accounting processes to divert revenues to other products and allocate costs from other business units to this product.

From (1) and (2), for a given equilibrium in pure strategies, the revenue and cost streams R and C are predictable ex ante.[16] Hence t^I and t^N are normally distributed with

$$Var(t^g) = (\sigma_c b_c^g)^2 + (\sigma_r b_r^g)^2, \qquad g = I, NI.$$

As in Holmström and Milgrom, the agent is assumed to be risk averse with CARA utility, so he maximizes

$$U_A^I = E(t^I) - Var(t^I) - e^2/2 \tag{3}$$

under integration, and

$$U_A^{NI} = E(t^{NI} - C) - Var(t^{NI}) - e^2/2 \tag{4}$$

under nonintegration. Similarly, the manager of the firm maximizes

$$U_M^I = R - E(t^I - C)$$

under integration, and

$$U_M^{NI} = R - E(t^{NI})$$

under nonintegration.

Expected Firm Profits. Finally, I assume that there is a competitive market of suppliers and employees at the contracting stage. The firm therefore can make a take-it-or-leave-it offer to the agent, where I normalize the reservation utility of the agent to zero. Expected profits under integration and nonintegration can therefore be written as

$$\pi^g = \Psi - \mathbb{C} + \int_0^1 I_i(\Delta_i - k_i)di + ve - e^2/2 - (\sigma_c b_c^g)^2 - (\sigma_r b_r^g)^2, \qquad g = I, NI.$$

Figure 6.1 summarizes the timing of the model.

Managerial Direction. In the model, Management sends cheap talk messages $m_i \in \{0, 1\}$, for $i \in [0, 1]$. One can verify that there always exists an equilibrium of the communication subgame where Management sends $m_i = 1$ if and only if $\Delta_i = 1$ and hence $I_i = 1$ is the efficient action.[17] I focus on this truthful equilibrium. A cheap talk message of $m_i = 1$ can then be interpreted as a request by management to take the coordinating action. Given truth-telling, a

---

[15] See Holmström and Milgrom (1987) for a justification of the linearity assumption.

[16] While a given coordination decision I_i is not predictable ex ante, there is a continuum of coordinating decisions I_i. Moreover, for a given equilibrium in pure strategies, each of these decisions is a deterministic function of k_i and Δ_i, both i.i.d. random variables.

[17] The incentive constraint to reveal that $\Delta_i = 0$ is that β^g, defined in (7), is smaller than 1. This is always satisfied at the optimum. A sufficient condition to reveal that $\Delta_i = 1$ is $1 - \beta^g \leq 1 - b_r^g$, which is also always satisfied at the optimum.

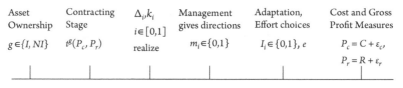

Asset Ownership	Contracting Stage	Δ_i, k_i $i \in [0,1]$ realize	Management gives directions	Adaptation, Effort choices	Cost and Gross Profit Measures
$g \in \{I, NI\}$	$t^g(P_c, P_r)$		$m_i \in \{0,1\}$	$I_i \in \{0,1\}, e$	$P_c = C + \varepsilon_c,$ $P_r = R + \varepsilon_r$

Figure 6.1 Time-line Moral Hazard Model

managerial direction to take a coordinating action will be followed by the agent if and only if

$$k_i b_c^I < b_r^I$$

under integration and

$$k_i(1 + b_c^{NI}) < b_r^{NI}$$

under nonintegration.[18] Given the foregoing incentive constraints, I define (the effectiveness of) *managerial direction* under integration and nonintegration by

$$\alpha^I \equiv b_r^I/b_c^I \quad \text{and} \quad \alpha^{NI} \equiv b_r^{NI}/(1 + b_c^{NI}). \tag{5}$$

Indeed, given that k is uniformly distributed on $[0, 1]$, α^I and α^{NI} are the probabilities that the agent follows the direction of management to take the coordinating action under integration and nonintegration, respectively. It follows that

$$\int_0^1 I_i(\Delta_i - k_i)di = p \int_0^{\alpha^g} (1 - k)dk = \frac{p}{2}\alpha^g (2 - \alpha^g) \tag{6}$$

under both integration and nonintegration.

Effort Choices From (3), effort under integration equals $e^I = vb_c^I$. From (4), effort under non-integration equals $e^{NI} = v(1 + b_c^{NI})$. It will be useful to denote *effort incentives* under integration and nonintegration by

$$\beta^I \equiv b_c^I \quad \text{and} \quad \beta^{NI} \equiv 1 + b_c^{NI}. \tag{7}$$

Under both structures, equilibrium effort is then given by

$$e^g = v\beta^g, \qquad g = I, NI. \tag{8}$$

Trade-off between Motivation and Coordination. In what follows, without loss of generality, I will optimize over β^g and α^g, that is "effort incentives" and "managerial direction," rather than the cost and revenue shares b_c^g and b_r^g. Substituting (5), (6), (7), and (8), expected profits under integration can be rewritten as

$$\pi^I = \Psi - \mathbb{C} + \frac{p}{2}\alpha^I (2 - \alpha^I) + \frac{v^2}{2}\beta^I(2 - \beta^I)$$
$$-\sigma_c^2(\beta^I)^2 - \sigma_r^2(\alpha^I\beta^I)^2, \tag{9}$$

---

[18] Given truth-telling, it is will be easy to verify that the agent never has an incentive to take a coordinating action when $m_i = \Delta_i = 0$.

whereas expected profits under nonintegration equal

$$\pi^{NI} = \Psi - \mathbb{C} + \frac{p}{2}\alpha^{NI}(2 - \alpha^{NI}) + \frac{v^2}{2}\beta^{NI}(2 - \beta^{NI}) \\ -\sigma_c^2(\beta^{NI} - 1)^2 - \sigma_r^2(\alpha^{NI}\beta^{NI})^2 \tag{10}$$

First-order conditions with respect to effort incentives (β^g) yield:

$$b_c^I \equiv \beta^I = \frac{v^2}{v^2 + 2\sigma_c^2 + 2\sigma_r^2(\alpha^I)^2}$$

and

$$1 + b_c^{NI} \equiv \beta^{NI} = \frac{v^2 + 2\sigma_c^2}{v^2 + 2\sigma_c^2 + 2\sigma_r^2(\alpha^{NI})^2}.$$

First-order conditions with respect to managerial direction (α^g) yield

$$\alpha^g = \frac{p}{p + 2\sigma_r^2(\beta^g)^2} \qquad g = I, NI.$$

An inspection of the above equalities yields the following implications:

Proposition 1

- $\beta^{NI} > \beta^I$ and $\alpha^I > \alpha^{NI}$: Effort incentives are larger under non-integration, but managerial direction is more effective under integration. Both are below first-best: $\beta^g \in (0,1)$ and $\alpha^g \in (0,1)$.
- Nonintegration features cost-plus contracting: the transfer to the supplier t^{NI} is increasing in the cost measure P_c. Integration features incentive contracting: the transfer to the employee t^I is decreasing in the cost measure P_c.

It is easy to verify that expected profits under integration, π^I, are supermodular in β^I, $(-\alpha^I)$, v, $(-p)$, and $(-\sigma_c^2)$. Similarly, expected profits under nonintegration are supermodular in β^{NI}, $(-\alpha^{NI})$, v, $(-p)$, and σ_c^2 for $\beta^{NI} \in [0,1]$. This yields the following comparative static results:

Proposition 2

- An increase in the value of effort, v, increases effort incentives, and decreases managerial direction. An increase in the importance of coordination, p, reduces effort incentives but increases managerial direction.
- Under nonintegration, an increase in the noisiness of cost measures, σ_c^2, increases effort incentives β^g and reduces managerial direction α^g. Under integration, opposite comparative statics hold.

This first set of results clearly shows a trade-off between motivation (incentives) and coordination. First, this trade-off is present for a given governance structure: more effort incentives come at the expense of less effective managerial direction, and both are at a second-best level at the optimum. In contracting with the agent (employee or supplier), management balances these two conflicting objectives. Interestingly, when contracting with a supplier, the cost measure is used to improve managerial direction, and transfers reward the supplier for having higher costs. This is akin to the cost-plus contracts studied in Bajari and Tadelis (2001). The aim of such "cost-plus" contracting is to improve the effectiveness of managerial direction. In contrast, when contracting in-house with an employee, the cost measure is used to increase motivation, and the employee is rewarded for reducing costs.

Second, this trade-off is also present between governance structures: integration results in better coordination, but nonintegration results in better motivation. This suggests that as coordination becomes more important, integration will be preferred, whereas nonintegration will be preferred when motivation become more important. The following proposition states this result formally:[19]

Proposition 3 An increase in the importance of cost-reducing effort, v, favors nonintegration. An increase in the importance of coordination, p, favors integration. For v sufficiently small, integration is always optimal, whereas for p sufficiently small, nonintegration is preferred.

Finally, the model allows us to analyze how integration decisions respond to the contractibility of input costs and gross profits. Consider first the contractibility of input costs. Using the envelope theorem, it follows from profit functions (9) and (10), that a better contractibility of input costs (a decrease in σ_c^2) favors integration if and only if

$$\beta^I > 1 - \beta^{NI}.$$

We further have that both β^I and β^{NI} are increasing in v and decreasing in p. Moreover, $\beta^I = 0 < 1 - \beta^{NI}$ for $v = 0$, whereas $\beta^I > 1 - \beta^{NI} = 0$ for $p = 0$. This yields the following result:

Proposition 4 The impact of a better contractibility of input costs, as measured by $1/\sigma_c^2$, depends on the value of effort v and the importance of coordination p.

---

[19] The comparative static result can be obtained by taking the derivative of the profit functions (9) and (10) with respect to v and p. Using the envelope theorem and the fact that $\beta^{NI}(2 - \beta^{NI}) > \beta^I(2 - \beta^I)$, but $\alpha^{NI}(2 - \alpha^{NI}) < \alpha^I(2 - \alpha^I)$, the result follows directly. It is further direct to show that integration (nonintegration) is optimal for $v = 0$ ($p = 0$). The last part of the proposition then holds by continuity.

Fix σ_r^2, then there exists a $\bar{v}(p, \sigma_r^2) > 0$ and $\bar{p}(v, \sigma_r^2) > 0$ such that a better contractibility of input costs favors integration if and only if $v > \bar{v}$ or $p < \bar{p}$.

Intuitively, a better contractibility of input costs has two opposite effects. On the one hand, it makes cost-plus contracting more efficient, and therefore allows for a better coordination under nonintegration. On the other hand, it allows for a more efficient provision of cost-cutting incentives to an employee, which favors integration. If the optimal level of effort incentives is relatively high (that is v is large or p is small), a better contractibility of input costs may then result in a shift from nonintegration to integration, but never the other way around. The opposite effect arises when optimal effort incentives are low.

Finally, consider the contractibility of gross profits, $1/\sigma_r^2$, which can also be interpreted as the ability to contract on performance measures other than costs, such as quality, compatibility, cooperation and so on, which are not rewarded by asset ownership. While no general results can be obtained,[20] some insight can be provided by focusing on cases where such performance measures are either very precise (σ_r^2 is small) or, instead, very noisy (σ_r^2 large):

Proposition 5 Assume $p > v^2$, then there exists $r_H > r_L > 0$, such that integration is preferred if performance measures on dimensions other than cost are very noisy, that is $\sigma_r^2 > r_H$, whereas nonintegration is preferred if such performance measures are very precise, that is, when $\sigma_r^2 < r_L$.

Proof Assume $1/\sigma_r^2 = 0$. Under nonintegration, then $\beta^{NI} = 1$ and $\alpha^{NI} = 0$. Under integration, we either have $\beta^I = 0$ and $\alpha^I = 0$, or $\beta^I \in (0, 1)$ and $\alpha^I = 0$. The latter case, however, is always dominated by nonintegration. From (9) and (10), one can then verify that integration will be preferred over nonintegration if and only if $p > v^2$. Continuity of profits in σ_r^2 implies that integration will be preferred for $p > v^2$ as long as σ_r^2 is large enough. Consider next $\sigma_r^2 = 0$. Nonintegration then achieves first best, as $\beta^{NI} = \alpha^{NI} = 1$, whereas effort is still second-best effort under nonintegration. Continuity of profits in σ_r^2 again implies that nonintegration will be preferred as long as σ_r^2 is sufficiently small.

Proposition 5 is strongly suggestive that a better contractibility of other dimensions than input costs favors using nonintegration, as this allows to exploit the strong cost incentives provided by asset ownership. In contrast, if

---

[20] Indeed, profits are not supermodular in $1/\sigma_r^2$.

those other dimensions are hard to measure, there is a trade-off between effort incentives and managerial direction.

In conclusion, the simple multitasking model above shows how, in a relative parsimonious way, moral hazard models can give content to a theory of managerial direction, where the decision to integrate or not reflects a trade-off between motivation and coordination. An informal statement of the trade-off between motivation and coordination can also be found in Roberts (2004, 103–8).

As important, the above model shows how moral hazard theories of the firm can deliver a number of testable and intuitive predictions. Particularly noteworthy are those related to contractibility of performance dimensions. While these results suggest that a better contractibility of output measures favors using the market (nonintegration), this is not necessarily the case for the contractibility of input costs. A better contractibility of costs mitigates agency problems both within firm boundaries, by allowing for more higher-powered incentives for cost reduction, and between firm boundaries, by allowing for more effective cost-plus contracting and, hence, better coordination.

2. Control Theories of the Firm

Moral hazard models make the extreme assumption that task allocation is fixed exogenously, and agents cannot be removed/replaced when they do not follow task directions. In reality, many important decisions taken by employees can be overturned by the firm's owners or their designated managers through the direct or indirect use of their residual control rights. Indeed, firm owners and top management tend to exercise residual control rights through selective intervention: they intervene when employees disobey important orders or directions.[21] For example, management may deny employees access to assets necessary for implementing decisions, funding or personnel may be withdrawn, and the employee may be fired, replaced, or reassigned. While control models share the assumption of moral hazard models that certain decisions are noncontractible, they take the polar position that those decisions are fully controlled by the firm owners or their designated managers.[22]

---

[21] One justification for the assumption in moral hazard models is that actions are not only noncontractible, but also nonobservable, and hence selective intervention is not feasible.

[22] An implicit assumption is further that authority over actions cannot simply be transferred contractually—ownership of assets and, hence, firm boundaries must matter. See Baker, Gibbons, and Murphy (2011) for a model in which contracts are used to move control rights across fixed firm boundaries

A straightforward implication from control models might seem that asset ownership, and hence control, should be allocated to the party whose interests are most aligned with total surplus maximization. Gibbons (2005, 212–13), for example, provides a formal model along those lines.[23] Taken literally, however, Gibbons's model is more a theory of *who* should own the assets of the firm rather than what the boundaries of that firm are.

A more powerful insight obtains when firm boundaries determine the objectives of firm owners—rather than the other way around. In particular, if firm owners can appropriate the noncontractible returns on the assets of the firm, as is the case in moral hazard models, it follows quite naturally that centralized asset ownership results in a better coordination of decisions than dispersed asset ownership. Some well-known papers which follow this logic to elucidate firm boundaries include Stein (1997) on internal versus external capital markets, and Hart and Holmström (2010) (HH) on firm scope.[24] In Stein (1997), integration results in a better ex post allocation of capital, but comes at the expense of reduced incentives for business unit managers.[25] In HH, the owners of integrated firms are better at exploiting economies of scale through standardization, but they do not internalize the private benefits of managers of individual business units. Both control models have in common that, in the presence of externalities, concentrated asset ownership may be valuable for coordination purposes.

In this section, I show how the improved coordination in integrated firms, highlighted in HH, may come at the expense of worse adaptation to a changing environment. For this purpose, I introduce asset ownership in the model of Alonso, Dessein, and Matouschek (2008) (ADM).[26] As in HH, decisions benefit from being coordinated in ADM, but the model introduces the notion that decisions need to be adapted to an uncertain environment.[27]

---

[23] See also Bester (2009) for a related model, which focuses on the allocation of decision rights in an organization but can be reinterpreted in terms of asset ownership.

[24] As in other control models, HH assume that parties simply exercise their decision rights without any bargaining with side payments. Rather than appealing to noncontractibility, they informally justify the no bargaining assumption by introducing "shading" (Hart and Moore 2008) in their model. An earlier version did not refer to shading, but simply assumed noncontractibility.

[25] See also Scharfstein and Stein (2000), Rajan et al. (2000), Stein (2002), Brusco and Panunzi (2005), Inderst and Laux (2005), and Friebel and Raith (2010).

[26] See also Rantakari (2008).

[27] In contrast, uncertainty plays no role in HH's theory of firm scope. Decision making is assumed to deviate from ex post surplus maximization for different reasons under integration and nonintegration, and the question in HH is which inefficiency is largest. Introducing uncertainty in their model would not alter this trade-off.

2.1 Adaptation and Firm Boundaries

Adaptation to a changing and uncertain environment is a central issue in transaction cost economics. As stated by Williamson (1985, 56):

> many of the interesting issues with which transaction cost economics is involved reduce to an assessment of adaptive, sequential decision-making [...] the basic proposition here is that governance structures differ in their capacities to respond effectively to disturbances.

In arguing that "adaptation is the central problem," Williamson (1996, 2002) frequently cites Hayek who famously maintained that "the economic problem of society is mainly one of adaptation to changes in particular circumstances of time and place" (Hayek 1945, 524). Hayek's argument, however, was very much that the market has adaptive capabilities which are superior to that of a centrally planned economy. Hayek emphasized not only the role of the price system in coordinating economic activity, but also that most decision-relevant information is dispersed and local in nature. In settings in which the relevant information is dispersed, it is far from clear why a centralized or integrated organization would be better at adapting to a changing environment than a decentralized or nonintegrated organization. [28]

Subsection 2.2 proposes a modified version of ADM to address the above question. In line with Hayek's focus on local information, the model assumes that the decision-relevant information is dispersed. Concretely, let there be two assets, one can think of two business units, each operated by a different agent who is privately informed about some local information pertaining to his unit. Each unit must implement a major decision whose effectiveness depends on how adaptive it is to the local information and how well coordinated it is with the decision of the other unit. Agents are employees, however, who do not own the assets they operate. They must therefore communicate their local information to the owner or owners of the business units, who control major decisions. [29] The question is whether there should be common ownership of assets with a single "boss" for both agents or dispersed ownership with each agent having his own boss.

---

[28] For example, many business practitioners have advocated that firms decentralize decision making in more competitive and turbulent environments. Some empirical evidence, such as Bloom et al. (2009), is consistent with this.

[29] Following the literature on firm boundaries, and in contrast to ADM or Dessein (2002), I assume that decision rights cannot be credibly delegated to employees. Decisions are therefore always taken by asset owners and I assume that an employee cannot be an owner.

If there were no communication frictions between employees and owners, concentrated ownership with a single boss would always be optimal. Indeed, such a single owner would then internalize all externalities between business units. Incentive conflicts between the firm owner and the agents who operate the business units, however, may make communication strategic and noisy.[30] Concretely, I assume that each agent maximizes the returns of the unit he operates, for example, because of career concerns or implicit incentives. In contrast, firm boundaries determine the objectives of the firm owners, who maximize the returns of the unit(s) under their control.

The optimal ownership structure is then driven by a trade-off between coordination and adaptation. Common ownership (integration) is valuable, as the single firm owner then internalizes externalities and ensures coordination. Common ownership, however, also results in decisions which are not very adaptive to local information, as the employees and the firm owner do not share the same objectives and, hence, communication is strategic and noisy. Important local information is thus lost under integration. In contrast, under dispersed ownership (nonintegration), each firm owner shares a common objective with his employee, and communication is friction-less. Owners of individual assets are then able to accurately adapt decisions to local information, but may fail to coordinate their decisions.[31]

Relative to GH, the proposed control model emphasizes the role of a central office or a common owner in coordinating decisions under integration. However, it also highlights the benefits of nonintegration in being more responsive to a changing environment. The adaptive benefits of markets (that is, dispersed asset ownership) can be contrasted with the entrepreneurial and incentivizing benefits emphasized in standard property rights or moral hazard models.

2.2 A Control Theory of the Firm

The following control model is adapted from ADM to include asset ownership. Consider two business units, 1 and 2, which can either be stand-alone firms or

---

[30] Stein (2002) and Friebel and Raith (2010) also consider dispersed information and strategic communication in models of resource allocation. Resource reallocation is assumed to be only feasible in integrated firms, however. Horizontal coordination and communication are therefore ruled out. In contrast, in ADM, the same production possibilities are feasible under both integration and nonintegration.

[31] Consistent with ADM, Simester and Knez (2002) provide evidence about a high-technology firm which indicates that the firm enjoys better coordination with its internal supplier, and that this partially determines which parts are made internally. As in the model, a major reason is that communication is much more distorted and strained, for strategic reasons, when it occurs across firm boundaries rather than within the firm.

belong to one and the same firm. Business Unit $j \in \{1, 2\}$ generates profits that depend on its local conditions, described by $\theta_j \in \mathbf{R}$, and on two decisions, $d_1 \in \mathbf{R}$ and $d_2 \in \mathbf{R}$. In particular, the profits of Business Unit 1 are given by

$$\pi_1 = K_1 - \alpha \, (d_1 - \theta_1)^2 - \delta \, (d_1 - d_2)^2, \tag{11}$$

where $K_1 \in \mathbf{R}_+$ is the maximum profit that the unit can realize. The first squared term captures the *adaptation loss* that Unit 1 incurs if decision d_1 is not perfectly adapted to its local conditions, that is, if $d_1 \neq \theta_1$, and the second squared term captures the *coordination loss* that Unit 1 incurs if the two decisions are not perfectly coordinated, that is, if $d_1 \neq d_2$. Coordination benefits can be interpreted as economies of scope when the two business unit choose more standardized processes, use more common inputs, or are more compatible with each other. I refer to ADM (as well as HH) for more discussion on the interdependence parameter δ. The parameter $\delta/\alpha \in [0, \infty)$ then measures the importance of coordination relative to adaptation. The profits of Unit 2 are similarly given by

$$\pi_2 = K_2 - \alpha \, (d_2 - \theta_2)^2 - \delta \, (d_1 - d_2)^2, \tag{12}$$

where $K_2 \in \mathbf{R}_+$ is the maximum profit that Unit 2 can realize.

Information: Each unit is run by an employee. Agent 1, the employee in charge of Unit 1, privately observes his local conditions θ_1 but does not know the realization of θ_2. Similarly, Agent 2, the employee in charge of Unit 2, observes θ_2 but does not know θ_1. It is common knowledge, however, that θ_1 and θ_2 are uniformly distributed on $[-s_1, s_1]$ and $[-s_2, s_2]$ respectively, with s_1 and $s_2 \in \mathbf{R}_+$, where the draws of θ_1 and θ_2 are independent. The private benefits of each employee are further assumed to be proportional to the profits of his unit, for example, because he can divert part of the profits of the unit as in Stein (1997) or HH. Note that this assumption can easily be endogenized by adding career concerns or a moral hazard problem to the model, where the profits of a business unit depend on the talent and/or effort of the employee.

Firm Boundaries and Asset Ownership: Following GH, firm boundaries matter as contracts are highly incomplete and asset ownership provides residual control and residual income rights. In particular, I assume that there are two clusters of assets: the assets of Business Unit 1 and assets of Business Unit 2. While d_1 and d_2 are noncontractible, ownership of the assets of business unit $i = 1, 2$, provides control over d_i. Similarly, profits are noncontractible but ownership of the assets of business unit i provides residual income rights over π_i. This assumption follows Hart (1988), Holmström and Milgrom (1991, 1994), Stein (1997), and HH.

Two ownership configurations are possible: Business Units 1 and 2 are jointly owned (*integration*), or Business Units 1 and 2 are independently owned (*nonintegration*). For simplicity, I assume that Agent 1 and Agent 2 cannot be asset owners, for example, because they are liquidity constrained. Given the above assumptions, under nonintegration, the owner of Business Unit 1 (owner 1) chooses d_1 and maximizes π_1 and owner of Business Unit 2 (owner 2) chooses d_2 and maximizes π_2. Under common ownership (integration), the common owner chooses d_1 and d_2 and maximizes $\pi_1 + \pi_2$.

Communication: Since d_1 and d_2 are noncontractible, decision makers are not able to commit to paying transfers that depend on the information they receive or to make their decisions depend on such information in different ways. Communication between the owner or owners and their better-informed employees therefore takes the form of an informal mechanism: cheap talk. I assume that both Agent 1 and Agent 2 send a private message to whomever owns their business unit. Under integration, Agent i and the common owner then have different objectives. As a result, communication is noisy, and, as is common in the literature, I will focus on the most informative equilibrium. In contrast, under nonintegration, Agent i and owner i share the same objectives. Hence there exists an equilibrium in which owner i perfectly learns θ_1. Under nonintegration, owner 1 and owner 2 may also benefit from communicating with each other to coordinate their choices of d_1 and d_2. I assume therefore that owner 1 and 2 simultaneously send a message to each other after communicating with their agent.[32] Since owner 1 and 2 have different objectives, this communication will be noisy and, again, I will focus on the most-informative cheap talk equilibrium.

The game is summarized in Figure 6.2. First, asset ownership is allocated to maximize total expected profits $E[\pi_1 + \pi_2]$. Under integration, there is one owner, who controls both decisions. Under nonintegration, there are two owners, who each control a different decision. Second, the two agents which operate the business units become informed about their local conditions, that is, they learn θ_1 and θ_2, respectively. Third, the agents privately communicate

Who owns business unit i = 1,2? Common or dispersed ownership?	Agent i observes θ_i	Agent i sends message to owner of business unit i	Owners of business units send messages to each other	Owner business unit 1 chooses d_1 Owner business unit 2 chooses d_2

Figure 6.2 Time Line Control Model

[32] Alternatively, under nonintegration, each agent $i = 1, 2$ could send a private message m_{ij} to each manager $j = 1, 2$.

with the owner of their business unit. Under nonintegration, the owners also communicate with each other. Finally, the decisions d_1 and d_2 are made by the owner(s). Each decision maker chooses the decision that maximizes his payoff given the information that has been communicated.

2.3 Firm Boundaries: Adaptation versus Coordination

The trade-off between integration (common ownership) and nonintegration (dispersed ownership) is now relatively straightforward: under nonintegration, objectives of owners and employees are aligned and communication is fluent. In contrast, under integration, objectives of the common owner and employees are nonaligned, and communication is noisy.

Profits under nonintegration, then, are as if employees effectively control decision making. They are therefore equivalent to the decentralization case in ADM with fully biased managers. Similarly, profits under integration are equivalent to those under centralization in ADM. The only difference with ADM is that decision rights are never formally delegated to employees. The objectives of an employee's boss, however, depend on firm boundaries and determine how much real authority an employee has.[33]

Given the above equivalence, I can refer to ADM for a formal characterization of decision making and communication equilibria under integration (centralization) and nonintegration (decentralization in ADM). Proposition 3 in ADM highlights an important trade-off between integration and nonintegration. On the one hand, under nonintegration, owner i is better informed about θ_i than the common owner under integration, as the latter must rely on noisy intrafirm communication. One can say that owner $i = 1, 2$, has better specialized knowledge than the common owner. On the other hand, the common owner is better informed about θ_j than manager $i \neq j$. Indeed, for any $\delta \geq 0$, intrafirm communication under integration is more informative than interfirm communication under nonintegration. One can say that the common owner has broader knowledge than owner 1 or 2. It follows that the common owner is better able to coordinate d_1 and d_2. A first insight is thus that common ownership results in broader knowledge by decision makers, whereas dispersed ownership results in in deeper and more specialized knowledge by decision makers.

Beyond the (equilibrium) differences in their information structure, the common owner and the individual owners also have different objectives. While the common owner maximizes joint expected profits in choosing d_1 and d_2, the

---

[33] Put differently, the ownership structure affects the real authority of agents and, hence, their incentives for information revelation. The real authority of an employee may also affect his incentives for information acquisition, as emphasized in Aghion and Tirole (1997). Introducing the need for information acquisition in the model would further enhance the benefits of nonintegration.

owners of individual business units maximize expected profits of their unit and do not take externalities into account. As a result, the decisions of owner 1 and 2 are too responsive to their information relative to first-best.

It follows that integrated firms are better at coordinating decisions than nonintegrated firms: d_1 and d_2 are more correlated under integration (common ownership) than under nonintegration (dispersed ownership). In contrast, under nonintegration, individual decisions are typically more correlated with the local information of their unit. The above logic suggests that integration will be preferred if and only if coordination is sufficiently important relative to adaptation. The following proposition, which is taken directly from ADM, shows that this is indeed the case.

Proposition 6 There exists a $\bar{\delta} > 0$ such that integration (common ownership) is strictly preferred if $\delta/\alpha > \bar{\delta}$ and nonintegration (dispersed ownership) is strictly preferred if $\delta/\alpha \in (0, \bar{\delta})$.

While the idea that integrated firms may be better at coordinating decisions is also present in Stein (1997), Hart and Moore (2005), and HH, the novel contribution of the above control model is the focus on the ability of nonintegrated firms to adapt to a changing environment. As such, the model gives content to the broad idea that information gets lost and distorted in large bureaucratic firms. The adaptive benefits of nonintegrated firms, highlighted in the above model, can be contrasted with the entrepreneurial and incentivizing benefits of nonintegrated firms emphasized in GH and property rights theory.

3. Conclusion

This paper has discussed some new directions in the theory of the firm that emphasize the role of bureaucratic decision making and centralized asset ownership in coordinating and directing economic activity. Following Grossman and Hart (1986), firm boundaries are defined based on the ownership of nonhuman assets, and the costs and benefits of integration are analyzed in a unified framework. The new approaches differ from Grossman and Hart, however, on at least two dimensions: first, actions are noncontractible and firm boundaries determine what actions are eventually undertaken. In contrast, the assumption of ex post contractibility and Coasian bargaining in Grossman and Hart implies that decision making is always efficient, regardless of the ownership structure. Second, asset ownership not only provides residual control rights but also affects the objectives of firm owners: firm owners can appropriate the returns on the assets they own and are responsible for the financial outlays associated with providing and maintaining the assets necessary for production. While there may exist contractible cost and revenue measures, these are not a perfect substitute for asset ownership.

In both approaches discussed, centralized or common asset ownership implies a better coordination of actions and decisions. The reason is that centralized asset ownership allows or facilitates managerial direction or command and ensures that firm owners take externalities between decisions into account. The models therefore introduce management and bureaucratic decision making inside a theory of the firm. Those coordination benefits of common ownership are contrasted with the benefits of dispersed asset ownership in providing higher-powered incentives (which, however, reduce coordination) and a better adaptation of decisions to an uncertain and changing environment (which require decentralized decision making and therefore, again, reduce coordination).

A major shortcoming of this essay is its lack of attention to at least three recent strands in the incomplete contracting literature. First, a few papers, such as Matouschek (2004), have introduced asymmetric information in the context of standard property rights models. Ex post bargaining is then not friction-less anymore and hence the allocation of residual control rights matters for ex post efficiency. Second, Hart and Moore (2008) and Hart (2009) introduce some behavioral elements where agents "shade" their performance if they feel mistreated in the contract execution stage. Asset ownership may play a role here to the extent it affects such feelings of entitlement. Again this strand of literature introduces ex post inefficiencies in a theory of the firm. Finally, I have ignored dynamic considerations and relational contracts (Baker, Gibbons, and Murphy, 2002, 2011; Levin, 2002), which can be fruitfully applied to shed light on firm boundaries. While these papers contain many valuable insights, this essay has instead focused on models that introduce a clear role for managerial direction and bureaucratic decision making in a theory of the firm.

References

Acemoglu, D., P. Aghion, R. Griffith, and F. Zilibotti. 2010. "Vertical Integration and Technology: Theory and Evidence." *Journal of the European Economic Association* 8: 989–1033.

Aghion, P., and R. Holden. 2011. "Incomplete Contracts and the Theory of the Firm: What Have We Learned over the Past 25 Years?" *Journal of Economic Perspectives* 25: 181–97.

Aghion, P., and J. Tirole. 1997. "Formal and Real Authority in Organizations." *Journal of Political Economy* 105: 1–29.

Alchian, A., and H. Demsetz. 1972. "Production, Information Costs, and Economic Organization." *American Economic Review* 62: 777–95.

Alonso, R., W. Dessein, and N. Matouschek. 2008. "When Does Coordination Require Centralization?" *American Economic Review* 98: 145–79.

Athey, S., and J. Roberts. 2001. "Organizational Design: Decision Rights and Incentive Contracts." *American Economic Review* 91: 200–205.

Bajari, P., and S. Tadelis. 2001. "Incentives versus Transaction Costs: A Theory of Procurement Contracts." *Rand Journal of Economics* 15: 385–95.

Baker, G., R. Gibbons, and K. J. Murphy. 2002. "Relational Contracts and the Theory of the Firm." *Quarterly Journal of Economics* 117: 39–83.

Baker, G., R. Gibbons, and K. J. Murphy. 2011. "Relational Adaptation." Working Paper, MIT.

Baker, G., and T. Hubbard. 2003. "Make versus Buy in Trucking: Asset Ownership, Job Design, and Information." *American Economic Review* 93: 551–72.

Baker, G., and T. Hubbard. 2004. "Contractibility and Asset Ownership: On-Board Computers and Governance in U.S. Trucking." *Quarterly Journal of Economics* 119: 1443–79.

Battacharyya, S., and F. Lafontaine. 1995. "Double-Side Moral Hazard and the Nature of Share Contracts." *Rand Journal of Economics* 26: 761–781.

Bloom, N., R., Sadun, and J. Van Reenen. 2009. "The Organization of Firms across Countries." Working Paper, LSE.

Bester, H. 2009. "Externalities, Communication and the Allocation of Decision Rights." *Economic Theory* 41: 269–96.

Brusco, S., and F. Panunzi. 2005. "Reallocation of Corporate Resources and Managerial Incentives in Internal Capital Markets." *European Economic Review* 49: 1659–81.

Coase, R. 1937. "The Nature of the Firm." *Economica* 4: 386–405.

Crawford, V., and J. Sobel. 1982. "Strategic Information Transmission." *Econometrica* 50: 1431–51.

Dessein, W. 2002. "Authority and Communication in Organizations." *Review of Economic Studies* 69: 811–38.

Dessein, W., L. Garicano, and R. Gertner. 2010. "Organizing for Synergies." *American Economic Journal: Microeconomics* 2: 77–114.

De Meza, D., and B. Lockwood. 1998. "Does Asset Ownership Always Motivate Managers? Outside Options and the Property Rights Theory of the Firm." *Quarterly Journal of Economics* 113: 361–86.

Furubotn, E., and S. Pejovich. 1974. *The Economics of Property Rights*. Cambridge, MA: Ballinger.

Friebel, G., and M. Raith. 2010. "Resource Allocation and Organizational Form." *American Economic Journal: Microeconomics* 2: 1–33.

Gertner, R., and R. Stillman. 2001. "Vertical Integration and Internet Strategies in the Apparel Industry." *Journal of Industrial Economics* 49: 417–40.

Gibbons, R. 2005. "Four Formal(izable) Theories of the Firm?" *Journal of Economic Behavior and Organization* 58: 200–45.

Grossman, S., and O. Hart. 1986. "The Costs and Benefits of Ownership: A Theory of Vertical and Lateral Integration." *Journal of Political Economy* 94: 691–719.

Hart, O. 1988. "Contracts and the Theory of the Firm." *Journal of Law, Economics and Organization* 4: 119–39.

Hart, O. 1995. *Firms, Contracts, and Financial Structure*. Oxford: Clarendon Press.

Hart, O. 2009. "Hold-Up, Asset Ownership, and Reference Points." *Quarterly Journal of Economics* 124: 301–48.

Hart, O., and B. Holmström. 2010. "A Theory of Firm Scope." *Quarterly Journal of Economics* 125: 483–513.

Hart, O., and J. Moore. 1990. "Property Rights and the Nature of the Firm." *Journal of Political Economy* 98: 1119–58.

Hart, O., and J. Moore. 2005. "On the Design of Hierarchies: Coordination versus Specialization." *Journal of Political Economy* 113: 675–702.

Hart, O., and J. Moore. 2008. "Contracts as Reference Points." *Quarterly Journal of Economics* 123: 1–48.

Hayek, F. 1945. "The Use of Knowledge in Society." *American Economic Review* 35: 519–30.

Holmström, B. 1999. "The Firm as a Subeconomy." *Journal of Law, Economics and Organization* 15: 74–102.

Holmström, B., and P. Milgrom. 1987. "Aggregation and Linearity in the Provision of Intertemporal Incentives." *Econometrica* 55: 303–28.

Holmström, B., and P. Milgrom. 1991. "Multitask Principal-Agent Analysis: Incentive Contracts, Asset Ownership, and Job Design." *Journal of Law, Economics and Organization* 7: 24–52.

Holmström, B., and P. Milgrom. 1994. "The Firm as an Incentive System." *American Economic Review* 84: 972–91.

Holmström, B., and J. Roberts. 1998. "The Boundaries of the Firm Revisited." *Journal of Economics Perspectives* 12: 73–94.

Holmström, B., and J. Tirole. 1988. "The Theory of the Firm." In *Handbook of Industrial Organization*, edited by R. Schmalensee and R. Willig. Amsterdam: North-Holland.

Holmström, B., and J. Tirole. 1989. "Transfer Pricing and Organizational Form." *Journal of Law, Economics, and Organization* 7: 201–28.

Inderst, R., and C. Laux. 2005. "Incentives in Internal Capital Markets: Capital Constraints, Competition, and Investment Opportunities." *Rand Journal of Economics* 36: 215–28.

Lafontaine, F., and M. Slade. 2007. "Vertical Integration and Firm Boundaries: The Evidence." *Journal of Economic Literature* 45: 629–85.

Levin, J. 2002. "Multilateral Contracting and The Employment Relationship." *Quarterly Journal of Economics* 117: 1075–103.

Marino, A., J. Matsusaka, and J. Zabjonik. 2010. "Disobedience and Authority." *Journal of Law, Economics and Organization* 26: 427–59.

Matouschek, N. 2004. "Ex Post Inefficiencies in a Property Rights Theory of the Firm." *Journal of Law, Economics and Organization* 20: 125–47.

Rajan, R., H. Servaes, and L. Zingales. 2000. "The Cost of Diversity: The Diversification Discount and Inefficient Investment." *Journal of Finance* 55: 35–80.

Rajan, R., and L. Zingales. 1998. "Power in a Theory of the Firm." *Quarterly Journal of Economics* 113: 387–432.

Rantakari, H. 2008. "Governing Adaptation." *Review of Economic Studies* 75: 1257–85.

Roberts, J. 2004. *The Modern Firm: Organizational Design for Performance and Growth*. Oxford: Oxford University Press.

Scharfstein D., and J. Stein. 2000. "The Dark Side of Internal Capital Markets: Divisional Rent-Seeking and Inefficient Investment." *Journal of Finance* 55: 2537–64.

Simester, D., and M. Knez. 2002. "Direct and Indirect Bargaining Costs and the Scope of the Firm." *Journal of Business* 75: 283–304.

Stein, J. 1997. "Internal Capital Markets and the Competition for Corporate Resources." *Journal of Finance* 52: 111–33.

Stein, J. 2002. "Information Production and Capital Allocation: Decentralized versus Hierarchical Firms." *Journal of Finance* 57: 1891–921.

Tadelis, S. 2003. "Complexity, Exibility, and the Make-or-Buy Decision." *American Economic Review* 92: 433–7.

Van den Steen, E. 2007. "The Cost of Incentives under Disagreement: Too Motivated?" Working Paper, Harvard Business School.

Van den Steen, E. 2010. "Interpersonal Authority in a Theory of the Firm." *American Economic Review* 100: 466–90.

Whinston, M. 2003. "On the Transaction Cost Determinants of Vertical Integration." *Journal of Law, Economics and Organization* 19: 1–23.

Whinston, M., and I. Segal. 2010. "Property Rights." Working Paper, Northwestern University.

Williamson, O. 1971. "The Vertical Integration of Production: Market Failure Considerations." *American Economic Review* 61: 112–23.

Williamson, O. 1975. *Markets and Hierarchies: Analysis and Antitrust Implications*. New York, NY: Free Press.

Williamson, O. 1985. *The Economic Institutions of Capitalism*. New York, NY: Free Press

Williamson, O. 1991. "Comparative Economic Organization: The Analysis of Discrete Structural Alternatives." *Administrative Science Quarterly* 36: 269–96.

Williamson, O. 2002. "The Theory of the Firm as Governance Structure: From Choice to Contract." *Journal of Economic Perspectives* 16: 171–95.

Woodruff, C. 2002. "Noncontractible Investments and Vertical Integration in the Mexican Footwear Industry." *International Journal of Industrial Organization* 20: 1197–224.

7

Discussion of Wouter Dessein's "Incomplete Contracts and Firm Boundaries: New Directions"

FRANCINE LAFONTAINE

Let me begin by thanking the organizers of the conference for inviting me to discuss Dessein (2014). As someone who does empirical work at the boundary of organizational economics and industrial economics, I found this paper particularly interesting. I hope that my comments will encourage other researchers interested in empirical analyses of property rights theory and organizational issues more generally, as well as those wanting to push the theory further along, to read it carefully.

In this paper, the author provides two "simplified" but formal models in the tradition of property rights theory that extend the theory by incorporating and giving a central role to managerial control and bureaucratic decision making. Both models also follow the PRT tradition in making clear what the integration and nonintegration options are and the trade-offs involved, namely, the benefits and costs associated with these options. Contrary to traditional PRT models, however, the two models proposed here assume that actions are "ex post" non-contractible. This in turn means that the capacity of managers or owners of assets to coordinate and control employee behavior—management's role in the models—is fundamentally different under integration compared with noninte-gration, a characteristic of the models that brings them closer to more informal transaction cost arguments, where the firm has traditionally been assumed to benefit from greater command and control capabilities.

While similar along the above dimensions, the two models proposed in the paper are quite distinct in other ways. In particular, the first model empha-sizes moral hazard issues and the resulting need for control, while the second focuses on the desirability of internalizing externalities among different entities by making them part of the same firm (common ownership or integration) versus not (dispersed ownership).

In addition to giving a role to management, the two models are of particular interest in my view because they provide clear testable implications, that is, patterns one can look for in data. The empirical literature on PRT is rather limited, in part because the predictions from these models are often less clear and more fragile to specific assumptions (see Lafontaine and Slade 2007, 658–660, for a discussion of relevant empirical work). By making the models rather straightforward, deriving and emphasizing specific predictions, and being explicit as to the sources of the trade-offs implied by the theories, Dessein makes it likely that empiricists can find contexts within which to test some of the predictions. This in turn can help distinguish among specific theories and help readers better understand how firms organize different types of transactions and for what purposes, which then can provide further fodder to theorists and empiricists alike.

In reading the paper, I was struck for example with the many ways I could connect the two types of models to what I know about franchising and the franchising literature. Although franchise contracts are not exactly like the supply contracts that Dessein had in mind, an interesting feature of franchise relationships is that they are characterized fundamentally by two types of "incentive" problems, which correspond well to the two types of issues addressed by Dessein's models.[1]

The first incentive problem in franchise contracting is the standard moral hazard problem: a firm wants a set of agents who each work hard at making their own establishment successful. Given the geographic dispersion of establishments in a chain, effort is not observable. This incentive problem can be addressed via an incentive contract, which is what franchising entails. Specifically, franchisees earn the profits of their local establishment after paying royalties, usually about 4–8 percent of establishment revenues. Note that such royalty payments make the franchisee bear all the costs, which means they are fully incentivized to keep costs low. As should be clear from the level of the royalty rates, they also keep most of the benefits from increasing sales.

But what do franchisors worry about once an individual is a franchisee and operates under these high-powered incentives? Franchisees are very cost-conscious, as they should be. They will oppose company policies that may be beneficial to the chain, from a coordination perspective, for example, if it is not clearly beneficial to them in their local market. In other words, franchisees might not take the actions that the chain would prefer they take for coordination purposes, whereas an employee manager faced with the same decision would be

---

[1] See Blair and Lafontaine (2005) for more on the nature of franchising and franchise contracts.

happy to comply as such an employee does not incur any cost of compliance. By relying on franchising, franchisors indeed gain the high-effort incentives, but they lose the capacity to direct and control the behavior of local agents as they could under integration. In that sense, in a very fundamental way, franchisors are faced with the trade-off between motivation and coordination that is central to the first type of model discussed in Dessein's paper.

Evidence about franchise contracting, moreover, is quite consistent with many of the predictions from the model. In proposition 2, the author states that increases in the value of effort provision by the franchisee will lead to more effort incentives. In proposition 3 he notes that the same increase in value of effort will lead to more nonintegration. Proposition 3 also implies that increases in the value of coordination—for example, increases in the value of making sure product offerings are consistent across locations to protect the brand—will lead to more integration. The evidence concerning franchising discussed in Lafontaine and Slade (2007) clearly supports these predictions.

Interestingly, and consistent with the foregoing discussion, the consequence of solving the effort incentive problem by making franchisees residual claimants is that they then act like the agents in the second type of model described by Dessein. Specifically, their objective function is then clearly different from that of the chain or franchisor, namely, they focus on maximizing profits locally and care little about the externalities that occur across establishments. Yet in the context of franchising, where the establishments all operate under a common brand, these externalities can be important. The second type of model developed by Dessein tells us that we should find less franchising in those systems where the externalities are greatest. The evidence to date is also quite consistent with this implication in that franchisors in industries where the externalities are expected to be greater, and franchisors with more high-value brands, indeed franchise less (see notably Brickley and Dark 1987; Lafontaine and Shaw 2005).

Although all these predictions and patterns make the models developed here particularly interesting, it is important to recognize that ex post adaptation and coordination can be achieved at least partly through contracting practices in addition to driving the decision of whether to integrate. In our review of the empirical literature on interfirm contracts, published in the *Handbook of Organizational Economics* (2012), Margaret Slade and I discuss a number of contracting practices, including some that are known in the antitrust literature as vertical restraints, whose goal is to constrain the behavior of parties to a contract. With these contract clauses, the local distributor, or division manager, or franchisee still is expected to behave according to their objective function, but must do so within the constraints imposed by the contract. The latter might include, for example, requirements that "old" products (e.g., beer at Anheuser-Busch and donuts at Dunkin Donuts) be thrown away when no longer fresh, with the cost of abiding by the policy borne entirely by the distributor or franchisee. In other words, while integration might eliminate the "control" problem, relying on it raises the problem of "effort incentives" again. In reality, the relationship often does not need to be brought in house for the coordination problems to be managed. Lafontaine and Raynaud (2002), for example, discuss a number of clauses in franchise contracts that they argue prevent the type of franchisee profit-maximizing behaviors that may harm the common brand. Of course, in some contexts, the value of the brand might be such as to still entice the principal to bring many relationships in house, but the point here is that there are contractual alternatives that lie somewhere between integration and nonintegration.

The possibility that the coordination or control problem be addressed by means other than integration is not discussed by Dessein basically because this is outside the scope of his paper. Indeed, unless the management somehow can punish agents for not abiding by the constraints in the contract, the types of clauses mentioned here are meaningless. For them to play a role requires that we complicate the models to bring us into the realm of court or self-enforcement and the type of dynamics that Dessein purposely put aside. He did this so he could achieve the goal he had set: to show that one can derive property rights theory–type models that give a role to management and generate relatively simple models with clear testable implications. Further refinements no doubt will be needed to give the models yet greater empirical content, but there is no doubt in my mind that the "new directions" that Dessein is providing are a very useful starting point.

References

Blair, Roger, and Francine Lafontaine. 2005. *The Economics of Franchising*. Cambridge: Cambridge University Press.

Brickley, James A., and Frederick H. Dark. 1987. "The Choice of Organizational Form: The Case of Franchising." *Journal of Financial Economics* 18: 401–20.

Dessein, Wouter. 2014. "Incomplete Contracts and Firm Boundaries: New Directions." *Journal of Law, Economics, and Organization*, 30(suppl. 1): i13–36. Reprinted in this volume as chapter 6.

Lafontaine, Francine, and Emmanuel Raynaud. 2002. "Residual Claims and Self enforcement as Incentive Mechanisms in Franchise Contracts: Substitute or Complements." In E. Brousseau and J. M. Glachant (eds.) *The Economics of Contract in Prospect and Retrospect*. Cambridge: Cambridge University Press.

Lafontaine, Francine, and Kathryn L. Shaw. 2005. "Targeting Managerial Control: Evidence from Franchising." *RAND Journal of Economics* 36: 131–50.

Lafontaine, Francine, and Margaret Slade. 2007. "Vertical Integration and Firm Boundaries: The Evidence." *Journal of Economic Literature* 45(3): 629–85.

Lafontaine, Francine, and Margaret Slade. 2012. "Inter-Firm Contracts: The Evidence." In R. Gibbons and J. Roberts (eds.) *Handbook of Organizational Economics*. Princeton, NJ: Princeton University Press.

8

Comment on "Incomplete Contracts and Firm Boundaries: New Directions" by Wouter Dessein

MICHAEL D. WHINSTON

It is a pleasure to be able to participate in this conference in honor of Sandy and Oliver's tremendous paper. I was Oliver's colleague for a number of years at Harvard, which was a great experience. Sandy taught my first graduate microeconomics course when I was an undergraduate at Penn, and I think it is fair to say that I would not have followed the same path had it not been for the excitement that he conveyed about microeconomics.

It is sometimes said that the key insight of Grossman and Hart (1986) is that property rights are key drivers of incentives. Although clearly true, that is an idea that was not new: it was present in nineteenth-century descriptions of the tragedy of the commons and even in Aristotle's writings. Rather, I would say there were three key contributions. First, Sandy and Oliver showed us that a useful way of thinking about the scope of the firm is in terms of the assets it controls. Second, the paper emphasized that ownership conveys bargaining power, and this can alter the marginal returns that parties foresee from investments in a relationship. Finally, Grossman and Hart (1986) provided for the first time a formal model in which the efficiency of the market and the firm were treated in a consistent and equally thorough fashion.[1]

I'll leave most of the empirical comments to Francine Lafontaine but will make just two quick points. First, in actual settings we frequently encounter investments that do not conform to the assumptions in the Grossman-Hart

---

[1] The power of formal models in influencing debate should not be underestimated. In antitrust analysis, for example, one reason the Chicago School's arguments about the impossibility of profitable yet inefficient exclusion proved so forceful was that for many years they were made with a coherent model, whereas those arguing otherwise had no models.

(and Moore) papers, known as the property rights theory. For example, the driver care considered in Baker and Hubbard (2004) is an investment in the future value of the truck, not a human capital investment, and as such redounds to the benefit of the truck's owner. Nonetheless, it is the property rights theory's *approach* to the problem that has proved so powerful. Second, the predictions one gets out of suitably generalized property rights theory models are often quite distinct from what comes out of the Williamson-style transactions cost theory. For example, in Baker and Hubbard's paper, the introduction of onboard computers to trucks reduces contractual incompleteness, and hence the level of quasirents, but is found to increase the level of integration (that is, it reduces driver ownership), contrary to what a Williamson-style analysis would predict. (My guess is that over time we will see more empirical applications that show effects that are consistent with the suitably generalized property rights theory, and not with transactions cost theory.)

Turning back to the theory, I think a useful way to think about what's going on is that we are trying to allocate ownership to eliminate externalities, or at least reduce their harmful effects. In fact, Sandy was the one who first taught me about externalities. In the chapter on property rights that Ilya Segal and I wrote for the *Handbook of Organizational Economics* we emphasized this point. It is simplest to see in more static models in which each agent can take certain inalienable actions and there is no bargaining at all (as in the first model in Dessein's paper). If property rights can be allocated to eliminate externalities—like dividing a common pasture and putting up fences—we can get first-best efficiency. More generally, a good allocation of property rights will encourage actions with positive externalities and discourage those with negative externalities. In the more complicated setting of the Grossman-Hart-Moore papers, direct externalities are assumed away, but bargaining introduces a new kind of externality. Relationship specificity implies that a party's investments generally have positive externalities as they increase the bargaining surplus (which other parties get a share of), and the optimal assignment of asset ownership aims to encourage the most important of those investments.

As terrific a paper as Grossman and Hart (1986) is, as well as Oliver's follow-up work with John Moore, the property rights theory does have some significant limitations. One is that the contracting environment is particularly stark, leaving out any possibility of incentive contracting. A second is that all returns are inalienable; after an acquisition the acquirer's returns rise only through changes in bargaining power, as opposed to simply the fact that the acquired firm's revenues and many costs are now the property of the acquirer. Of course, these two omissions are related, for if, say, the revenue stream were perfectly contractible, then it would not be clear why a shift in its ownership due to an acquisition would make any difference at all. Finally, it is not clear how to apply the theory to large firms in which the workers and managers rarely have significant owner-ship stakes. Part of the reason relates to the two previous issues—if managers don't have large stakes, then integration can matter only if it alters managerial incentives and/or control rights.

As one example of how this can matter, consider the fact that in the property rights theory the *direction* of integration matters—that is, *it matters who buys whom*. But if the owners are all individuals who take no actions, it is not clear why this would be, at least from the standpoint of the very stark world of the property rights theory.[2]

Dessein's paper pushes in directions that address some of these limitations of the property rights theory. In his first model, ownership changes who bears the firm's costs, but these costs can be imperfectly reallocated, as can revenue streams, through incentive contracts that are based on noisy measures of perfor-mance. I like how the model, which builds on the multitask/incentive systems approach of Holmström, Milgrom, and Roberts, offers a richer model of an organization that includes the ability to write incentive contracts, and yet still provides a reason why the shift of return streams that accompanies integration is not fully offset through contracting (because relying on the imperfect mea-sures of these streams introduces risk-bearing costs).[3] At the same time, I am less convinced that the model is about "coordination," as nothing would change if it were a priori known that all of the actions I should be taken. Indeed, a reasonable interpretation of that simpler model would be that there is a trade-off between cost reduction effort (e) and quality enhancement (I), which affect measured costs in opposite directions, and that because of the noisy performance mea-sures integration shifts the agent's actions toward more quality enhancement and less cost reduction.

In contrast, the second model, which is closely related to Dessein's very nice paper with Ricardo Alonso and Niko Matouschek, is much more about coor-dination. There, integration changes the incentives of the decision makers who have control, and thereby affects the quality of communications between the organization's members. The result is a model that provides a much richer pic-ture of what goes on in large organizations and how integration can matter for that.

Limitations notwithstanding, I think it's fair to say that Grossman and Hart (1986) has really had a huge effect in moving our understanding forward on

---

[2] That said, I think that in reality it really does matter who buys whom—it matters for the merged firm's direction, and it matters to the future careers of the managers involved. Indeed, we often see that while the manager of the acquired firm is given some seemingly important position at the time of the merger, a year later he or she is gone.

[3] In this regard, it is a much nicer approach than simply assuming the owner can skim all of the returns, making incentive contracting useless.

these issues and, equally important, in energizing people to work on these issues themselves. It was clearly a tremendous success, for which Sandy and Oliver deserve both our congratulations and thanks.

References

Alonso, R., W. Dessein, and N. Matouschek, "When Does Coordination Require Centralization?," *American Economic Review*, March 2008, 145–179.

Baker, G.P and T.N. Hubbard, "Contractibility and Asset Ownership: On-Board Computers and Governance in U.S. Trucking," *Quarterly Journal of Economics*, November 2004, 1443–1480.

Dessein, Wouter, "Incomplete Contracts and Firm Boundaries: New Directions." *The Impact of Incomplete Contracts on Economics.* (2016): XX–XX.

Grossman, S., and O. Hart 1986. "The Costs and Benefits of Ownership: A Theory of Vertical and Lateral Integration." *Journal of Political Economy* 94: 691–719.

Hart, O. and J. Moore. "Property Rights and the Nature of the Firm." *Journal of Political Economy* (1990): 1119–1158.

Hart, O., *Firms, Contracts, and Financial Structure*. Oxford: Oxford University Press, 1995.

Segal, I. and M.D. Whinston, "Property Rights," Chapter 3 in R. Gibbons and J. Roberts, eds., *Handbook of Organizational Economics*, Princeton University Press, 2013.

PART 3

INCOMPLETE CONTRACTS
AND INTERNAL ORGANIZATION

9

Incomplete Contracts and the Internal Organization of Firms

PHILLIPE AGHION, NICHOLAS BLOOM, AND JOHN VAN REENEN

Grossman and Hart (1986) developed the incomplete contracts approach to analyze the costs and benefits of vertical integration, which could explain why firms have boundaries, and why not all transactions are taking place within a single firm. The basic idea is that contracts cannot specify all states of nature or all actions in advance, or there are states of nature or actions which cannot be verified ex post by third parties, and which therefore are not ex ante contractible. They used this approach to develop theories of ownership and vertical integration. When contracts cannot specify all possible uses of an asset, the contract must ex ante leave some discretion over the use of the assets: in other words it must allocate ownership of the asset to one or the other party. The benefit of integration is that the owner avoids hold-up by the other party, which in turn will enhance her incentives to invest in the relationship. The cost is that the other party will tend to under-invest in the relationship.

In this paper we show how the incomplete contract approach can be used to think about the internal organization of firms. The first half has a theoretical focus; we look at how formal and real authority are allocated between the firm's owner and its employees, between the top managers and subordinates, and between firms and financiers. We also examine how the allocation of authority affects communication within the firm.

This paper was prepared for the "Grossman and Hart at 25" conference in Brussels. We are grateful for comments by our discussants, John Roberts and Bentley MacLeod, the editor and two anonymous referees, and research assistance from Megha Patnaik. We would like to thank the Economic and Social Research Council for their financial support through the Centre for Economic Performance. The empirical part builds heavily on joint work with Raffaella Sadun. A more detailed working paper version is available online as Aghion et al. (2013).

In the second half of the paper we analyze some of the empirical literature, examining first the determinants of organization (focusing on delegation/decentralization) from the perspective of the Grossman-Hart approach and its extensions, and second the effects of decentralization on firm performance. The emphasis is on looking at "stylized facts" from large-scale econometric studies of firms rather than at case studies. Case studies are helpful in suggesting theoretical approaches and mechanisms, but are poor for hypotheses testing as they are small in number and highly selective. As with the theory, we also look at decentralization *within* firms, rather than the more commonly studied issue of boundaries of the firm or vertical integration, which was the original motivation for Grossman and Hart (1986).[1] We find some support for aspects of the incomplete contracts approach in the importance of the congruence of preferences and firm heterogeneity for decentralization. However, we acknowledge that there are many other stylized facts from the empirical decentralization literature that may require alternative theoretical perspectives.

The structure of this paper is as follows. Section 1 examines theory. We look at delegation and authority (1.1), financial contracting (1.2), and delegation and the informational content of decision making (1.4).[2] Section 2 examines the empirical determinants of firm decentralization, focusing on some predictions of the theory (such as the importance of preference congruence as proxied by trust). Section 3 analyzes the effect of decentralization on firm performance. In Section 4 we conclude and suggest areas for future research.

1. Theory

1.1 A model of Delegation and Authority in Organizations

1.1.1 Basic Model

Real authority, that is, the ability to make decisions, requires information. But acquiring information in turn requires time and effort. Thus, for example, the CEO of a big holding company that consists of several horizontally integrated units, can only devote limited attention to each unit, which in turn implies that more real authority will lie with downstream agents in each unit. In fact, increasing the "span of control" is one way in which a top manager can commit to leave more real authority, and therefore more initiative, to her subordinates in various branches of activity. More generally, it is the design of the organization,

---

[1] See Lafontaine and Slade (2008) for a comprehensive review of the empirical literature on this.

[2] In Aghion et al. (2013) Appendices A and C we also discuss work on academia and multidivisional firms.

together with the allocation of formal decision rights, that will determine how real authority is distributed within the firm.

The issue of real versus formal authority and of the implications of this distinction for the optimal design of firm organization is addressed by Aghion and Tirole (1997) using an incomplete contracts/property rights approach.

Their basic framework involves two parties: P (principal) and A (agent). It is assumed that *formal authority* can be allocated contractually (e.g., shareholders allocate authority to the board of directors). In turn, boards allocate authority to management—and management to different layers of management, and so on. By contrast, *real authority* is exerted by the party which has information; this may be the party with formal authority, but not neccessarily so. Contractual incompleteness is again key to the whole analysis: contracts signed ex ante between P and A cannot specify particular project choices, as these are not verifiable by third parties.

After the contract is signed, both P and A can invest in information acquisition: by investing effort $\frac{1}{2}E^2$, P acquires information with probability E. Similarly, by investing effort $\frac{1}{2}e^2$, A acquires information with probability e. An important parameter in the analysis of the costs and benefits of delegating formal (or real) authority to A is the degree of congruence between P's and A's preferences. Let α denote the probability that P's preferred project is also A's preferred project (call this congruence between the two parties' preferences), and suppose that a party gets zero utility if the other party chooses her preferred project and preferences are not congruent. Finally, assume that an uninformed party will never pick a project at random as this might be too risky.

The timing of moves is as follows. First, the two parties sign a contract that allocates formal authority to one party, either P or A. Then, both parties invest in information acquisition, that is, P and A choose E and e, respectively. Then, if she acquires information, the party with no formal authority proposes a project to the party with formal authority. The party with formal authority then either picks her preferred project (if she herself has acquired information) or she picks the project proposed to her by the party without formal authority if she did not acquire information. It is in this latter case that real authority differs from formal authority, since the project is actually chosen by the party *without* formal authority (the party with formal authority is uninformed and therefore can only rubberstamp the other party's project proposal).

P delegating formal authority to her agent A involves a cost and a benefit. The cost is that the agent may choose a project which the principal does not prefer. This is the *loss of control* effect. The benefit is that delegating formal authority to the agent encourages her to invest more effort (i.e., higher e) in information acquisition. This is the *initiative* effect. Which effect dominates depends upon the congruence parameter α: there exists a cut-off value α^* such that for $\alpha < \alpha^*$, the first effect dominates, and it is better for P to retain formal authority, whereas for $\alpha > \alpha^*$, the second effect dominates and it is better for P to delegate formal authority to A.

Since preference congruence turns out to be so critical for decentralization decisions, we examine this in the empirical section where there does appear to be some compelling evidence for the importance of empirical proxies for congruence, such as trust. Below we show that this is a robust prediction of generalizations to the basic theoretical approach.

1.1.2 Extensions

Subsequent to Aghion and Tirole (1997; AT), several papers have analyzed the allocation of formal authority internally in organizations. We shall describe some of these attempts in the next subsections. At this stage, let us mention a first attempt by Hart and Moore (1999; HM). HM analyze the optimal allocation of authority in multilayer hierarchies. Their model is one where by assumption, upstream agents are less likely to get new ideas (getting an idea in HM is like obtaining information in AT) due to their higher span of control. However, when they do get an idea, this idea has higher potential because of their greater span. HM then show that it is optimal to have "chains of commands," whereby whenever they have an idea, upstream agents (the "generalists") have priority rights over implementing the idea; only if they don't gave an idea can downstream agents (the "specialists") have their say on which action to implement. The intuition is that although upstream agents are less likely to get a new idea, having priority control rights makes sure that they are in control of all the assets downstream, which in turn allows them to fully realize the idea's potential. But if they fail to get a new idea, then the next downstream agent on each branch of the hierarchy should have her say if she has an idea, and so on, moving down in the hierarchy.

So far, we have concentrated on the allocation of formal authority within organizations. However, going back to AT, it could be that delegating formal authority to A is too costly to P, for example, because with arbitrarily small probability, A might take some very costly action. In that case P will always want to retain formal authority, but yet she may want to commit herself not to invest too much in information acquisition, so as to preserve the A's incentives to invest in e even though she keeps formal authority with herself. One way to achieve such commitment is through the choice of *span of control*. More specifically, by increasing the span of control, that is, the number of agents and activities under her supervision, the principal will commit to limiting how much effort she devotes to acquiring information on each particular activity. This in turn will encourage initiative by agents on each activity, as they anticipate that the principal will ignore their proposals less often (as she will not have acquired the relevant information). The choice of the optimal span of control by the principal at date zero is in turn subject to the same trade-off between the principal's loss of control and the agents' initiatives as above. This trade-off also underlies other features of organizational design, such as the role of intermediaries, the costs and benefits of having multiple principals on some activities, or the optimal combination of tasks within teams.

The idea that the design of organizations can serve as a commitment device to delegate (real) authority, is further explored by Acemoglu et al. (2007), who use it to test their theory of the determinants of decentralization on French and British firm-level panel data (see section 2 for more empirical detail). The model, closely related to AT, is one in which the owner of a firm in a given sector can learn about the outcome of an investment decision through observing other firms in the same sector, or by relying on the superior information of down-stream agents (or on downstream agents' effort to acquire information) within the firm. The more precise the public information acquired through observing other firms in the same sector, the less a firm needs to delegate control to its better informed agent. This simple observation delivers a rich set of predictions on the determinants of decentralization. In particular it suggests that older firms should delegate less, as these firms will have had time to learn from more prede-cessors in the same sector. It also suggests that greater the firm heterogeneity in the same sector, the more a firm in that sector should delegate control as what it observes from other firms is less likely to be relevant for its own choices (if firms are very different it is harder for them to learn from each other). Finally, it suggests that a firm closer to the technological frontier should delegate control more, as it is more likely to face problems that have not been solved before by other firms in the same sector. In the empirical section we discuss the empirical tests of these three predictions and show that they all receive support in the data.

Even if decentralization was the efficient choice due to characteristics of the firm's environment, Baker et al. (1999) emphasize that delegation is often informal because the corporate head quarters (CHQ) must usually sign off on decisions. The issue is whether the CHQ credibly commits to allowing the plant manager to effectively make important decisions and does not override the plant manager (in order to establish her reputation of not interfering). Thus, the extent of decentralization is the outcome of a repeated game between the CHQ and manager. Again, trust may facilitate a cooperative outcome to this repeated game, which suggests that regions or countries which have higher levels of trust should enjoy greater firm decentralization.

Another reason delegating formal authority within firms may be difficult is explained by Bolton and Dewatripont (2011): nothing prevents a principal (the owner of a firm) who delegates formal authority to an agent to revert her decision at any time. Bolton and Dewatripont point to the so-called business judgment rules, which prevent courts from enforcing contracts between several parties within the same firm. On the other hand, there are instances where transfer of formal authority can be enforced nevertheless. First, if this transfer is accompanied by a transfer of information from the principal to the agent, then this information transfer guarantees irreversibility of the transfer of control (see Aghion et al. 2004 for a more detailed discussion of this point). Second, in a more dynamic context, principals may want to establish a reputation for not reverting control allocation decisions over time, precisely to keep the option of credible control transfers in the future. Third, as stressed by Hart and Holmström (2010), taking control back from an agent causes the agent to become aggrieved which in turn may induce the agent to "shade," that is, to take unobservable actions which are damaging to the firm. Finally, as pointed out by Bolton and Dewatripont (2011), there are at least two examples of contracting situations where business judgment rules do not apply: financial contracting, that is, contracts between a firm and its investors, which we discuss in the next subsection, and universities, where the faculty are protected by contracts and tenure commitments which grants them academic freedom (see Aghion et al. 2008 and Appendix A of Aghion et al. 2013).

1.1.3 Summary and Empirical Implications

There are many other important theoretical aspects of firm delegation stemming from GH and AT. The next two subsections will focus on finance and information, as space constraints prevent us from elaborating on other important areas such as academia and multidivisional firms (the Appendices of Aghion et al. 2013 summarize these contributions).

As a general point, although decentralization models in the GH-AT tradition generate a rich set of predictions, it is fair to say that relatively few of these have been subject to rigorous empirical examination. One main reason for this is that it is hard to develop empirical analogs of theoretical objects such as decentralization, information, and communication in one firm, let alone in large-scale databases suitable for econometric analysis. In section 2 we focus on some areas where empirical progress has been made.

1.2 Financial Contracting and the Role of Contingent Control Allocations

Since the work of Modigliani and Miller (1958)—which suggested that the mix of debt and equity a firm has does not affect its value—economists have wondered why most firms have some combination of debt and equity financing. Debt has certain tax advantages (interest is typically tax deductible for the firm but dividend payments are not), yet corporate debt was prevalent even before corporate income tax existed. Why would firms have debt, then?

Aghion and Bolton (1992) develop an incomplete contracts model which provides a rationale for holding debt. They argue that the mix of debt and equity financing divide up the states of the world where debt and equity holders have control of the firm's assets. When times are good, and cash flows are sufficient to meet interest payments, equity holders have control. When times are bad, debt holders get control.

Suppose that an entrepreneur needs to finance a project that costs $K = 10$. She does not have private wealth and thus needs funding from an outside investor. The investor cares only for monetary benefits, whereas the entrepreneur only draws private benefits from taking various actions. Actions are not verifiable by a third party and therefore cannot be contracted upon ex ante. Hence, all the initial contract can do is allocate control rights between the two parties. The timing of the relationship between the entrepreneur and the investor can be described as follows. At the contracting stage, the two parties write a financial contract which allocates control rights. The contract must be "feasible," that is, it must satisfy the investor's ex ante participation constraint (she must get at least as much as her outside option in expectation). Then the state of nature is realized. Suppose there is a good state θ_g and a bad state θ_b, each of which can occur with probability 1/2, and which state is realized is verifiable by a third party. Then an action must be chosen. Suppose that only two actions can be chosen: a_1 and a_2. Action a_1 maximizes monetary revenue in all states, whereas action a_2 maximizes private benefits in all states. For example, let $\pi(a, \theta)$ denote the monetary profit from taking action a in state θ, and $B(a)$ denote the private benefit from taking action a in any state θ and suppose that

$$\pi(a_1, \theta_g) = 11, \pi(a_1, \theta_b) = 13,$$
$$\pi(a_2, \theta_g) = 10, \pi(a_2, \theta_b) = 6,$$

and

$$B(a_1) = 2 < B(a_2) = 4.$$

The first-best involves a_1 being chosen in state θ_b and a_2 being chosen in state θ_g, since

$$B(a_1) + \pi(a_1, \theta_b) = 15 > 10 = B(a_2) + \pi(a_2, \theta_b),$$

whereas

$$B(a_1) + \pi(a_1, \theta_g) = 13 < 14 = B(a_2) + \pi(a_2, \theta_g).$$

We can now compare three governance structures, which correspond to three types of financial contracts. Entrepreneur control (e.g., as implemented through issuing nonvoting shares), would lead to action a_2 being chosen in all states, but this would violate the investor's participation constraint since

$$\frac{1}{2}(6) + \frac{1}{2}(10) = 8 < 10 = K.$$

The investor has cash, which he might use to convince the entrepreneur to take action a_1 in state θ_b. However, if most of the bargaining power at the renegotiation stage lies with the entrepreneur, the prospect of ex post renegotiation will not help satisfy the investor's ex ante participation constraint. In this case, entrepreneur control is not ex ante feasible. How about investor control (e.g., as implemented through issuing voting equity)? In this case the investor will choose action a_1 in all states, even though action a_2 is the first best action in state θ_b, that is, the action that maximizes the sum of monetary and private benefits in that state. Now, can the entrepreneur renegotiate the action from a_1 to a_2 in state θ_g? The answer is no, simply because the entrepreneur has no cash she can use to bribe the investor into changing his choice of action. Investor control satisfies the investor's participation constraint, since

$$\frac{1}{2}(11) + \frac{1}{2}(13) = 12 > 10 = K.$$

However it is not first-best, as total surplus would be maximized by having action a_1 taken in state θ_b and action a_2 taken in state θ_g.

Now, consider a contract that specifies a contingent allocation of control—to the entrepreneur in state θ_g and to the investor in state θ_b. This contract will lead to action a_1 being taken in state θ_b and action a_2 being taken in state θ_g. Contingent control can in turn be implemented through a debt contract that transfers control from the entrepreneur to the investor in state θ_b.

The idea that contingent control can help align incentives goes beyond financial contracting. For example Bolton and Dewatripont (2011) restate the Aghion-Bolton model as one of a headquarter who commits to replace a divisional manager only in some states of nature (e.g., in state θ_b for the above notation). Under this reinterpretation $(B(a_2) - B(a_1))$ can be seen as the private cost for the division manager of closing down his unit and thus having his employees laid off, rather than maintaining the unit in operation. This contingent arrangement reduces the expected monetary losses of the headquarters and simultaneously internalizes the private costs of closing down units. In a context where the information about θ could be manipulated by the division managers, for example, through account manipulation or through risky decision making (gambling for resurrection) so as to avoid being replaced, contingent control can help mitigate the problem by offering a guarantee to divisional managers. Another guarantee is to give managers a stake in the firm's profits even when they are being replaced (see Bolton and Dewatripont 2011; Garicano 2000).

1.3 Delegation as a Way to Improve the Informational Content of Decision Making

Dessein (2002) analyzes how the allocation of control can help incorporate the agent's information into decision making in a situation where the agent has private information. In contrast to Aghion and Tirole (1997), there is no information acquisition effort by the agent or the principal, therefore in Dessein's model the allocation of authority is not so much a tool to motivate the agent (as in Aghion and Tirole) or to give a supplier incentives to make relationship specific investments (as in Grossman and Hart). The main insight of Dessein (2002) is that in a world with asymmetric information and contractual incompleteness, the delegation of authority from a principal to an agent is often the best way to elicit the agent's private information.

In Dessein's setting the agent is assumed to be better informed, but with preferences over decisions that are not fully congruent with those of the principal. If the principal has authority (i.e., if she holds the decision rights), which Dessein refers to as "centralization," then the agent communicates his information "strategically" in order to tilt the principal's decision. Centralization thus results in information loss. However, while "delegating" control to the agent avoids this information loss, it also makes the agent's biased decision making prevail. Delegation thus results in a loss of control. Dessein (2002) shows that for a broad range of parameters, the loss of control under delegation matters less than the loss of information under centralization. In particular, the smaller the agent's bias (i.e., the more congruent the principal's and agent's objectives are), or the larger the agent's informational advantage, or the more uncertainty there is, the more likely it is that delegation is optimal.

An important assumption in Dessein (2002) is that under "principal authority," the principal cannot commit to not taking the decision which she believes maximizes her expected utility. She can, however, commit to "delegate" control rights to the agent. This is consistent with the incomplete contracting assumption that actions or decisions are noncontractible, even when control allocation is contractible. Delegation can then be interpreted as a commitment device from the principal to use the agent's information in the way that best fits the agent's objectives. While delegation results in biased decision-making (this is the *loss of control* effect) it ensures that decision making responds more to the agent's information. Compare this with centralized authority, which ensures an unbiased decision from the principal's point of view but encourages the agent to distort his information in order to influence the principal.

Information communication is modeled using Crawford and Sobel (1982)'s model of strategic communication. Since decisions are noncontractible and information is assumed to be soft, communication between the agent and principal takes the form of "cheap talk." However, strategic communication can be informative if there is sufficient preference alignment between the agent (the sender) and the principal (the receiver). Dessein's contribution can be seen as one of introducing control-rights considerations in strategic communication games, with the idea that delegation induces communication by the agent to become less "strategic," although at the cost of noncongruent decision making.

The result that delegation dominates when the agent's bias is small is not fully obvious: communication between the agent and principal is also better under centralization in that case, as the agent gains less by distorting information when her preferences are more congruent with those of the principal. Yet Dessein (2002) shows that under general conditions, as long as the bias of the agent is sufficiently small, delegation is always strictly preferred over centralization. For some specific cases, such as the leading example in Crawford and Sobel (1982), Dessein (2002) obtains the striking result that communication never takes place at the optimum: as long as preferences are sufficiently congruent, the principal is strictly better off avoiding communication (and the resulting information distortions) altogether, by committing to delegate control to the agent.

Overall, this paper provides an important rejoinder to the central insight of the property rights literature that the cost of integration (or centralization) are the reduced incentives to either make relationship-specific investments (Grossman and Hart) or to acquire information (Aghion and Tirole). In Dessein (2002), the cost of centralization (e.g., through integration), is the distortion and loss of information.

2. Empirical Evidence on the Determinants of Decentralization

Recent empirical interest in decentralization has been stimulated by the growth of a substantial body of evidence that documents persistence performance differences among firms, even in narrowly defined industries (see Syverson 2011; Gibbons and Roberts 2012; Aghion et al. 2013, Appendix C). Could these differences be due to different organizational structures within firms? This section is organized as follows. Subsection 2.1 focuses on the measurement of firm decentralization, 2.2 on the impact of trust on decentralization, 2.3 on empirical implication of learning models for decentralization, and 2.4 documents more general "stylized facts" of decentralization. We formally discuss identification issues in more detail in Appendix D of Aghion et al. (2013).

2.1 Measuring Firm Decentralization

A key factor in any organization is who makes decisions. A centralized firm is one were decisions are all taken at the top of the hierarchy, and a decentralized firm is where decision-making is more evenly dispersed throughout the corporate hierarchy.[3]

How can the concept of decentralization be implemented empirically? One way is to look at the organization charts of firms ("organogram") as graphical representations of the formal authority structure. One of the best studies in this area is Rajan and Wulf (2006) who use the charts of over 300 large U.S. corporations during 1987–1998 to examine the evolution of organizations (e.g., the number of people who directly report to the CEO as a measure of the span of control). Unfortunately, as Max Weber and (more recently as discussed above) Aghion and Tirole (1997) stressed, formal authority is not the same as real authority; the organogram may not reflect where real power lies.[4]

Observing whether a firm is decentralized into profit centers is useful, as this is a formal delegation of power—the head of such a business unit will be judged by the CEO on the basis of the unit's profitability. Similarly if the firm is composed of cost (or revenue) centers this indicates less decentralization as only costs (or revenue) are likely to be under control of the manager. If the firm does not even delegate responsibility to a cost or revenue center this indicates a very centralized company. Acemoglu et al. (2007) use this distinction to classify firms in their empirical work on French and British firm panel data.

Whether a company is organized into profit centers is a rather crude indicator of decentralization. A better (but more costly) approach is to directly survey firms. Bloom et al. (2012b) measure decentralization between the plant manager and the CHQ. They asked plant managers about their decisions over investment (maximum capital investment that could be made without explicit sign off from central headquarters), hiring, marketing, and product introduction (the latter three on a scale of 1–5). This was conducted at the same time as the Bloom and Van Reenen (2007) management survey.

Bloom et al. (2012b) constructed an empirical summary of decentralization combining these four measures into a single index by z-scoring each individual

---

[3] An extreme case of decentralized "organization" is an idealized market economy where atomistic individuals make all the decisions and form spot contracts with each other. The origin of many of the debates on decentralization have their origins in the 1930s, over the relative merits of a market economy relative to a centrally planned one.

[4] We focus on decentralization as distinct from managerial spans of control. These are distinct concepts—the span and depth (number of levels) of a hierarchy are compatible with different power relationships between the levels. Nevertheless, there is some evidence that the move towards delayering over the past 20 years has been associated with decentralization (see Rajan and Wulf 2006).

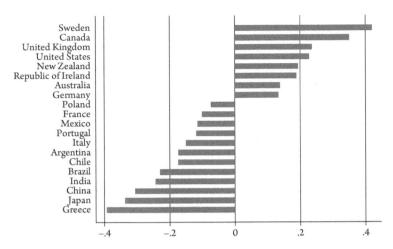

Figure 9.1 Decentralization is higher in Scandanavia and Anglo-Saxon countries, and lower in Asia and Southern Europe. Source: Histogram of decentralization across firms within each country. The definition of decentralization follows Bloom et al. (2012b), with data updated to 2010 from www.worldmanagementsurvey.com

indicator and z-scoring the average (so that the index has zero mean and unit standard deviation). We followed their approach but combine their data with additional waves of the World Management Survey conducted in 2007 and 2009 covering eight more countries.

Figure 9.1 shows that decentralization varies substantially across countries, with the United States, the United Kingdom, and Northern European countries being the most decentralized and Southern European and Asian countries the least. There is an even wider spread of decentralization across firms *within* every country, as shown in Figure 9.2.

Decentralization extends beyond just plant managers and the CHQ. For example, one can also consider the autonomy of workers from the plant manager following Bresnahan et al. (2002). Proxies for this dimension of decentralization include questions indicating greater worker control over the pace of work and over the allocation of tasks.

2.2 Trust (Congruence of Preferences)

The Aghion-Tirole approach offers a natural implementation of incomplete contracts to study decentralization within firms. One key parameter in fostering decentralization is the congruence of preferences between principal and agent. Other theoretical developments following Grossman-Hart such as Baker et al. (1999) also support this idea. Finding empirical proxies for the congruence parameter is challenging, but one possibility is to use measures of trust. In recent years, economists have started to take cultural factors more seriously

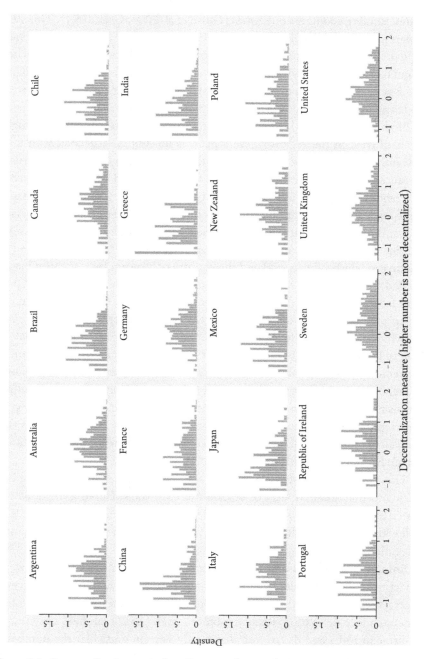

Figure 9.2 Decentralization varies heavily across firms within every country.
Source: Histogram of decentralization across firms within each country. The definition of
decentralization follows Bloom et al. (2012b), with data updated to 2010 from
www.worldmanagementsurvey.com

in determining economic outcomes (Guiso et al. 2006; Greif 1994). This stems in part from the influence of Putnam's (1993) work on the importance of social capital. Empirically, generalized social trust as a proxy for social capital has been found to be associated with many positive economic outcomes (e.g., see Knack and Keefer 1997 on trust and growth or Guiso et al. 2009 on trust and foreign trade and investment).

Bloom et al. (2012b) examine the importance of trust, finding that higher levels of trust in the region where a plant is located is associated with a significantly greater degree of decentralization. As in many other papers, trust is measured using the standard indicators from the World Values Survey which asks random samples of individuals about generalized trust. These external measures are matched to plant locations to obtain a measure of trust in the region. The authors also exploit the fact that their data contains many subsidiaries of multinational firms to construct measures of trust in the country of origin (the multinational's headquarters) and the country of location (where the affiliate is located). Both of these seem to matter for decentralization, but the most powerful factor is the *bilateral* trust between country pairs, that is, the degree to which people from the subsidiary's parent country trust people in the country where the plant is located. Multinationals locating in countries that are seen to be relatively highly trusted (after country location and origin dummies are removed), are significantly more likely to decentralize. For example, even though the United Kingdom is overall a relatively high-trust country, multinationals headquartered in the United States (where Britain has a relatively good trust reputation) tend to decentralize more toward their British affiliates than equivalent multinationals headquartered in France (where for historical reasons Britain has a relatively bad trust reputation).

These results suggest that trust can affect the internal structures of global firms and that some aspects of organization are transplanted abroad, as suggested by recent theories of international trade (e.g., Helpman et al. 2004). It fits well with the idea that the congruence of preferences is a major determinant of delegation.

Enforcement of contracts should further foster decentralization, and we do in fact observe more delegation where there is stronger rule of law.[5] However, contracts are never perfectly enforceable, which leaves a role for trust to help generate more delegation. Recently, Bloom et al. (2012) ran field experiments on firms in India and discovered that family size (in particular the number of adult male family members) was the key determinant of firm size, probably due to the importance of trust. Owners only trusted other family members to make

---

[5] See Bloom et al. (2009). More generally on the importance of law and reputation on contract enforceability see MacLeod (2007).

major managerial decisions as they worried that outsiders would steal from the firm. Hence, the supply of (trusted) male family member time was typically the binding factor for firm growth.

2.3 Learning

In the theory section we discussed an extension to the Aghion-Tirole approach when considering how firms could learn either from other firms or from themselves. Acemoglu et al. (2007) examine three predictions from their model: (i) delegation should be greater when the industry is more heterogeneous (so it is harder to learn from others); (ii) the firm is close to the frontier (so that there are fewer other firms to learn from); and (iii) the firm is younger (so it has less experience to learn from its own mistakes). Acemoglu et al. (2007) measure decentralization using both formal measures of whether firms are organized into profit centers as discussed above (for French firms) and direct survey measures of the power managers have over hiring decisions (for British firms). In both samples they find decentralization is more likely in industries that are more heterogeneous and for firms that are younger or closer to the technological frontier.

These results are illustrated in Figures 9.3–9.5 where the y-axis has the average degree of decentralization in different bins of the relevant variables.

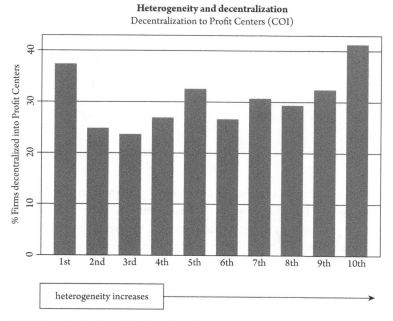

Figure 9.3 Decentralization is higher when heterogeneity is greater. Source: Acemoglu et al. (2007)

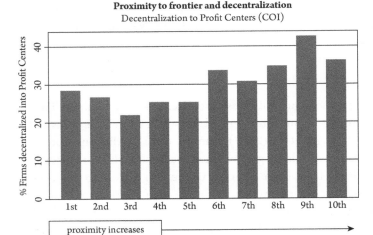

Figure 9.4 Decentralization is higher when plant are closer to the TFP frontier.
Source: Acemoglu et al. (2007)

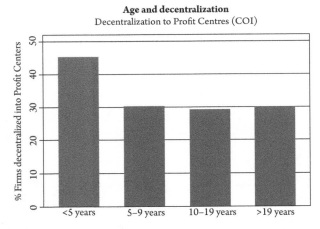

Figure 9.5 Decentralization is higher in younger plants. Source: Acemoglu et al. (2007)

In Figure 9.3 there is a reasonably clear positive relationship after the second decile between decentralization and heterogeneity (as measured by the dispersion of firm productivity growth). In Figure 9.4 decentralization appears to be higher among firms closer to the technological frontier (as measured by the distance of the firm's productivity from the leading firm in the four digit industry). That firms closer to the frontier should delegate more may also explain why subsidizing higher education, in particular graduate education, is more likely to be growth-enhancing if universities are more decentralized (see for example Aghion et al. 2009). Figure 9.5 shows that older firms look more centralized than younger firms, possibly because they have learned better what to do, so there is less need of delegation to a local manager who is better informed but may not pursue the principal's interests.

2.4 Other Empirical Factors Influencing Decentralization

The development of the incomplete contracts approach as applied to firm decentralization appears to have some confirmation in the data. The congruence of preferences (as proxied by trust) and heterogeneity (making it harder to learn) both seem to foster decentralization. There are many other findings in the literature on the empirical determinants of decentralization. These are not so obviously implications of the Grossman-Hart approach, but it is worth considering them.

2.4.1 Firm Size and Scope

Some basic factors determine decentralization. All else equal, a larger firm will require more decentralization than a small firm. A sole entrepreneur does not need to delegate because she is her own boss, but as more workers are added, doing everything herself is no longer feasible. Penrose (1959) and Chandler (1962) stressed that decentralization was a necessary feature of larger firms, because CEOs do not have the time to take every decision in large firms (see also Geanakoplos and Milgrom 1991). Similarly as firms expand in their scope both geographically and in product space, local information will become more costly to transmit, so this will also favor decentralization.

Most empirical findings support this. Bloom et al. (2012b) find that firm size and plant size are both associated with a significant increase in their decentralization index. Furthermore, plant managers in subsidiaries of foreign multinationals have more autonomy than similar plants of domestic non-multinationals. They interpret this as an indicator that managing at a distance is harder, inducing headquarters to give more autonomy to local managers.

2.4.2 Human Capital

Many models would predict that human capital should be associated with decentralization. For example, more skilled workers will have greater ability to take on more responsibility. When the environment changes due to new technologies and organizational change is required, skilled workers may be better at learning how to cope with the new organizational structure.

There is generally a robust and positive association of decentralization and skills. For example, Bloom et al. (2012b) measure skills by the proportion of people who hold a college degree and find this to be significantly correlated with decentralization. Caroli and Van Reenen (2001) examine the relationship between skills and organization in some detail, arguing in favor of "skill-biased organizational change": that is, increases in the supply of human capital will tend to increase delegation. To tackle the endogeneity problem, they use information on the differential price of skilled versus unskilled labor in the local market (as indicated by the wage differential between college educated workers and other individuals). They argue that this skill premium is partially driven by exogenous shifts in the supply of unskilled workers. For their sample of UK and French firms they find that regions where skill premia are higher have a lower probability of decentralization.

2.4.3 Information and Communication Technologies (ICT)

Garicano (2000) formalizes the idea of the firm as a cognitive hierarchy. There are a number of problems to be solved and the task is how to solve them in the most efficient manner. The simplest tasks are performed by those at the lowest level of the hierarchy, and the "exceptional" problems are passed upward to an expert. The cost of passing problems upward is that communication is expensive. The benefit of passing the problem upward is that it reduces the cognitive burden on lower level employees.

This framework was designed to address the impact of ICT on firm organization. Interestingly, information technologies have different implications for decentralization than communication technologies. Consider again the decentralization decision between the CHQ and plant manager. When communication costs fall (for example through the introduction of e-mail or company intranets), it is cheaper for the plant manager to refer more decisions to the CHQ. So communication technologies should cause *centralization*. By contrast, technologies that make it easier for the plant manager to acquire information (e.g., enterprise resource planning software, ERP like SAP) means that *decentralization* should increase. An example would be LexisNexis in law firms, which enables junior lawyers to quickly find relevant cases without consulting a more senior associate or partner.

Bloom et al. (2009) test this theory and find considerable empirical support. Computer networks (reducing communication costs) significantly decrease decentralization to plant managers, whereas tools to help managers access more information (like ERP) significantly increase decentralization.[6]

---

[6] The magnitude of the effect is substantial. An increase in ERP usage by 60% (the average difference in ICT between Europe and the United States) increases a plant manager's autonomy by an amount equivalent to the increase in U.S. college graduates between 1990 and 2000.

2.4.4 Product market competition

Some authors such as Acemoglu et al. (2007) argue that a cause of the aggregate increase in more decentralized organizations is rapid technological change. An alternative explanation is that globalization and deregulation have increased the degree of product market competition which has in turn stimulated organizational change. The theory is ambiguous here. If competition has made swift decisions more important, then this will increase the salience of local knowledge, leading to greater decentralization under the framework discussed above (e.g., Aghion and Tirole, 1997). Similarly if competition aligns the incentives of agents more with the principal, then the costs of decentralization may also fall. There are countervailing forces, however. For example, a larger number of firms in an industry aids yardstick competition, but it may also help learning in the Acemoglu et al. (2007) framework, which will reduce the need to decentralize.

The empirical evidence, however, seems more clear-cut. Bloom et al. (2010) find a robust positive association between competition and decentralization using industry import competition, the inverse of the industry Lerner index, or simply the number of perceived competitors. A similar positive correlation was reported in Acemoglu et al. (2007) and Marin and Verdier (2008, 2009). All of these are cross-sectional studies, so the positive coefficient on competition could simply reflect unobserved variables correlated with competition. Guadalupe and Wulf (2009) try to tackle this endogeneity problem using the Rajan and Wulf (2006) panel data set on the changing organizational structure of firms over time. They argue that the Canada U.S. Free Trade Agreement in 1989 constitutes an exogenous increase in competition for U.S. firms in industries where tariffs were removed. Exploiting this policy experiment reveals that competition is associated with their proxy for decentralization.

3. Organizational Practices and Firm Productivity

How can researchers identify the effects of organizational structure (e.g., decentralization) on firm performance?[7]

3.1 Correlations of Performance and Organizational Practices: The Basic Identification Problem

Consider the basic production function as

$$q_{it} = \alpha_l l_{it} + \alpha_k k_{it} + a_{it},\qquad(1)$$

---

[7] Aghion et al. (2013) Appendix D discusses general identification issues in this literature in more detail.

where q is ln(output), l is ln(labor), and k is ln(capital) of firm i at time t. Assume that we can write the TFP term a_{it} as

$$a_{it} = \alpha_0 + \beta m_{it} + u_{it}, \tag{2}$$

where m_{it} is an organizational feature of the firm (such as decentralization) and u_{it} is an unobserved error. Together these equations imply

$$q_{it} = \alpha_0 + \alpha_l l_{it} + \alpha_k k_{it} + \beta m_{it} + u_{it}. \tag{3}$$

This of course contains several assumptions. It assumes that the relevant organizational factor enters linearly, whereas organization could instead be affecting the coefficients on the other factor inputs, and many theories (e.g., of complementarity) would generate the same predictions. We discuss these below. We will assume that we can deal with the econometric problems in estimating the coefficients on the production function so that we have a consistent measure of total factor productivity (see Ackerberg et al. 2006, for a discussion of recent contributions). Note that OLS estimates of equation (3) will generally be biased, as $E(m_{it} u_{it} \neq 0)$.

The traditional strategy is to assume that m_{it} is a firm fixed effect. So one approach is simply to recover average firm TFP under this assumption and project it on some cross-sectional measure of management m_i. This will indicate whether there is an association between the two measures, but not whether the relationship is causal. For example, Bloom and Van Reenen (2007) show that there is a robust relationship between TFP and their measure of management quality, but they interpret this as an "external validity" test of the quality of the management data rather than as any causal relationship.

An analogous strategy if there are time-varying measures of organization is to treat all the correlated unobservables as fixed, that is, $u_{it} = \eta_i + \varepsilon_{it}$ with $E(m_{it} \eta_i) \neq 0$ but $E(m_{it} \varepsilon_{it}) = E(m_{it} \varepsilon_{it-1}) = 0$. Then the fixed effect model estimated in (say) first differences would be

$$\Delta a_{it} = \beta \Delta m_{it} + \Delta \varepsilon_{it}, \tag{4}$$

which can be consistently estimated by OLS.

There are a huge number of studies that have correlated various aspects of the firm's performance on various aspects of its organizational form (e.g., the survey in Lazear and Oyer 2012). The better studies use micro data and pay careful attention to measurement issues and need to control for many covariates. For example, Cappelli and Neumark (2001) and Black and Lynch (2001) examine various aspects of "high-performance" workplaces, mostly relating to employee involvement, teamwork, and meetings. Both papers look across many industries and find no direct effect of these measures on performance (in contrast to many case studies). As we discuss below, Ichniowski et al. (1997), however, examined management practices and performance in 37 U.S. steel mills over time and found a link between upgrading to bundles of modern practices and improved performance, so the correlation evidence is mixed.

There remain several serious problems. First is the data constraint that measuring organization is hard and finding data with time series variation even harder. Second, the management proxies are measured with error, so this will cause attenuation toward zero if the measurement error is classical. This bias is exacerbated in first differences. Third, and most seriously, the factors that cause variation in the propensity to adopt organizational practices will also likely be correlated with those affecting TFP so the assumption is unlikely to hold in most cases. The bias could be upward or downward (e.g., if firms doing badly are more likely to innovate organizationally as argued by Nickell et al. 2001).

There is no simple solution to these endogeneity problems as we fundamentally need some exogenous identifying variation. Bloom et al. (2012) implemented a gold standard randomized control trial in Indian textile plants. The intervention was by high-quality management consultants to improve a range of management practices (as in Bloom and Van Reenen 2007) which appeared to dramatically improve productivity. Most of the quasi experiments have been in labor economics. A good example is Lazear (2000) who looked at the introduction of a pay for performance system for windshield installers in the Safelite Glass Company. Lazear found that productivity increased by around 44%, with about half of this due to selection effects and half from the same individuals changing behavior. More recently, Bandiera et al. (2007, 2009) engineered a change in the incentive pay system for managers in farm. They have no contemporaneous control group, but can examine the behavior of individuals before and after the introduction of the incentive scheme. Productivity rose by 21% mainly with at least half due to improved selection (the managers allocated more fields to the ablest workers rather than to their colleagues).

3.2   Complementarities between Organizational Practices

One of the key reasons firms may find it difficult to adjust their organizational form is that there are important complementarities between sets of organizational practices. Milgrom and Roberts (1990) build a theoretical structure where such complementarities (or more precisely, super-additivities) mean that firms optimally choose clusters of practices that "fit together." When the environment change so that an entrant firm would use this group of optimal practices, incumbent firms will find it harder—they will switch either a large number of practices together or none at all.

This has important implications for productivity analysis. The effects of introducing a single practice will be heterogeneous between firms and depend on what practices they already use. This implies that linear regressions of the form of equation (4) may be misleading. To see this, consider two practices, m^1 and m^2, whose relationship with productivity is such that TFP increases only when both are used together.

$$a_{it} = a_0 + \beta_1 m_{it}^1 + \beta_2 m_{it}^2 + \beta_{12}(m_{it}^1 \times m_{it}^2) + u_{it}. \tag{5}$$

One version of the complementary hypothesis is $\beta_1 > 0$, $\beta_2 < 0$, and $\beta_{12} > 0$, that is, the disruption caused by just using one practice (m_{it}^2) could actually reduce productivity. A regression which omits the interaction term may $m_{it}^1 \times m_{it}^2$ find only a zero coefficient on the linear terms.

The case study literature emphasizes the importance of complementarities. Testing for their existence poses some challenges, however, as pointed out most clearly by Athey and Stern (1998). A common approach is a regression of practice 1 (m_{it}^1) on practice 2 (m_{it}^2) with a positive covariance (conditional on other factors) indicating complementarity. It is true that complements will tend to covary positively, but this is a very weak test. There could be many other unobservables causing the two practices to move together. We need an instrumental variable for one of the practices (e.g., Van Biesebroeck 2007), but this is hard to obtain as it is unclear what such an instrument would be, that is, could it be legitimately excluded from the second-stage equation? In classical factor demand analysis we would examine the cross-price effects to gauge the existence of complements versus substitutes, that is, does demand for practice 1 fall when the price of practice 2 rises (all else equal)? There remains the concern that the price shocks could be correlated with the productivity shocks, but such an assumption is weaker than assuming unobserved shocks to the firm's choice of practices are uncorrelated. Unfortunately, such tests are particularly hard to implement because there are generally no market prices for the organizational factors typically considered.

An alternative strategy is to work straight from the production function (or performance equation more generally). Consider the productivity equation after substituting in multiple practices:

$$q_{it} = \alpha_0 + \alpha_l l_{it} + \alpha_k k_{it} + \beta_1 m_{it}^1 + \beta_2 m_{it}^2 + \beta_3(m_{it}^1 \times m_{it}^2) + u_{it}. \tag{6}$$

Ichniowski et al. (1997) estimate a version of equation (6) using very disaggregate panel data on finishing lines in U.S. steel mills, using 11 human resource practices (including incentive pay, recruitment, teamwork, job flexibility, and rotation). Their measure of productivity is based on downtime—the less productive lines were idle for longer. They find that introducing one or two practices has no effect on productivity, but introducing a large number together significantly raises productivity. Although the endogeneity problem is not eliminated, the controls for fixed effects, looking within one firm and using performance data, helps reduce some of the more obvious sources of bias.

3.3 The Role of ICT Again

One of the key productivity puzzles of recent years has been why the returns to the use of information and communication technologies appear to be so high and so heterogeneous between firms and between countries. For example, Brynjolfsson and Hitt (2003) find that the elasticity of output with respect to ICT capital is far higher than its share in gross output (see also Stiroh 2002). One explanation for this is that effective use of ICT also requires significant changes in firm organization. Changing the notation of (6) slightly, we could write

$$q_{it} = \alpha_0 + \alpha_l l_{it} + \alpha_k k_{it} + \beta_c c_{it} + \beta_m m_{it}^2 + \beta_{cm}(c_{it} \times m_{it}) + u_{it}, \qquad (7)$$

with the hypothesis that $\beta_{cm} > 0$. This is broadly the position of papers in the macro literature explaining the faster productivity growth of the United States than Europe after 1995 (e.g., Jorgenson et al. 2008).

Bresnahan et al. (2002) try to test this directly by surveying large U.S. firms on decentralization and team work (for a cross section) and combining this with data on ICT (from a private company Harte-Hanks), and productivity from Compustat. They find evidence that $\beta_{cm} > 0$, that is, that computer capital is more productive when firms have greater decentralization and team work. Bloom et al. (2012a) broaden the sample to cover both U.S. and firms in seven European countries, and find evidence of complementarity of ICT with people management. They also show that their results are robust to controlling for firm fixed effects. Careful econometric case studies (e.g., Baker and Hubbard 2004; Bartel et al. 2007) also identify differential productivity effects of ICT depending on organization form. Lemieux et al. (2009) show that one particular people management practice, performance pay, is becoming increasingly important in the United States and has a significant impact on widening inequality. They suggest that the spread of ICT innovations has facilitated the adoption of performance pay techniques.

3.4 The Role of Human Capital

One of the reasons for the renewed interest in organizational change by labor economists was the attempt to understand why technology seemed to increase the demand for human capital, thus contributing to the rise in wage inequality experienced by the United States, United Kingdom, and other countries since the late 1970s. Many theories have been proposed (see Autor et al. 2003, for a review), but one hypothesis is that lower IT prices increased decentralization for the reasons outlined in Garicano (2000), and decentralization leads to an increase in inequality (Garicano and Rossi-Hansberg 2012). Further, decentralization is complementary with skills for at least three reasons. First, skilled workers are more able to analyze and synthesize new pieces of knowledge, so the benefits of local processing of information are enhanced. Additionally, skilled workers are better at communicating, which reduces the risk of duplication of information. Second, the cost of training them for multitasking is lower, and they are more autonomous and less likely to make mistakes. Finally, workers who are better educated may be more likely to enjoy job enrichment, partly because they expect more from their job in terms of satisfaction.

This has three main implications:

1. Decentralization leads to skill upgrading within firms. This is due to the fact that the return to new work practices is greater when the skill level of the workforce is higher.
2. A lower price of skilled labor will accelerate the introduction of organizational changes.
3. Skill intensive firms will experience greater productivity growth when decentralizing.

Caroli and Van Reenen (2001) find support for all three predictions. They estimate production functions (with the relevant interactions), skill share equations, and organizational design equations. A novel feature of this approach is that because labor is traded in a market, it is possible to use local skill price variation to examine complementarity issues. They find that higher skill prices make decentralization less likely, consistent with "skill-biased organizational change."

4. Conclusions

We began by surveying the theoretical literature on the organization of firms and the optimal decentralization of decision rights within firms. We discussed how the concept of incomplete contracts shapes this organization of decision making within firms. In particular, the inability to contract over all possible states of the world leads principals to delegate control to agents as a way to ex ante commit to letting agents expropriate some of the returns from costly activities, like collecting information on the best actions to take.

We then overviewed some of the empirical evidence on the organization and management of firms, focusing on decentralization. We looked at within-firm organization, especially decentralization following the theoretical survey, and we also looked at econometric studies, focusing on large-scale firm databases rather than case studies. There has recently been a number of papers measuring management and organizational practices across firms and countries. Like productivity, decentralization varies a lot across firms and countries (e.g., Scandinavian and Anglo-Saxon firms are more decentralized than those from Asia and Southern Europe). A number of factors highlighted in the incomplete contract theory are shown to be important for accounting for differences in firm organization—in particular heterogeneity and the congruence of preferences (as proxied by trust). Several other factors appear robustly positively correlated with decentralization, such as product market competition, human capital, and firm size.

In terms of future work, we see two areas of opportunity. First, there is a need to match up empirical work more closely with the theory. Until recently, comprehensive data sets on measures of organization across many firms and countries were unavailable. Now that this gap in the core data infrastructure is being covered, there is a great opportunity for testing some of the theories of organizational economics. This is challenging, first because many of the important aspects in the environment emphasized in the theoretical literature are hard to match into empirical counterparts, and second because identifying the causal relationship between organizational changes and firm outcomes like productivity and growth is difficult. Even with strong measurement and tight links to theory, it is essential to identify the direction of causality in some of stylized empirical results we have identified above—for example, do skilled managers enable more decentralized decision making, or are skilled managers attracted to more decentralized firms? We see the theory and empirics of the organization of the firm as one of the key growth areas in economics over the next 25 years.

References

Acemoglu, D., P. Aghion, C. Lelarge, J. Van Reenen, and F. Zilibotti. 2007. "Technology, Information and the Decentralization of the Firm." *Quarterly Journal of Economics* 122: 1759–99.

Ackerberg, D., C. L. Benkard, S. Berry, and A. Pakes. 2007. "Econometric Tools for Analyzing Market Outcomes." *Quarterly Journal of Economics* 122(4): 1759–99.

Aghion, P., N. Bloom, and J. Van Reenen. 2013. "Incomplete Contracts and the Internal Organization of Firms." NBER Working Paper 18842.

Aghion, P., and P. Bolton. 1992. "An Incomplete Contracts Approach to Financial Contracting." *Review of Economic Studies* 59(3): 473–94.

Aghion, P., M. Dewatripont, and P. Rey. 2004. "Transferable Control." *Journal of the European Economic Association* 2(1): 115–38.

Aghion, P., M. Dewatripont, and J. C. Stein. 2009. "Academic Freedom, Private-Sector Focus, and the Process of Innovation." *RAND Journal of Economics* 39: 617–35.

Aghion, P. and J. Tirole. 1997. "Formal and Real Authority in Organizations." *Journal of Political Economy* 105: 1–29.

Alonso, R., W. Dessein, and N. Matouschek. 2008. "When Does Coordination Require Centralization?," *American Economic Review* 98(1): 145–79.

Athey, S., and S. Stern. 1998. "An Empirical Framework for Testing Theories about Complementarity in Organizational Design." NBER Working Paper No. 6600.

Atkeson, A., and P.J. Kehoe. 2005. "Modeling and Measuring Organization Capital." *Journal of Political Economy* 113(5): 1026–53.

Autor, D. H., F. Levy, and R. J. Murnane. 2003. "The Skill Content of Recent Technological Change: An Empirical Exploration." *Quarterly Journal of Economics* 118(4): 1279–333.

Baily, M. N., C. Hulten, and D. Campbell. 1992. "Productivity Dynamics in Manufacturing Establishments." *Brookings Papers on Economic Activity: Microeconomics* 4: 187–249.

Baker, G. P., R. Gibbons, and K. J. Murphy. 1999. "Informal Authority in Organizations." *Journal of Law, Economics, and Organization* 15(1): 56–73.

Baker, G. P., and T. N. Hubbard. 2004. "Contractibility and Asset Ownership: On-Board Computers and Governance in US Trucking." *Quarterly Journal of Economics* 11(4): 1443–79.

Bandiera, O., I. Barankay, and I. Rasul. 2007. "Incentives for Managers and Inequality among Workers: Evidence from a Firm Level Experiment." *Quarterly Journal of Economics* 122(2): 729–73.

Bandiera, O., I. Barankay, and I. Rasul. 2009. "Social Connections and Incentives in the Workplace: Evidence from Personnel Data." *Econometrica* 77(4): 1047–94.

Bartel, A. C., C. Ichiniowski, and K. Shaw. 2007. "How Does Information Technology Affect Productivity? Plant-Level Comparisons of Product Innovation, Process Improvement and Worker Skills." *Quarterly Journal of Economics* 12 (4): 1721–58.

Bartelsman, E. J., and P. J. Dhrymes. 1998. "Productivity Dynamics: US Manufacturing Plants, 1972–1986." *Journal of Productivity Analysis* 9(1): 5–34.

Bartelsman, E. J., and M. Doms. 2000. "Understanding productivity: Lessons from Longitudinal Microdata." *Journal of Economic Literature* 38(3): 569–94.

Bartelsman, E. J., J. C. Haltiwanger, and S. Scarpetta. 2009. "Cross-Country Differences in Productivity: The Role of Allocation and Selection." NBER Working Paper 15490.

Black, S. E., and L. M. Lynch. 2001. "How to Compete: The Impact of Workplace Practices and Information Technology on Productivity." *Review of Economics and Statistics* 83(3): 434–45.

Bloom, N., B. Eifert, A. Mahajan, D. McKenzie, and J. Roberts. 2013. "Does Management Matter? Evidence from India." *Quarterly Journal of Economics* 128: 1–51.

Bloom, N., L. Garicano, R. Sadun, and J. Van Reenen. 2009. "The Distinct Effect of Communication Technology and Information Technology on Firm Organization." NBER Working Paper 14975.

Bloom, N., C. Genakos, R. Martin, and R. Sadun. 2010. "Modern Management: Good for the Environment or Just Hot Air?," *Economic Journal* 120(544): 551–72.

Bloom, N., C. Genakos, R. Sadun, and J. Van Reenen. "Management Practices across Firms and Countries." *Academy of Management Perspectives* 26(1): 12–33.

Bloom, N., T. Kretschmer, and J. Van Reenen. 2009. "Work-Life Balance, Management Practices and Productivity." In Richard Freedman and Kathryn Shaw (eds.) *International Differences in Business Practices and the Productivity of Firms*. Cambridge, MA: NBER.

Bloom, N., C. Propper, S. Seiler, and J. Van Reenen. 2010. "The Impact of Competition on Management Quality: Evidence from Public Hospitals." NBER Technical Report.

Bloom, N., R. Sadun, and J. Van Reenen. 2009. "The Organization of Firms across Countries." CEP Discussion Paper dp0937.

Bloom, N., R. Sadun, and J. Van Reenen. 2010. "Does Product Market Competition Lead Firms to Decentralize?," *American Economic Review* 100(2): 434–8.

Bloom, N., R. Sadun, and J. Van Reenen. 2012a. "Americans Do I.T. Better: US Multinationals and the Productivity Miracle." *American Economic Review* 102(1): 167–201.

Bloom, N., R. Sadun, and J. Van Reenen. 2012b. "The Organization of Firms across Countries." *Quarterly Journal of Economics* 127(4): 1663–705.

Bloom, N., and J. Van Reenen. 2007. "Measuring¹and Explaining Management Practices across Firms and Countries." *Quarterly Journal of Economics* 122(4): 1351–408.

Bolton, P., and M. Dewatripont. 2011. "Authority in Organizations: A Survey." Working Paper.

Bresnahan, T. F., E. Brynjolfsson, and L. M. Hitt. 2002. "Information Technology, Workplace Organization, and the Demand for Skilled Labor: Firm-Level Evidence." *Quarterly Journal of Economics* 117(1): 339–76.

Brynjolfsson, E., and L. M. Hitt. 2003. "Computing Productivity: Firm-Level Evidence." *Review of Economics and Statistics* 85(4): 793–808.

Cappelli, P., and D. Neumark. 2001. "Do High-Performance Work Practices Improve Establishment-Level Outcomes." *Industrial and Labor Relations Review* 54: 737–75.

Caroli, E., and J. Van Reenen. 2001. "Skill-Biased Organizational Change? Evidence from a Panel of British and French Establishments." *Quarterly Journal of Economics* 116(4): 1449–92.

Chandler, A. D. 1962. *Strategy and Structure: Chapters in the History of American Enterprise.* Cambridge, MA: MIT Press.

Crawford, V. P., and J. Sobel. 1982. "Strategic Information Transmission." *Econometrica: Journal of the Econometric Society* 50: 1431–51.

Criscuolo, C., J. Haskel, and R. Martin. 2003. "Building the Evidence Base for Productivity Policy Using Business Data Linking." *Economic Trends* 600: 39–51.

Dessein, W. 2002. "Authority and Communication in Organizations." *Review of Economic Studies* 69(4): 811–38.

DiNardo, J., and D. S. Lee. 2004. "Economic Impacts of New Unionization on Private Sector Employers: 1984–2001." *Quarterly Journal of Economics* 119: 1383–441.

Foster, L., J. Haltiwanger, and C. Syverson. 2008. "Reallocation, Firm Turnover, and Efficiency: Selection on Productivity or Profitability?" *American Economic Review* 98: 394–425.

Garicano, L. 2000. "Hierarchies and the Organization of Knowledge in Production." *Journal of Political Economy* 108(5): 874–904.

Garicano, L., and T. Hubbard. 2009. "Earnings Inequality and Coordination Costs: Evidence from U.S. Law Firms." Working Paper

Garicano, L., and E. Rossi-Hansberg. 2012. "Organizing Growth." *Journal of Economic Theory* 147: 623–56.

Geanakoplos, J., and P. Milgrom. 1991. "A Theory of Hierarchies Based on Limited Managerial Attention." *Journal of the Japanese and International Economies* 5(3): 205–25.

Gibbons, R., and J. Roberts. 2012. *Handbook of Organizational Economics.* Princeton, NJ: Princeton University Press

Gibrat, R. 1931. *Les Inégalités Economiques.* Paris: Sirey.

Greif, A. 1994. "Cultural Beliefs and the Organization of Society: A Historical and Theoretical Reflection on Collectivist and Individualist Societies." *Journal of Political Economy* 102(5): 912–950.

Grossman, S. J., and O. D. Hart. 1986. "The Costs and Benefits of Ownership: A Theory of Vertical and Lateral Integration." *Journal of Political Economy* 94(4): 691–719.

Guadalupe, M., and J. Wulf. 2010. "The Flattening Firm and Product Market Competition: The Effect of Trade Liberalization on Corporate Hierarchies." *American Economic Journal: Applied Economics* 2(4): 105–27.

Guiso, L., P. Sapienza, and L. Zingales. 2003. "People's Opium? Religion and Economic Attitudes." *Journal of Monetary Economics* 50(1): 225–82.

Guiso, L., P. Sapienza, and L. Zingales. 2004. "The Role of Social Capital in Financial Development." *American Economic Review* 94(3): 526–56.

Guiso, L., P. Sapienza, and L. Zingales. 2006. "Does Culture Affect Economic Outcomes?," *Journal of Economic Perspectives* 20(2): 23–48.

Guiso, L., P. Sapienza, and L. Zingales. 2009. "Cultural Biases in Economic Exchange?," *Quarterly Journal of Economics* 124(3): 1095–131.

Hart, O. D., and B. Holmström. 2010. "A Theory of Firm Scope." *Quarterly Journal of Economics* 125(2): 483–513.

Hart, O. D., and J. Moore. 1999. "On the Design of Hierarchies: Coordination versus Specialization." LSE-Sticerd Discussion Paper TE/99/375.

Helpman, E., M. J. Melitz, and S. R. Yeaple. 2004. "Export versus FDI with Heterogeneous Firms." *American Economic Review* 94(1): 300–16.

Hsieh, C. T., and P. J. Klenow. "Misallocation and Manufacturing TFP in China and India." *Quarterly Journal of Economics* 124(4): 1403–48.

Ichniowski, C., K. Shaw, and G. Prennushi. 1997. "The Effects of Human Resource Management Practices on Productivity: A Study of Steel Finishing Lines." *American Economic Review* 87(3): 291–313.

Jorgenson, D. W., M. S. Ho, and K. J. Stiroh. 2008. "A Retrospective Look at the US Productivity Growth Resurgence." *Journal of Economic Perspectives* 22(1): 3–24.

Klette, T. J., and Z. Griliches. 1996. "The Inconsistency of Common Scale Estimators when Output Prices are Unobserved and Endogenous." *Journal of Applied Econometrics* 11: 343–61.

Knack, S., and P. Keefer. 1997. "Does Social Capital Have An Economic Payoff? A Cross-Country Investigation," *Quarterly Journal of Economics* 112(4): 1251–88.

Lafontaine, F., and M. E. Slade. 2010. "Inter-Firm Contracts: Evidence." In E. Gibbons and D. J. Roberts (eds.) *Handbook of Organizational Economics*, pp. 958–1013. Princeton, NJ: Princeton University Press.

Lazear, E. 2000. "Performance Pay and Productivity." *American Economic Review* 90(5): 1346–61.

Lazear, E., and P. Oyer. 2012. "Personnel Economics." In E. Gibbons and D. J. Roberts (eds.) *Handbook of Organizational Economics*, pp. 479–519. Princeton, NJ: Princeton University Press.

Lemieux, T., W. B. MacLeod, and D. Parent. 2009. "Performance Pay and Wage Inequality." *Quarterly Journal of Economics* 124(1): 1–49.

MacLeod, W. B. 2007. "Reputations, Relationships and Contract Enforcement." *Journal of Economic Literature* 45(3): 597–630.

Marin, D., and T. Verdier. 2008. "Power Inside the Firm and the Market: A General Equilibrium Approach." *Journal of the European Economic Association* 6(4): 752–88.

Marin, D., and T. Verdier. 2009. "Power in the Multinational Corporation in Industry Equilibrium." *Economic Theory* 38(3): 437–64.

Milgrom, P., and J. Roberts. 1990. "The Economics of Modern Manufacturing: Technology, Strategy, and Organization." *American Economic Review* 80(3): 511–28.

Modigliani, F., and M. H. Miller. 1958. "The Cost of Capital, Corporation Finance and the Theory of Investment." *American Economic Review* 48(3): 261–97.

Nickell, S., D. Nicolitsas, and M. Patterson. 2001. "Does Doing Badly Encourage Management Innovation?," *Oxford Bulletin of Economics and Statistics* 63(1): 5–28.

Penrose, E. T. 1959. *The Theory of the Growth of the Firm.* New York: Wiley.

Prescott, E. C., and M. Visscher. 1980. "Organization Capital." *Journal of Political Economy* 88(3): 446–61.

Putnam, R. 1993. "The Prosperous Community." *American Prospect* 4(13): 35–42.

Rajan, R. G., and J. Wulf. 2006. "The Flattening Firm: Evidence from Panel Data on the Changing Nature of Corporate Hierarchies." *Review of Economics and Statistics* 88(4): 759–73.

Solow, R. M. 1957. "Technical Change and the Aggregate Production Function." *Review of Economics and Statistics* 39(3): 312–20.

Stein, J. 1997. "Internal Capital Markets and the Competition for Corporate Resources." *Journal of Finance* 52: 111–33.

Stiroh, K. 2002. "Reassessing the Role of IT in the Production Function: A Meta-Analysis." Federal Reserve Bank of New York Working Paper.

Syverson, C. 2010. "What Determines Productivity?," *Journal of Economic Literature* 49(2): 326–65.

Van Biesebroeck, J. 2007. "Complementarities in Automobile Production." *Journal of Applied Econometrics* 22(7): 1315–45.

Walker, F. A. 1888. "On the Source of Business Profits: A Reply to Mr. Macvane." *Quarterly Journal of Economics* 2(3): 263–96.

10

Comments on Aghion, Bloom, and Van Reenen, "Incomplete Contracts and the Internal Organization of Firms"

JOHN ROBERTS

For a long time, economists referred to "the theory of the firm," by which they meant an explanation of the determinants of the boundaries of the firm, particularly the vertical boundaries.[1] Of course, the phenomenon of the firm is much richer than this specific focus would suggest, and there is in fact much more to the economic analysis of the firm. In particular, there is now a substantial literature, both theoretical and empirical, on firms' internal organization.[2]

Much of this literature involves models where incomplete contracting is central. In this, it derives ultimately from Grossman and Hart (1986). So it is entirely appropriate to have a chapter in this volume (chapter 9) on the role of incomplete contracting on at least one aspect of internal organization, namely, delegation and the locus of decision rights, and on the empirical evidence related to delegation. To have the chapter coauthored by one of the leading theorists in organizational economics and two of the leading empiricists studying the subject is a special treat.

The paper has a theory section and then empirical and econometric parts. I focus mostly on the first and the empirical implications following from it.

The theory section involves four subsections. The first presents Aghion and Tirole (1997) on "formal versus real authority" and the problem of inducing an agent to collect information. The second treats a number of issues under the rubric of "extensions" (of Aghion-Tirole). The third involves the

---

[1] Wrapped up in such discussions was often a specification of what was meant by a firm and theories as to why these things exist.

[2] See, for example, the first 20 chapters of Gibbons and Roberts (2013).

Aghion and Bolton (1992) model of state-contingent allocations of decision rights in financial contracting, supplemented with a suggestion from Bolton and Dewatripont (2013) that the model could be interpreted as applying to whether a manager will be fired or her division closed. Finally, the fourth section discusses Dessein (2002), which models cheap talk by a privately informed agent in the Aghion-Tirole context and asks if the agent should simply be allowed to make the choices rather than communicate his private information strategically.

The Aghion-Tirole model is very well known, so there is no point summarizing it here. A key assumption that shows up elsewhere needs to be noted, however: that the principal is able to commit to allowing the agent to make decisions. Doing so in this framework motivates the agent to develop information, because he knows he will get to choose the alternative he likes best rather than being overruled by the principal. The key empirical implication of the model is that closer alignment between the tastes of the principal and agent favors giving the decision to the agent. The Dessein extension has essentially the same empirical implications.

While the financing of the firm is a central question in the economics of the firm, the Aghion-Bolton model of financial contracting has nothing to do per se with *internal* organization and delegation. Meanwhile, note that the Bolton-Dewatripont reinterpretation employs the assumption from Aghion-Tirole that the principal can commit to give authority to the manager in some states.

The "extensions" discussion mentions the Hart and Moore (2005) model of the allocation of decision rights between "generalists" and "specialists." Although this paper has some interesting empirical implications, many of which conform to practice, it does not seem to be much about delegation per se, and indeed, it does not figure in the empirical section.

More directly related to delegation, the authors also discuss the extension of Aghion-Tirole offered in Acemoglu et al. (2007), where rather than gathering information herself, the principal can observe the practices of other firms in the same industry. This variation leads to several empirical implications, notably that delegation is favored in younger firms that have yet to learn much about themselves, as well as in firms in more heterogeneous environments and those operating nearer the technological frontier, for both of which observing others is less informative. The basic logic of the argument in Acemoglu et al. suggests that there should also be more delegation when there are fewer firms in the industry (so there is less information available from others' choices) and when the industry is geographically dispersed (so observation of others is more difficult), but these are not addressed in the original paper or in the empirical results reported in the chapter.

The "extensions" subsection also discusses an important idea that was in the original Aghion-Tirole paper, that raising the cost to the principal of gathering information when she has formal authority would motivate the agent, because he would be less likely to be overruled. Here the authors suggest that expanding the principal's span of control could accomplish this. There is no formal model, but presumably they have in mind a set-up where there are potentially multiple agents, each of whom can acquire information about independent, noncompeting projects, as can the principal. However, the costs of expanding the span of control are not discussed, so the empirical implications are not completely obvious.

The last subject in the extensions subsection concerns the crucial assumption already noted and used consistently through the literature discussed here: that the principal can commit to allowing the agent to make decisions. The authors recognize that this is a questionable assumption, and they note that Baker et al. (1999) and later Bolton and Dewatripont (2013) observe that typically the principal can always overrule the agent, even if she has said that he has formal authority. This is not just a minor point, however. Instead, it is a crucial and highly problematic element of the main theories discussed here, which—as noted—assume just the opposite.

In fact, the "business judgment rule" means that the courts will simply not enforce policies or agreements to allocate authority within a firm to a unit or its manager. Such delegation can be withdrawn at will. Moreover, the general requirement that only "legal persons" can enter into contracts limits contractual allocations of authority even more (see Kornhauser and Macleod 2013). Unless the agent is a separate legal entity (as was suggested in Aghion-Tirole), there can be no contract, and any delegation of powers is not enforceable.[3] So models where contracting on the allocation of decision rights is possible are very problematic if they are meant to apply to internal organization.

Given this, if delegation within the firm is to be credible and lasting, it needs to be based on reputation concerns (as was suggested by Baker et al. and Bolton and Dewatripont).[4] The difficulty here is that once we move into the repeated-game context usually used to examine reputations, many other alternative organizational arrangements become possible. For example, the principal might cede decision making to the agent, but direct him to search diligently and, whenever he becomes informed, choose the principal's preferred alternative. If the principal knows the effort the agent exerted and whether he became informed, then it would seem easy for her to control his behavior in a repeated

---

[3] This is well understood in business. For example, at one point energy company BP produced a document on how the firm was to be managed. The section on delegation was absolutely clear that any delegation could be revoked at any time and without any explanation, although such behavior was discouraged.

[4] Or, as the authors suggest, on the idea of "aggrievement" leading to "shading," as proposed by Hart and Holmström (2010). Essentially, this would seem to require repeated dealings, too.

game. Even with much less information, she could use a review strategy (see, for example, Sugaya 2012) to estimate if the agent was disobeying too often, in which case he could be terminated. Such alternatives might be better than simple delegation.

For the agent to care about being terminated, of course, he must be receiving some rents. In the repeated game, the opportunity to select his preferred outcome occasionally might generate these. As well, the principal might pay the agent.

In fact, the lack of compensation contracts is a major gap in this literature on delegation. There needs to be an examination—probably in a repeated context—of the use of compensation to motivate and control behavior under delegation. Such an analysis might be very informative for empirical work. Whether the empirical implications of the one-shot models with commitment would extend to these richer models is unclear.[5]

The empirical part of the paper focuses first on defining and measuring decentralization in firms. Examination of organization charts and the adoption of profit centers are suggested as possibilities and are used later, but the authors place greatest emphasis on the results of surveys, particularly those by Bloom et al. (2012). This work offers a measure of delegation based on plant managers' answers to survey questions about how much autonomy they have in decisions about investment, marketing, hiring, and new product introduction.

As noted, the primary prediction of the Aghion-Tirole line of work is that closer alignment of the preferences of the principal and agent should favor delegation. Using "trust" (as measured in the World Values Survey) as a proxy for alignment, Bloom et al. find strong support for the prediction across countries. Companies based in countries with higher levels of trust are more decentralized, and multinationals decentralize more in countries with higher trust levels. The authors thus argue that the alignment prediction is supported.

The issue is whether trust is the best proxy for alignment. Answering this would seem to depend on understanding the reason for the divergence of interests. For example, if the agent is a manager, his market value might be increased if he is seen to be running lots of large investment projects. In this case, he may favor larger projects or more frequent investment. Then alignment will be greater if the market cannot observe the projects he runs. Also, if the agent is

---

[5] Gibbons et al. (2013) discuss a range of other papers on decentralization and delegation. In some of these (for example, Harris and Raviv 2005), the positive connection of alignment and decentralization can be broken. As well, in richer models such as Alonso et al. (2008), Rantakari (2008), and Freibel and Raith (2010), the underlying trade-offs, the comparative statics and the ensuing empirical predictions are much more complicated than in the simple models considered in this chapter. Also of importance is Van den Steen's (2010) quite distinct explanation for the allocation of decision rights.

compensated on the value of the investment to the principal, alignment would be closer. It would seem to be worthwhile to give more thought to this issue.

The Acemoglu et al. paper carried out the tests of its predictions (about young firms, ones in more heterogeneous environments, and those operating close to the technology frontier) and found general support in samples of British and French firms.

The authors also offer a useful survey of other empirical work on decentralization and the linkages to factors other than incomplete contracting, including information and communications technology, human capital, competition, and size. For the most part, the theory that would rationalize these linkages is poorly developed. They then provide a very nice discussion of the problems of doing econometric analyses of organizational design matters and their link to performance. This is a very helpful drawing together of the subject.

All told, this is a chapter well worth reading.

References

Acemoglu, D., P. Aghion, C. Lelarge, J. Van Reenen, and F. Zilibotti. 2007. "Technology, Information and the Decentralization of the Firm." *Quarterly Journal of Economics* 122: 1759–99.

Aghion, P., and P. Bolton. 1992. "An Incomplete Contracts Approach to Financial Contracting." *Review of Economic Studies* 59: 473–94.

Aghion, P., and J. Tirole. 1997. "Formal and Real Authority in Organizations." *Journal of Political Economy* 105: 1–29.

Alonso, R., W. Dessien, and N. Matoushek. 2008. "When Does Coordination Require Centralization?" *American Economic Review* 98: 145–79.

Baker, G., R. Gibbons, and K. J. Murphy.1999. "Informal Authority in Organizations." *Journal of Law, Economics, and Organization* 15: 56–73.

Bloom, N., R. Sadun and J. Van Reenen. 2012. "The Organization of Firms across Countries." *Quarterly Journal of Economics* 127: 1663–705.

Bolton, P., and M. Dewatripont. 2013. "Authority in Organizations." In R. Gibbons and J. Roberts (eds.) *The Handbook of Organizational Economics*. Princeton, NJ: Princeton University Press, pp. 342–72.

Dessein, W. 2002. "Authority and Communication in Organizations." *Review of Economic Studies* 69: 811–38.

Friebel, G., and M. Raith. 2010. "Resource Allocation and Organizational Form." *American Economic Journal: Microeconomics* 2: 1–33.

Gibbons, R., N. Matoushek, and J. Roberts. 2013. "Decisions in Organizations." In R. Gibbons and J. Roberts (eds.) *The Handbook of Organizational Economics*. Princeton, NJ: Princeton University Press, pp. 373–431.

Grossman, S., and O. Hart. 1986. "The Costs and Benefits of Ownership: A Theory of Vertical and Lateral Integration." *Journal of Political Economy* 94: 691–719.

Harris, M., and A. Raviv. 2005. "Allocation of Decision-Making Authority." *Review of Finance* 9: 353–83.

Hart, O., and B. Holmström. 2010. "A Theory of Firm Scope." *Quarterly Journal of Economics* 125(2): 483–513.

Hart, O., and J. Moore. 2005. "On the Design of Hierarchies: Coordination versus Specialization." *Journal of Political Economy* 113: 675–702.

Kornhauser, L., and W. B. MacLeod. 2013. "Contracts between Legal Persons." in R. Gibbons and J. Roberts (eds.) *The Handbook of Organizational Economics*. Princeton, NJ: Princeton University Press, pp. 918–57.

Rantakari, H. 2008. "Governing Adaptation." *Review of Economic Studies* 75: 1257–85.

Sugaya, T. 2012. *The Folk Theorem in Repeated Games with Private Monitoring*. Dissertation, Princeton University.

Van den Steen, E. 2010. "Interpersonal Authority in a Theory of the Firm." *American Economic Review* 100: 466–90.

11

The Empirical Implications of the Grossman-Hart Model: Comments on "Incomplete Contracts and the Internal Organization of Firms" by P. Aghion, N. Bloom and J. Van Reenen

W. BENTLEY MCLEOD

It is not only a great pleasure to have the opportunity to participate in this conference in honor of Sandy Grossman and Oliver Hart, it is also a great pleasure to have the chance to comment on the work of three very distinguished economists. The purpose of "Incomplete Contracts and the Internal Organization of Firms" is to review the theoretical and empirical implications of incomplete contracts theory for the level of decentralization in a firm. The first part of the paper (section 1) reviews models of authority with asymmetric information. In these models agents choose the degree of delegation based on the information held by the agent, and the effect that this information has on effort (Aghion and Tirole 1997) or on the quality of decision making (Dessein 2002). In these papers, like Grossman and Hart (1986) (GH), it is shown that the allocation of authority has efficiency consequences.

Section 2 discusses the empirical literature that relates features of the environment, such as the level of trust, to the level of decentralization in the firm. Section 3 discusses a literature that measures the impact that decentralization within the firm has on firm profits.

Aghion et al. (2014)'s review, though inspired by GH and the incomplete contracts literature, focuses on the role of information flows within the firm.

I thank Patrick Legros for very helpful comments.

In this note I fill in the front end of this review, and begin with a discussion of the origins of formal incomplete contracts theory (Simon 1951). I then show how GH provides the Simon model with a more rigorous foundation for the importance of authority.

Next I present a simplified version of GH and show how one can use the Rubin/Holland model of causal inference (Holland 1986) to derive some testable implications from the theory. I then use these observations to make some comments regarding the literatures that are reviewed in sections 3 and 4 of Aghion et al. (2014). Specifically, I point out that the Rubin/Holland model could be more widely used to clearly distinguish between casual inference and results that are empirical questions and results that are very interesting, but mainly descriptive.

1. The Theory of Authority

The first formal model of incomplete contracts is due to Simon (1951). Relying on his extensive practical experience with organizations, he observed that in complex environments planning is expensive, and hence it may be cheaper to wait for more information before making a decision. He used this idea to model the employment relationship as one in which the precise job requirements are determined after employment. The problem is that once employed, the firm may ask the workers to carry out tasks that are very unpleasant; to deal with this Simon suggested that an employment contract gives *limited* discretion to the employer.

In his model decentralization occurs via the sales contract, a contract that specifies the characteristics of the good in advance. This has the benefit of lower production costs ex ante, but possibly higher costs ex post if an event occurs that make the conditions of the sales contract inefficient. This creates a trade-off in that the sales contract has a cost because it is not flexible enough, while the employment contract has a cost in that the choices by the employer do not take into account an employee's opportunity cost.

An important observation in GH is that parties to a bilateral agreement are always free to alter the terms ex post. As Hart and Moore (1988) illustrate, a contract can be viewed as creating default allocation ex post, from which parties can bargain. Thus, while the different contracts in the Simon model may lead to different ex post payoffs, once renegotiation is introduced, the trade-off in the Simon model disappears (see MacLeod 2002). This result can be viewed as another version of the Coase (1960) theorem—in the absence of transactions costs the initial allocation of property rights do not matter for the efficiency of the relationship.

The contribution of GH is to highlight the role that authority over residual decision rights has for investment. They show that the initial allocation of authority has implications for performance that cannot be undone through ex post renegotiation. Thus, the allocation of decision rights and the extent to which one person has full authority or authority is split between different assets will vary with relative importance of the relationship specific investments made by each party. This analysis was significantly extended and generalized by Hart and Moore (1990). In this comment I briefly discuss how to use the Rubin/Holland model to go from this theory to some testable hypothesis.

2. GH Theory in a Nutshell

Since all models are false, the real issue is not whether a model is correct in some abstract sense but whether it can be used to improve on previous models.[1] In this regard the Coase theorem plays an import role in organizational economics by providing a counterfactual against which to test organizational models, such as the GH model. Coase hypothesized that in the absence of transactions costs, the initial allocation of property rights and legal liability can have no effect on economic efficiency. This perspective puts on the table a null hypothesis that can be used to test for the presence of transaction costs.

This is a relatively standard approach in many areas of economics. For example, the competitive model is the (false) benchmark against which we compare models with imperfect competition. The rational choice model is the benchmark against which behavioral economists develop their models. By exploring how a benchmark model fails we can begin to build better models.

Now consider the case of a building project where one person is the principal who knows or cares about the characteristics of the building, and the other is the general contractor with the equipment and manpower to build the project. As in the GH model, each agent makes specific investment a_i, $i \in \{P, C\}$, where P is the "principal" and C is the "general contractor." Let us consider how variations in the importance of their investments affect the performance of different organizational forms.

One possibility is that P is a large firm that acts as its own general contractor. An example would be a university that has its own architects for small projects, and brings in tradespeople as subcontractors. In such a case the university is a general contractor with complete control over how the project is executed. We call this P-integration or PI.

---

[1] Even in physics it is well recognized that models are good, but imperfect representations of reality. Wolfgang Pauli once quipped regarding a colleague's work that "Not only is it not right, it's not even wrong!" (Peierls 1960).

A second case would be a market relationship where the principal and contractor negotiate on a project-by-project basis. This case is denoted by no-integration or NI. The third and final case is one where the firm is a developer that produces a standard building product for market, such as a tract home in a housing development. In this case, the final good (house) is produced with no contract with the final buyer, and hence there is no ex ante investment by the final owner of the house. This case is denoted as C-integration or CI for short.

2.1 A Formal Model

Formally, the incentive to integrate is modeled by letting $\lambda \in [0, 1]$ represent the relative importance of specific investments. For example, it might represent the ability to track a truck with goods in transit, as in Baker and Hubbard (2004). The payoffs in the GH model can be defined by:[2]

$$B_P \left(a_P, \phi_1 \left(q_P, q_C \right) | \lambda \right) = q_P q_C \left(\lambda a_P + \left(1 - \lambda \right) a_C \right) - \frac{a_P^\alpha}{\alpha}, \tag{1}$$

$$B_C \left(a_P, \phi_2 \left(q_P, q_C \right) | \lambda \right) = -c q_P q_C - \frac{a_C^\alpha}{\alpha}. \tag{2}$$

The sunk costs are given by $\frac{a_i^\alpha}{\alpha}$, where $\alpha > 1$ is a measure of how quickly those costs rise with investment. The ex post choice is whether to trade or not, given by $q_i \in \{0, 1\}$. The variable cost of production is given by c, and it is assumed to be sufficiently small that trade is always optimal.

If the principal owns the contractor's assets (case PI) then she can set both q_C and q_P. Similarly, if the contractor owns the principal's assets (case CI) then he can set both q_P and q_C. Under no integration, the principal is free to choose q_P and the contractor chooses q_C. Investments are assumed to be noncontractible.

Consider four allocations, denoted by $j \in \{E, NI, P, C\}$. When $j = E$ this is the efficient "Coasean" allocation. The no-integration allocation is $j = NI$. In this case each party gets 50% of the returns from renegotiation. Under $j = P$ the principal owns the assets, and hence the contractor earns only her outside option, assumed to be independent of her investment. Finally $j = C$ is the allocation when the contractor owns the assets, and we get the symmetric case to P ownership. Let $W_j (\lambda)$ be the total welfare for $j \in \{E, NI, P, C\}$. The optimal investment into asset P yields a net benefit of:

$$V (\lambda) = \left(\frac{\alpha - 1}{\alpha} \right) \lambda^{\frac{\alpha}{\alpha - 1}}.$$

Using this and the formula for value given by expressions (4) and (5) in GH, it is straightforward to show that total welfare as a function of organizational form is as shown in Table 11.1.

---

[2] Here the notation is taken from equation (1) in GH.

Table 11.1 **Effects of Integration**

Organizational Form	$W_j(\lambda)$
Coasean (E)	$V(\lambda) + V(1-\lambda) - c$
No integration (NI)	$\beta(\alpha)(V(\lambda) + V((1-\lambda))) - c$
P-integration (PI)	$V(\lambda) - c$
C-integration (CI)	$V(1-\lambda) - c$

Here the term $\beta(\alpha)$ has the features that $\lim_{\alpha \to 1^+} \beta(\alpha) = 0$ and $\lim_{\alpha \to \infty} \beta(\alpha) = 1/2$.[3] Under no integration both parties invest, but at a rate lower than under the first best. Under P-integration only the principal invests, while only the contractor invests under C-integration.

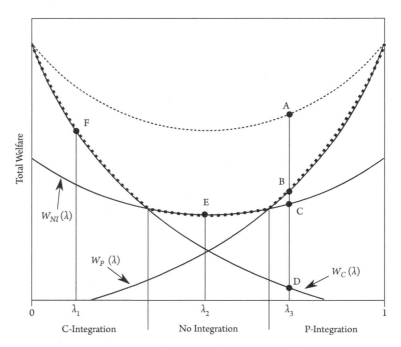

Importance of Asset 1 Relative to Asset 2 (λ)

Coase Theorm Prediction ($W_E(\lambda)$) ----------

GH Theory Prediction
$max\{W_{NI}(\lambda), W_P(\lambda), W_C(\lambda)\}$ ·······

Figure 11.1 Predictions of Grossman-Hart Model

[3] With no integration parties split the returns evenly, and the optimal investment by the principal is $a_P^{NI} = \left(\frac{\lambda}{2}\right)^{\frac{1}{\alpha-1}}$ (similarly for the agent). It follows that $\beta(\alpha) = \frac{2\alpha-1}{\alpha-1} 2^{\frac{\alpha}{1-\alpha}} \in (0,1)$.

The implications of the theory are illustrated in Figure 11.1. The x-axis has the relative importance of assets P and C, with λ going from 0 (only asset C is relationship specific) to 1 (only asset P is relationship specific). The y-axis is welfare in dollars. The top line corresponds to the payoff at the efficient, Coasean solution where property rights do not matter. In this example the payoff falls and then rises. This has no particular significance except to illustrate that even if we have data with a measure that can be interpreted as λ we cannot in general expect there to be any relationship between the measure of asset specificity and payoffs.

Next we have three curves that correspond to the payoffs in the GH model under the three asset allocations. The parameter α is set so that each of the three asset structures is optimal for some value of λ. Observe that for low values of λ the model predicts that it is second-best efficient for the contractor to own all this assets. For intermediate values no integration is second-best efficient, and then finally for high values having the principal own all the assets is second-best efficient.

3. Empirical Implications

Next, let us explore the GH model in the context of the Rubin/Holland causal model.[4] Though the Rubin/Holland model is deceptively simple, it is quite helpful in precisely highlighting the empirical content of a theory. It assumes that there is a unit to be treated U (e.g., person, firm, country), a potential treatments T (e.g., drug, law change, organizational change) and potential outcomes Y (e.g., health, profits, growth). Let $Y(U, T)$ be the outcome when treatment T is applied to unit U. The *causal effect* of treatment T_t^1 relative to treatment T_t^2 at date t is

$$CE(U, T_t^1, T_t^2) = Y(U, T_t^1) - Y(U, T_t^2).$$

This expression captures exactly the information one would like to have when making a decision between treatments T^1 and T^2. Notice that these are indexed by date t—the causal effect requires comparing outcomes from treatments administered at the same time! Without some sort of time machine, this is clearly impossible. Holland (1986) calls this the "fundamental problem of causal inference."[5] Much of modern empirical work can be viewed as proposing different solutions to this problem—with every solution requiring some theoretical

---

[4] See Holland (1986). Imbens and Rubin (2011) provide a book-length treatment.
[5] Holland (1986, 947).

assumption (namely, a plausible but unprovable hypothesis) that leads to the identification of a causal effect.[6]

In economic theory one typically supposes that preferences and payoff possibilities are exogenous, and then one works out the equilibrium allocation given this information. Given that neither preferences nor the technology are observable in practice, it is not generally obvious what are the empirical implications of such a theory. The Rubin/Holland model provides a solution.

In the context of the GH model, a natural unit of analysis is the pair of assets $\{A_1, A_2\}_\lambda$, indexed by $\lambda \in [0, 1]$. Notice that λ is a characteristic of the asset. The possible treatments are the three organizational forms $j \in \{NI, P, C\}$. Notice that the Coasean case is not a treatment, but the hypothesis that the treatment will have no effect. In this model the outcome variable is total welfare $W_j(\lambda)$. We now consider the possible testable implications of the theory.

Section 3 of Aghion et al. (2014) discusses various determinants of decentralization in the firm. For example, they observe that "trust can affect the internal structures of global firms." Trust as used here is a characteristic of the firm, and what is being asked is whether firms with different measures of trust have different levels of decentralization. Holland (1986, 946) points out that one need to distinguish between a treatment (the decentralization choice) and unit characteristic (trust in the firm). For example, he observes that gender cannot be a treatment, and hence not a cause of an effect.

To measure the causal effect of gender, one would first have an individual apply for a job, observe the outcome, and then change their gender and do the application again. In that case, the difference in employment outcomes would be "caused" by the change in gender. Such an experiment is in general not possible. Rather, the usual treatment is to change the information available to the employer and look at the causal effect of the information treatment on the employer (the "unit"). For example, Goldin and Rouse (2000) consider the treatment to have musicians play behind a screen or not, while Bertrand and Mullainathan (2004) manipulate the surnames of job applicants. In these examples gender or race is never a cause or treatment. Rather the cause is the change in information that the treatment unit/employer receives, and the outcome is the employment decision.

In the context of the GH model, the parameter λ corresponds to an observable characteristic like trust or degree of complementarity discussed in section 3 of Aghion et al. (2014). Figure 11.1 illustrates that the theory predicts that if the

---

[6] Holland discusses a number of these. They include assumptions such as the effect does not change over time or that one can identify characteristics of the units that allow one to suppose that the effects are the same for units with the same characteristics. This is essentially what one does when running a regression with a large number of control variables.

characteristics of the assets vary from λ_1 to λ_2 and then to λ_3, then the outcome moves from F to E and then to B. This results in a move from C-integration (CI) to no-integration (NI) and finally P-integration (PI). Notice that this prediction consists of a joint hypothesis: first, that payoffs vary with the level of integration, and second, that the agents choose the most efficient arrangement.

However, observing variation in organization form as a function of λ does not prove or disprove the GH model. It could be the case that the Coasean hypothesis is correct, in which case the observed variation in organizational form may be due to factors completely unrelated to the hold-up problem. What we can see from figure 11.1 is that the strong implication of the GH model does not come from the variation in λ, but from the variation in profits conditional on organizational form. That is, the causal effect of P-integration (PI) relative to no integration (NI) is defined by:

$$CE\left(\{A_1, A_2\}_\lambda, PI, NI\right) = W_P(\lambda) - W_{NI}(\lambda).$$

To *measure* the causal effect we would have to find some way to carry out an experiment that *constrains* the choice made by parties. Assuming this experiment can be carried out, it provides a rather strong and clean test of the GH model. Comparing points B and C in Figure 11.1, we see that the GH model predicts $CE\left(\{A_1, A_2\}_{\lambda_3}, PI, NI\right) > 0$. In contrast if the Coasean hypothesis were correct then $CE\left(\{A_1, A_2\}_{\lambda_3}, PI, NI\right) = 0$.

In practice it may not be possible to measure λ with any precision, in which case we may not know where we are in Figure 11.1. What we do know is that if we were able to carry out this experiment, then the Coasean model would be rejected in favor of the GH model (assuming these are the only two alternatives) if we find that $CE \neq 0$ for some λ.

It is certainly useful to measure how organizational form varies with some characteristic, as is done in section 3 of Aghion et al. (2014), but one has to be very cautious when interpreting such observations as having a causal interpretation. They provide in section 4 a more direct test of decentralization theory because they ask if there is any evidence of changes in management practices affecting firm productivity. A nice example of a good research design is the important work of Bloom et al. (2012). They report the result of an experiment where firms are treated with free consulting services, and find strong evidence that these services provide a positive causal effect on firm performance. It would be be useful to know why since we are still faced with the dual hypothesis issue discussed above. If indeed firms are profit maximizing, then why are they not already choosing the most efficient management practices?

In the labor literature these issues have long been studied in the context of the Roy model. We now know that in general one cannot identify a causal effect from observed data without some rather stringent conditions (see for example Heckman and Honore 1990).[7] Appendix C of Aghion et al. (2014) discusses the general point that the organizational literature has not yet made identification a central issue, an observation that extends to the literature on hold-up.

An example of a nonexperimental paper that makes some progress is Card et al. (2014). They measure the extent to which workers and firms share rents in the Veneto region of Italy. In this paper the unit is the union-firm pair, and the outcome is the rent share for each group. The treatments are shocks to firm productivity. To provide a causal estimate of the rent-sharing rule, Card et al. (2014) argue that variations in sales by industry outside of the Veneto region are exogenous and hence can be used as an instrument for rents in bargaining pair.[8]

Grout (1984) shows that if there are no binding commitments between parties, then we can expect trade unions to capture some of the rents from firm investment in physical capital, leading to underinvestment by the firm. At the time he wrote his paper, trade unions in the United Kingdom did not use long-term contracts—contracts were of fixed durations, and then renegotiated from scratch when a new contract was needed. The goal of the paper was to illustrate the implications of this rule for investment. In contrast, Card et al. (2014) find no evidence of this form of hold-up in Italy. Rather union-firm pairs share the rents from the relationship after subtracting the cost of investments made by the firm.

This does not necessarily imply that the GH insight on the importance of ownerships is incorrect. A key assumption in GH is that parties in a long-term relationships efficiently renegotiate contract terms and conditions. Crawford (1988) has shown that if parties can enter into binding short run commitments, then it is possible to have an efficient long term contract. This suggests that what may be driving the Card et al. (2014) result is the ability of parties to make short-term commitments, and not hold-up per se (Card et al. (2014) provides a nice model to illustrate how this would work). This leads to a clear, open, empirical question—what is the causal impact of a change in the contracting possibilities set on organizational form and performance?

The studies discussed in Aghion et al. (2014) show that we are beginning to have a large portfolio of data sets with information on organizational form. From the Rubin/Holland model we learn that for each data set both the GH model and the theory reviewed in Aghion et al. (2014) can be used to explore

---

[7] See also MacLeod (2013) for a discussion of the Roy model in the context of measuring the performance of economic systems.

[8] Angrist et al. (1996) show how to view instrumental variables estimates through the lens of the Rubin/Holland model.

an almost unlimited set of questions, the answers to which may help us better understand the causal impact of integration/centralization upon performance.

References

Aghion, P., N. Bloom, and J. Van Reenen. 2014. "Incomplete Contracts and the Internal Organisation of Firms." *Journal of Law, Economics, and Organization*, 30(suppl. 1):. Reprinted in this volume as chapter 9.

Aghion, P., and J. Tirole. 1997. "Formal and Real Authority in Organizations." *Journal of Political Economy* 105(1): 1–29.

Angrist, J. D., G. W. Imbens, and D. B. Rubin. 1996. "Identification of Causal Effects Using Instrumental Variables." *Journal of the American Statistical Association* 91(434): 444–55.

Baker, G. P., and T. N. Hubbard. 2004. "Contractibility and Asset Ownership: On-Board Computers and Governance in U. S. Trucking." *Quarterly Journal of Economics* 119(4): 1443–79.

Bertrand, M., and S. Mullainathan. 2004. "Are Emily and Greg More Employable than Lakisha and Jamal? A Field Experiment on Labor Market Discrimination." *American Economic Review* 94(4): 991–1013.

Bloom, N., B. Eifert, A. Mahajan, D. McKenzie, and J. Roberts. 2012. "Does Management Matter? Evidence from India." *Quarterly Journal of Economics* 128(1): 1–51.

Card, D., F. Devicienti, and A. Maida. 2014. "Rent-Sharing, Holdup, and Wages: Evidence from Matched Panel Data." *Review of Economic Studies* 81: 84–111.

Coase, R. A. 1960. "The Problem of Social Cost." *Journal of Law and Economics* 3: 1–44.

Crawford, V. P. 1988. "Long-Term Relationships Governed by Short-Term Contracts." *American Economic Review* 78(3): 485–99.

Dessein, W. 2002. "Authority and Communication in Organizations." *Review of Economic Studies* 69(4): 811–38.

Goldin, C., and C. Rouse. 2000. "Orchestrating Impartiality: The Impact of 'Blind' Auditions on Female Musicians." *American Economic Review* 90(4): 715–41.

Grossman, S. J., and O. D. Hart. 1986. "The Costs and Benefits of Ownership: A Theory of Vertical and Lateral Integration." *Journal of Political Economy* 94(4): 691–719.

Grout, P. 1984. "Investment and Wages in the Absence of Binding Contracts: A Nash Bargaining Approach." *Econometrica* 52(2): 449–60.

Hart, O. D., and J. H. Moore. 1988. "Incomplete Contracts and Renegotiation." *Econometrica* 56(4): 755–85.

Hart, O. D., and J. H. Moore. 1990. "Property Rights and the Nature of the Firm." *Journal of Political Economy* 98: 1119–58.

Heckman, J. J., and B. E. Honore. 1990. "The Empirical Content of the Roy Model." *Econometrica* 58(5): 1121–49.

Holland, P. W. 1986. "Statistics and Causal Inference." *Journal of the American Statistical Association* 81(396): 945–60.

Imbens, G. W., and D. B. Rubin. 2011. *Causal Inference in Statistics and Social Sciences.* Oxford: Oxford University Press.

MacLeod, W. B. 2002. "Complexity and Contract." In E. Brousseau and J.-M. Glachant (eds.) *Economics of Contract in Prospect and Retrospect*, 213–40. Cambridge: Cambridge University Press.

MacLeod, W. B. 2013. "On Economics: A Review of *Why Nations Fail* by D. Acemoglu and J. Robinson and *Pillars of Prosperity* by T. Besley and T. Persson." *Journal of Economic Literature* 51(1): 116–43.

Peierls, R. E. 1960. "Wolfgang Ernst Pauli. 1900–1958." *Biographical Memoirs of Fellows of the Royal Society* 5: 175–92.

Simon, H. A. 1951. "A Formal Theory of the Employment Relationship." *Econometrica* 19: 293–305.

PART 4

INCOMPLETE CONTRACTS AND CORPORATE FINANCE

12

Corporate Finance, Incomplete Contracts, and Corporate Control

PATRICK BOLTON

It is a great pleasure to write this essay in celebration of Sandy Grossman's and Oliver Hart's classic 1986 article "The Costs and Benefits of Ownership: A Theory of Vertical and Lateral Integration." To appreciate the importance and novelty of their contribution, it is helpful to put it into context of their earlier research and the state of economic theory at the time. Among the hottest research topics in economic theory in the early 1980s were general equilibrium (GE) theory, rational expectations, and information economics (mechanism design). Both Grossman and Hart had made several important contributions in these general areas. Hart's thesis was in the area of GE theory with incomplete markets, and in the early 1980s he was working on GE with imperfect competition. One central conceptual issue arising in GE with incomplete markets or imperfect competition is what the objective function of the firm is and to what extent there can be shareholder unanimity. Grossman and Hart had written several major articles on this topic. They had also made important contributions on implicit labor contracts and involuntary unemployment, and on a general characterization of the Principal-Agent problem with moral hazard.

Much of this work appeared in the most prestigious journal at the time (*Econometrica*) and achieved the highest standards of mathematical rigor and generality. Indeed, both Grossman and Hart were seen as belonging to an elite group of young theorists taking over the field of economic theory from the founding giants of mathematical economics: Kenneth Arrow, Frank Hahn, Gerard Debreu, and Robert Aumann. It is important to emphasize that there is virtually no hint in this earlier work of the ideas Grossman and Hart were about

I am grateful to two anonymous referees and the editor (Al Klevorick) for very helpful comments.

to develop in their 1986 article, which by all appearances is a complete break from their earlier research both methodologically and conceptually.

What explains this sharp break? What prompted Grossman and Hart to embark on this path-breaking endeavor? There are mainly two motivations. First, although Oliver Hart has long had a deep interest in Coase's (1937) theory of the firm and the early managerial theories of the firm of Penrose (1958), Baumol (1959), Cyert and March (1963), and Williamson (1964), he was not persuaded by these managerial perspectives of the firm. He thought that as theories they failed because they were too detailed, descriptive, with too many different variables, to lend themselves as useful analytical tools. He was thinking of how to formulate an analytically simple theory of the firm.

Second, the ultimately unsatisfactory outcome of Grossman and Hart's work on the principal agent problem (Grossman and Hart, 1983) must have played an important role in prompting them to change direction. Why did this theory lead to an unsatisfactory outcome? After all, as a piece of mathematical analysis, this is a brilliant achievement solving in one swoop both a fundamental nonexistence problem in principal agent problems, and a methodological flaw with the first-order approach pointed out by James Mirrlees (1974, 1999). The unsatisfactory outcome is that the theory in full generality yields no robust predictions on the shape of optimal incentive contracts, and it produces no robust comparative statics results.

In other words, the theory says that the shape of the optimal incentive contract a principal offers an agent write is highly sensitive to the specific environment the parties find themselves in and is likely to be incredibly complex. Far more complex than anything one can see in reality, and far less robust than the fairly standard incentive contracts one typically observes. This concern is clearly voiced in the survey of contract theory by Oliver Hart and Bengt Holmström (1987) delivered at the World Congress of the Econometric Society of 1985:

> Indeed, the economic credibility of the contractual approach may be called into question when, as often happens, optimal contracts become monstrous state-contingent prescriptions. How are such contracts written and enforced?
>
> (Hart and Holmström 1987, 74)

and

> The main [concern] is its sensitivity to distributional assumptions. It manifests itself in an optimal sharing rule that is complex, responding to the slightest changes in the information content of the outcome x.

Such "fine-tuning" appears unrealistic. In the real world incentive schemes do show variety, but not to the degree predicted by the basic theory.

(Hart and Holmstrom 1987, 90)

Interestingly, in response to this critique the contract theory literature has taken two separate directions, which even today remain in competition, and confusingly, sometimes overlap. The first direction taken by Grossman and Hart (1986) is pragmatic and simply limits contractual complexity by imposing plausible exogenous contract enforcement constraints. This is the *incomplete contracts* approach they pioneered. The second direction is fundamentalist and seeks to endogenously derive simple and realistic optimal contracts—such as linear incentive contracts—from a complex dynamic programming problem in which the agent has a rich action set. This is the approach pioneered by the optimal security design literature following Townsend (1979) and by Holmström and Milgrom (1987) in the context of dynamic principal agent problems.

Both approaches have been important in shaping corporate finance theory post Grossman and Hart (1986). The incomplete contracts approach, which Philippe Aghion and I embraced, has allowed us to address issues of (contingent) control allocation and renegotiation which had been absent from previous discussions of corporate finance and financial contracting. My other work with David Scharfstein turns out to have contained both elements of the incomplete contracts approach and elements of the limited commitment approach, as subsequent work by DeMarzo and Fishman (2007) and DeMarzo and Sannikov (2006) has highlighted.

Before discussing the incomplete contracts literature in corporate finance, I begin with a brief summary of the state of corporate finance theory before GH (1986). I then turn to a discussion of some of the main themes of the corporate finance theory literature post GH and evaluate the relative merits of the incomplete contracts and dynamic programming approaches. I shall argue that while both approaches have considerably improved our understanding of the dynamics of corporate finance, they still lack operational and practical relevance. Unlike the trade-off theory inherited from Modigliani and Miller—which has huge practical relevance, despite the fact that tax considerations may, paradoxically, not be first-order in determining firms' financing choices—the more modern incentive and incomplete contracting approaches—which arguably focus on more first-order issues—have so far had a limited operational impact. That is, while incomplete contracting approaches capture important dimensions of corporate financial decisions (as recent empirical research has revealed), they do not offer an operational methodology that can be used by practitioners. I will conclude by suggesting a way forward in closing this important gap, based on recent work of mine with Hui Chen and Neng Wang.

1. Modigliani and Miller and the Foundations of Corporate Finance

Modern corporate finance practice is founded on Modigliani and Miller's (1958) classic article on the cost of capital. In this article they lay out a methodology for valuing investments and argue that the value of a firm is independent of how the firm is financed. Economists have mostly focused on the famous Modigliani and Miller (MM) irrelevance theorem, stating that when capital markets are competitive and efficient, and when there are no taxes and bankruptcy costs, then the way a firm is financed is irrelevant. That is to say, under these conditions the value of a firm is independent of its liability structure, and depends only on the value of its assets. The MM irrelevance theorem, already implicit in Arrow and Debreu's (1954) proof of existence of a general competitive equilibrium, is a central proposition in general equilibrium theory, which pins down the objective function of a firm (and ensures shareholder unanimity).

In the real world, of course, some key conditions of the theorem are not met, in particular the presence of taxes and bankruptcy costs. Therefore, the way firms are financed in practice is not irrelevant to their value. Nevertheless, the Modigliani and Miller logic and their approach to determining a firm's cost of capital has still proved to be of enormous practical value. I am referring here to their famous *weighted average cost of capital* (*WACC*), and their approach to valuation based on discounting a firm's *free cash-flow* using WACC. Combined with a suitable asset pricing model (most often in practice the capital asset pricing model, CAPM), and correcting for taxes, the discounted cash flow approach using WACC is today the most widely used approach to valuation and corporate investments (see Graham and Harvey 2001).

This approach to valuation is closely linked with a simple theory of the optimal capital structure of the firm: the *trade-off* theory (see Miller 1977; Brennan and Schwartz 1978; DeAngelo and Masulis 1980; a Leland 1994), which is still widely accepted. According to this theory, debt is a cheaper source of capital for the firm after tax if one ignores bankruptcy costs. If it were not for deadweight bankruptcy costs, it would be efficient for the firm to finance itself only with debt. In the presence of bankruptcy costs, the optimum debt-equity ratio is determined by equating the marginal tax shield benefit of debt with the expected marginal bankruptcy cost.

The trade-off theory assumes that the firm's cash flow is observable and verifiable, and that any promised debt repayment satisfying the firm's limited liability constraint is enforceable. Models of the trade-off theory typically assume that debt is a fixed claim (fixed coupon payments plus principal), which is independent of the firm's realized earnings, and equity is a claim entitling the owners to the firm's free cash flow net of debt obligations. These models also typically assume that the (stochastic) evolution of the firm's cash flow is predetermined and reduce the firm's financing problem to an optimal allocation problem of the firm's cash flow to the holders of debt and equity, the tax authorities and nature (in the form of deadweight costs of bankruptcy).

This is a highly reductive theory of corporate finance, which misses many key determinants of leverage. For example, U.S. corporations extensively relied on debt financing in the nineteenth century, even though bankruptcy could be extremely costly and there were no tax shield benefits to offset expected bankruptcy costs. By the trade-off theory they should have stayed away from debt financing altogether. More generally, just as the CAPM, the trade-off theory has found limited empirical support (see, e.g., MacKie-Mason 1990; Rajan and Zingales 1995). Yet the trade-off theory, especially in its dynamic version following Leland (1994), retains a central place in corporate finance, mainly because it offers the most operational approach available to the determination of the firm's optimal capital structure and to the valuation of risky debt. True, the Leland (1994) model predicts excessively high leverage ratios, but the more dynamic formulation in Goldstein, Ju, and Leland (2001) is able to predict reasonably accurate debt levels and credit spreads.

2. Grossman and Hart: Incomplete Contracts and Corporate Control

How is the corporate finance theory landscape changed after Grossman and Hart (1986)? One central dimension missing from the MM approach to corporate finance discussed above is ownership and control. The MM approach remains silent on how a firm's cash flow is determined. It takes the cash flow as given and asks only how it should be allocated among different claimants and how it should be valued. In contrast, the incomplete contracts approach to corporate finance seeks to understand corporate control and how the exercise of control is affected by the firm's choice of financing.

This is a richer and significantly more complex theory than the trade-off theory. I argue that it has yielded important new conceptual insights, but that it has so far had only a marginal operational impact. As much as chief financial officers (CFOs) feel that they need to understand the MM approach to corporate finance, they have so far not shown much interest in the more modern theories of corporate finance that emphasize adverse selection, moral hazard, incomplete contracts, and control. It is not that they are unaware of the importance of these issues, but that the theory so far has offered little operational guidance. There is little doubt that corporate decision makers understand the importance of incentives and control, but it is fair to say that for the most part they have not relied on the finance theory literature on these issues to inform their decisions. Before dealing with corporate finance following Grossman and Hart (1986) I must briefly discuss the agency theories of corporate finance, which provide a first analysis of the endogenous determination of a firm's cash flow.

2.1 Adverse Selection and Moral Hazard

Jensen and Meckling (1976) provide the first formal analysis of the incentive implications of a firm's choice of capital structure. They start from Berle and Means's (1932) observation that if the managers in control of a firm's operations own only a small fraction of the company's stock, they are likely to run the firm inefficiently, or at least not in shareholders' best interests. They then suggest an argument in favor of debt financing, which has later become the main justification for leveraged buyouts (LBOs): by financing a firm with debt, managers are able to retain concentrated equity ownership in the firm, and thus are incentivized to invest in future cash flows that enhance shareholder value. However—they continue—too much debt financing creates its own incentive problems, excess risk-taking, so that the optimal leverage ratio for the firm trades off the moral hazard benefits in terms of better investment incentives for managers against the excess risk-taking incentives for shareholders of highly levered firms. Excess risk-taking by highly levered firms has, alas, become an all too familiar notion after the financial crisis of 2008.

Another familiar cost faced by highly indebted borrowers is *debt overhang*, a concept first formally analyzed by Myers (1977). Highly indebted borrowers facing the risk of financial distress will pass up valuable investment opportunities or even sell assets at fire sale prices. To reduce the risk of debt overhang, it may thus be desirable for firms not to borrow too much. Also, should a firm end up with too much debt on its books it may be desirable for borrower and lender to renegotiate or restructure some of this debt. This latter observation provides the main economic justification for the existence of bankruptcy reorganization and debt resolution procedures.

Next to these theories of capital structure based on moral hazard problems, Myers and Majluf (1984) have proposed a powerful theory based on asymmetric information or adverse selection. They argue that the firm as an issuer of claims on the firm's cash flow has to overcome investors' suspicion that the firm may be trying to sell overpriced claims. This is easiest to do if the firm is able to issue safe debt (say, senior, short-term, collateralized, debt-like repos), for issuer and investors alike ought to be able to easily value such a safe fixed-income instrument. If safe debt is unavailable the next easiest claim to value is risky debt, or possibly convertible debt, and the hardest claim to value may be equity. That is, equity may be the hardest claim to value as it may be the most information-sensitive claim. Which is why Myers and Majuf—under their pecking order theory—propose that equity claims should only be issued as a last resort and that firms should first use internally generated funds, then safe debt, and then if needed risky debt.

These theories are an important advance over the simple trade-off theory and considerably improve our understanding of corporate finance. However, it should come as no surprise that the pure agency theories of corporate finance encounter similar conceptual difficulties as the principal agent theory à la Grossman-Hart (1983). Indeed, a central problem with agency theories of corporate finance, as Dybvig and Zender (1991) have emphasized, is that it is perfectly possible to separate the choice of capital structure of the firm from the problem of optimally incentivizing a firm's manager by directly designing an optimal compensation contract for the CEO. Under an optimal incentive contract, which admittedly may be very complex and sensitive to the special circumstances a firm finds itself in, it is possible to address directly all relevant moral hazard and adverse selection issues, so that capital structure choice again becomes irrelevant, or is determined by the trade-off theory. In sum, the firm's capital structure is relevant for managerial incentives, and therefore also for corporate control, only if incentive and financial contracting is limited by enforcement constraints; that is, only if contracts are incomplete.

2.2 Incomplete Contracts and Corporate Control

2.2.1 *Contingent Control Allocation*

This last observation is the starting point of the analysis in Aghion and Bolton (1992), which develops a theory of capital structure choice based on the problem of optimal allocation of corporate control. The analysis starts by assuming that not all actions available to a manager and not all states of the world are describable (ex ante) in a contract or verifiable. If some future action choices cannot be specified in a contract, this creates a problem of control, as some actions (and states of the world) left out of the initial contract will have to be determined ex post. This further raises the question: who is charged with taking these actions? In other words, who is in control? But this is only the starting point, as the next question is why it is relevant at all who is in control? In our bilateral contracting problem with an entrepreneur and a financier, allocations of control to one or the other party would have to lead to different outcomes for control to matter at all. Different outcomes presuppose different objectives, which could be fully aligned neither through ex ante contracting nor through ex post renegotiation.

Our first approach to this second question was to assume that the entrepreneur and financier had different beliefs about which investments were preferable. Based on casual observation, we assumed that the entrepreneur was generally more optimistic about the success of risky investments than was the financier. This difference of opinions combined with the assumption of limited liability (and limited wealth of the entrepreneur) naturally gives rise to conflicting objectives, which cannot be fully aligned through contracting. It also gives rise to a plausible contingent control allocation.

The entrepreneur seeks to keep control in the states of the world where the difference of opinions is largest; that is, where she is likely to be much more optimistic about success than the financier. She is willing to give up control in states of the world where differences of opinion are smaller. To the extent that differences of beliefs are likely to increase as the venture's prospects improve, this contingent control allocation could be implemented through debt financing, whereby the financier gains control in the event of default and otherwise the entrepreneur retains control. It could also be implemented through staged transfers of control under a venture capital (VC) contract.

As simple and plausible as this solution seemed to us, the contract theory community at the time was not ready to accept two departures from orthodoxy in the same paper: incomplete contracts and differences of opinion. We received almost unanimous advice to change the model and do away with differences of opinion. So instead of modeling differences in objectives arising from different beliefs, we modeled them as arising from the presence of *private benefits*: we assumed that the entrepreneur derives both financial returns and private benefits from the venture, while the investor derives only financial returns. In a way, this new model is more general, as differences of opinion can be mapped into financial returns and a particular form of private benefits, but vice versa, it is not always possible to transform an objective function combining financial rewards plus private benefits into an objective function with no private benefits but differences of beliefs.

Our model delivers predictions on the separation of cash flow and control rights that are consistent with common contractual clauses in VC contracts, as Kaplan and Stromberg's (2003) study of VC contracts revealed. It also delivers predictions on cash inventory management under investor control, showing that it may be optimal for the entrepreneur to accumulate cash reserves that may be used to induce the investor to choose an investment with high private benefits for the entrepreneur. While these are valuable qualitative insights, the model remains in many ways too abstract and general to be an operationally useful analytical tool. Part of the difficulty lies in the somewhat vague notion of private benefits. The other difficulty is that the enforcement limits on financial contracts are exogenously imposed in a somewhat arbitrary fashion. There is also the conceptual difficulty revealed by Maskin and Tirole (1999) that when an action or state of the world is observable to the contracting parties but not to a court (or judge) it can still be made verifiable through a suitable revelation mechanism.

2.2.2 Limited Commitment

For all these reasons it is not completely surprising that most of the subsequent literature on incomplete contracts in corporate finance has focused on narrower models in which private benefits are associated with some form of stealing or cash flow diversion. The pertinent image here is that of the cashier who is able to discreetly lift a few bills from the cash till. This literature also downplays the observable but not verifiable distinction and focuses on what is now generally referred to as a limited commitment problem that the borrower faces due to her limited ability to commit to repay a loan.[1]

In Bolton and Scharfstein (1990) we explore such a model of limited commitment, where the firm's realized earnings are private information. To elicit truthful reporting of high realized earnings the financier must then offer a carrot to the firm. In our model this carrot takes the form of allowing the firm access to new loans that are necessary to continue operating the business when the firm repays its old loans. Hart and Moore (1994, 1998) also explore a model of limited commitment, in which, however, repayment of old loans is elicited with a stick: the threat of liquidating the firm if it does not repay its loan quickly enough.

Perhaps the main conceptual innovation of limited commitment models is a better understanding of the mechanics of debt default. Under the MM approach, default is assumed to occur when the firm is insolvent; that is, when debt liabilities exceed the value of the firm's assets (see, e.g., Merton 1974). This is a natural assumption if financial contracts are perfectly enforceable, for if the firm were to default when it is still solvent then debtholders could simply enforce payment by seizing the firm's assets. In contrast, under limited commitment it is possible to separate default from insolvency and distinguish between liquidity and strategic defaults.

The former is a situation where the firm is forced to default due to a cash shortage and the latter one where the firm chooses to default and force a debt

---

[1] Another related approach to private benefits proposed by Holmström and Tirole (1997, 1998) is not directly related to stealing, but indirectly through *shirking*. By shirking the manager obtains private benefits in the form of reduced effort costs and *'diverts'* (i.e. does not produce) the financial returns promised to investors.

restructuring because it is in its interest even though it is able to service the existing debt. Allowing for strategic default is a major conceptual breakthrough because it draws attention to an important practical aspect of debt design that is completely absent from the MM approach, namely, the protections that creditors require in the form of seniority, collateral, security interests, and covenants. These are all protections that increase the likelihood that creditors will be repaid by reducing the probability of a strategic default and by increasing the creditors' bargaining position in a future debt renegotiation. While the importance of debt covenants and subordination priorities has long been recognized by legal scholars (see, e.g., Schwartz 1998) economists have only started incorporating these protections in limited commitment models of debt. Under the MM approach and the trade-off theory all the firm's debts should be junior, unsecured debt. Indeed, these debts would give the firm all the tax shields it wants and would minimize bankruptcy costs, as these debts are relatively easy to restructure or dilute with new debt issues.

2.2.3 Debt Structure

In Bolton and Scharfstein (1996) we show how the threat of strategic default can be mitigated by having a well-protected, dispersed debt structure, which is difficult to renegotiate simply because it is more difficult to bring many people around a bargaining table. We also show that depending on the risk of a liquidity default, the firm may or may not want to structure its debt to make it difficult to restructure: if the risk of a liquidity default is high the firm may be better off with a debt structure that is easy to restructure, while if the risk of a liquidity default is low the firm may prefer to have debt that is hard to renegotiate.

In Bolton and Freixas (2000, 2006) we apply these ideas further and distinguish between expensive (due to intermediation costs) bank relationship-lending, which is flexible and easy to restructure, and cheaper bond issues, which are, however, more difficult to restructure. We then derive a partial equilibrium of the financial system with coexistence of a banking sector and securities markets. In this equilibrium riskier firms rely on bank lending as an important source of funding, because they value the flexibility it offers, while safer firms rely more on bond financing. This model lends itself, in particular, to an analysis of monetary policy through the lending channel.

In a series of related articles, Diamond and Rajan (2000, 2001, 2005) also build on the idea of debt dispersion to counteract a threat of strategic default, to develop a limited commitment theory of banking, bank fragility, and monetary policy. In the process they substantially upgrade the classic theory of banking as liquidity transformation of Diamond and Dybvig (1983): while in Diamond and

Dybvig banks offer demand deposits to savers as a liquidity service, in Diamond and Rajan banks offer demand deposits as a disciplining device, to facilitate exit by disgruntled investors should the bank make bad loan decisions or be a weak debt collector. In their theory, bank fragility becomes a commitment device in a world of limited commitment, helping banks make more efficient loans than nonintermediated lenders who are vulnerable to ex post strategic default and debt renegotiation.

Limited commitment models of debt point to the importance of debt renegotiation, a topic that has mostly been ignored by the MM approach. One could argue, of course, that as a first approximation this is a valid omission. However, recent empirical studies suggest that debt renegotiation is an important issue in practice. For example, Roberts and Sufi (2009) find that the vast majority of corporate long-term debt (over 90%) is renegotiated before maturity in response to changes in the firm's environment. They also find that debt design reflects the parties' anticipation of future renegotiation, and attempts to allocate bargaining power on a state-contingent basis. Similarly, Rauh and Sufi (2010) highlights that firms' debt structures vary systematically with underlying firm risk and that riskier firms have more complex and more collateralized debt structures.

Interestingly, a more recent MM-based literature has incorporated elements of strategic default into their models. Thus, Anderson and Sundaresan (1996) consider a problem of debt valuation in a dynamic setting in which the borrower can strategically default. Not surprisingly, they find that both the default frontier and debt design are modified relative to the Merton (1974) model. Similarly, Mella-Barral and Perraudin (1997) analyze a continuous-time model of debt à la Leland (1994) with strategic default and find that the pricing of debt is significantly affected by the possibility of strategic debt renegotiation. Their model, in particular, provides more accurate estimates of credit spreads than other structural models without strategic default.

2.2.4 *Nonexclusivity*

This first generation of debt structure models takes a comprehensive contracting approach to the design of debt structure: the number of creditors and the seniority structure are optimally determined ex ante in a multilateral (incomplete) contract with the borrower. The implicit premise in this literature is that the debt structures we observe are efficient from an ex ante perspective. A more recent, second generation of debt structure models relaxes the assumption of ex ante comprehensive contracting and adds another dimension of contractual incompleteness, namely, that debt structure is the equilibrium outcome of a debt contracting game with nonexclusivity.

The notion of nonexclusivity refers to the fact that a borrower may be able to borrow from a second set of creditors without the agreement from the first set of lenders. The analysis of equilibrium debt structures under nonexclusivity can be formulated as a common agency game with externalities (see Bernheim and Whinston 1985, 1986a, 1986b; Segal 1999). Not surprisingly, in the presence of externalities the equilibrium outcome of the contracting game will generally be inefficient. In the context of a corporate debt structure problem, when new debts are piled onto old debts, the expected payoff of old creditors is affected, as the new debts may increase the probability of default and reduce the recovery value of old debts in default. Since new creditors do not take account of this externality on old creditors, there tends to be too much debt in an equilibrium with nonexclusivity (see, e.g., Bizer and DeMarzo 1992, for an early analysis of borrowing with nonexclusivity from multiple lenders). This is why nonexclusivity is a major concern for creditors, and to the extent possible creditors will attempt to protect themselves against future lending by the firm through various forms of debt covenants in the debt contract.

The efficiency of corporate debt structures and corporate borrowing thus depends to a large extent on the protection offered by debt covenants. The effectiveness of debt covenants, in turn, depends on how easy they are to enforce and how comprehensive an exclusion they provide. In short, the area where the issue of (endogenous) contractual incompleteness perhaps matters most, when it comes to debt contracts, is the design and enforcement of debt covenants.

As we argue in Ayotte and Bolton (2011), a critical distinction between property rights and contractual rights lies at the heart of the nonexclusivity problem. Following legal scholarship we define a property right as a right in rem, that is, a right enforceable against third parties (future potential lenders), while a contractual right is a right in personam, that is, a right enforceable only against the parties to the contract. Property law limits which rights can be enforced against third parties. The property rights of creditors come mainly in the form of security rights on collateral that has been perfected (i.e., liens on assets that have been registered, and for which, therefore, third parties have been notified). All other debt covenants, whether they are negative pledge clauses, limitations on new investments, or acceleration clauses are contractual rights only against the borrower. In other words, they can be enforced only through legal actions against the borrower (e.g., through injunctions) and they have no force in bankruptcy against new lenders.

Debt covenants are costly to enforce because they require continuous monitoring of the borrower by the lender. As we argue, the reason property rights law is structured in this way is to provide basic protections to new lenders against expropriation by old lenders. Indeed, debt covenants can be hard to find in a lengthy debt contract, and if all covenants were enforceable against new lenders, these lenders would face potentially huge expropriation risk, which could lead to severe credit rationing in equilibrium.

Given that most covenants are costly to enforce, lenders concerned about non-exclusivity prefer to rely on the property rights offered by liens (collateral and security interests). For many borrowers, however, such as financial firms, there are too few tangible assets that can be used as collateral. For these borrowers, covenants may also be too costly to enforce. As a result, these borrowers may be forced to maintain highly inefficient debt structures. These can take the form of excessively short-term debt, as Brunnermeier and Oehmke (2010) have argued in the context of corporate borrowing (and Bolton and Jeanne 2009 in the context of sovereign borrowing), or debt that is excessively difficult to restructure (Bolton and Jeanne 2007). Note that according to this theory of debt structure, bank fragility arising from short-term liabilities may be an inefficient equilibrium outcome caused by nonexclusivity and not necessarily an optimal outcome to discipline bank lending, as in Diamond and Rajan (2000).

2.2.5 Equity Structure

Just as they open the way to a theory of debt structure, incomplete contracting and limited commitment models of corporate finance also provide a foundation for a theory of equity ownership structure. Thus, Fluck (1998) shows how equity can emerge as an open-ended claim receiving a regular dividend payment in a self-enforcing equilibrium in a limited commitment environment in which firm managers can divert cash. Similarly, Myers (2000), and more recently Lambrecht and Myers (2010), develop a theory of dividend payments as a way of preempting a hostile takeover. Incomplete contracting theories of equity structure can also be divided into efficient equity structure design theories and inefficient equilibrium equity structure theories.

Among the former theories, Admati, Pfleiderer, and Zechner (1994) and Bolton and von Thadden (1998) argue that concentrated ownership in the hands of a large block-holder may be an optimal ownership structure when monitoring of management is important. An alternative theory of limited controlling-block size and optimal managerial entrenchment (implemented, e.g., through poison-pills) by Burkart, Gromb, and Panunzi (1997) and Pagano and Roell (1998) is that managers' discretion needs to be protected to some extent to give them optimal incentives to originate new investment opportunities.

Among the latter theories, Bebchuk (1999) and Shleifer and Wolfenzon (2002) argue that ownership concentration arises as an inefficient equilibrium outcome driven by the block-holder's inability to commit not to divert cash from the firm and desire to protect valuable private benefits of control.

3. An Assessment

As the foregoing brief discussion of the corporate finance theory literature after Grossman and Hart (1986) suggests, the introduction of limited commitment into the MM framework has substantially enriched our understanding of corporate control, corporate debt structure, leverage, and equity structure. As a positive theory of corporate finance, the limited commitment theory offers new predictions, many of which have been borne out in empirical studies. In particular, the studies on debt covenants by Roberts and Sufi (2009), Chava and Roberts (2008), Nini, Smith, and Sufi (2009), and Bienz, Faure-Grimaud, and Fluck (2012) show that the contingent allocation of control rights through debt covenants is a common practice that has significant effects on corporate investment and financing decisions.

As a normative theory, the limited commitment approach also offers a useful framework to assess legal interventions shaping equity and debt structures. However, normative analyses based on limited commitment models are often constrained by the lack of realism of these models with respect to the core assumption of nonverifiability of cash flows, investments, and states of nature. In reality, both investments and earnings are partially verifiable. Moreover, the contracting parties can spend resources to make them more verifiable. Also, the contractual incompleteness of debt contracts in practice is endogenous and is not simply the outcome of a technological or institutional constraint.

As a result, the contracts, financial structures, and legal rules observed in reality sometimes bear only a distant resemblance with the contracts derived in the theory. While a good theory inevitably leads to such simplifications and abstractions, these, of course, also make a normative analysis more difficult. Still, relative to the MM framework of complete markets (with or without asymmetric information), the introduction of incomplete contracts and limited commitment has considerably enriched our understanding of corporate finance practice and corporate law.

The one major weakness of limited commitment and agency theories of corporate finance, however, is that they are not operational. Unlike the MM approach (and the trade-off theory), agency and limited commitment models do not offer a methodology that practitioners can use. This is why 35 years after the publication of Jensen and Meckling (1976) agency, information, and control issues remain marginal and esoteric topics confined to advanced corporate finance classes. These issues are often treated more like an afterthought, something that is mentioned as a caveat following a systematic and thorough valuation exercise based on the MM approach.

As a result, agency issues are often overlooked in practice simply because there is no simple quantitative methodology available to handle them. My view, therefore, is that before we pursue further refinements of the theory to put it on stronger foundations we need to make more progress on making the theory more operational, even if this means taking shortcuts. The structural models following Leland (1994) offer one direction, but they need to be augmented to introduce simple forms of agency costs and limited commitment.

I have recently become involved in a research project in that direction with my work with Hui Chen and Neng Wang (Bolton Chen, and Wang 2011, 2013). Basically what we do is build a corporate finance problem around a continuous-time, stochastic version of the neoclassic q theory of investment à la Hayashi (1982) (which assumes MM neutrality), by simply adding a reduced-form cost of external financing. Granted, this cost could be derived from first principles in a model along the lines of DeMarzo et al. (2010), but our point is that this would involve a more complex model, which would too quickly distract from the goal of developing an operational theory.

As is easy to see, an external cost of financing creates a role for corporate cash balances and risk management along the lines suggested by Froot, Scharfstein, and Stein (1993). Indeed, in our dynamic model the critical state variable is the firm's cash-to-capital ratio (a variable that is easy to construct and track from a firm's balance sheets). When this ratio is very high the firm behaves like a financially unconstrained firm, and when it is low the firm engages in various forms of dynamic hedging, underinvests, possibly sells assets at fire-sale prices, and as a last resort raises costly external financing.

There is no fundamental conceptual innovation in this model. However, the model straightforwardly lends itself to a quantitative analysis, and by carefully calibrating the key parameters of the model (which can all be easily observed or estimated) one can provide concrete prescriptions to firms on how much they should invest, how they should manage their cash balances, how much they should engage in dynamic hedging, and how they should finance their investments. This is only a start and this is a highly simplified model. Still, it is a richer and more realistic model than the dynamic *trade-off theory* model, and it can provide a quantitative methodology that allows practitioners to take account of agency and limited commitment problems.

4. Conclusion

By introducing a way of modeling incomplete contracts, and by proposing a simple theory of the firm based on the allocation of residual rights of control, Grossman and Hart's 1986 article has opened the way for formal economic theory to address important issues that had almost exclusively been left to corporate law, management, accounting, and sociology of organizations scholars.

At the same time, their article has drawn attention to a largely neglected issue in economics, namely, limits to contracting that arise from contract enforcement constraints (as opposed to asymmetric information and incentive constraints). By emphasizing contract enforcement constraints, their article has helped ground the more abstract and general economics of contracts literature in a more institutionally realistic context. Even though it is now 25 years since the publication of their article, this process is still under way and far from complete. There is still too little communication, for my taste, between legal scholars and economists. Still, by taking a bold pragmatic step and introducing somewhat ad hoc (but plausible) constraints on contracting, Grossman and Hart have profoundly changed the field of contract and institutional economics. They have made it more relevant and rescued the field from "monstrous state-contingent prescriptions."

References

Admati, A., P. Pfleiderer, and J. Zechner. 1994. "Large Shareholder Activism, Risk Sharing, and Financial Market Equilibrium." *Journal of Political Economy* 102: 1097–130.

Aghion, P., and P. Bolton. 1992. "An Incomplete Contracts Approach to Financial Contracting." *Review of Economic Studies* 59: 473–94.

Anderson, Ronald W., and Suresh Sundaresan. 1996. "Design and Valuation of Debt Contracts." *Review of Financial Studies* 9(1): 37–68.

Arrow, Kenneth J., and Gerard Debreu. 1954. "Existence of an Equilibrium for a Competitive Economy." *Econometrica* 22(3): 265–90.

Ayotte, Kenneth, and Patrick Bolton. 2011. "Optimal Property Rights in Financial Contracting." *Review of Financial Studies* 24(10): 3401–33.

Baumol, William J. 1959. *Business Behavior, Value and Growth*. New York: Macmillan.

Bebchuk, Lucian. 1999. "A Rent Protection Theory of Corporate Ownership and Control." NBER Working Paper 7203.

Berle, A. A., and G. Means. 1932. *The Modern Corporation and Private Property*. New York: Macmillan.

Bernheim, B. D., and M. D. Whinston. 1985. "Common Marketing Agency as a Device for Facilitating Collusion." *RAND Journal of Economics* 16: 269–81.

Bernheim, B. D., and M. D. Whinston. 1986a. "Common Agency." *Econometrica* 54: 923–42.

Bernheim, B. D., and M. D. Whinston. 1986b. "Menu Auctions, Resource Allocation, and Economic Influence." *Quarterly Journal of Economics* 101(1): 1–31.

Bienz, Carsten, Antoine Faure-Grimaud, and Zsuzsanna Fluck. 2012. "Bond Covenants and the Defeasance of Control Rights." http://www1.american.edu/academic.depts/ksb/finance realestate/mrobe/Seminar/Fluck.pdf

Bizer, D. S., and P. M. DeMarzo. 1992. "Sequential Banking." *Journal of Political Economy* 100: 41–61.

Bolton, Patrick, Hui Chen, and Neng Wang. 2011. "A Unified Theory of Tobin's q, Corporate Investment, Financing, and Risk Management." *Journal of Finance* 66(5): 1545–78.

Bolton, Patrick, Hui Chen, and Neng Wang. 2013. "Market Timing, Investment, and Risk Management." *Journal of Financial Economics* 109(1): 40–62.

Bolton, Patrick, and Xavier Freixas. 2000. "Equity Bonds and Bank Debt: Capital Structure and Financial Market Equilibrium under Asymmetric Information." *Journal of Political Economy* 108(2): 324–51.

Bolton, Patrick, and Xavier Freixas. 2006. "Corporate Finance and the Monetary Transmission Mechanism." *Review of Financial Studies* 19: 829–70.

Bolton, Patrick, and Olivier Jeanne. 2007. "Structuring and Restructuring Sovereign Debt: The Role of a Bankruptcy Regime." *Journal of Political Economy* 115 (6): 901–24.

Bolton, Patrick, and Olivier Jeanne. 2009. "Structuring and Restructuring Sovereign Debt: The Role of Seniority." *Review of Economic Studies* 76 (3): 879–902.

Bolton, Patrick, and David S. Scharfstein. 1990. "A Theory of Predation Based on Agency Problems in Financial Contracting." *American Economic Review* 80: 93–106.

Bolton, Patrick, and David S. Scharfstein. 1996. "Optimal Debt Structure and the Number of Creditors." *Journal of Political Economy* 104: 1–25.

Bolton, Patrick, and Elu von Thadden. 1998. "Blocks, Liquidity and Corporate Control." *Journal of Finance* 53: 1–25.

Brennan, M. J., and E. S. Schwartz. 1978. "Corporate Income Taxes, Valuation, and the Problem of Optimal Capital Structure. " *Journal of Business* 51(1): 103–14

Brunnermeier, Markus K., and Martin Oehmke. 2010. "The Maturity Rat Race." NBER Working Paper Series w16607. http://ssrn.com/abstract=1727088.

Burkart, Mike, Denis Gromb, and Fausto Panunzi. 1997. "Large Shareholders, Monitoring and the Value of the Firm." *Quarterly Journal of Economics* 113: 693–728.

Chava, Sudheer, and Michael R. Roberts. 2008. "How Does Financing Impact Investment? The Role of Debt Covenants." *Journal of Finance* 63(5): 2085–121.

Coase, Ronald. H. 1937. "The Nature of the Firm." *Economica* 4(16): 386–405.

Cyert, R., and J. March. 1963. *A Behavioral Theory of the Firm.* Englewood Cliffs, NJ: Prentice Hall.

DeAngelo, H., and R. W. Masulis. 1980. "Optimal Capital Structure under Corporate and Personal Taxation." *Journal of Financial Economics* 8: 3–29.

DeMarzo, Peter M., and Michael J. Fishman. 2007. "Optimal Long-Term Financial Contracting." *Review of Financial Studies* 20 (6): 2079–128.

DeMarzo, Peter M., Michael Fishman, Zhiguo He, and Neng Wang. 2010. "Dynamic Agency and the *q* Theory of Investment." *Journal of Finance* 57(6): 2295–340.

DeMarzo, Peter M., and Yuliy Sannikov. 2006. "Optimal Security Design and Dynamic Capital Structure in a Continuous-Time Agency Model." *Journal of Finance* 61(6): 2681–724.

Diamond, Douglas W., and Philip Dybvig. 1983. "Bank Runs, Deposit Insurance, and Liquidity." *Journal of Political Economy* 91: 401–19.

Diamond, Douglas W., and Raghuram G. Rajan. 2000. "A Theory of Bank Capital." *Journal of Finance* 55: 2431–65.

Diamond, Douglas W., and Raghuram G. Rajan. 2001. "Liquidity Risk, Liquidity Creation, and Financial Fragility: A Theory of Banking." *Journal of Political Economy* 109: 289–327.

Diamond, Douglas W., and Raghuram G. Rajan. 2005. "Liquidity Shortage and Banking Crisis." *Journal of Finance* 60: 615–47.

Dybvig, Philip H., and Jaime F. Zender. 1991. "Capital Structure and Dividend Irrelevance with Asymmetric Information." *Review of Financial Studies* 4: 201–19.

Fluck, Zsuzsanna. 1998. "Optimal Financial Contracting: Debt versus Outside Equity." *Review of Financial Studies* 11(2): 383–418.

Froot, Kenneth, David Scharfstein, and Jeremy Stein. 1993. "Risk Management, Coordinating Corporate Investment, and Financing Policies." *Journal of Finance* 48: 1629–58.

Goldstein, Robert, Nengjiu Ju, and Hayne Leland. 2001. "An EBIT-Based Model of Dynamic Capital Structure." *Journal of Business* 74: 483–512.

Graham, John R., and Campbell R. Harvey. 2001. "The Theory and Practice of Corporate Finance: Evidence from the Field." *Journal of Financial Economics* 60: 187–243.

Grossman, Sanford, and Oliver Hart. 1983. "An Analysis of the Principal-Agent Problem." *Econometrica* 51: 7–45.

Grossman, Sanford, and Oliver Hart. 1986. "The Costs and Benefits of Ownership: A Theory of Vertical and Lateral Integration." *Journal of Political Economy* 94: 691–719.

Hart, Oliver, and Bengt Holmström. 1987. "The Theory of Contracts." In T. F. Bewley (ed.) *Advances in Economic Theory: Fifth World Congress. Econometric Society Monographs Series, No. 12*, 71–155. Cambridge: Cambridge University Press.

Hart, Oliver, and John Moore. 1994. "A Theory of Debt Based on the Inalienability of Human Capital." *Quarterly Journal of Economics* 109: 841–79.

Hart, Oliver, and John Moore. 1998. "Default and Renegotiation: A Dynamic Model of Debt." *Quarterly Journal of Economics* 113: 1–41.

Hayashi, Fumio. 1982. "Tobin's Marginal q and Average q: A Neoclassical Interpretation." *Econometrica* 50: 215–24.

Holmström, Bengt, and Paul Milgrom. 1987. "Aggregation and Linearity in the Provision of Intertemporal Incentives." *Econometrica* 55: 303–28.

Holmström, Bengt, and Jean Tirole. 1997. "Financial Intermediation, Loanable Funds, and the Real Sector." *Quarterly Journal of Economics* 112(3): 663–91.

Holmström, Bengt, and Jean Tirole. 1998. "Private and Public Supply of Liquidity." *Journal of Political Economy* 106: 1–40.

Jensen, Michael C., and William H. Meckling. 1976. "Theory of the Firm, Managerial Behavior, Agency Costs and Ownership Structure." *Journal of Financial Economics* 3: 305–60.

Kaplan, Steven N., and Per Strömberg. 2003. "Financial Contracting Theory Meets the Real World: An Empirical Analysis of Venture Capital Contracts. " *Review of Economic Studies* 70(2): 281–315.

Lambrecht, Bart M., and Stewart C. Myers. 2010. "A Lintner Model of Dividends and Managerial Rents." AFA 2011 Denver Meetings Paper. http://ssrn.com/abstract=1571081.

Leland, Hayne E. 1994. "Corporate Debt Value, Bond Covenants and Optimal Capital Structure." *Journal of Finance* 49: 1213–252.

MacKie-Mason, Jeffrey K. 1990. "Do Firms Care Who Provides Their Financing?" In Glenn Hubbard (ed.) *Asymmetric Information, Corporate Finance, and Investment*. Chicago: University of Chicago Press.

Maskin, Eric, and Jean Tirole. 1999. "Unforeseen Contingencies and Incomplete Contracts." *Review of Economic Studies* 66: 83–114.

Mella-Barral, Pierre, and William Perraudin. 1997. "Strategic Debt Service." *Journal of Finance* 52(2): 531–56

Merton, Robert C. 1974. "On the Pricing of Corporate Debt: The Risk Structure of Interest Rates." *Journal of Finance* 29(2): 449–70.

Miller, Merton. 1977. "Debt and Taxes." *Journal of Finance* 32: 261–76.

Mirrlees, James. 1974. "Notes on Welfare Economics, Information and Uncertainty." In M. Balch, D. McFadden, and S.Wu (eds.) *Essays in Equilibrium Behaviour under Uncertainty*. Amsterdam: North-Holland.

Mirrlees, James. 1999. "The Theory of Moral Hazard and Unobservable Behaviour, Part 1." *Review of Economic Studies* 66: 3–21.

Modigliani, Franco, and Merton Miller. 1958. "The Cost of Capital, Corporation Finance, and the Theory of Investment." *American Economic Review* 48: 261–97.

Myers, Stewart C. 1977. "The Determinants of Corporate Borrowing." *Journal of Financial Economics* 5: 147–75

Myers, Stewart C. 2000. "Outside Equity. " *Journal of Finance* 55(3): 1005–37.

Myers, Stewart C., and Nicholas S. Majluf. 1984. "Corporate Financing and Investment Decisions When Firms Have Information that Investors Do Not Have." *Journal of Financial Economics* 13: 187–221.

Nini, Gregory, David Smith, and Amir Sufi. 2009. "Creditor Control Rights and Firm Investment Policy. " *Journal of Financial Economics* 92(3): 400–20.

Pagano, Marco, and Ailsa Röell. 1998. "The Choice of Stock Ownership Structure: Agency Costs, Monitoring, and the Decision to Go Public." *Quarterly Journal of Economics* 113(1): 187–225.

Penrose, Edith T. 1958. *The Theory of the Growth of the Firm*. New York: Wiley.

Rajan, Raghuram, and Luigi Zingales. 1995. "What Do We Know about Capital Structure? Some Evidence from International Data." *Journal of Finance* 50: 1421–60.

Rauh, Joshua, and Amir Sufi. 2010. "Capital Structure and Debt Structure. " *Review of Financial Studies* 23(12): 4242–80.

Roberts, Michael, and Amir Sufi. 2009. "Renegotiation of Financial Contracts: Evidence from Private Credit Agreements." *Journal of Financial Economics* 93(2): 159–84.

Schwartz, Alan. 1998. "Priorities and Priority in Bankruptcy." *Cornell Law Review* 82: 1396–419.

Segal, Ilya. 1999. "Contracting with Externalities." *Quarterly Journal of Economics* 114: 337–88.

Shleifer, Andrei, and Daniel Wolfenzon. 2002. "Investor Protection and Equity Markets." *Journal of Financial Economics* 66: 3–27.

Townsend, Robert M. 1979. "Optimal Contracts and Competitive Markets with Costly State Verification." *Journal of Economic Theory* 21: 265–93.

Williamson, Oliver E. 1964. *The Economics of Discretionary Behavior: Managerial Objectives in a Theory of the Firm.* Englewood Cliffs, NJ: Prentice Hall.

13

Discussion of Patrick Bolton's "Corporate Finance, Incomplete Contracts, and Corporate Control"

EFRAIM BENMELECH

The seminal work of Grossman and Hart (1986) changed the landscape of corporate finance by giving impetus to an extensive theoretical literature that analyzes financial decisions from an incomplete contracting perspective. In particular, the incomplete contracts approach has been successful in developing theories that motivate the use of debt contracts. The paper by Patrick Bolton (chapter 12)—one of the most influential contributors to this literature—offers an in-depth review and assessment of the incomplete contracts approach to financial contracting.

When Oliver Hart wrote his 2001 *Journal of Economic Literature* survey "Financial Contracting," the empirical evidence was just beginning to accumulate.[1] In the past few years the field has benefited from the availability of data on syndicated loans, commercial real estate loans, and asset-backed securities, which have enabled microlevel studies of financial contracting.[2] In this short discussion I review the empirical evidence on the role that collateral plays in financial contracts.

Incomplete Contracts and Collateral

Most of the theory on the role of collateral in secured lending has focused either on situations where borrowers exhibit moral hazard or on situations

---

[1] One exception is Kaplan and Stromberg's (2003) influential empirical paper.

[2] For example, see Assuncao, Benmelech, and Silva (2014), Benmelech (2009), Benmelech and Bergman (2008, 2009), Benmelech, Garmaise, and Moskowitz (2005), Djankov et al. (2007), Kaplan and Stromberg (2003), Qian and Strahan (2007), and Roberts and Sufi (2009a,b).

of adverse selection. The nature of the financial friction in these models yields differential theoretical predictions. When the financial friction is one of adverse selection and asymmetric information, high-quality firms are predicted to employ collateral when borrowing, whereas firms of low quality are predicted to borrow using unsecured debt. For example, the optimal contract in Bester (1985) is one in which risky borrowers pay a high interest rate but are not required to put down any collateral, while safer borrowers put down some collateral and pay a lower interest rate.

In contrast to the predictions relying on adverse selection and hidden information, models that are based on moral hazard predict that lower quality firms are required to use collateral when raising capital, whereas higher quality firms are able to borrow without it. In essence, collateral is used to increase borrowers' pledgeable income and hence helps in obtaining external finance and reducing its price. The empirical evidence suggests that, consistent with the moral hazard models, low-quality borrowers are those more likely to post collateral (see, e.g., Berger and Udell 1990; John, Lynch, and Puri 2003).

Collateral is of central importance in the incomplete contracting literature. In particular, collateral allows the creditor to recover, at least partially, a loan made to a debtor (see, e.g., Aghion and Bolton 1992; Shleifer and Vishny 1992; Hart and Moore 1994, 1998; Bolton and Scharfstein 1996). This threat of asset liquidation motivates debtors to avoid default. Thus, in the incomplete contracting literature, asset liquidation values play a key role in both the ex ante determination of debt contracts as well as the ex post determination of debt payments. In a series of papers with coauthors we test empirically predictions from the incomplete contracts literature and find that consistent with the models, collateral liquidation values determine the ex post strategic behavior of borrowers, as well as the ex ante pricing of these contracts, their maturity structure, debt capacity, and number of creditors.

Collateral Values and Renegotiations

In Benmelech and Bergman (2008) we document empirically the conditions under which airlines renegotiate aircraft leases in the United States. We first develop an incomplete contracting model of financial contract renegotiation based on Hart and Moore (1998) and then estimate it using data on the airline industry in the United States. The model has two testable implications. First, firms will be able to credibly renegotiate their financial commitments only when their financial situation is sufficiently poor. Second, when a firm's financial position is sufficiently poor, and hence its renegotiation threat is credible, a reduction in the liquidation value of assets increases the concessions the firm obtains in renegotiation. We proceed by empirically analyzing renegotiation of aircraft leases by U.S. airlines. Aircraft leases are a natural environment for test-ing renegotiation-based models since in bankruptcy lessors are relieved from the automatic stay provision that affects most creditors. These lessors, therefore, have the ability to quickly repossess their assets if a firm defaults on its lease pay-ments, which matches nicely the stylized assumption in much of the theoretical literature. Our results emphasize the importance of the incomplete contracting perspective to real-world financial contract renegotiation. The ability of firms to renegotiate their financial commitments depends heavily on their bargain-ing position vis-à-vis liability holders. This bargaining position is determined, in turn, by both the credibility of threats made during renegotiation and by the outside option of the bargaining parties.

Collateral Values and Financial Contracting

The value of the creditor's option to foreclose on collateral affects both his willingness to provide financing and the terms on which financing is extended. Incomplete contracting models of debt financing predict that the terms of debt financing depend on the collateral liquidation values. The following are some of the central empirical predictions arising from these models.

- Prediction 1. Debt levels increase in collateral liquidation values (Shleifer and Vishny 1992; Hart and Moore 1994).
- Prediction 2. The promised debt yield decreases in asset liquidation values, controlling for the debt level.
- Prediction 3. Debt maturity increases in collateral liquidation value (Shleifer and Vishny 1992; Hart and Moore 1994).
- Prediction 4. Firms borrow from multiple creditors when liquidation value is low and from a single creditor when liquidation value is high (Bolton and Scharfstein 1996; Diamond 2004).

Benmelech and Bergman (2009) analyze the effect of collateral redeployabil-ity on the pricing of loans using a novel data set of secured debt issued by U.S. airlines. Airlines in the United States issue tranches of collateralized debt obli-gations, which take a variety of formats known as equipment trust certificates, Enhanced Equipment Trust Securities, and pass through certificates. These debt instruments pledge aircraft from an airline's fleet as collateral and have served as the main source of external financing for U.S. airlines since the mid-1990s. Matching aircraft serial numbers hand collected from filing prospectuses to a database on worldwide aircraft, we obtain detailed information about the char-acteristics of all aircraft serving as underlying collateral. For each debt tranche, this information is then used to construct measures of collateral redeployability.

Benmelech and Bergman (2009) show that debt tranches that are secured by more redeployable collateral exhibit lower credit spreads, higher credit ratings, and higher loan-to-value ratios—an effect that our estimates show to be economically sizable. The results thus suggest that—consistent with predictions 1 and 2—the ability to pledge collateral, in particular redeployable collateral, lowers the cost of external financing and increases debt capacity.

Moreover, Benmelech (2009) investigates the effect of assets' liquidation values on capital structure by exploiting the diversity of track gauges in nineteenth-century North American railroads. The abundance of track gauges limited the redeployability of rolling stock and track to potential users with similar track gauge. Furthermore, potential demand for both rolling stock and tracks was further diminished when many railroads went under equity receiverships. Consistent with prediction 3, Benmelech (2009) shows that the potential demand for a railroad's rolling stock and tracks was a significant determinant of debt maturity and the amount of debt that was issued by railroads.

These results are not confined only to the airline and railroad industries. Benmelech, Garmaise and Moskowitz (2005) analyze the effect of liquidation values on debt contracting using a unique data set of commercial property loan contracts. The empirical identification strategy employs commercial zoning regulation to capture the flexibility of a property's permitted uses as a measure of an asset's redeployability or value in its next best use. Within a census tract, Benmelech, Garmaise, and Moskowitz (2005) find that more redeployable properties receive larger loans with longer maturities and durations, lower interest rates, and fewer creditors, controlling for the property's type, sales price, and earnings-to-price ratio. These results are consistent with all of the incomplete contracting–based predictions listed above on the relation between collateral values and debt financing terms.

In a recent paper, Assuncao, Benmelech, and Silva (2014) analyze the effects of a credit reform in Brazil on the auto credit market. The development of the Brazilian auto loan market faced several impediments. Chief among them was the inefficient process of repossession and resale of autos when borrowers defaulted on their loans. Banks were allowed to repossess the autos of borrowers who failed to repay their loans. However, the banks could not resell repossessed cars without court approval. As a result, the time from the repossession of a car to its resale by the bank averaged more than two years. In August 2004, the Brazilian government announced a broad credit reform that, among other legal changes, eased the resale of repossessed autos.

Assuncao, Benmelech, and Silva (2014) show that consistent with predictions 1, 2, and 3, the legal change has led to larger loans with lower credit spreads, longer maturities, and higher leverage. The authors also find that the credit reform led to the "democratization" of credit in that borrowers with lower income, with higher risk, and who are self-employed were more likely to obtain a loan after the law was implemented. These results shed light on the consequences of a credit reform, highlighting the crucial role that collateral and repossession play in the liberalization and democratization of credit markets.

Conclusion

The incomplete contracting approach to financial contracting provided a rich setting for the analysis of debt contracts. One of the main contributions of this literature is to emphasize the important role that collateral plays in debt financing. Collateral liquidation value affects the ex ante willingness to provide financing and the terms on which credit is extended as well as the ex post determination of debt payments that are affected by contract renegotiations and strategic default. The ultimate strength of any economic theory lies in its ability to explain real-world outcomes. The ample empirical evidence that has accumulated in recent years provides strong support for the incomplete contracting approach to financial contacts.

References

Aghion, Philip, and Patrick Bolton. 1992. "An Incomplete Contracts Approach to Financial Contracting". *Review of Economic Studies* 59: 1472–94.

Assuncao, Juliano, Efraim Benmelech, and Fernando S. S. Silva. 2014. "Repossession and the Democratization of Credit." *Review of Financial Studies* 27: 2661–89.

Benmelech, Efraim. 2009. "Asset Salability and Debt Maturity: Evidence from Nineteenth-Century American Railroads." *Review of Financial Studies* 22(4): 1545–83.

Benmelech, Efraim, and Nittai K. Bergman. 2008. "Liquidation Values and the Credibility of Financial Contract Renegotiation: Evidence from U.S. Airlines." *Quarterly Journal of Economics* 123(4): 1635–77.

Benmelech, Efraim, and Nittai K. Bergman. 2009. "Collateral Pricing." *Journal of Financial Economics* 91(3): 339–60.

Benmelech, Efraim, Mark Garmaise, and Tobias J. Moskowitz. 2005. "Do Liquidation Values Affect Financial Contracts? Evidence from Commercial Zoning Laws." *Quarterly Journal of Economics* 120(3): 1121–54.

Berger, Allen, and Gregory F. Udell. 1990. "Collateral, Loan Quality and Bank Risk". *Journal of Monetary Economic* 25: 21–42.

Bester, Helmut. 1985. "Screening vs. Rationing in Credit Markets with Imperfect Information". *American Economic Review* 75: 850–55.

Bolton, Patrick, and David D. Scharfstein. 1996, "Optimal Debt Structure and the Number of Creditors." *Journal of Political Economy* 104(1): 1–25.

Diamond, Douglas. 2004. "Presidential Address, Committing to Commit: Short-Term Debt When Enforcement Is Costly". *Journal of Finance* 59: 1447–79.

Djankov, Simeon, Caralee McLiesh, and Andrei Shleifer. 2007. "Private Credit in 129 Countries". *Journal of Financial Economics* 84: 299–329.

Grossman, Sanford, and Oliver Hart. 1986. "The Costs and Benefits of Ownership: A Theory of Vertical and Lateral Integration". *Journal of Political Economy* 94: 691–719.

Hart, Oliver. 2001. "Financial Contracting." *Journal of Economic Literature* 39(4): 1079–100.

Hart, Oliver, and John Moore. 1994. "A Theory of Debt Based on the Inalienability of Human Capital". *Quarterly Journal of Economics* 109: 841–79.

Hart, Oliver, and John Moore. 1998. "Default and Renegotiation: A Dynamic Model of Debt". *Quarterly Journal of Economics* 113: 1–41.

John, Kose, Anthony Lynch, and Manju Puri. 2003. "Credit Ratings, Collateral, and Loan Characteristics: Implications for Yield". *Journal of Business* 76: 371–409.

Kaplan, Steven N., and Per Stromberg. 2003. "Financial Contracting Theory Meets the Real World: Evidence from Venture Capital Contracts". *Review of Economic Studies* 70: 281–316.

Qian, Jun, and Philip E. Strahan. 2007. "How Laws and Institutions Shape Financial Contracts: The Case of Bank Loans". *Journal of Finance* 62: 2803–34.

Roberts, Michael, and Amir Sufi. 2009a. "Renegotiations of Financial Contracts: Evidence from Private Credit Agreements." *Journal of Financial Economics* 93(2): 159–84.

Roberts, Michael, and Amir Sufi. 2009b. "Financial Contracting: A Survey of Empirical Research and Future Directions." *Annual Review of Financial Economics* 207–26.

Shleifer, Andrei, and Robert W. Vishny. 1992. "Liquidation Values and Debt Capacity: A Market Equilibrium Approach". *Journal of Finance* 47: 143–66.

14

Why the Incomplete Contract Approach Is Important for Finance

LUIGI ZINGALES

Before starting with my comments, I would like to make a small rejoinder to Steve Kaplan's piece (chapter 16). We have just observed the ultimate test of any theory in finance—not Google citations, not Web of Science citations—but making into Steve Kaplan's MBA lectures. For two reasons, that is truly the ultimate test of success. First, because it is not easy for any theory to make it into an MBA class, especially a case class like the one Steve teaches, and second, because Steve is especially skeptical and demanding with any theory. I remember the first year I arrived in Chicago, Steve sat through my PhD class. When I taught Grossman-Hart and Hart and Moore, he jumped on the distinction between "observable" and "verifiable." Skeptical, Steve challenged it right away: "What is this distinction between observable and verifiable? Give me an example!" Before I could actually think, I responded, "What happened between you and your wife last night was observable to both parties, but not verifiable in court." He was not convinced and he asked for a "business" example. So, I am glad that many years later, he bought into the framework.

More seriously, Patrick Bolton gave an excellent representation of how important the incomplete contract approach has been in corporate finance (see chapter 12). In the past 60 years, there have been four big approaches: (1) Modigliani and Miller (M&M) with taxes, (2) asymmetry of information/agency, (3) incomplete contracts, and (4) behavioral. In summarizing what the incomplete contract approach created by GMH framework has meant for the corporate finance literature, I focus on four aspects.

The first one is the connection between corporate finance and theory of the firm. This connection is crucial in all three dimnsions of corporate finance: capital stucture, corporate govenanance, and valuation.

Let us start with capital structure. I do not want to be disrespectful to Modigliani and Miller, since I consider their contribution fundamental; yet one could paraphrase M&M in the following way: "postulating the existence of a firm that has no reason to exist as a combined entity, the total value of this firm is the same if we keep it together or we break it apart." In other words, in the M&M paradigm, there is no reason why firms exist to begin with. So whether you keep this firm together, break it apart, or slice its cash flow in many different ways, it does not really matter.

The asymmetric information/agency framework is not much better in this respect, nor is the behavioral approach. If you really want to understand corporate finance and why slicing cash flow or allocating control are important, you have to understand why being a firm is important. For example, absent renegotiation frictions, the cost of financial distress is really the cost of breaking apart a firm. If you do not have a theory of why it makes a difference for a firm to exist, it is very hard to have a theory of why it is costly to break this firm apart, that is, a theory of what the costs of financial distress are, past some renegotiation costs.

Only in the incomplete contract approach do we have an endogenous explanation of why breaking a firm into pieces can have costs and benefit: it changes the incentives to undertake human capital investment specific to the firm. Certainly, other approaches can attach an explanation of why there are positive and negative synergies, but it is indeed an add-on, completely orthogonal to the financing decision. In the GHM framework, the same forces that drive the cost and benefits of integration drive the cost and benefit of financing.

The underlying theory of the firm is equally important for corporate governance. Why is there a corporate governance "problem"? Why does Adam Smith's invisible hand not automatically provide a solution? We need governance because firms are different from markets and unless you have a theory of why firms are different from markets, it is very hard to have a theory of why you need to govern those firms and why different types of governance make a difference.

Finally, a key part of corporate finance is valuation. A theory of the firm is very important for valuation as well. Much of the value in modern firms does not derive from their assets in place, but from their growth opportunities. The real problem is to whom those opportunities belong.

Think about Oprah Winfrey: she was working for a TV station and decided to create her own channel. As a result of her decision to leave, the investment opportunity did not belong to the channel she was working for, but rather belonged to her. There are a lot of similar examples. Many investment banks acquired others hoping to acquire their employees and clients. But the key employees left and so did the clients, leaving the acquirers with an empty shell. So who owns the growth opportunities and even the future cash flow is a key element in valuation. The incomplete contract approach is the only framework I know of that tries to deal with the problem of who owns these growth opportunities. I have tried to highlight these points several years ago (Zingales 2000). Yet more needs to be done on this front.

The second key contribution of the incomplete contract approach is its definition of control rights. I will not spend much time here because all the literature has emphasized this aspect, and correctly so. A related point that perhaps has been less emphasized is that control rights are much more important in countries where the law is not enforced promptly and/or in an unbiased fashion. This is why, as a young student, I fell in love with Oliver Hart's teaching: his theories resonated immediately with me, coming from a country where the law is not enforced effectively and, as a result, control is extremely important.

The third key insight of the Grossman and Hart framework, crucial not only to corporate finance but to the economic literature in general, is its emphasis on the importance of renegotiation. Elu von Thadden was very right when he said that the euro is an example of an incomplete contract. It is also a wonderful example of how limited our ability to commit is. If you are not a European, you might not know that there is a no-bailout clause enshrined in the German constitution, which prevents Germany from participating in any bailout of other European countries. Nevertheless, when the Greek crisis exploded, what did Europe do? It bailed out Greece. It is hard to imagine a commitment stronger than enshrining something in a constitution, and not in just any constitution, but in the German constitution. In spite of this very hard commitment mechanism, renegotiation took place.

The emphasis on renegotiation that the incomplete contract literature brought to finance is extremely important. In the venture capital world, you write contracts that have basically very little hope of being enforced in the way they are written. They are just a threat. They set the stage for future renegotiations, very much in the spirit of Aghion, Dewatripont, and Rey (1994).

For example, a typical clause in venture capital contracts gives the venture capitalist (VC) the right to sell back her shares to the firm at a given price at a predetermined time in the future. When this clause is inserted, the VC has no intention to exercise it. The first reason is that the return on investment will not be so great. A second reason is that the firm is liquidity constrained and will never be able to buy back the VC. So why do VCs regularly insert this clause? It is not because they expect to enforce it. It is simply because it sets the stage for future renegotiation. It gives the VC a valuable threat point that influences the division of the ex post surplus in her favor. We could not fully appreciate the importance of this point without the incomplete contract framework.

The fourth, and more controversial, aspect of the incomplete contracts' contribution to corporate finance involves the application of this framework to publicly traded corporations. In particular, the topic of in whose interest public companies should be run is very controversial. If a Martian came to Earth, was taught Grossman and Hart (1986) and Hart and Moore (1990), and then was asked whether investors or workers should own the control rights in a public corporations, the answer would be obvious: the workers. In the GHM framework, ownership should be allocated to motivate the most valuable *noncontractible* investments. It is very hard to argue that financial investments are noncontractible. Thus, ownership should belong to either management or the workers, but not to any outside financier. Yet, in their corporate governance survey Shleifer and Vishny (1997) arrive at the exact opposite conclusion: control rights should belong to the outside financiers because they are the people who are most likely to be expropriated. Ironically, Shleifer and Vishny justify this conclusion on the basis of. . . Grossman and Hart (1986). Their argument is not necessarily wrong, but it relies on an extrapolation of the GHM framework, not fully spelled out. The success of a theory is also measured by the way it is extended and overinterpreted. Thus, this debate is a tribute to the GHM framework.

Yet there is a reason the best applications of the GHM framework are in entrepreneurial finance. Entrepreneurs have to make very important human capital investments. The GHM framework is perfect in this context. In publicly traded corporations, however, it is much more difficult to apply it. In the typical modern corporation, ownership and control are separated: control is held by managers and ownership is held by people who do not make any human capital-specific investment to the firm: the shareholders. Starting from the original version of the theory, it is a bit hard to explain what it means to separate ownership from control, since ownership is defined as control. Raghu and I have tried to extend the original theory in this direction a bit (Rajan and Zingales 1998, 2001), but much more needs to be done.

References

Aghion, Philippe, Mathias Dewatripont, and Patrick Rey. 1994. "Renegotiation Design with Unverifiable Information." *Econometrica* 62(2): 257–82.

Grossman, Sanford J., and Oliver Hart. 1986. "The Costs and Benefits of Ownership: A Theory of Vertical Integration." *Journal of Political Economy* 94(4): 691–719.

Hart, Oliver, and John Hardman Moore. 1990. "Property Rights and the Nature of the Firm." *Journal of Political Economy* 98(6).

Rajan, R., and L. Zingales. 1998. "Power in a Theory of the Firm." *Quarterly Journal of Economics* 113: 387–432.

Rajan, R., and L. Zingales. 2001. "The Firm as a Dedicated Hierarchy: A Theory of the Origins and Growth of Firms." *Quarterly Journal of Economics* 116: 805–52.

Shleifer, A., and Robert W. Vishny. 1997. "A Survey of Corporate Governance." *Journal of Finance* 52(2).

Zingales, L. 2000. "In Search of New Foundations." *Journal of Finance* 55: 1623–53.

PART 5

INCOMPLETE CONTRACTS
AND BUSINESS FIRMS

15

Oliver Hart's Contributions to the Understanding of Strategic Alliances and Technology Licensing

JOSH LERNER

This discussion explores the way in which Oliver Hart's insights have informed our understanding of the role of strategic alliances and licensing. These institutions have become increasingly important in high-technology industries. The work of Oliver, his coauthors, and his students have shed light on the structuring of these agreements, as we discuss here.

At the outset, it is worth highlighting the complexity of these agreements, which reflects the costly and uncertain nature of technology projects. The complexity and unpredictability of the research presents challenges in drafting enforceable agreements that specify the contributions of each party in the face of all contingencies. A great deal of innovation has been devoted to the design of these contracts, which makes it difficult to generalize about this phenomenon.

Despite these difficulties, understanding strategic alliances is critical to those who wish to understand high-technology industries. The availability of equity from public investors for new high-tech firms has been variable, with cycles of boom and bust characterizing the sector. During periods with little financing activity, young high-tech firms suffer tremendous financial stresses and have few alternatives for raising capital other than strategic alliances.

Furthermore, the economic importance of technology alliances has been increasing. While obtaining a comprehensive view of alliance financing is exceedingly difficult, tabulations suggest that alliances are the dominant source of external financing for R&D by young firms in many industries, including

I thank participants in Grossman & Hart @ 25 conference in Brussels for helpful comments, especially Steve Kaplan. Parts of this essay are based on earlier works. Financial support was provided by the Division of Research at Harvard Business School and the U.S. National Science Foundation.

advanced materials, information technology, and telecommunications. Surveys of corporate research managers suggest that alliances will be an increasingly important mechanism through which R&D is financed in the years to come.

Nowhere is this trend clearer than in biotechnology, where alliances with pharmaceutical firms have become the single largest source of financing, accounting for several billion dollars of funds annually. The economic importance of these transactions is also shown by the willingness of firms to spend substantial amounts litigating them and the size of the damage awards: for example, Genentech and Eli Lilly's dispute over their alliance to develop human growth hormone, which led to the filing of at least six lawsuits between 1987 and 1993.

Why Are Alliances and Licensing so Important?

Academic technology transfer officers and executives at technology companies often face the challenge of commercializing early stage technologies with tremendous promise. But a variety of considerations make it difficult to raise financing from traditional sources—such as banks and public investors—for some of the most potentially profitable and exciting technologies. As a result, in many cases these companies are required to turn to strategic alliances for financing. These difficulties can be sorted into four critical factors: uncertainty, asymmetric information, the nature of firm assets, and the conditions in the relevant financial and product markets.

The first of these issues, uncertainty, is a measure of the array of potential outcomes for a company or project. The wider the dispersion of outcomes, the greater the uncertainty. By their very nature, young technology companies are associated with significant levels of uncertainty: only a relative handful of innovations actually become commercial products, and a small subset of these proves to be profitable. The extent of intellectual property protection that a new product will receive is also often very uncertain. High uncertainty means that entrepreneurs and investors cannot confidently predict what the company will look like in the future. Uncertainty affects the willingness of investors to contribute capital, the desire of larger firms to license unproven technologies, and the decisions of firms' managers.

The second factor, asymmetric information, is distinct from uncertainty. Because of his or her day-to-day involvement with the technology, a scientist knows vastly more about his or her discovery's prospects than do prospective investors. Various problems develop in settings where asymmetric information is prevalent. For instance, the entrepreneur may take detrimental actions that outsiders cannot observe, perhaps undertaking a riskier strategy than initially suggested or not working as hard as the investor expects. The entrepreneur might also invest in projects that build up his reputation at the investors' expense.

Asymmetric information can also lead to selection problems. The scientist who makes a potentially important discovery may exploit the fact that he knows more about the project or his abilities than his investors do. Licensees may find it difficult to distinguish between truly revolutionary technologies and impractical ones. Without the ability to screen out unacceptable projects, outsiders are unable to make efficient and appropriate decisions choices regarding where to invest. These problems have been particularly severe in new technology development because of the scientific complexity of developing new products and processes.

The third factor is the nature of the assets. Firms that have tangible assets—for example, machines, buildings, land, or physical inventory—may find financing easier to obtain or may be able to get more favorable terms. The ability to abscond with the firm's source of value is more difficult when it relies on physical assets. When the most important assets are intangible, raising outside financing or entering into strategic alliances may be more challenging. In most technology industries, firms have tended to rely on patent protection to protect their assets. Those firms that have relied on trade secrets or informal know-how have found attracting investors or entering into licensing agreements to be very difficult.[1]

Market conditions also play a key role in determining the difficulty of financing firms. Both the capital and product markets may be subject to substantial variations. The supply of capital from public investors and the price at which this capital is available may vary dramatically. These changes may be a response to regulatory edicts or shifts in investors' perceptions of future profitability.

As a result of all these problems, technology firms often have little choice but to turn to corporations for financing. A corporation with a related line of business can overcome many of these information problems by undertaking extensive due diligence prior to the transaction and monitoring the firm afterward. The corporation may have assets, such as sales forces and manufacturing know-how, which young firms lack and yet are essential to the successful introduction of a new product. Small, research-intensive firms frequently rely on

---

[1] For instance, trade secrets offer exceedingly narrow intellectual property protection, only shielding against misappropriation: "the acquisition of a trade secret by a person who knows or has reason to know that the trade secret was acquired by improper means" (Milgrim, 1993). Thus, a firm cannot sue a rival who discovers its trade secret independently or through reverse engineering (disassembling a device to discover how it works). This is unlike patent protection, which allows the awardee to prosecute others who infringe, regardless of the source of the infringers' ideas. Pooley (1989) notes that very few "naked" trade secret licenses are observed, suggesting that the information covered only through this narrow property right is difficult to transfer in an arm's-length exchange.

alliances with larger corporations to avoid having to build these capabilities, which may take years to develop. Furthermore, the ongoing operations of the corporate partner may enable it to overcome some of the problems associated with the intangible nature of the young technology firm's assets.

Described in this manner, these problems may appear to be quite abstract. But they have very real implications for academic technology managers or corporate executives seeking to commercialize early stage technologies. They may find investors unwilling to invest the time and resources to examine early technologies or offering only modest payments in exchange for large stakes in innovations that the scientists, technology transfer officers, and company executives believe to be quite valuable. In the remainder of this section, I summarize the evidence regarding these claims.

This set of suggestions has been examined in a variety of work. Most directly relevant is the work of Pisano (1990), who examines pharmaceutical firms' choices between developing new drugs in house versus through alliances in the case of 92 drug development projects. He demonstrates that the insights of contracting theory (Grossman and Hart 1986) are highly relevant here. In particular, when there are few small biotech firms working in the field, the pharmaceutical company is more likely to undertake the project in house. This is consistent, he argues, with the theoretical suggestions that "hold-up" problems—that is, efforts by one of the parties to renegotiate the contract on more favorable terms after the agreement is signed—will be greater in this setting. Pisano also finds evidence that firm-specific factors are critical in the decision to undertake alliances.

How Are Alliances Structured?

A second broad question that this essay considers is the manner in which alliances are structured. Here, the setting mirrors closely the incomplete contracting theory developed in Grossman and Hart (1986) and Hart and Moore (1988) and summarized in Hart (1995).

A typical assumption is that it is impossible for the two parties to write a verifiable contract specifying the effort and final output of the two parties that could be enforced in a court of law. This is because there are many possible contingencies, all of which cannot be anticipated at the time the contract is drafted. Because of this nonverifiability problem, these models argue that it is optimal for ownership of the project to be assigned to the party with the greatest marginal ability to affect the outcome. This party, who will retain the right to make the decisions that cannot be specified in the contract, should also receive any surplus that results from the project. Because of this incentive, the party will make the decisions that maximize—or come close to maximizing—the returns from the project.

Aghion and Tirole (1994) adapt this general model to a R&D alliance between two firms. As long as the R&D-performing firm has the initial bargaining power or does not face capital constraints, the results are as discussed before: the control rights are assigned to the party whose marginal contribution to the project's success is greatest. When the financing firm has the initial bargaining power and the R&D firm is capital constrained, however, a different pattern may emerge. In particular, if it is optimal for the property rights to be transferred to the R&D firm, the best outcome will not be achieved: the financing firm will be willing to transfer ownership, but the cash-constrained R&D firm will not have enough resources to compensate the financing firm. As a result, an inefficient allocation of the property rights occurs, with the financing firm retaining the rights to the invention.

Research by new firms has numerous features that resemble the setting depicted in the theoretical literature on incomplete contracts. Technology projects—particularly early stage efforts—are highly complex and uncertain, making it very difficult to specify the features of the product to be developed. As one executive relates: "Redefining the work when the unexpected happens, as it invariably will, [is essential]. Research is by its very nature an iterative process, requiring constant reassessment depending on its findings. If there is a low risk of unexpected findings requiring program reassessment, then it is probably not much of a research program" (Sherbloom 1991, 220–21).

Similarly, the complexity and unpredictability of the research presents challenges in drafting an enforceable agreement that specifies the contributions of the R&D firm. In particular, firms that contract to perform R&D in alliances frequently have ongoing research projects of their own in addition to the contracted efforts. In case of a dispute, it may be difficult for the financing firm to prove that the R&D firm has employed alliance resources to advance projects that are not part of the alliance.

This class of models suggests a variety of empirical implications. In general, among alliances where informational asymmetries are greater, the period during which the R&D firm maintains active control over the project should be longer.

Lerner and Merges (1998) examine the determinants of control rights within a sample of 200 alliances. They analyze the share of 25 key control rights allocated to the financing firm by regressing the assigned number of rights on independent variables denoting the project stage and financial conditions, as well as controls for a variety of alternative explanations. Consistent with the incomplete contracting framework, the greater the financial resources of the R&D firm, the fewer control rights are allocated to the financing firm. For instance, a one standard deviation increase in shareholders' equity at the mean of the independent variables leads to an 11% drop in the predicted number of control rights assigned to the financing firm. Evidence regarding the relationship between control rights and the stage of the project at the time the alliance is signed is less consistent with existing theory. Projects in their early stages at the time of alliance formation actually assign significantly less control to the R&D firm.[2]

It should be noted, however, that in some important respects these agreements deviate from the classic model of incomplete contracts. Robinson and Stuart (2007) highlight the extent to which these agreements often contain provisions that are impossible to verify or simply unobservable. Why these provisions are included are somewhat of a mystery: they suggest that the contracting parties may anticipate threatening to terminate agreements or engaging in litigation.[3] These findings anticipate some of the issues discussed in Halonen-Akatwijuka and Hart (2013) and Lerner and Malmendier (2010).

Lerner, Shane, and Tsai (2003) explore the impact of the financing environment at the time an agreement was signed on the success of the agreement. They show that in periods when financing availability was strong, agreements were more successful, whether measured by the probability that the drug in development advanced to the next stage in the clinical trials or was approved. They show that the effect was more pronounced in those agreements where the biotechnology company received little of the control, as the incomplete contracting view suggests. This helps address concerns that the result is driven by shifts in an unobserved third factor. Lerner, Shane, and Tsai also examine the likelihood of renegotiation. If it would maximize innovative output to assign control to the small biotech company, but this allocation of control is precluded by financial market conditions, then we should see a distinct pattern in renegotiations. In particular, when financing conditions improve for biotechnology firms, those agreements assigning the bulk of the control to the major pharmaceutical firm should be disproportionately renegotiated. The empirical results are consistent with this pattern.

What Is the Evidence from Field Research?

Another important source of information on alliances is case study research. The conclusions of these cases are often not as "neat" as statistical analyses that are crafted to examine a particular question, but field-based analyses can generate a

---

[2] Although this study is confined to the biotechnology industry, patterns in information technology are similar: see Elfenbein and Lerner (2003, 2012).

[3] An interesting theoretical look at the impact of the threat of termination on alliance contracts is in Panico (2011).

variety of insights. In this section, I highlight the experiences of three companies that have been examined in case studies. Although not exhaustive of the case study literature on alliances, they suggest the richness of insights that field-based research can provide.

These three young companies all were developing advanced human therapeutics and grappling with the challenges posed by alliances. The biotechnologies pursued by the three firms are quite different: antigen-based allergy drugs (ImmuLogic Pharmaceutical Corporation), advanced drug delivery mechanisms (ALZA Corporation), and monoclonal antibody–based treatments of inflammation (Repligen Corporation). There were considerable differences in the location and sophistication of strategic partners and the development stages of the technologies.

One point that these cases—consistent with the literature discussed already—was how the allocation of control rights are determined both by concerns about behavior after the alliance is signed and by relative bargaining power. One alliance that may be considered successful[4] in many respects was Repligen's May 1992 alliance with Eli Lilly regarding a very early stage effort to develop a monoclonal antibody–based treatment of inflammation after heart attacks (Kane and Lerner 1994). In the Repligen-Lilly alliance, three control rights were the subjects of protracted negotiations. The first was the management of clinical trials—the right to decide which drugs would be pursued and when. A second was the control over the marketing strategy, an arena in which Lilly had extensive experience and Repligen only a slight acquaintance. Finally, both parties wished to control the process development and ultimate manufacturing of the drug.

The terms of the alliance that emerged from the negotiations appeared to assign the control rights to the parties whose behavior would have the greatest impact on the product development effort. Repligen was allowed a great deal of control over developing the lead product candidate, an area where it had considerable experience, but tangential product development activities were subject to extensive review by Lilly. Lilly was assigned control over all aspects of marketing, and Repligen was assigned all manufacturing control rights unless it encountered severe difficulties with regulators.

Other alliances illustrate the importance of the relative bargaining power of the two parties. An example was the January 1978 alliance between ALZA and

---

[4] The net-of-market return for Repligen in the three-day window around the announcement of the transaction in May 1992 was +9%, and that of Lilly +2%. These increases can be compared to the +2.1% reaction to 55 announcements of R&D initiatives by high-technology firms found by Chan et al. (1997). The early stage project succeeded in getting its lead product candidate into Phase I trials in just 13 months. After extending the project in June 1995, however, Lilly canceled its involvement three months later, citing shifting internal priorities.

Ciba-Geigy (Angelmar and Doz 1988; Lerner and Tufano 1993). At the time of the alliance, ALZA faced a major financial crisis. The firm had little more than $1 million in the bank, was spending $2 million more per month than it was receiving in revenues, had nearly exhausted its credit line, was in violation of several loan covenants, and was precluded from a sale of equity to the public by unfavorable market conditions and the perception that they had been excessively optimistic in its earlier communications with investors and analysts.

The alliance assigned almost total control to the Swiss pharmaceutical giant. Ciba-Geigy was given a supermajority on the joint board that reviewed and approved potential research projects, the right to license and manufacture any of ALZA's current or future products, the ability to block any other alliances that ALZA proposed to enter, and 8 of the 11 seats on ALZA's board of directors. In addition, Ciba-Geigy received a new class of preferred shares. If converted into common stock, the new preferred shares would represent 53% of the equity in ALZA. Until conversion, however, Ciba-Geigy had 80% of the voting rights, an allocation that allowed it to employ ALZA's tax losses.

At the same time, it is reasonable to believe that concerns about the postalliance behavior of ALZA also motivated Ciba-Geigy to demand strong control rights. ALZA's leaders had displayed little ability to direct the firm's research effort over the course of the 1970s. This may have led Ciba-Geigy to conclude that the benefits of allocating control rights to ALZA's management were limited. Despite the strict control rights contractually assigned to Ciba-Geigy, there were frequent disputes between the two firms as ALZA researchers sought to either circumvent the pharmaceutical firm's middle management or ignored their instructions outright. Frustrated by these problems, Ciba-Geigy agreed to terminate the alliance and sell its equity back to ALZA in November 1981.

A contrasting illustration is presented by ImmuLogic (Lerner, 1992). In March 1991, the firm was considering entering into an alliance or raising equity in an initial public offering. One concern that led the company to decide to go public was that a potential strategic partner might exploit its relatively weak financial condition. In other words, ImmuLogic feared that a pharmaceutical company might obtain numerous concessions on key governance and financial issues by protracting the negotiations until ImmuLogic was close to running out of capital. It consequently deferred negotiating an alliance to develop and market its allergy drugs until it went public in May 1991. The firm announced an alliance with Marion Merrell Dow in December 1991, which allowed ImmuLogic to retain numerous control rights, such as an equal role in planning marketing strategy in the United States: *In Vivo* magazine hailed the transaction as "push(ing) the limit of the biotech deal . . . a partnership in fact as well as name" (quoted in Lerner 1992, Teaching Note 5-293-118, 7). Just as ALZA's relinquishment of almost total control to Ciba-Geigy was largely a consequence of its weak financial position, ImmuLogic's ability to obtain these control rights reflected its financial strength.

These cases also emphasize three issues that are not generally highlighted in the theoretical literature in incomplete contracting. One is the interaction between the allocation of control rights and the financial terms of the transactions. For instance, in the negotiations that led to Repligen's retention of control over manufacturing, the firm agreed to an alteration in its compensation. Repligen accepted a lower royalty than originally envisioned (5% of the sales price) but agreed to supply the drug to Lilly at a price (about 15% of the sales price) above what it believed its true manufacturing cost would be. Repligen agreed to reduce the price it charged Lilly if it was able to manufacture the drug for less, but only if its cost was below 8% of the sales price.

A second interesting and unexplored aspect is the apparent signal that the allocation of control rights provided to potential investors and other outsiders. Both ImmuLogic and Repligen highlighted their retention of key control rights in the press releases announcing the transactions described here. Their ability to obtain these rights attracted favorable comments in the trade press and analyst reports alike. These patterns suggest a richer set of interactions than theoretical treatments of these issues imply.

The third relates to the structure of the payments between the financing and the R&D firm. The design and implementation of incentive schemes in general is a major focus of the finance and economics literature, but payments in alliances have been little examined except in theoretical works (e.g., Gallini and Wright 1990; Kamien and Tauman 1986). This lack of attention is a reflection of the difficulty in analyzing them. The payments typically are of several types: an initial up-front payment, a purchase of equity (which the financing firm may be able to force the R&D firm to repurchase if the alliance is unfruitful) or warrants, commitments to contract for R&D on specific topics, milestone payments contingent on the achievement of technological and marketing objectives or the renewal of the agreement, and a royalty on the eventual sales generated by the product. Assessing the expected net present value of these payments is very difficult. The magnitude and timing of eventual sales that the project will generate are difficult to anticipate. The amount of the R&D to be contracted for is often ambiguous. Alliances may also include contingent payments for remote outcomes. The rationale for their inclusion is that firms frequently report—and analysts tabulate when assessing firms—the sum of all precommercialization payments from new alliances, whether the funds are likely to be received or not.

These contractually specified contingent payments may thus convey important strategic benefits, even if the probability of payment is very low. Clearly, this is a difficult but important area for research.

This discussion has sought to suggest the importance, richness, and complexity of alliances and licensing in the technology industry, and the way that it illustrates the work of Oliver Hart and his colleagues.

References

Aghion, Phillipe, and Jean Tirole. 1994. "On the Management of Innovation." *Quarterly Journal of Economics* 109: 1185–207.

Angelmar, Reinhard, and Yves Doz. 1988. "Ciba-Geigy/Alza Case Series" (including "Advanced Drug Delivery Systems: Alza and Ciba-Geigy," A through F; "Alza Corporation," A and B; "Ciba-Geigy Limited: Pharmaceutical Division," A through C). Unnumbered INSAED case studies.

Chan, Su H., John W. Kensinger, Arthur J. Keown, and John D. Martin. 1997. "Do Strategic Alliances Create Value?" *Journal of Financial Economics* 46: 199–221.

Elfenbein, Daniel W., and Josh Lerner. 2003. "Ownership and Control Rights in Internet Portal Alliances, 1995–1999." *RAND Journal of Economics* 34, 356–69.

Elfenbein, Daniel W., and Josh Lerner. 2012. "Exclusivity, Contingent Control Rights, and the Design of Internet Portal Alliances." *Journal of Law, Economics, and Organization* 28: 45–76.

Gallini, Nancy, and Brian D. Wright. 1990. "Technology Transfer under Asymmetric Information." *RAND Journal of Economics* 21: 237–52.

Grossman, Sanford J., and Oliver D. Hart. 1986. "The Costs and Benefits of Ownership: A Theory of Lateral and Vertical Integration." *Journal of Political Economy* 94: 691–719.

Halonen-Akatwijuka, Maija, and Oliver Hart. 2013. "More Is Less: Why Parties May Deliberately Write Incomplete Contracts." Working Paper no. 19001, National Bureau of Economic Research.

Hart, Oliver D. 1995. *Firms, Contracts, and Financial Structure.* New York: Oxford University Press.

Hart, Oliver D., and John Moore. 1988. "Incomplete Contracts and Renegotiation." *Econometrica* 56: 755–85.

Kamien, Morton, and Yair Tauman. 1986. "Fees versus Royalties and the Private Value of a Patent." *Quarterly Journal of Economics* 101: 471–93.

Kane, David, and Josh Lerner. 1994. "Repligen Corporation: January 1992." Harvard Business School Case No. 9-294-082 (and Teaching Note 5-295-137).

Lerner, Josh. 1992, "ImmuLogic Pharmaceutical Corporation." Harvard Business School Cases No. 9-293-066 through 9-293-071 (and Teaching Note 5-293-118).

Lerner, Josh, and Robert P. Merges. 1998. "The Control of Technology Alliances: An Empirical Analysis of the Biotechnology Industry." *Journal of Industrial Economics* 46: 125–56.

Lerner, Josh, Hilary Shane, and Alexander Tsai. 2003. "Do Equity Financing Cycles Matter? Evidence from Biotechnology Alliances." *Journal of Financial Economics* 67: 411–46.

Lerner, Josh, and Peter Tufano. 1993. "ALZA and Bio-Electro Systems." Harvard Business School Cases No. 9-293-24 through 9-293-127 (and Teaching Note 5-296-060).

Lerner, Josh, and Ulrike Malmendier. 2010. "Contractibility and Contract Design in Strategic Alliances." *American Economic Review* 100: 214–246.

Milgrim, Roger M. 1993. *Milgrim on Trade Secrets.* New York: Matthew Bender.

Panico, Claudio. 2011. "On the Contractual Governance of Research Collaborations: Allocating Control and Intellectual Property Rights in the Shadow of Potential Termination." *Research Policy* 40: 1403–11.

Pisano, Gary P. 1990. "The R&D Boundaries of the Firm: An Empirical Analysis." *Administrative Science Quarterly* 35: 153–76.

Pooley, James. 1989. *Trade Secrets: A Guide to Protecting Proprietary Business Information.* New York: American Management Association.

Robinson, David T., and Toby E. Stuart. 2007. "Financial Contracting in Biotech Strategic Alliances," *Journal of Law and Economics* 50: 559–96.

Sherbloom, James P. 1991. "Ours, Theirs, or Both? Strategic Planning and Deal Making." In R. Dana Ono (ed.) *The Business of Biotechnology: From the Bench to the Street.* Stoneham, MA: Butterworth-Heinemann, pp. 213–24.

16

Incomplete Contracts and Venture Capital

STEVE KAPLAN

I'm going to talk about the setting of corporate finance theories that we've already heard something about. We have been talking about venture capitalists as the empirical analog to principals in theory. Accordingly, I will go through what Per Strömberg and I have learned in our studies of venture capitalists. Then I'm going to talk about the practical implications of incomplete contracting. I think the commenters so far have been overly negative on the extent of those practical implications. In fact, incomplete contracting theories have first-order practical implications in venture capital financing. They have been particularly useful in what what I teach my students and what I tell entrepreneurs in practice. Finally, I'll repeat some of the unresolved issues and questions that I have, some of which have been mentioned already.

So what's the setting for venture capital financings? The setting includes an entrepreneur who has an idea but no money and an investor who has money but no ideas. In addition, there are often information differences preinvestment—particularly uncertainty about investment and entrepreneur quality, as well as moral hazard issues postinvestment. The key question is how the investor can profitably fund the entrepreneur's idea.

Since Grossman-Hart, we've understood that decision or control rights are important. In the subsequent corporate finance theories, two different strands have incorporated this. In papers like Aghion-Bolton (1992) and Dewatripont-Tirole (1994), the state is observable and verifiable by a third party. Control is state dependent in that it tends to go to the entrepreneur in good states and the financiers in bad states. Hart-Moore (1990 and 1994) and Bolton-Scharfstein (1990), on the other hand, are different in that the state is observable but not verifiable. In those two papers, the optimal security is debt. There are no equity-like claims. If the entrepreneur pays, the entrepreneur has control; if the entrepreneur does not pay, the lender takes control.

Ernst-Ludwig Van Thadden mentioned research that was consistent with the Hart-Moore setting. He did not talk about the Aghion-Bolton setting. I'm going to talk about both because I think the differences are both interesting and important.

So, what was the state of play when Per Strömberg and I started to think about all these things? There were many theories in 2000, but there was very little evidence. Of course, that's why we wrote our paper [Kaplan and Strömberg (2003)]. We thought that venture capitalists were particularly good empirical analogs to the theory.

First, the venture capitalists are sophisticated at contracting. When you read a contract, you can see that it is very very detailed and has clearly gone through substantial negotiations.

Second, venture capitalists have strong incentives to maximize value because a large share of their compensation comes from the profits on their investments and the ability to raise subsequent funds (which is also based on investment success). As we know, the venture capitalists made a great deal of money in the 1990s. Although the analogy is not perfect because venture capitalists are subject to some agency issues, Oliver concluded in his 2001 survey [Hart (2001)] that venture capitalists were indeed a good place to look. So we did.

We studied more than 200 venture capital financing rounds. We described and tried to measure cash flow rights, control rights, liquidation rights, and the contracting space. What did we find? It was very clear that the VCs separately allocated cash flow rights, control rights, board rights, voting rights, and liquidation rights. The venture capitalists used convertible securities most frequently, but they also implemented those different rights with different kinds of securities. Some used a combination of preferred and common stock. Others used different classes of common stock. Crucially, control rights and liquidation rights mattered a great deal and were quite distinct from cash flow rights.

In a typical contract, control rights were allocated such that if the company performed poorly, the venture capitalist got full control. As performance improved, control started shifting away from the venture capitalist toward the entrepreneur. If the company did really well, the venture capitalist control rights went away, as did the liquidation rights. Furthermore, all of these rights were frequently contingent on observable measures of both financial and nonfinancial performance.

What do our results mean? First, incentives matter. That was good for the old agency/corporate finance literature. At the same time, control rights clearly mattered a lot. That means the contracts are incomplete in some sense. In addition, the cash flow rights and control rights were consistently separated.

Although we didn't perform an explicit test, the contracts looked remarkably like the contracts in Aghion-Bolton and Dewatripont-Tirole. Because the contracts were equity contracts, they looked much less like the contracts in Hart-Moore, suggesting that venture capital is not a good setting for Hart-Moore-type models and assumptions.

There's another paper I've written that is worth mentioning. Per, Frederic Martel, and I looked at contracts internationally [Kaplan, Martel and Strömberg (2007)]. We compared the contracts in a number of countries outside the United States to those in the United States. We found that although the non-U.S. contracts included control rights and liquidation rights, those rights were somewhat less strong than in the United States.

Consistent with the story in LaPorta et al. (1997), the differences correlated somewhat with legal regimes. At the same time, however, there was a stronger relation between contracts and venture capitalist experience. Venture capitalists who used the U.S. (Aghion-Bolton)–style contracts used the same contracts not only in the United States but everywhere they invested. You can interpret this as a horse race of Grossman-Hart, Aghion-Bolton against LLSV. In this setting, Grossman-Hart and Aghion-Bolton were big winners over LLSV. I believe Oliver likes this result.

These results also suggest that the U.S. model works everywhere, particularly as long as there is some enforceability of contracts. It is worth noting that the countries included both largely developed countries and some developing countries as well.

Now, what are the practical implications? These results provide some very practical guidance for entrepreneurs. I often hear (or read about) entrepreneurs who complain that venture capitalists are evil, rapacious people because if the company isn't performing, the VCs kick out the entrepreneur. I have met some entrepreneurs who are very angry about venture capitalists. The theory and empirical results provide a coherent explanation for these entrepreneurs.

As an example, one of my colleagues had a cousin who was raising venture capital. He was complaining that he didn't like these contracts because they were rapacious. We sent him my paper with Per. After he read it, he said, "Ah, now I understand. These contracts make a huge amount of sense. And, I understand what rights and terms are negotiable and what are not." So it turned out to be very useful in that case. It is also useful in teaching potential entrepreneurs and venture capitalists.

The other finding that is very useful is that on contingencies. If there's a difference of opinion between the entrepreneur and investor, the theory helps show us we can use those differences of opinion to negotiate a contingent contract. That is very consistent with what happens in practice. Just understanding this can help entrepreneurs and investors negotiate more effective contracts.

What's unresolved or could be improved? I would like to see theorists pay more attention to the realism of their assumptions. Theorists tend to be overly cavalier about their assumptions—particularly those concerning observability and verifiability. You've heard that from Patrick that different assumptions make sense in different settings. I'd like to see theorists being more thoughtful about that. In particular, there are many instances in developed countries and even in emerging economies where you see contracts that are written on observables. They must be verifiable (at least to some extent) because they're in the contracts and they get executed.

References

Aghion, Phillippe, and Patrick Bolton, 1992, "An incomplete contracts approach to financial contracting", *Review of Economic Studies*, 77: 338–401.

Bolton, Patrick, and David Scharfstein, 1990, "A theory of predation based on agency problems in financial contracting", *American Economic Review*, 80: 94–106.

Dewatripont, Matthias, and Jean Tirole, 1994, "A theory of debt and equity: Diversity of securities and manager-shareholder congruence", *Quarterly Journal of Economics* 109: 1027–1054.

Hart, Oliver, 2001, "Financial Contracting." *Journal of Economic Literature.*

Hart, Oliver, and John Moore, 1990, "Property rights and the Nature of the Firm." *Journal of Political Economy* 98, 1119–1158.

Hart, Oliver, and John Moore, 1994, "A Theory of Debt Based on the Inalienability of Human Capital", *QuarterlyJournal of Economics* 109, 841–879.

Kaplan, Steven, Fredric Martel and Per Strömberg, 2007, "How Do Legal Differences and Learning Affect Financial Contracts?" *Journal of Financial Intermediation*, Volume 16, 273–311.

Kaplan, Steven and Per Strömberg, 2003 "Financial Contracting Theory Meets the Real World:Evidence From Venture Capital Contracts," *Review of Economic Studies*, Volume 70, 281–316.

LaPorta, R., Lopez-de-Silanes, F., Shleifer, A., Vishny, R., 1997. Legal determinants of external finance. J. Finance 52, pp. 1131–1150.

17

Incomplete Contracts and the Role of Small Firms

JEREMY C. STEIN

Let me begin by saying that it's a great pleasure to be able to take part in honoring Sandy and Oliver, and I'm grateful to the organizers for including me in this conference. What I thought I would try to do is give a sense of where and how my own thinking has been most influenced by Sandy and Oliver's work. At the risk of being overly concrete, I will focus on one specific empirical observation that has long struck me as a first-order fact that is difficult to come to grips with, unless one appeals to the insights that are at the heart of the Grossman-Hart-Moore (GHM; Grossman and Hart 1986; Hart and Moore 1990) paradigm.

My one observation is this: if you look across a range of industries—from the most innovative to the lowest-tech—you often see a striking coexistence of firms of wildly different sizes, from mom-and-pop firms to global giants. Banking is one example: the largest U.S. banks have assets on the order of $2 trillion. And at the same time, there are roughly 2,000 banks with assets under $100 million. Homebuilding is another case in point: on the one hand, approximately 40 percent of the people who work in the construction business work for small local builders; these are firms with 20 or fewer employees. On the other hand, there are big publicly traded homebuilding companies like Toll Brothers, which was producing something like 8,000 to 10,000 homes a year in the period before the financial crisis.

There are many other industries one could point to, from restaurants, to florists, to retail stores. One reason for emphasizing banking and homebuilding is that these are industries where one might a priori think that financial market frictions would tend to create strong economies of scale, and hence would tend to lead to markets dominated by large firms. In banking, Diamond (1984) points to large-scale diversification as being one of the keys to making delegated monitoring work. Similarly, in homebuilding, a small builder who is highly lever-aged and who has much of his net worth tied up in a few properties is extremely vulnerable to local house price downturns, something that would appear to be a serious competitive disadvantage. Consider the following quote from Toll Brothers' 2010 annual report:

> We have always competed primarily with small and mid-sized private builders. After five years of a depressed housing market, most private builders have been severely weakened and many have gone out of business. Even the best ones are suffering from limited access to capital. . . . We believe our strong balance sheet and access to capital will continue to give us an advantage and distinguish us from the tens of thousands of other builders in our industry.

So the basic question to be asked is this: what is it that allows very large and very small firms to coexist in these sorts of industries? More specifically, if one takes seriously the idea that financial constraints are important, and that they can create significant economies of scale for the largest firms, what is the diseconomy on the other side of the equation that balances things out? Alternatively, what is the key advantage of decentralization relative to integration?

To oversimplify, let me contrast two views. The first, which I will label the "entrepreneurship" view, is that little firms are nothing more than big-firm wannabes. In other words, they are little simply because while they might hope to get big someday, they are not there yet—either because of financial con-straints, or time to build, or lack of accumulated skill and know-how. In this view, the size distribution at any point in time is in part the product of histor-ical shocks, and the biggest firms are the ones that have had a series of positive draws of, for example, profitability, and productivity.

The alternative view might be called "small is beautiful." In this view, the size distribution of firms in an industry represents a steady-state equilibrium, one in which there are some advantages to being small which offset whatever scale economies come from easier access to finance and other factors. Some support for the idea that small is beautiful comes from recent work by Hurst and Pugsley (2011). Using survey data from the Panel Study of Entrepreneurial Dynamics, they document that the majority of small business owners do not aspire to grow significantly; rather their ex ante plan is to stay small, with only a handful of employees. Moreover, when asked about why they started the business in the first place, the leading motives cited were ones that on the surface seemed non-pecuniary, with the dominant answers being "be own boss" and "enjoy the work, have passion for it."

One might stop there, and say that we have a theory of small firms based on the observation that people enjoy being their own boss and derive some nonmonetary benefit from doing so. Of course, this leaves the nonmonetary benefit—which is effectively a black box—to carry a lot of explanatory weight in some industries, because again, there is a presumption that it has to offset considerable economies of scale.

Here is where I find the GHM paradigm to be extraordinarily helpful—in thinking about what exactly the "costs of a boss" are and how they manifest themselves in ways that ultimately may have significant pecuniary, as well as non-pecuniary implications. Simply put, the key insight of the theory is that authority and initiative are complements. When small business owners talk about the passion they have for their work, implicit in that is the premise that a loss of autonomy and decision rights might dull their incentives, and reduce their creativity: why would you work as hard on developing your brilliant ideas if there is a risk your boss may second-guess you and prevent you from implementing them? If there's one thing that we as academics ought to be able to relate to, it's just this point. The GHM framework is ideally suited for analyzing this set of issues.

Moreover, the theory can do more than just rationalize the existence of small firms. It can make specific predictions for where and when these cost-of-a-boss effects are likely to be most pronounced, and hence to have the most significant influence on firm size. In some of my own work (Stein 2002), I have built on GHM and on Aghion and Tirole (1997), and tried to flesh out the proposition that giving people autonomy is particularly important in industries or in settings where it matters a lot to be able to gather soft information. My notion of soft information follows Hayek (1945, 524): "the sort of knowledge with which I have been concerned is knowledge of the kind which by nature cannot enter into statistics and therefore cannot be conveyed to any central authority in statistical form."

There is no reason to believe that having a boss reduces all kinds of effort; to the contrary, it might actually induce agents to work very hard at doing things that allow them to lobby their bosses for more resources. In terms of information production, this sort of lobbying would correspond to the production of hard information: that which, in Hayek's words, can be credibly conveyed to a central authority. By contrast, the production of soft information—which is by its nature more subjective and less transmittable—is likely to suffer when agents do not have the authority to act on the basis of the information they have produced. So in cases where soft-information production is particularly valuable, we ought to be more likely to observe either smaller firms or more decentralization within larger firms.

In the banking industry, one area where soft-information production is likely to be especially important—and hence where small banks may have a valuable role to play—is in lending to small firms, whose prospects are often difficult to evaluate based on hard information like formal accounting data. Consistent with the theory, Berger et al. (2005) document that small banks use a different lending technology than large banks when it comes to making small business loans, relying more on geographic proximity and interpersonal contact, and less on accounting records; moreover this personalized lending technology appears to be more effective in relaxing credit constraints for their borrowers. Going further, Liberti and Mian (2009) find that even within the same bank, loan applications that have to be passed further up the hierarchy for approval rely less on the soft, subjective assessments of individual credit officers and more on hard, objective data. This latter finding is striking support for the hypothesis that decentralized authority helps encourage the production of soft information.

Closely related is the work by Chen et al. (2004) on the mutual fund industry. They find that small mutual funds tend to outperform large mutual funds on average, and that this outperformance tends to come from their better ability to evaluate the stocks of the smallest, most geographically proximate firms—that is, those firms where it would seem plausible that local, on-the-ground information, as opposed to statistical analysis, would be most useful.

What about my other leading example, homebuilding? Here I know of less in the way of empirical research on the role of soft information. But one tentative hypothesis would be that in this industry, soft information has to do with, say, the local and sometimes very personal nature of the zoning and permitting process—what steps one needs to take to acquire an undeveloped parcel of land and get it approved and developed to the point that it is ready for construction to begin. If so, the prediction of the theory would be that small builders are at a comparative advantage in areas where new lots are scarce and idiosyncratic in their development requirements, whereas large builders are at a comparative advantage where there are larger tracts of available land, or where the development process is more homogeneous.

Finally, let me touch on a theoretical nuance that is right up the alley of the GHM paradigm. I have been emphasizing the proposition that when soft information is valuable, it becomes more important to give autonomy and decision rights to local, on-the-ground managers. But why does this require the firm in question to be small? Why can't the same decentralization of decision rights be credibly implemented inside a larger firm, thereby capturing the benefits of both soft information as well as whatever economies of scale go along with firm size? Two points are worth noting. First, to the extent that one of the reasons for being a big firm is access to capital, top management of such a firm cannot credibly alienate its right to reallocate capital across divisions. In such a setting, *complete* decentralization of decision rights is likely to be impossible. If a line manager within one unit of the firm has a project that she would like to pursue, she cannot be assured that senior management will not reallocate capital away from her unit and toward another part of the firm, thereby shelving her project. This implies that if one wants to maximize the incentives of on-the-ground managers, there is likely to be some role for firm size as the ultimate credible decentralization mechanism.

Second, however, *partial* decentralization of decision rights within a larger firm may well be feasible, in which case the theory speaks to the effects of different organizational structures on local incentives. For example, Berger et al. (2005) find that small banks that are housed inside large bank holding companies appear to behave more like stand-alone small banks, in that they are more successful in fostering customer relationships based on soft information. Thus the partial decentralization associated with a holding company structure seems to be complementary to soft-information acquisition, consistent with the theory. Similarly, Chen et al. (2004) find that in the mutual fund industry, small funds located inside large fund families nevertheless behave like small funds—they do better at picking small geographically proximate stocks.

To conclude: one of the central contributions of the GHM paradigm is that it has provided us with a clearer understanding of the root sources of diseconomies of scale, and hence of the virtues of small firms. I have argued that one specific application of the theory is in the area of soft-information production, with the key idea being that a lack of control rights particularly discourages the acquisition and use of soft, on-the-ground information. This interpretation of GHM leads to what one might call a "Hayekian" view of the role of small firms: they may not be so much entrepreneurial enterprises on their way to being much bigger firms, or even major engines of job creation, but they may nevertheless play a crucial role in marshaling the myriad forms of soft information that are dispersed throughout the economy.

References

Aghion, Philippe, and Jean Tirole. 1997. "Formal and Real Authority in Organizations." *Journal of Political Economy* 105: 1–29.

Berger, Allen N., Nathan H. Miller, Mitchell A. Petersen, Raghuram G. Rajan, and Jeremy C. Stein. 2005. "Does Function Follow Organizational Form? Evidence from the Lending Practices of Large and Small Banks." *Journal of Financial Economics* 76: 237–69.

Chen, Joseph, Harrison Hong, Ming Huang, and Jeffrey D. Kubik. 2004. "Does Fund Size Erode Mutual Fund Performance? The Role of Liquidity and Organization." *American Economic Review* 94: 1276–302.

Diamond, Douglas W. 1984. "Financial Intermediation and Delegated Monitoring." *Review of Economic Studies* 51: 393–414.

Grossman, Sanford J., and Oliver D. Hart. 1986. "The Costs and Benefits of Ownership: A Theory of Vertical and Lateral Integration." *Journal of Political Economy* 94: 691–719.

Hart, Oliver D., and John Moore. 1990. "Property Rights and the Nature of the Firm." *Journal of Political Economy* 98: 1119–58.

Hayek, Friedrich A. 1945. "The Use of Knowledge in Society." *American Economic Review* 35: 519–30.

Hurst, Erik, and Benjamin Pugsley. 2011. "What Do Small Businesses Do?" *Brookings Papers on Economic Activity* (Fall): 73–142.

Liberti, Jose, and Atif Mian. 2009. "Estimating the Effect of Hierarchies on Information Use." *Review of Financial Studies* 22: 4057–90.

Stein, Jeremy C. 2002. "Information Production and Capital Allocation: Decentralized versus Hierarchical Firms." *Journal of Finance* 57: 1891–921.

PART 6

INCOMPLETE CONTRACTS
AND INDUSTRIAL ORGANIZATION

18

Contracts, Ownership, and Industrial Organization: Past and Future

PATRICK LEGROS AND ANDREW F. NEWMAN

1. Introduction

In his iconic textbook Scherer (1980) offered a description of industrial organization (IO) with which most economists would still agree:

> [IO is] concerned with how productive activities are brought into harmony with society's demands for goods and services through some organizing mechanism such as a free market, and how variations and imperfections in the organizing mechanism affect the degree of success achieved by producers in satisfying society's wants. (1)

A decade later, the *Handbook of Industrial Organization* was more specific, referring to its subject as "the broad field within microeconomics that focuses on *business behavior* and its implications both for market structures and processes, and for public policies" (xi, emphasis added).

In view of these definitions, an outside observer might be surprised by the very primitive view of the business firm—the "neoclassical black box"—that continues to dominate the field, particularly considering the explosive growth in the theory and evidence about firms that followed the work of Williamson (1971, 1975), Grossman and Hart (1986), Hart and Moore (1990), and

This is a revised version of a survey presented at the conference *Grossman and Hart 25* on June 24–26, 2011 at the Université libre de Bruxelles. We thank our discussants Mathias Dewatripont and Kai-Uwe Kühn, two referees, and the audience for their valuable comments. Legros benefited from the financial support of the Communauté Française de Belgique (project ARC00/05-252). For their hospitality and support, Newman is grateful to the Yale Economic Growth Center and the Brown Population Studies and Training Center.

others. Instead, when assessing how business behavior affects prices, quantities, productivity, welfare, and other economic outcomes, IO economists have overwhelmingly identified the "imperfection in the organizing mechanism" with market power.[1] Yet *imperfections within firms*, the subject of organizational economics, are also a very natural source of imperfection in the organizing mechanism, and it is striking how small a role these have played in answering the central questions of IO.

Why should this be? To some extent, it appears to be a historical accident. Charismatic economists like George Stigler dismissed behavioral and organizational approaches to the firm because of their lack of formal modeling and poor empirical validation (Perelman 2011); this favored market power as the root of all distortion. Oligopoly theory, fueled by game-theoretic advances, led to significant theoretical and empirical agendas for IO researchers and also found a natural audience among policy makers, who had justifiable antitrust concerns about rising industries such as information technology or recently deregulated ones such as airlines. For tractability, this approach was mainly based on the neoclassical, cost-minimizing firm-as-production-function. In the already complex environment of oligopoly, richer organizational considerations were rarely introduced, and when they were they were mainly viewed as instruments for securing a competitive advantage.[2]

In parallel to this formal oligopoly literature, the transaction cost approach (TCE) descended from Klein et al. (1978) and Williamson (1975) introduced incomplete contracting ideas into IO and led to a large empirical literature that validated the role of contracting imperfections as a source of distortion. But the lack of formalization continued to limit the influence of contracting ideas in academic IO (e.g., Joskow 2010). Grossman and Hart's seminal property-rights-theoretic article (1986), which at long last introduced a formal way to discuss firm boundaries and showed how ownership of assets and the allocation of control affects firm performance, led a wave of formal theorizing about the internal organization of firms that continues to this day.

---

[1] The many IO textbooks that have been written in the past 30 years typically follow the same plan. The author acknowledges that the received view of the firm is an abstraction, that it is actually nonsense to talk of the "behavior of a firm": after all, only individuals can have behavior, and a "firm" is a place where different stakeholders have conflicting interests, where contracts are incomplete (the term seemed to have appeared in textbooks in the 1970s). After emphasizing that the assumption of a firm as a cost-minimizing single decision maker is empirically invalid, as well as theoretically suspect, and after reviewing more modern theories of the firm and managerial behavior (often taking up 10% of the book's pages), the rest of the textbook then abruptly ignores all of this, and the theory and empirics of industrial performance are developed on the basis of neoclassical firms.

[2] The major exception was a literature, which we survey in section 2.1, that maintained a skeptical stance on the proposition that competition necessarily leads to distortion-free performance.

Despite this wealth of literature, the connection between organizational economics and IO variables like prices and quantities is infrequently explored, as is the effect of organizations on consumer welfare or other measures of industry performance. For several reasons the time has come to develop an organizational industrial organization (OIO) that embeds incomplete contracting ideas into IO. Such an agenda will articulate how control-right allocations, firm boundaries, and other elements of internal organization can be the main determinants of firm conduct and market performance, whether or not there is market power in the industry.

- The methodological criticisms of the 1940s–1960s are no longer valid. We are equipped with robust and rich organizational theories, and data sets quantifying organizational variables (e.g., vertical integration, delegation) are becoming available. In fact, recent empirical work in industries as diverse as airlines, concrete, and trucking emphasizes the relation between ownership structures and prices or performance.

- Another empirical IO literature documents persistent heterogeneity in firm performance within as well as across industries and countries (Syverson 2011). This begs for explanation, something that neoclassical firm models are ill equipped to provide. Organizational economics seems to provide hope for coherence on this issue; indeed, it has long maintained that understanding heterogeneity is one of, if not *the*, central question of the field.[3] But it is difficult to see how one can address organizational and profitability differences without embedding multiple organizations in a market, the essence of the OIO approach.

- The force of public opinion and policy makers' concerns have shifted in response to new economic realities. Recent industry failures, including the corporate accounting scandals of the 2000s; plane crashes in the United States; lead-painted toys from China; and, most devastatingly of all, the global financial crisis have been ascribed to unaccountable managers, misaligned ownership structures, or outsourcing – in short organizational design flaws – rather than to monopoly power. Much of this criticism is focused on areas where the firms themselves face significant competition. Indeed, managers often blame competitive pressures when they are brought to account for their organizations' failures.

---

[3] "How easy it is for an inefficient manager to dissipate the differentials on which profitability rests, and that it is possible, with the same technical facilities, to produce with a great variety of of costs, are among the commonplaces of business experience which do not seem to be equally familiar in the study of the economist" (Hayek 1945, quoted in Williamson 1990).

- Nascent efforts at developing an OIO already suggest that market conditions or industrial structure matter for organizational design. At the same time, organizational design will affect the productivity of firms, hence eventually the total industry output, the quality of products and information about this quality for consumers. Organizational design matters for consumers, hence for IO.

The survey comprises two main parts. In a first, we review two of the main questions that have been addressed by papers introducing organizational considerations into IO. These past efforts have dealt with the disciplining effect of market competition for incentive provision and the use of organizations as strategic variables. In a second part, we argue that an organizational approach to IO provides new insights about endogenous heterogeneity, price, and quantity variables as well as consumer welfare even in the simplest competitive market setting. Furthermore, in that part we will also show how IO matters for organization theory.

2. Organizations and IO: Questions from the Past

In the 1980s, the parallel advances in oligopoly and contract theory provided fertile ground to revisit questions asked in the 1960s, in particular about the disciplining effect of the market on managers (Machlup 1967). The first part of this section discusses the literature on this and related questions. Though limited in terms of the organizational design elements it considered – principally managerial compensation schemes were studied – what became clear from that work is that simple intuitions such as Machlup's, that competition always improves managerial discipline, are only partially correct because they ignore the endogeneity of organizational design. Incentive provision may complement the disciplining effect of the market. But incentives may also substitute for the market: for instance, when demand is low, managers may work harder to avoid bankruptcy, but shareholders may then be less willing to provide strong incentives to managers. Both theoretical and empirical work suggest that, unlike in the neoclassical case, there may be a nonmonotonic relationship between competition and managerial effort provision.

These results are significant for their implication that it is not generally possible to study neoclassical firms and hope that the resulting behavior and response to shocks or changes in the environment will replicate that of organizational firms. Hence, some form of OIO modeling is needed to assess industry performance, particularly if one is interested in organizational design elements beyond compensation schemes, such as delegation or ownership structure.

The second broad topic that has received significant attention so far in the literature is the use of organizational design as an instrument for gaining market power. The classic IO policy question of the effects of mergers, both vertical and horizontal, figures most prominently here. A smaller literature observes that with separation of ownership and control, financial contracting will matter, both internally to the firm and strategically in its interaction with other firms. We review these literatures in the second part of this section.

Our broad conclusion will be that relatively few organizational variables have been considered so far, and that we are therefore short of having a broad understanding of the relationship between the organization of firms and industry variables like prices and quantities, or consumer welfare.

2.1 Does Competition Matter for Organizations?

In the early 1980s, the main theoretical apparatus for studying internal organization was the principal agent (P-A) model and this is perhaps why the analysis of Machlup's conjecture has taken place mainly in the framework of incentive provision, a "firm" being simply a P-A relationship. We first review the main theoretical arguments suggesting an effect of the degree of competition on incentive provisions. We then consider applications of these ideas to different questions in IO, such as spatial competition and industrial policy. The applications underscore the nonmonotonic relationship between competition and incentive provision.

2.1.1 *The Nonmonotonic Theoretical Relationship between Competition and Incentives*

As Nalebuff and Stiglitz (1983a,b) and Harris and Holmström (1982) show, competition allows relative performance evaluation in agency problems. The owner is better off since he obtains more information and incentive schemes are stronger, but effort change is nonmonotonic because it depends on the cost of implementing incentive schemes (e.g., on the underlying distribution of signals). This type of yardstick competition generally requires significant information about the individual performance of other firms, as well as knowledge of the characteristics of the other firms in order to filter relevant information from the market.

Hart (1983) considers a situation where managers have high or low productivity and can exert effort to achieve profit targets. He introduces an index of competition by assuming that in addition to managerial firms, neoclassical firms are present in the market. For neoclassical firms, productivity is observable; this implies that neoclassical firms produce a high output level when productivity is high and a low output level when productivity is low. If there is cost correlation across firms, when the managers' type is high, the presence of neoclassical firms will increase the supply in the market and therefore put downward pressure on prices, making it more difficult for managers to hide their type, eventually leading them to exert more effort.

The product market price transmits information about the fundamentals of the economy. While Hart (1983) shows that there is indeed a positive effect of competition (measured by the mass of neoclassical firms in the market) on effort provision, Scharfstein (1988) shows that the opposite result can be achieved if we abandon the assumption of infinite risk aversion made in Hart (1983): in this case, a lower product market price may actually make the monetary transfer to the manager costlier, and lower effort provision becomes optimal for owners.

Schmidt (1997) departs from yardstick competition or cost correlation, and, as in the corporate finance literature (e.g., Aghion and Bolton 1992), considers a model where owners may decide to close down the firm and bankruptcy creates an opportunity cost for managers—the loss of private benefits for instance. Effort of the manager takes the form of a reduction in the probability that the cost of production is high; more effort makes it less likely that profits are low. Owners observe the cost realization and a signal about the market environment; they can therefore compute the expected profit of the firm if they decide not to liquidate. A low cost will lead to positive profits, but a high cost will lead to negative profits if the signal is low enough. Therefore, there is bankruptcy only if there is high cost and the signal is low. Anticipating this, the manager chooses his effort, trading off his cost of effort and the private loss from bankruptcy. In this framework, more competition implies a higher probability of bankruptcy (e.g., a first-order stochastic shift in the signal distribution).

Contrary to Hart (1983) and Scharfstein (1988) who focus on an insurance-incentive trade-off, Schmidt (1997) considers risk-neutral managers with limited liability and focuses on a rent extraction-incentive trade-off. Depending on the outside option of the manager, the individual rationality (IR) condition may or may not bind in the optimal contract. When the IR condition binds, the owners are forced to provide more attractive compensation to the manager to meet his outside option; in turn, this leads to higher effort provision. By contrast, when the individual rationality constraint does not bind, the owners do not need to compensate the manager for the increasing risk of bankruptcy since he is already getting a rent. If the difference between the expected profits with low and high costs decreases when there is more competition, the marginal benefit of high effort decreases from the owner's point of view. This rent reallocation effect of competition may then induce the owners to implement a lower effort for the manager.

The essence of the link between competition and incentives can be captured in the following simple example, where we abstract from competition per se and represent the firm's environment, which it views as exogenous, by a parameter π that varies positively with demand or the market price or inversely with the degree of competition. Consider a "firm" (principal-agent relationship) in which the agent exerts effort $a \in [0,1]$ at quadratic cost $G(a) = a^2/2$, has a zero outside option, and is protected by limited liability. There are two periods; effort generates a *high* or *low* signal at the end of the first period; the probability of the high signal is a. A high signal indicates that the output in the second period will be 1, a low signal that it will be $1/4$. Beside effort, there are no other costs of production. Therefore the profit from production is π after a high signal and $\pi/4$ after a low signal.

At the beginning of period 2 the principal may liquidate the unit and obtain a value of L for its assets; to simplify, this liquidation value is independent of π. If the firm continues to produce in the second period, the agent obtains a private benefit of B, which is also independent of π.[4]

A wage contract in the first period is a pair $(0, w)$ of wages contingent on the signal observed; by limited liability wages must be nonnegative, and standard arguments show that 0 is the optimal wage in case of a low signal; w, to be determined is the wage following a high signal.[5] If $\pi < L$, the firm will be liquidated independently of the signal; hence the principal sets $w = 0$, the agent exerts effort $a = 0$, and there is no output produced. There are therefore two possible regimes with positive production in the second period:

- If $L < \pi < 4L$, the firm is liquidated only after a low signal. In this case, the expected utility of the agent is $U^A = a(w + B) - G(a)$ and that of the principal is $U^P = a(\pi - w) + (1-a)L$. The agent's optimal effort level is $a = w + B$: substituting $w = a - B$ in the principal's utility, we have $U^P = a\pi + (1-a)L - a(a - B)$ which is maximized at $\frac{\pi - L + B}{2}$, but because we have $w = a - B$, limited liability together with $a \leq 1$ imply that the optimal choice of effort for the principal is $a^*(\pi) = \min\left\{\max\left\{\frac{\pi - L + B}{2}, B\right\}, 1\right\}$.
- If $\pi > 4L$, the firm is not liquidated after either signal and the expected utility of the agent is $U^A = aw + B - G(a)$. The agent will get the private benefit for any signal, and therefore his optimal effort is $a = w$. It follows that $U^P = a(\pi - a) + (1 - a)\pi/4$ while $U^A = \frac{a^2}{2} + B$. Hence the unconstrained optimum for the principal is $a^*(\pi) = \frac{3\pi}{8}$ if $\pi \leq 8/3$ and is $a = 1$ if $\pi \geq 8/3$.

For prices between $\pi = L$ and $\pi = 4L$, incentives are already provided by the threat to liquidate in case of a low signal: high incentives for effort provision may

---

[4] Since B is not contractible and the agent has no wealth, there is no scope for renegotiation: the agent cannot "bribe" the principal for not liquidating the firm.

[5] Note that because incentives for the agent are the strongest when the firm is liquidated in the low state, the principal has no reason to try to commit not to liquidate the assets when the signal is *l*.

be easily provided because the minimum effort the agent would take is equal to B. By contrast, for prices higher than $\pi = 4L$, incentives must be provided by high wages, which come out of the profits of the principal, simply because he cannot punish the agent by committing to liquidate. If the private benefit is large enough relative to the liquidation value, the effort level may be non-monotonic with respect to π, consistent with the results in the literature where liquidation threat is endogenous to the degree of competition. For instance if $B = 1, L = 1/2$, effort is equal to zero for $\pi \leq 1/2$, to 1 for $\pi \in (1/2, 2)$, to $3\pi/8$ for $\pi \in (2, 8/3)$, and to 1 for π greater than $8/3$. We will see in section 3 that this nonmonotonicity in effort has nontrivial consequences for the industry supply.

2.1.2 Applications

P-A Firms in Spatial Oligopolies Raith (2003) analyzes a free entry oligopoly model on a Salop circle where firms are P-A relationships in a linear-normal-exponential environment: the principal is risk neutral, the agent is risk averse with CARA utility, profits are shared linearly, and the cost realization has a normal distribution with a mean decreasing with effort. As is well known, in such a setting riskier signals about the agent's effort result in weaker incentives being provided. Empirical work on this link is in fact less assertive on this point (e.g., Lafontaine and Slade 2007 who collect the empirical evidence; see also Prendergast 2002 and Ackerberg and Botticini 2002). Raith's model reconciles the empirical results by emphasizing two types of risks that have opposite influence on effort provision. First, there is the usual agent's risk in P-A models implying that a noisier environment makes incentives less powerful. However, there is also a firm's risk, since the variance of profits is also a function of the shocks. More risk may deter entry, increasing profitability for the incumbents and therefore encouraging them to provide higher powered incentives. Taking both effects into account may yield nonmonotonicities similar to those found by Schmidt (1997) or Scharfstein (1988).

Industrial Policy Aghion et al. (1997) point out that organizational firms—subject to agency problems—are affected in an opposite way than neoclassical firms by industrial policy or competition policy (see also Aghion et al. 1999). For instance, competition policy (assumed to lead to an increase in the number of firms) will tend to decrease the R&D effort of neoclassical firms – the Schumpeterian effect – but will lead to an increase in the effort of organizational firms – the Machlup effect we have discussed previously. This suggests that property right considerations may indeed change the way industrial policy should be conducted. However, ownership boundaries are exogenous in this work, which may limit the robustness of the policy conclusions.

2.1.3 Evidence

The agency approach and the theoretical ambiguity between competition and different aspects of organization have inspired a significant amount of empirical research (see the recent book Aghion and Griffith 2008 for a survey of that literature). For example, Nickell et al. (1997) finds that competition and corporate governance may be substitutes. Guadalupe and Wulf (2010) finds that increasing competitiveness following a trade reform resulted in significant "flattening" of reporting structures inside firms as well as higher powered executive pay. Cunat and Guadalupe (2005, 2009) obtain similar findings, using changes in exchange rates to show that the power of executive pay schemes increases with the degree of competition. Variation in takeover regulation allows Giroud and Müeller (2009) to uncover a positive relationship between competitiveness (Herfindahl index) and cost performance. In contrast to these "monotonic" empirical findings, which possibly reflect insufficient data variation, Aghion et al. (2006) provide evidence that the degree of vertical integration may have an inverted-U relationship with the level of product market competition.

2.1.4 What Have We Learned?

A common theme in these papers is that changing market conditions, like a downward pressure on prices, may increase effort provision *assuming that the incentive scheme is kept constant* but may also discourage the owners, or whoever is responsible for defining the incentive scheme, from offering strong incentive schemes. If the latter effect is strong enough, it may overturn the benefits of competition for the provision of effort in organizational firms. It is therefore the *endogeneity of incentive schemes* that introduces nonmonotonicity into the relationship between competition and organizational design.

This last point is of fundamental importance to the development of a more general organizational IO, one that goes beyond models of the firm as a P-A relationship. For instance, vertical and lateral integration, which surely are among the leading candidates for OIO treatment, may be subject to similar theoretical nonmonotonicities. A more general message from the literature we have reviewed so far is that external forces shape organizational choice, and one may have to look outside the firm in order to understand how it is organized.

2.2 Ownership, Internal Organization, and Contracts as Strategic Variables in Oligopolies

Because internal organization has an effect on a firm's performance, it also affects the best responses of firms in strategic settings and could be construed as yet another tool in firms' strategic portfolios, along with prices, capacity, advertising, or R&D investments, and so on. For instance, one may be tempted to think of internal organizational choices that are output-enhancing as a commitment to be a more aggressive competitor, very much as a cost-reducing investment is a commitment to produce more.

Part of the literature has looked at the problem of using delegation as commitment in oligopolies. However, it has also been pointed out that because delegation decisions, like other aspects of organizational design, are endogenous, and in particular flexible and renegotiable, they may have limited commitment value. Hence internal organization should not be treated at the same level as other variables like R&D or capacity building. This makes OIO quite challenging in oligopoly settings and also begs the question of whether internal organization would matter in the absence of market power.

Another strand of literature addresses the possibility of commitment through financial contracts. There, debt may serve as a foreclosure instrument in imperfectly competitive settings. But as the corporate finance and macro literatures make clear, the importance of debt extends far beyond its role in bolstering market power.

Ownership rights may also create commitment, particularly when ownership is understood as in Grossman-Hart-Moore (GHM) to be coupled with the right to make decisions, including the right to design the organization and incentive scheme: the owner can then commit to decisions that are sequentially rational for him or her, subject to potential renegotiations. However, ownership may also restrict the ability not to interfere with other agents' decisions, which constrains the design of internal organization, in particular delegation of tasks (Aghion and Tirole 1997; Baker et al. 1999).[6]

Independently of their theoretical roles as commitment devices, delegation and debt have received little attention from industrial policy makers. Not so for integration, which attracts immediate scrutiny by antitrust authorities. We review the literature on integration as a foreclosure instrument in the second subsection. Here, as in the literatures on delegation and debt, imperfect competition is a key element of the analysis, and this prompts the question of whether integration decisions could be "inefficient" in competitive settings.

---

[6] For instance, lack of ownership may limit the desire of inventors to share their idea with a financier or an expert for fear of being expropriated. Biais and Perotti (2008) argue that joint ownership by the inventor and the expert serves as a commitment to share information and for the expert not to steal that information. However, this commitment value disappears for "really good" ideas. Also in the context of R&D, Aghion et al. (2008) argue that differences in control rights allocations between the private and the public sector effectively create a boundary between fundamental or early stage research and development or later stage research and serves as a commitment device for scientists to pursue their own interests for fundamental research.

2.2.1 *Strategic Commitment Devices: Delegation and Debt*

Delegation Following an influential paper by Fershtman and Judd (1987) (see also Vickers 1985; Sklivas 1987), a series of papers has considered the possibility that owners delegate strategic decisions to managers while at the same time controlling these decisions by using incentive schemes.[7] Fershtman and Judd (1987) consider incentive schemes in a Cournot oligopoly where the variable part is a convex combination of the profit π_i and the sales S_i made by the firm; that is, the manager's compensation is proportional to $\alpha\pi_i + (1 - \alpha)S_i$. For simplicity, consider a duopoly. After each firm's owners choose α_1, α_2, managers then choose their individual quantities q_1, q_2. The owners then can choose whether to observe quantities, but yardstick competition is not allowed. One reason for delegation could be the managers' superior information about the demand level, something they will learn after incentive contracts are agreed on.

In this framework, if $1 - \alpha$ is positive, a manager will be more aggressive in increasing sales; by contrast if $1 - \alpha$ is negative, managers will want to reduce sales. However, if firm 1 has $1 - \alpha_1 < 0$, the owners of firm 2 will want to provide sales incentives ($\alpha_2 < 1$) to their manager to push firm 1's manager to decrease his quantities further; anticipating this, firm 1's owners should provide sales incentives to their manager for otherwise they will lose market share. Hence, in the equilibrium of the incentive game between owners, both α_i are less than 1. It follows that the commitment to an incentive scheme prior to quantity choices of managers eventually leads to higher output levels and lower profit levels for the owners than when there is no delegation. The authors also consider environments with differentiated goods or uncertainty about costs; in the latter case they can show that as the number of firms becomes large, equilibrium incentive schemes converge to $\alpha = 1$, that is, managers behave in a profit-maximizing way.[8]

Fershtman and Judd (1987) endogenize the behavior of firms in choosing profit maximization or sales maximization, and therefore complete the literature of the 60s that assumed rather than derived a non–profit-maximizing behavior of firms. However, their analysis begs the question of commitment of owners to incentive schemes. Indeed, the explicit assumption of observability of incentive schemes by all firms and the implicit assumption that owners do not renegotiate the contract with managers are de facto creating commitment but are often

---

[7] This idea of using contracting with third parties to commit to actions is also present in Brander and Lewis (1986)

[8] Reitman (1993) has shown that when managerial contracts can also include stock options, Cournot outcomes can be restored. On the role of managerial compensation and stock options for dynamic competition see Spagnolo (2000) who shows, theoretically, that deferred stock options facilitate collusion since they effectively make the managers more patient.

strong assumptions (see Dewatripont 1988; Caillaud et al. 1995 for the possibility of using contracts as precommitments when renegotiating contracts cannot be prevented).

In an incomplete contract framework, if ex ante contracts cannot be made contingent on future state realizations, delegation rights must be independent of the state realization (by assumption) while ownership provides more flexibility ex post, in particular on whether individual divisions should be delegated the right to decide in a particular state. The *decision to delegate* is therefore a function of the ownership structure and the "owner" may prefer to wait to delegate than to commit to do so in the initial contract (if commitment is possible). This is a point that is well understood in the applications of incomplete contracting to corporate finance (e.g., Aghion and Bolton 1992; Dewatripont and Tirole 1994), but that is somewhat obscured in simple models since issues of delegation are brought in from an internal organization perspective while issues of (ownership) integration are brought in from a boundary of the firm perspective. This link may be more apparent when there are many dimensions on which to decide[9] or when there is a dynamic relationship between owners and managers. For instance, legal rights can be transferred to another party for some dimensions only or an agent may retain the ability to take noncontractible actions that affect the quality of the final product independently of ownership (see Legros and Newman 2008 for a model along these lines).

In imperfectly competitive markets, Wickelgren (2005) shows that the owner may want to create competition between two divisions that produce differentiated products. This balances effort incentives versus internal price competition, leading to a situation similar to what would happen with nonintegration and yardstick competition for managers. Alonso et al. (2008) assume commitment to decision rights allocations in a model where a unique price has to be set for two divisions producing differentiated products with linear demand functions and where managers have private information about the level of the demand. If there is delegation, the right to choose the price is given to the manager facing the flattest demand function, but delegation arises only if the slopes of the demand functions are sufficiently different.

Commitment to delegation therefore supposes that the owners have protected the manager to whom they delegate from interfering with his decisions. This could be done by transferring the legal right to make decisions on the asset (which is very close to ownership). It could also be done for incentive compatibility reasons.

Lafontaine and Slade (2007) is one of the few papers considering ownership as a strategic variable. This is done in the specific context of franchising,

---

[9] Or as in Tadelis (2002) when the "design" is complex and requires ex post adjustments.

where the owner of an intangible asset (e.g., the McDonald's brand) benefits when franchisees make specific investments. They show that the owner may want to have independent franchisees to provide a yardstick to evaluate the performance of franchises he owns. This is one rationale for what we will soon call "endogenous heterogeneity" in organizational forms.

Returning to the issue of commitment, Aghion and Tirole (1997) and Baker et al. (1999) articulate two different mechanisms by which an owner may indeed commit not to overturn decisions made by an employee if there is delegation. In Aghion and Tirole (1997), it is because the employee may have (endogenously) better information and they show that in some instances it is better to give an agent "real authority" than to give him "legal or formal authority": real authority means that decisions made by the agent will not be overruled by the principal, whereas formal or legal authority means that the principal cannot intervene in the decision made by the agent. The cost of giving formal authority to the agent is the loss of control when the principal knows that the decision taken is not the right one, the benefit is that it increases the incentives of the agent to acquire information. In Baker et al. (1999), commitment not to interfere with decisions made by agents under delegation is sustained through relational contracting, and they show when this is better than the legal commitment generated by divestiture.

Finally, outside regulation as corporate governance guidelines may constrain the internal organization of firms and the possibility to mitigate the conflict of interests between different stakeholders. There is a recent literature on the role that corporate governance may play and its relation to competition (see for instance, Vives 2000; Allen and Gale 2000). Some "natural experiments" (Bertrand and Mullainathan 2003; Giroud and Müller 2009) suggest that managers are indeed pursuing a "quiet life": after regulation that prevents takeovers or sales of assets, there seems to be a significant increase in input costs, including workers salaries, and therefore managerial discretion seems indeed to be a source of cost inflation in firms. The results in Giroud and Müeller (2009) suggest that the effect is more pronounced in less competitive industries (as measured by the Herfindahl index),[10] but they do not seem to control for the potential changes in internal organization or incentive schemes that may have followed the regulatory change.

Debt Jensen and Meckling (1976) have highlighted the agency cost of debt: borrowers will tend to discount low profit realizations and may therefore engage in projects that have a negative present value. Yet as we have seen in section 2.1,

---

[10] The use of the Herfindahl index for measuring the intensity of competition is borrowed from the Cournot model but is not necessarily a good measure for other market structures, or, as Farrell and Shapiro (1990) have argued, when assets can be traded.

increasing the risk of bankruptcy may also serve as a disciplining device for managers in agency models and Grossman and Hart (1982) show that debt can be used as a bonding device in P-A models since the risk of bankruptcy increases in the case of low profit realizations. In an influential paper Brander and Lewis (1986) argue that there is a nontrivial relationship between the debt-equity ratios and the performance of a duopoly: on one side, debt will induce firms to discard profits in low states that lead to bankruptcy and therefore pursue strategies that increase the profit levels in the good states but, on the other side, firms will pursue strategies that give them a competitive advantage and drive out of the market other firms that have a high debt-equity ratio. This leads to more aggressive behavior in Cournot oligopolies and less aggressive behavior in Bertrand oligopolies, but in both cases the profit increases with the use of debt.

While the result that debt makes oligopolistic firms more aggressive has been challenged by different authors, both theoretically and empirically.[11] the general idea that financial structure has consequences for the strategic behavior of firms is an important message for IO (see the recent survey by Lyandres 2006).

In this literature, financial contracting would have no role to play absent market power. By contrast, Bolton and Scharfstein (1990) make financial contracts a necessary instrument of entry by firms: entrepreneurs may need to borrow to invest in capital expansion or plant creation. Financial contracting is imperfect because repayment cannot be made contingent on output realizations. While the costly state verification problem prevents financial contracting in a static framework, when there is more than one period the threat of closing the firm if it claims to have low output can generate incentives for repayment. In this

---

[11] As Showalter (1995) shows, the effect of debt on strategic behavior depends not only on the substitution or complementarity of the strategic variables but also on the type of uncertainty firms face. Brander and Lewis (1986) consider demand uncertainty, and Showalter (1995) shows that with cost uncertainty firms become less aggressive. Faure-Grimaud (2000) considers endogenous financial contracts and shows that the Brander and Lewis (1986) effect of debt making firms more aggressive competitors is offset by the cost of financial instruments in a Cournot oligopoly. Povel and Raith (2004) also consider endogenous debt contracts and introduce an expected cost of liquidation that is increasing in the amount of default: this makes the equity holder liable for low-profit states and reduces the agency cost of debt, which would suggest that firms with debt may be less aggressive. Jacob (1994) shows that issuing long-term debt may be an instrument for collusion: since contrary to Brander and Lewis (1986) firms are engaged in a long-term competition, high profit realizations make the firm less aggressive since the opportunity cost of competitive wars, following deviations from collusion, is larger. The difference of results is illustrative of the different predictions in oligopoly theory when one goes from a static analysis to a dynamic analysis: in general, "bad" equilibrium outcomes in a static setting, like more aggressively in setting low prices, help in a dynamic context since they provide a credible punishment in the case of deviations.

On the empirical side, Chevalier (1995) uses supermarket data and shows that an LBO announcement has a positive effect on the market value of competitors, suggesting that debt softens competition; see also Dasgupta and Titman (1998).

framework, finance has an active role to play, whether or not there is market power, but in the latter case, finance leads to a rationale for predation. Indeed, if another firm in the industry does not need to borrow for entry, because it has "deep pockets," it may engage in predation by increasing the probability of low output levels and therefore forcing the other firm into bankruptcy for lack of debt repayment. Optimal financial contracts now balance this threat of predation and the agency problem due to the state verification problem. This paper is representative of the literature combining finance and IO (see also Fudenberg and Tirole 1986; Katz 1991).

In section 3.3, we will discuss something that the literature rarely addresses, which is the use of side payments needed to reallocate surplus in contractual negotiations, including the transfer of ownership rights. Broaching it directly opens up novel issues concerning the relationship between liquidity distribution and organizational choices in an industry.

2.2.2 *Using Integration to Foreclose Competitors*

Policy makers long suspected that mergers might be motivated primarily by the firms' desire to enhance their market power. While the argument is not difficult to grasp in the horizontal case, the theoretical case for vertical foreclosure resisted formal treatment for a surprisingly long time. Arguably, by the time it was successfully broached, the Chicago school, bolstered in part by arguments for the productivity benefits of vertical integration advanced by Klein et al. (1978) and Williamson (1971, 1975, 1985), had succeeded in allaying antitrust authorities' fears, for the merger guidelines with respect to vertical integration had become fairly lax. Nevertheless the theoretical cases are worth examining, because they hint at how a full OIO analysis of the simultaneous determination of market structure and firm boundaries may proceed.

Hart and Moore (1990) provide one of the first formal treatments of the role of integration as a foreclosure instrument. In their basic model, two downstream firms $D1$, $D2$ sell a homogeneous product under constant returns and can produce one unit of output for each unit of input they buy. Contracts between an upstream firm U and a downstream firm for the provision of input levels can be in two-part tariffs, thereby eliminating the traditional IO "double marginalization" motive for integration, and it is not possible to for a downstream firm to write contracts preventing the upstream firm from selling to another downstream firm, to abstract from exclusive dealing (later this assumption is relaxed when they compare integration to exclusive dealing). Nevertheless contracts are incomplete, in that there is a large number of possible input types and uncertainty over which one will be appropriate to trade, making it too costly to write contingent trade and pricing contracts. Allocating control over assets is therefore the only way to influence ex post behavior, in particular, pricing of the input.

When the two downstream firms are separate units, even a monopoly upstream seller cannot obtain more profit than is generated under Cournot competition. Indeed, for any quantity of input q_1 purchased by D_1, the monopolist U maximizes his revenue from selling inputs to $D2$ by offering that firm $q_2 = B_2(q_1)$, the best response of $D2$ to q_1; anticipating this, $D1$ will be willing to pay at most $\pi_1(q_1, B_2(q_1))$ to U. If $D2$ has the same expectations, it is optimal for U to offer the Cournot quantities to the downstream firms. If however U integrates with $D1$, the merged entity will internalize the profit made by $D1$ and therefore will prefer to sell the monopoly quantity and not to supply $D2$: integration generates commitment not to sell to the other downstream firm. As Hart and Tirole argue, the commitment generated by integration is superior to that of exclusive contracting clauses because it allows for greater flexibility. For instance, if there is another, less efficient, upstream supplier $U2$, an integrated firm $(U1, D1)$ can compete with $U2$ to serve $D2$, something that an exclusive contract would not allow. A "contingent" contract that would limit the quantities sold to $D2$ may also be difficult to implement in practice since it requires a high degree of information.[12]

They generalize their model to allow for fixed costs of entry or operation by upstream and downstream firms and profit sharing in case of integration. They show that more efficient firms have more incentives to integrate, which in turn leads to a "bandwagon" effect that leads the other upstream-downstream pair to integrate as well: since the profits of the nonintegrated downstream firm decrease, absent integration, this firm may exit; it is then in the interest of the other upstream firm to integrate with it and share the costs of investment to rescue its market.

In other variants of the basic model, Hart and Tirole consider situations where each upstream firm has a fixed capacity upstream ("scarce supplies") or downstream ("scarce needs"), while each D_i needs only one unit of input. Integration modifies the bargaining positions of the parties: integrated firms have a higher bargaining power since they benefit from supply assurance and therefore the nonintegrated firms will tend to have lower profits and lower incentives to invest.

The analysis highlights the importance of endogenizing rather than assuming commitment and entry, as was done in the literature. For instance, in the symmetric case where the upstream firms have the same marginal cost of production,

---

[12] See McAfee et al. (1989) and Marx and Shaffer (2004) for an analysis of the possibility of commitment through nondiscrimination clauses. See also Segal (1999, 2003) for a general analysis of contracting with externalities.

Ordover et al. (1990) show that integration is beneficial, in contrast to the results in Hart and Tirole (1990). This is because the ability of the integrated firm to commit not to supply to the other downstream firm eliminates competition between the upstream firms to supply to the other downstream firms, eventually benefitting both the integrated firm and the other upstream firm.[13]

Bolton and Whinston (1993) show that in a multilateral situation integration may serve the dual role of protecting a party from opportunism ex post and reinforcing market power of the party with scarce resources. Suppose that each of $D1, D2$ needs a unit of input but that U has a single unit to distribute. Downstream firms make investments x_1, x_2 at cost $c(x_i)$. The willingness to pay of consumers for a product can be either high, and equal to $v_H(x)$ or low and equal to $v_L(x)$, where $\max_x v_L(x) < \min_x v_H(x)$.

The demand realizations are perfectly correlated: with equal probability demand realizations are $(v_H(x_1), v_L(x_2))$ or $(v_L(x_1), v_H(x_2))$. Allocating the input to the downstream firm facing the highest willingness to pay of consumers is efficient and total welfare is $\frac{1}{2}v_H(x_1) + \frac{1}{2}v_H(x_2) - c(x_1) - c(x_2)$. Therefore the marginal incentives for investment of the firms are $c'(x_i) = \frac{1}{2}v'_H(x_i)$. With nonintegration, each downstream firm will compete for the input à la Bertrand, and therefore the highest value firm will pay the second highest value; hence conditional on having the highest value the net surplus of downstream firm D_1 is $v_H(x_1) - v_L(x_2)$ and his expected payoff is $\frac{1}{2}(v_H(x_1) - v_L(x_2)) - c(x_1)$ implying the same marginal incentive to invest as in the social optimum. Hence investment levels with nonintegration are efficient.

But while nonintegration leads to efficient investment levels, it is not always stable, since the upstream firm and a downstream firm may strictly gain by integrating. Suppose that $U, D1$ integrate; the vertical structure has a surplus of $v_H(x_1)$ with probability $1/2$ (in this case $D2$ does not produce) and a surplus of $v_L(x_1)$ with probability $1/2$ ($D2$ purchases the input from the vertical structure at the opportunity value of $v_L(x_1)$). Hence the expected surplus of the vertical

---

[13] The literature has embraced the idea that integration facilitates commitment. For instance, O'Brien and Shaffer (1992) consider the case of a single upstream producers and downstream firms competition à la Bertrand (hence avoiding the usual "double marginalization" motive for integration). They assume that the upstream firm cannot commit to recontracting and therefore that retail prices will be smaller than under integration, even if the upstream firm can choose two-part tariffs, providing a new rationale for vertical restraints linked to contract incompleteness. Alexander and Reiffen (1995) identify the strategic values of different price and nonprice vertical restraints, as well as the role of external enforcement mechanisms, like regulation. Schmitz and Sliwka (2001) assumes that the supplier of a good can invest to enhance quality, which will increase the value to the buyer and also the residual value of the asset in case bargaining fails, and in a degree of specificity, which also enhances the value of the good to the buyer but decreases the residual value in case of failure of bargaining. Integration depresses incentives to invest but increases specificity, while nonintegration has opposite effects.

structure is $\frac{1}{2}(v_H(x_1) + v_L(x_1)) - c(x_1)$: the marginal incentive to invest increases by $v'_L(x_1)/2$ with respect to nonintegration. Note that the incentives to invest of $D2$ are the same as with nonintegration since he has the same expected surplus function. However, because the investment of $D1$ increases, the equilibrium value of $D2$ decreases (and by a larger amount than the equilibrium payoff to the vertical structure increases since investment choices are not first best).

These papers combine two effects present in the literature: an efficiency motive for integration (see Lafontaine and Slade 2007 for a survey of the literature) and market foreclosure or raising rivals' cost strategic considerations. Empirically, it is difficult to disentangle the two effects; for instance, highly concentrated markets are prone to foreclosure effects but are also often also characterized by relation-specific investments, implying therefore also an efficiency role for integration (see the discussion of the different results in the empirical literature in Joskow 2010).

3. OIO: Questions for the Future

Despite the long history of contact between theories of the firm based on incomplete contracting and IO, the two areas are far from integrated, so to speak. One view would be that this is just fine: organizational considerations are brought in when they are most naturally needed, as for merger activity or for understanding when vertical integration may lead to foreclosure. Complementary to this view is the position that incorporating richer views of the firm into models of market power will make things much more complicated without adding much new insight beyond what one could obtain by maintaining this "arm's length relationship" between organizational economics and industrial organization.

What these positions fail to address is whether the imperfections inside firms that make organizational design relevant can *by themselves* generate insights, explanations, and testable implications that are not predicated on market power. To test the waters, we shall assume away market power altogether, and consider an environment of price-taking competition. The exercise shows that incomplete contracting can shed light on at least the following basic questions:

- **How does organizational design affect the most basic economic quantities** of interest to IO economists, namely, prices, quantities and consumer welfare?
- **Can market conditions affect organizational design** in the absence of market power, and if so, how?
- **Can we explain heterogeneity** of organizational forms with its accompanying productivity differences among firms?

- **Can OIO provide a practical proving ground** for competing organizational theories?
- **How does an organizational industry differ from a neoclassical one** in the way it absorbs and propagates shocks to fundamentals?
- **What are the policy implications** of the answers to these questions?

Neither space nor the present state of knowledge permit complete discussion of answers to all of these questions. But recent models in the literature and the rudimentary representations and extensions that we present here provide grounds for optimism that these questions can be usefully addressed.

3.1 An OIO Example

Consider as a building block the model of Hart and Holmström (2010) (HH) where final goods are produced with two complementary inputs; call them *A* and *B*. Input suppliers are an indivisible collection of assets and workers, overseen by a manager. During the course of the relationship, ex ante noncontractible production decisions will have to be made. The important point is that these decisions need to be coordinated to enhance output: it is not so important what decision is chosen in each unit, as long as it fits what is happening in the other.[14] The organizational problem arises from a conflict of interest over what decision is optimal. For instance, if *A* represents product development and *B* manufacturing, then product designs that are easy for *A* to develop may be difficult for *B* to manufacture, and vice versa. This could be an effect of the nature of technology, the result of past training and experience, a concern over reputation, or even a difference in beliefs about the best course of action (i.e., "vision").

Thus, if each retains control over his own decisions (which is interpreted as nonintegration), there will tend to be poor coordination: if the two managers were to maximize profit by picking perfectly matched actions, each would want to deviate by moving (at least slightly) in his preferred direction. The coordination problem can be "solved" via integration. HH depart from G-H in a second way here, by assuming that integration involves a sale of assets not to one of *A*, *B* but rather to a third-party professional manager who then acquires decision rights over both *A* and *B*. The professional manager is concerned only about the enterprise's revenue and will therefore have incentives to maximize it by perfectly coordinating decisions. The problem is that this imposes costs on the *A* and *B* managers in terms of private benefits.

---

[14] In contrast to Grossman and Hart (1986), HH assume that ex post bargaining with unlimited side transfers is not feasible since agents use contracts as reference points and would feel aggrieved if they do not get the best outcome under the initial contract.

Note the potential significance of this model in light of some recent empirical work by Atalay et al. (2012). They survey intrafirm shipping data for U.S. manufacturers. The surprising finding is that among domestic firms, very few of the inputs produced by one subsidiary are shipped to other subsidiaries of the same firm, implying that vertical integration does not comprise single supply chains (for multinational firms, the traditional picture, wherein one subsidiary produces an input that is consumed by the next firm in the chain, does seem to hold up). Rather, the picture of vertically integrated firms that emerges is that of a portfolio of input suppliers, with each subsidiary selling to its own market, in which the common owner provides certain (unmeasured) managerial services. While these findings are controversial, if true, they may cast some doubt on the empirical relevance of the hold-up problem as a major determinant of firm boundaries, at least among U.S. domestic manufacturers.

The HH model is consistent with these findings, and indeed with Atalay et al.'s own explanation for vertical integration as a conduit for (unobserved by them) managerial services. Several suppliers that are related because they produce complementary goods but are not actually transacting with each other might nevertheless benefit from services that conform to a single style or fit a common standard, say for brand recognition, marketing and distribution, logistics and so on. But it is harder to see how a hold-up problem could arise or spot adaptation decisions would need to be made if the input produced by A is not actually being shipped to B in equilibrium. This does not mean, of course, that hold-up problems are irrelevant. But incomplete contract models articulated around a trade-off between coordination of decisions versus private costs of these decisions may provide a reasonable and simple benchmark model for performing market analysis.

We now embed the basic model in a product market setting, along the lines of Legros and Newman (2013).[15] Consider a market composed of a large number of HH-style enterprises (A, B), each of which takes the market price P for the (single) product as given. The price is determined endogenously in the model

---

[15] Earlier attempts to explain the pattern of outsourcing in industries when there is incomplete contracting include McLaren (2000) and Grossman and Helpman (2002). Both papers proceed in the Williamsonian tradition where integration alleviates the hold-up problem at an exogenous fixed cost. McLaren (2000) observes that when the market for specialized inputs thickens, there are fewer opportunities for hold-up and therefore a greater tendency for nonintegration. This generates strategic complementarities between organizational choices and the possibility of multiple vertical industry equilibria. It also predicts that globalization, interpreted as market thickening, leads to nonintegration and outsourcing. Grossman and Helpman (2002) develop similar trade-offs in a monopolistic competition model with search frictions and study how parameters such as demand elasticities and search efficiency affect the choice of ownership structure. It also addresses the heterogeneity question, but in contrast to what we show below, it finds simultaneous presence of integration and nonintegration in an industry to be nongeneric.

via a market clearing condition, and A's are willing to participate as long as they have a nonnegative payoff. There are three noncontractible production "styles," $L, M,$ or R that can be adopted in each unit. If they make the same choice, the quantity produced is 1. If their choices differ by one (e.g., $\{L, M\}$) the output is $\lambda < 1$, by two ($\{L, R\}$) it is λ^2. A's costs of L, M, R are $0, c, C$, while B's are $C, c,$ 0 where $2 < \frac{C}{c} < \frac{1+\lambda}{\lambda}$.

A contract between an A and a B specifies an ownership structure, that is, whether the enterprise is integrated or not, and a fixed (independent of output but not necessarily of the ownership structure) transfer that A receives from B which is just large enough to induce A to participate (Legros and Newman 2013 considers general contingent sharing rules).

Under nonintegration, A and B choose their production decisions simultaneously once the fixed transfer has been made. Since the transfer is fixed, it has no effect on decision making, and we can therefore represent the payoffs in the postcontracting subgame by the matrix (A is the row player, B the column player)

Player B :

		L	M	R
	L	$0, P - C$	$0, \lambda P - c$	$0, \lambda^2 P$
Player A :	M	$-c, \lambda P - C$	$-c, P - c$	$-c, \lambda P$
	R	$-C, \lambda^2 P - C$	$-C, \lambda P - c$	$-C, P$

A's dominant strategy is to play L, and it is straightforward to verify that since the parametric assumptions on $\lambda, C,$ and c imply $\frac{C-c}{1-\lambda} < \frac{C}{1-\lambda^2} < \frac{c}{\lambda(1-\lambda)}$, B plays R when $P < \frac{C}{1-\lambda^2} \equiv \hat{P}$ and L when $P \geq \hat{P}$, yielding payoffs for B of $\lambda^2 P$ if $P < \hat{P}$ and $P - C$ if $P \geq \hat{P}$. Note that in this equilibrium A has a payoff of zero and therefore the transfer he receives is equal to zero.

Under integration, a professional manager with zero opportunity cost, whose payoff is increasing in income but is indifferent about $L, M,$ and R, purchases the assets via fixed transfers, thereby acquiring control of decisions and access to the revenue stream, which he maximizes. Since he is indifferent among $(L, L), (M, M), (R, R)$, we assume that he picks the efficient choice, which is (M, M), as $2c < C$.

Since A would incur a cost of c under integration, the transfer B pays is equal to c, and B's payoff is $P - 2c$. This exceeds B's payoff under nonintegration when fully conceding to A (i.e., playing L), which is $P - C$. However, as we have seen, B does not always want to concede under nonintegration. If $P - 2c < \lambda^2 P$, or $P < \frac{2c}{1-\lambda^2} \equiv P^* < \hat{P}$, then under nonintegration, the managers play (L, R), and B therefore prefers nonintegration. But if $P \geq P^*$, then integration is preferred by B to nonintegration, regardless of how it is played in equilibrium. Thus, *the choice of ownership structure depends on the market price.*

The reason for this result is very simple: at low prices $(P < P^*)$, nonintegration is not well coordinated and produces little, but this is of little consequence to the managers because extra output generated by integration valued at a low price would not offset the private costs. At moderate prices $(P^* < P < \hat{P})$, the gain in revenue from more efficient production is worth the higher private cost of integration. And at the highest prices, $(P > \hat{P})$, integration is chosen not because it is more productive in terms of output but because it imposes lower private costs on B who would otherwise concede fully to A.

Observe that when when $P \geq \hat{P}$, the "transaction cost" associated with nonintegration, that is, the cost of transacting across firm boundaries, is C, which is generated only from private costs. However, when $P < \hat{P}$, the transaction cost is $(1 - \lambda^2) P$, which results from lost output. Thus, *the nature as well as the size of the cost of transacting in the supplier market depends on the price in the product market.* Meanwhile transacting within firm boundaries (integration) always generates a private cost of $2c$. Since transaction costs depend on the price, so does the least-cost ownership structure, which as we noted above is integration when $P > P^*$ and nonintegration when $P < P^*$.

We turn now to the market equilibrium. Observe that an individual enterprise's supply correspondence is $\{\lambda^2\}$ for $P < P^*$, $\{1\}$ for $P > P^*$, and $\{\lambda^2, 1\}$ for $P = P^*$. Suppose that an industry is composed of a large number (continuum with unit measure) of enterprises just like this one. Then the industry supply will also be $\{\lambda^2\}$ for $P < P^*$ and $\{1\}$ for $P > P^*$, and will be $[\lambda^2, 1]$ for $P = P^*$.

This "organizationally augmented" supply (OAS) curve embodies not only the usual price-quantity trade-off, but also the organizational design: as we move along the supply starting at $P = 0$, we have nonintegration for $P < P^*$ and integration for $P > P^*$. Moreover, at $P = P^*$, managers are indifferent between the two ownership structures. Since any mix of nonintegrated and integrated firms would make managers happy at this price, the supply is "horizontal" there. See Figure 18.1, where we have also added a standard demand curve.

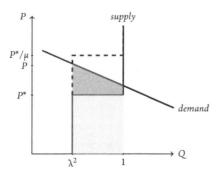

Figure 18.1 The Organizational Augmented Supply Curve $(\mu < 1)$

Note that the cost of production which is simply the managers' private costs is represented by the area under the supply curve: under nonintegration $(P < P^*)$ it is zero and under integration it is $2c$, which is equal to $(1 - \lambda^2)P^*$.

In the figure, we have also indicated the supply when firms are "managerial," in the sense that managers accrue only $\mu < 1$ of the revenue, with the rest accruing to shareholders. In this case, nonintegration is chosen for $\mu P < P^*$, integration for $\mu P > P^*$. It follows that the supply curve is now an "upward translation" (dashed in the figure) of the original supply. But cost is represented as before, by the area under the $\mu = 1$ supply.

The competitive market equilibrium condition, quantity supplied = quantity demanded, then determines not only price but also the ownership structures of all the enterprises. Thus in industry equilibrium, ownership structure determines supply while simultaneously demand determines ownership structure. We can now begin to provide answers to some of our questions:

- **Market conditions affect organizational design**. When demand is low, the enterprises will be nonintegrated. When it is high they will be integrated. Thus, just as in the vertical foreclosure literature discussed in section 2.2, *there is a positive correlation between integration and the price level*. However, here the causality runs the other way, from prices to integration.[16]
- **Organizational design affects industry performance**. This is implicit in the very shape of the OAS: since nonintegrated enterprises produce less than integrated ones, the choice of ownership structure has bearing on industry output and equilibrium price. In fact,
- **Competitive equilibrium ownership structures need not maximize welfare**. As long as there is separation of ownership and control $(\mu < 1)$, the market equilibrium is not generally surplus efficient. *The welfare loss is greater the more elastic is the demand*: this is the opposite of the relationship between demand elasticity and deadweight loss for a neoclassical monopoly. This suggests that corporate governance and policies to regulate it will have implications for *consumers* and industry performance.
- **Productivity-relevant organizational heterogeneity is endogenous**. For a "generic" set of demand curves the equilibrium price will be P^* and there will be simultaneously some integrated firms and some nonintegrated enterprises. Thus even though every enterprise is fundamentally identical, there is *heterogeneity of organization and concomitant heterogeneity in performance* (output).

[16] Mindful of this reverse causality, Alfaro et al. (2014) exploit variation in "most favored nation" import tariffs, which increase prices but are arguably exogenous to vertical integration, to show that price levels do affect the level of integration; at least within the range of variation of their data, their results show a positive relationship between integration and price, as in this model.

Heterogeneity of performance among firms has attracted an enormous amount of attention in several literatures, including IO and OE (see e.g., Gibbons 2006, 2010; Syverson 2011), and thus it is worthwhile investigating whether and to what extent ownership structure might account for it. On the qualitative side, the model suggests that endogenous differences in ownership structure may go part way toward explaining heterogeneity. On the quantitative side, the model also suggests that the degree of heterogeneity is clearly sensitive to demand: for low or high enough demands, there is uniformity of ownership structure, but in between most common measures of organizational or productivity variation would vary continuously with demand. Whether this or other organizational IO models could account for a substantial proportion of observed performance variation remains to be seen.

The endogenous heterogeneity result is a simple consequence of market clearing where there is a discontinuity in individual supply due to the performance differences of the two ownership structures.[17] Indeed, it is the performance difference that is responsible for the (genericity of) equilibrium heterogeneity: without it, the supply would be continuous and there would be no reason for firms not to have identical ownership structures.

3.2   OIO as a Proving Ground for Organization Theory

Although pertinent, the HH model is only one of many organizational models one could consider when trying to develop an OIO. Other models of organizations will tend to generate different relationships between IO variables, such as prices and quantities, and organizational variables, such as the degree of integration. In other words, one may have different OAS curves for different organizational models. We now provide two examples in which the predicted relationship among organizational and industry performance variables differ from the monotonic ones generated by the model in the previous subsection.

3.2.1   A Nonmonotonic Relationship between Price and Integration

As a first illustration, consider the previous model but assume now that integration entails a loss of productivity, which we represent by supposing that

---

[17] Another explanation for heterogeneity in organizational forms, also based on the inherent discreteness of integration choices, is offered by Gibbons et al. (2012), which views equilibrium heterogeneity in ownership structures as the result of a particular resolution to the "Grossman-Stiglitz problem" (Grossman and Stiglitz 1980). In their (rational expectations) model, market prices aggregate information, but depending on their ownership structure, that information is differentially generated by firms. Equilibrium requires that some firms invest in information gathering and some do not, which in turn entails that there is heterogeneity in ownership structure.

output under integration is $\sigma < 1$ times the output under nonintegration, given the same production choices. This could be a reduced-form representation of a number of organizational costs that have been discussed in the literature, including costs of communication within hierarchical organizations (see the survey by Dessein 2013); perfunctory managerial behavior in the face of HQ authority (as in the contractual literature on aggrievance, e.g., Hart and Moore 2008); influence activities by the managers trying to persuade the neutral HQ to decide things their way (Milgrom 1987); resource diversion by HQ itself; or many of the costs of integration cited by Williamson (1985).

This loss affects only integration, and surplus in this case is $\sigma P - 2c$. It is then straightforward to verify that when $P < \hat{P} \equiv \frac{C}{1-\lambda^2}$, integration dominates only if $P > P_0 \equiv \frac{2c}{\sigma-\lambda^2}$, and when $P > \hat{P}$, integration dominates only if $P < P_1 \equiv \frac{C-2c}{1-\sigma}$. It turns out that $P_0 < \hat{P}$ if and only if $\hat{P} < P_1$, and this happens whenever σ is not too small:

$$\sigma > \lambda^2 + (1 - \lambda^2)\frac{2c}{C}.$$

In this case, the organizational choice is not monotonic in price, since integration is chosen only when $P \in [P_0, P_1]$. Moreover, integration no longer outperforms nonintegration (in terms of profit, revenue or output). This raises the possibility that there can be "too much" integration as well as too little, even in a perfectly competitive environment: if managers and HQ claim only a share μ of revenue, as discussed, then for prices in between $\hat{P}/\mu$ and P_1/μ, there is integration even though nonintegration produces more output.

Beyond generating nonmonotonicity in organizational forms with respect to prices, this example highlights the importance of the managerial market in explaining organizational forms and industry performance. If σ is interpreted as "managerial skill," more skilled HQs increase the range $P_1 - P_0$ of prices in which integration occurs. The determination of ownership structure, particularly the degree of heterogeneity, may then be related to the supply of managerial talent.

3.2.2 A Nonmonotonic Industry Supply

In the example in section 2.1.1 there is a trade-off between the strength of incentives provided by the market and the provision of incentives within the firm, which affects the effort level of the agent. Suppose that π coincides with the market price P, and consider the special case of a private benefit of $B = 1$ and a liquidation value of $L = 1/2$. If the price is lower than $1/2$, the firm is always liquidated and the agent has no incentive to exert effort. If the price is in the interval $(1/2, 2)$, the firm is liquidated only if there is a low signal, making the agent willing to exert effort even if he does not have a wage incentive. When the price is greater than 2, however, the principal cannot commit to liquidate the firm, and incentives have to be provided via contingent wages. But such wages are costly for the principal, and for prices close to 2 he will not want to provide full incentives to the agent; as the price increases, the principal strengthens incentives. This creates a nonmonotonicity in effort level, but more telling a nonmonotonic industry supply curve, as illustrated in Figure 18.2.[18]

Embedding this simple P-A model into a market generates novel theoretical effects at the industry level. More important, the example suggests that empirical estimation of supply curves may offer a way to falsify specific organizational models.

3.3 Surplus Division and Financing Asset Purchases

Trading assets requires making compensatory transfers, but as we saw in section 2.2.1, agency problems or incomplete contracting make financing of ex ante transfers through debt or other financial contracts costly. Lump-sum transfers are almost universally more desirable. This is not a problem if enterprises have large amounts of cash, which is a strong assumption in most settings. This raises the question of what happens in the general case when cash endowments are small relative to the value of the transactions.

As we detail below, cash endowments have often played an important role in the literature, because cash facilitates the emergence of "efficient" organizations. However, because the analysis is often cast in a partial equilibrium framework (the role of cash for a given relationship), it ignores the change in the bargaining positions of the parties when *other* firms have different cash endowments. After

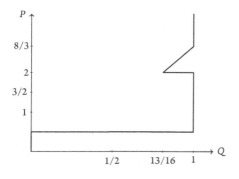

Figure 18.2 A Nonmonotonic Industry Supply

---

[18] De Meza and Southey (1999) provides an early example of a nonmonotonic OAS. It considers an environment in which the organizational choice involves the degree of input monitoring, as in Banerjee and Newman (1993) and Legros and Newman (1996). All three papers admit the possibility of coexistence of organizational forms and excessive monitoring in equilibrium.

a review of the literature we turn to a model in which the distribution of cash has consequences for the organization of the industry. In particular "more cash" on average does not necessarily imply "more efficient contracting" on average.

3.3.1 The Role of Cash Endowments in the Literature

Limited cash endowments is a central assumption in the corporate finance literature: it is one of the main reasons for an entrepreneur to engage into financial contracts. The literature has emphasized that some forms of financing may have better incentive effects than others, as in the debt versus equity comparison in Jensen (1986).

Organizational design involves assigning control rights and pecuniary payoffs in particular patterns. It was the chief insight of Aghion and Bolton (1992) to recognize that the same is true of financial contracts. For instance, debt and equity contracts have different ways of bundling ownership rights with return streams. Equity holders keep control of the firm's assets as long as they can repay the debt, in which case they obtain the residual stream of profits. If they cannot repay the debt, creditors obtain control, as well as the residual value, of the assets. Since control rights and return streams generate distinct incentives, debt and equity contracts may be dominated by financial securities that bundle control and return stream rights in other ways (e.g., Dewatripont and Tirole 1994). The literature on financial contracting, which is surveyed in Bolton (2013), shows that in general even the best designed financial security will be less efficient than a cash transfer.

In agency settings, it is well understood that agent's limited liability creates a rent extraction motive for the principal. For instance, even if the surplus maximizing ("first best") effort is implementable, the principal may choose to implement a smaller effort in order not to give rents to the agent. When the outside option of the agent is large, however, this rent extraction motive is disciplined, since the principal will need to give a sufficient share of the surplus to the agent. As we have seen earlier in the model of Schmidt (1997), whether the rent extraction motive is present has implications for whether the degree of product market competition covaries with the degree of managerial incentive provision. Hence, both the cash holdings and the bargaining positions (outside options) of the parties matter. While cash holdings can be observable, the bargaining positions of the stakeholders in the firm are more difficult to assess, and they are often a function of what happens outside the firm, in particular on what other firms do. This makes an OIO approach important for identifying the effects of limited cash holdings.

Beyond its effect on incentives in principal-agent models, the rent extraction motive also influences organizational choices and their efficiency. For instance, when the outside option of the agent is low, the principal may favor investing in a costly monitoring technology to avoid (or reduce) the moral hazard problem and paying rents to the agent, whereas when the outside option is high, the principal forgoes monitoring because the necessarily high expected wage he pays already provides incentives (Acemoglu and Newman 2002; Legros et al. forthcoming). In an incomplete contract framework, integration decisions may be a nontrivial function of the cash holdings of the parties and, as the moral hazard example suggests, of their bargaining positions.[19] This suggests that ownership allocation may be coupled with additional constraints on the use of the assets or on the design of the renegotiation process,[20] and that the macroeconomy, or any shock that may change the value of outside options, will affect ownership allocation and the performance of firms.

In an application to R&D ventures, Aghion and Tirole (1994) show theoretically how cash constraints distort contracting and allocation of property rights to parties involved in joint R&D efforts: if the research unit is cash constrained and does not have a strong bargaining power, the customer will not be willing to transfer ownership of the unit, despite the performance gain.

These papers focus on one relationship, assuming specific bargaining positions of the different parties. As we have argued, this limits the scope of positive analysis since bargaining positions are in general endogenous, reflect the organizational choices of other firms, and also reflect the distribution of cash endowment: in an equilibrium of the industry, bargaining positions and organizational choices are jointly determined. An illustration of this point is the role that the distribution of liquidity endowments may have on contractual choices in moral hazard settings.[21]

---

[19] De Meza and Lockwood (1998) show that in the Grossman and Hart (1986) model, if agents have outside options at the negotiation stage, many of the results are qualitatively different. For instance, ownership should not necessarily go to the agent whose investment is the "most important." See also Chiu (1998) who shows that *not having* ownership may increase investment incentives. The difference with Grossman and Hart (1986) and Hart and Moore (1990) is that they "bundle" outside options and threat point in the ex post bargaining while Chiu (1998) follows the bargaining literature tradition that views the outside option as the payoff to the agent if he *quits* the bargaining table while the threat point is the (discounted) payoff the bargainer obtains *before* negotiation is terminated. Having ownership leads to a high outside option and the bargaining process specifies that when the outside binds (that is the outside option is greater than the ongoing payoff) the player obtains his outside option. This implies that having a high outside option, hence having ownership, weakens incentives to invest.

[20] As in Aghion et al. (1994).

[21] See Banerjee and Newman (1993) for an early illustration of this point in a model where a principal has to decide whether to invest in a monitoring technology for his agent. The role of the distribution of cash endowments for organizational choices in an industry is emphasized in Legros and Newman (1996).

3.3.2 *Surplus Division and the Spillover Effects of the Cash Distribution*

Let us go back to a situation similar to that in Grossman and Hart (1986) and suppose that under nonintegration the parties have noncontractible payoffs $v_i^N, i = A, B$ while under integration, and transfer of property rights to A they have $v_i^I, i = A, B$, where $v_A^I > v_A^N, v_B^I < v_B^N$, then the owner of the B asset is willing to relinquish ownership only if A is able to perform a transfer of $v_B^N - v_B^I > 0$. As long as both A and B have enough cash, or can borrow from the financial market without distorting ex post decisions it follows that A and B will choose the ownership structure that maximizes the total surplus: that is, integration arises only if $v_A^I + v_B^I > v_A^N + v_B^N$. However, if either A or B has limited cash holdings, debt financing for the purchase of assets will be distortionary since the debt repayment tends to reduce the marginal return from decisions, and the surplus efficient ownership structure need not emerge.[22] We assume for simplicity that debt is so distortionary that it is not used for ex ante transfers.

For B to agree to integration, it must obtain a lump-sum transfer of at least $t^* = v_B^N - v_B^I$. If this is the only relationship in the industry, then as the cash holding of firm A increases, integration is more likely: the size of the surplus generated in the industry is increasing in the cash of firm A. This is the usual "partial equilibrium" intuition one gets from corporate governance: cash in the relationship creates a *positive contracting externality*.

Suppose now that there are two assets A_1, A_2 and that the owners of these assets have different cash holdings $l_1 \le l_2$. Assets are identical in terms of their productive capacity: as long as an asset A_j is combined with an asset B, the payoffs are given by $v_A^k, v_B^k, k = I, N$. If an asset A_j is not in a relationship with an asset B, his payoff is equal to zero. Because there are two assets of type A, one of them will be left unmatched; since $l_1 \le l_2$, the owner of A_1 is at a competitive disadvantage and will be left unmatched. Assuming that $l_1 \le v_A^N$, the most that this owner can offer to the owner of B is $v_B^N + l_1$, and this is therefore what B will want to obtain to be in relationship with A_2. Hence, $v_B^N + l_1$ is the outside option of B in a relationship with A_2 while the outside option of A_2 is zero.

A_2 would prefer to have integration, but B will be willing to accept integration only if he receives a transfer t_2 from A_2 satisfying $v_B^I + t_2 \ge v_B^N + l_1$, that is, if $l_2 \ge t_2 \ge t^* + l_1$, where the left inequality is the cash constraint for the owner of A_2. As l_1 increases, the condition is less likely to be satisfied. For instance, starting from a situation where $l_2 = t^* + l_1$, increasing l_1 by 2δ and increasing l_2 by δ will lead to a violation of the condition; more cash in the industry

---

[22] Bolton and Whinston (1993) also show that if we consider more than three parties, the "efficient" ownership structure may fail to arise even if parties can make ex ante lump-sum payments as long as payments for reallocation of property rights cannot be made contingent on future sales of assets.

will lead to nonintegration. Similarly, a redistribution of liquidity from l_2 to l_1 will also lead to nonintegration. This is a new role for cash: cash in the industry may create a *negative contracting externality* on firms, even if they all benefit from cash injection. Note that as l_1 increases, A_2 effectively loses market power in its relationship with B; as a result A_2 is less likely to have power inside the firm, and surplus division within the firm should be more equal, leading eventually to different organizational choices.

This example illustrates two important points, the first one being well understood in contract theory, the second rather less so.

Surplus Division With finite cash endowments, the organizational choice does not necessarily maximize total surplus because it depends on the distribution of surplus.

Spillovers While cash helps improve contracting in a given relationship, it may generate negative externalities on other relationships because it affects the distribution of surplus.

In the remainder of this subsection, we discuss these two effects in greater depth.

3.3.3 Surplus Division in U.S. Trucking

In the above example, the role of an increase in l_1 is to shift the terms of trade between the A's and the B's. There are other ways to generate such a shift, for instance by introducing better opportunities for the A's in other industries. The recent history of the trucking industry provides an illustration.

In the 1980s and 1990s the trucking industry in the United States experienced a shift away from drivers who owned their own trucks toward employee drivers. This organizational change has been attributed to various technological developments, such as the introduction of on-board computers, which offered both better monitoring of driver actions and greater flexibility in dispatching, permitting more efficient use of trucks (Baker and Hubbard 2004). By the early 2000s, the prevalence of owner operators and use of on-board computers had stabilized. But more recently, the industry has begun to shift some control back to drivers. Between 2004 and 2006, carriers began offering drivers such perks as the right to travel with spouses or to outfit their cabs with satellite televisions. Since drivers decide whether and when to exercise these rights, they constitute an increase in their control. The question is why there has been a shift of control allocations in trucking without an apparent technological shift.

A possible answer comes from the observation that an important alternative employment for truckers is construction, which experienced a boom in the early 2000s. Thinking of the drivers as the A's, and the construction-*cum*-trucking firms as the B's, the increase in the outside options of drivers from the construction boom implies they more surplus in trucking, and the question is how the transfer from firm to driver is accomplished.

The obvious solution would have been to raise the drivers' wages, which would correspond to increasing cash side payments. However, trucking as well as construction are notoriously cash-strapped industries, with invoice payments coming long after workers have been paid and services rendered. An alternative is to increase the size of drivers' contingent shares, but this is costly both because it reduces the incentives of other members of trucking firms, and because it imposes more risk on drivers. Borrowing to increase the wage bill is similarly (in fact, likely more) costly, as we have discussed. This leaves control rights as the least costly means of transferring surplus from firms to drivers.[23]

3.3.4 Spillovers

In section 3.3.2 it was shown that shocks to some firms (A_1) may lead to reorganization in *other* firms $(B-A_2)$, even if those firms have experienced no shocks. This is because of a spillover effect: through the market, shocks to some firms are transmitted to others, possibly inducing them to reorganize. As we saw, the distribution of liquidity, and not just its average level, may have an important role to play in the determination of an industry's organizational structure.

Even if there is no effect on the organization of firms, the distribution of liquidity will affect the ability of the private sector to channel funds to entrepreneurs.[24] One of the exciting avenues for future research would be to couple the imperfections in the financial market with the endogenous determination of the organizations of firms.

Shocks to cash holdings are not the only source of organizational spillover effects. Referring again to the model in section 3.3.2, suppose there is a technological shock to asset A_1, which becomes more productive: under both forms of

---

[23] Legros and Newman (2004), a working paper version of Legros and Newman (2008), contains a model that generalizes the one in section 3.3.2 and shows that with risk-neutral A's and B's, (1) adjusting contingent sharing rules is less distortionary than using debt to finance a side payment and (2) transferring control or ownership of assets is less distortionary than adjusting sharing rules over a wide range of divisions of the surplus. With risk-averse A's, the appeal of control transfers over share adjustments is likely to be even greater.

[24] For instance, Holmström and Tirole (1997) analyze the effect of credit crunches when firms have different liquidity endowments. Firms with large liquidity can borrow from an (uninformed) capital market, but firms with less liquidity—hence less collateral—have to borrow from intermediaries using a costly monitoring technology. Credit crunches affect low-liquidity firms' ability to borrow, increasing the cost of monitoring and the spread in interest rates paid by high- and low-liquidity firms. Their results are consistent with stylized facts, in particular the fact that the 1990–1991 change in bank lending is correlated with a change in the equity value of the banking sector. See also the recent book Holmström and Tirole (2011) for a survey of the literature on this point.

organization the payoffs to both asset holders increase by δ. By contrast, asset A_2 is not subject to a shock. Then, if $l_1 + \delta < l_2$, the outside option of B is now $v_B^N + l_1 + \delta$. Hence, if $l_2 \in (t^* + t_1, t^* + t_1 + \delta)$, in the relationship (A_2, B) there would have been integration before the productivity shock but after the shock there will be nonintegration. We would observe a change in organization for the relationship (A_2, B) despite the fact that its technology is unchanged: *it is the change in technology of other firms that leads to the reorganization of the firm.*

In some cases the reorganization of some firms in the industry following technological shocks may *absorb* the potential gains from increased productivity. Since the newly nonintegrated enterprise produces less than it did before, the net output of the industry is smaller than it would be had organization been exogenous. Legros and Newman (2013) provides an example in which uniform shocks (say a 10% productivity increase for every firm) leads to a 10% increase in industry output, while a doubling of the productivity of 10% of the firms, by lowering the price and inducing the remaining firms to switch from integration to nonintegration, results in *no* increase in industry output, something that would be exceedingly difficult to obtain with neoclassical (or even exogenously organizational) firms. This kind of "reorganizational dampening" may manifest itself as "mismatch" between technology and organization (since technology inside the organization is not wholly responsible for organizational form), and may account for some empirical puzzles, such as the missing productivity gain from information technology that was widely discussed in the 1990s (Brynjolfsson et al. 2002).

4. Conclusion

Twenty-five years ago, Holmström, and Tirole (1989) wrote an extensive survey on the theory of the firm and covered most of the aspects present at this 2011 conference. A sign of the success of the incomplete contract paradigm is the fact that it is no longer practical to write a survey of the theory of the firm that would encompass all of the dimensions covered in 1989. In particular, corporate finance, internal organization, and applications to industrial organization and international trade are receiving specific treatments: the tremendous growth in knowledge over the past 25 years has resulted in considerable specialization and dis-integration, as it were. What recent theory and empirics suggest, however, is that a fuller understanding of the positive and normative consequences of firm boundaries and other organizational variables calls for more reintegration. Section 3 goes one way in this direction, and provides some answers as to why an organizational IO warrants further development. Generally, organizational choices matter for scale, scope, and performance of firms, and equilibrium often requires heterogeneity in these choices, even across firms with seemingly identical characteristics. The organization of a single firm depends on how all other firms are organized, because that affects the bargaining positions of asset holders when they negotiate integration decisions. Sometimes this dependence leads to reorganizational dampening of technological innovation, which results in little or no gain in industrial productivity.

There are many aspects of industrial organization that we do not consider in this survey, either because they would require a survey of their own or because they have yet to be addressed in the literature. For an example of the first, we have not reviewed the literature on regulation and procurement, topics that are clearly important domains of application of the incomplete contracting paradigm, given the role that the state can play in opening markets to competition, in regulating competition or in engaging in contracting relationship with the private sector.[25] For an example of the second, a unified theory of industrial market structure and ownership structure is high on the agenda but has yet to emerge.

References

Acemoglu, Daron, and Andrew F. Newman. 2002. "The Labor Market and Corporate Structure." *European Economic Review* 46: 1733–56.

Ackerberg, Daniel A., and Maristella Botticini. 2002. "Endogenous Matching and the Empirical Determinants of Contract Form." *Journal of Political Economy* 110: 564–91.

Aghion, Philippe, and Patrick Bolton. 1992. "An Incomplete Contracts Approach to Financial Contracting." *Review of Economic Studies* 59: 473–94.

Aghion, Philippe, Mathias Dewatripont, and Patrick Rey. 1994. "Renegotiation Design with Unverifiable Information." *Econometrica* 62: 257–82.

Aghion, Philippe, Mathias Dewatripont, and Patrick Rey. 1997. "Corporate Governance, Competition Policy and Industrial Policy." *European Economic Review* 41: 797–805.

Aghion, Philippe, Mathias Dewatripont, and Patrick Rey. 1999. "Competition, Financial Discipline and Growth." *Review of Economic Studies* 66: 825–52.

Aghion, Philippe, Mathias Dewatripont, and Jeremy C. Stein. 2008. "Academic Freedom, Private-Sector Focus, and the Process of Innovation." *RAND Journal of Economics* 39: 617–35.

Aghion, Philippe, and Rachel Griffith. 2008. *Competition and Growth: Reconciling Theory and Evidence.* Cambridge, MA: MIT Press.

Aghion, Philippe, Rachel Griffith, and Peter Howitt. 2006. "Vertical Integration and Competition." *American Economic Review* 96: 97–102.

Aghion, Philippe, and Jean Tirole. 1994. "The Management of Innovation." *Quarterly Journal of Economics* 109: 1185–209.

Aghion, Philippe, and Jean Tirole. 1997. "Formal and Real Authority in Organizations." *Journal of Political Economy* 105: 1–29.

Alexander, Cindy R., and David Reiffen. 1995. "Vertical Contracts as Strategic Commitments: How Are They Enforced?" *Journal of Economics Management Strategy* 4: 623–49.

Alfaro, Laura, Paola Conconi, Harald Fadinger, and Andrew F. Newman. 2014. "Do Prices Determine Vertical Integration?" NBER Working Paper 16118.

---

[25] Incomplete contract setting has been applied to procurement or public-private partnerships (see Hart et al. 1997; Hart 2003; Dewatripont and Legros, 2005; Iossa and Martimort, 2008); to the allocation of ownerships in a regulatory setting, with public production by a private firm (Besley and Ghatak, 2001); to the provision of pure or impure public goods (Francesconi and Muthoo, 2011).

Allen, F., and D. Gale. 2000. "Corporate Governance and Competition." In Xavier Vives (ed.) *Corporate Governance*. Cambridge: Cambridge University Press.

Alonso, Ricardo, Wouter Dessein, and Niko Matouschek. 2008. "Centralization versus Decentralization: An Application to Price Setting by a Multi-Market Firm." *Journal of the European Economic Association* 6: 457–67.

Atalay, Enghin, Ali Hortacsu, and Chad Syverson. 2012. "Why Do Firms Own Production Chains?" NBER Working Paper 18020.

Baker, George, Robert Gibbons, and Kevin J. Murphy. 1999. "Informal Authority in Organizations." *Journal of Law, Economics, and Organization* 15: 56–73.

Baker, George, and Thomas Hubbard. 2004. "Contractibility and Asset Ownership: On-Board Computers and Governance in US Trucking." *Quarterly Journal of Economics* 119: 1443–79.

Banerjee, Abhijit V., and Andrew F. Newman. 1993. "Occupational Choice and the Process of Development." *Journal of Political Economy* 101: 274–98.

Bertrand, Marianne, and Sendhil Mullainathan. 2003. "Enjoying the Quiet Life? Corporate Governance and Managerial Preferences." *Journal of Political Economy* 111: 1043–75.

Besley, Timothy, and Maitreesh Ghatak. 2001. "Government versus Private Ownership of Public Goods." *Quarterly Journal of Economics* 116: 1343–72.

Biais, Bruno, and Enrico Perotti. 2008. "Entrepreneurs and New Ideas." *RAND Journal of Economics* 39: 1105–25.

Bolton, Patrick. 2013. "Corporate Finance, Incomplete Contracts, and Corporate Control." In Supplement 1, *Journal of Law, Economics, and Organization* 30: i64–117.

Bolton, Patrick, and David S. Scharfstein. 1990. "A Theory of Predation Based on Agency Problems in Financial Contracting." *American Economic Review* 80: 93–106.

Bolton, Patrick, and M. Whinston. 1993. "Incomplete Contracts, Vertical Integration, and Supply Assurance." *Review of Economic Studies* 60: 121–48.

Brander, James A., and Tracy R. Lewis. 1986. "Oligopoly and Financial Structure: The Limited Liability Effect." *American Economic Review* 76: 956– 70.

Brynjolfsson, Erik, Lorin M. Hitt, and Shinkyu Yang. 2002. "Intangible Assets: Computers and Organizational Capital." *Brookings Papers on Economic Activity* 2002: 137–81.

Caillaud, Bernard, Bruno Jullien, and Pierre Picard. 1995. "Competing Vertical Structures: Precommitment and Renegotiation." *Econometrica* 63: 621–46.

Chevalier, Judith. 1995. "Capital Structure and Product-Market Competition: Empirical Evidence from the Supermarket Industry." *American Economic Review* 85: 415–35.

Chiu, Y. Stephen. 1998. "Noncooperative Bargaining, Hostages, and Optimal Asset Ownership." *American Economic Review* 88: 882–901.

Cunat, Vicente, and Maria Guadalupe. 2005. "How Does Product Market Competition Shape Incentive Contracts?" *Journal of the European Economic Association* 3: 1058–82.

Cunat, Vicente, and Maria Guadalupe. 2009. "Globalization and the Provision of Incentives inside the Firm: The Effect of Foreign Competition." *Journal of Labor Economics* 27: 179–212.

Dasgupta, Sudipto, and Sheridan Titman. 1998. "Pricing Strategy and Financial Policy." *Review of Financial Studies* 11: 705–37.

De Meza, David, and Ben Lockwood. 1998. "Does Asset Ownership Always Motivate Managers? Outside Options and the Property Rights Theory of the Firm." *Quarterly Journal of Economics* 113: 361–86.

De Meza, David, and Clive Southey. 1999. "Too Much Monitoring, Not Enough Performance Pay." *Economic Journal* 109(454): 126–39.

Dessein, Wouter. 2013. "Incomplete Contracts and Firm Boundaries: New Directions." In Supplement 1, *Journal of Law, Economics, and Organization* 30: i13–36.

Dewatripont, Mathias. 1988. "Commitment through Renegotiation-Proof Contracts with Third Parties." *Review of Economic Studies* 55: 377–89.

Dewatripont, Mathias, and Patrick Legros. 2005. "Public-Private Partnerships: Contract Design and Risk Transfer." EIB papers.

Dewatripont, Mathias, and Jean Tirole. 1994. "A Theory of Debt and Equity: Diversity of Securities and Manager-Shareholder Congruence." *Quarterly Journal of Economics* 109: 1027–54.

Farrell, Joseph, and Carl Shapiro. 1990. "Asset Ownership and Market Structure in Oligopoly." *RAND Journal of Economics* 21: 275–92.

Faure-Grimaud, Antoine. 2000. "Product Market Competition and Optimal Debt Contracts: The Limited Liability Effect Revisited." *European Economic Review* 44: 1823–40.

Fershtman, Chaim, and Kenneth L. Judd. 1987. "Equilibrium Incentives in Oligopoly." *American Economic Review* 77: 927–40.

Francesconi, Marco, and Abhinay Muthoo. 2011. "Control Rights in Complex Partnerships." *Journal of the European Economic Association* 9: 551–89.

Fudenberg, Drew, and Jean Tirole. 1986. "A 'Signal-Jamming' Theory of Predation." *RAND Journal of Economics* 17: 366–76.

Gibbons, R. 2006. "What the Folk Theorem Doesn't Tell Us." *Industrial and Corporate Change* 15: 381–6.

Gibbons, Robert. 2010. "Inside Organizations: Pricing, Politics, and Path Dependence." *Annual Review of Economics* 2: 337–65.

Gibbons, Robert, Richard Holden, and Michael Powell. 2012. "Organization and Information: Firms' Governance Choices in Rational Expectations Equilibrium." *Quarterly Journal of Economics* 127: 1813–41.

Giroud, Xavier, and Holger M. Mueller. 2009. "Does Corporate Governance Matter in Competitive Industries?" *Journal of Financial Economics* 59: 312–31.

Grossman, Gene, and Elhanan Helpman. 2002. "Integration versus Outsourcing in Industry Equilibrium." *Quarterly Journal of Economics* 117: 85–120.

Grossman, Sanford, and Oliver Hart. 1982. " Corporate Financial Structure and Managerial Incentives." In John McCall (ed.) *The Economics of Information and Uncertainty*, 107–140. Cambridge, MA: NBER, UMI.

Grossman, Sanford J., and Oliver D. Hart. 1986. "The Costs and Benefits of Ownership: A Theory of Vertical and Lateral Integration." *Journal of Political Economy* 94: 691–719.

Grossman, Sanford J., and Joseph E. Stiglitz. 1980. "On the Impossibility of Informationally Efficient Markets." *American Economic Review* 70: 393–408.

Guadalupe, Maria, and Julie Wulf. 2010. "The Flattening Firm and Product Market Competition: The Effect of Trade Liberalization on Corporate Hierarchies." *American Economic Journal: Applied Economics* 2: 105–27.

Harris, Milton, and Bengt Holmström. 1982. "A Theory of Wage Dynamics." *Review of Economic Studies* 49: 315–33.

Hart, Oliver. 1983. "The Market Mechanism as an Incentive Scheme." *Bell Journal of Economics* 14: 366–82.

Hart, Oliver. 2003. "Incomplete Contracts and Public Ownership: Remarks, and an Application to Public-Private Partnerships." *Economic Journal* 113: C69–76.

Hart, Oliver, and Bengt Holmström. 2010. "A Theory of Firm Scope." *Quarterly Journal of Economics* 125: 483–513.

Hart, Oliver, and John Moore. 1990. "Property Rights and the Nature of the Firm." *Journal of Political Economy* 98: 1119–58.

Hart, Oliver, and John Moore. 2008. "Contracts as Reference Points." *Quarterly Journal of Economics* 123: 1–48.

Hart, Oliver, Andrei Shleifer, and Robert Vishny. 1997. "The Proper Scope of Government: Theory and an Application to Prisons." *Quarterly Journal of Economics* 112: 1127–61.

Hart, Oliver, and Jean Tirole. 1990. "Vertical Integration and Market Foreclosure." *Brookings Papers on Economic Activity: Microeconomics* 1990: 205–86.

Hayek, Friedrich. 1945. "The Use of Knowledge in Society." *American Economic Review* 35: 519–30.

Holmström, Bengt, and Jean Tirole. 1989. "The Theory of the Firm." In R. Schmalensee and R. Zillig (eds.) *Handbook of Industrial Organization*, 61–133. Amsterdam: Elsevier.

Holmström, Bengt, and Jean Tirole. 1997. "Financial Intermediation, Loanable Funds, and the Real Sector." *Quarterly Journal of Economics* 112: 663–91.

Holmström, Bengt, and Jean Tirole. 2011. *Inside and Outside Liquidity*. Cambridge, MA: MIT Press.

Iossa, Elisabetta, and David Martimort. 2008. "The Simple Micro-Economics of Public-Private Partnerships. " CEIS Working Paper 139.

Jacob, Glazer. 1994. "The Strategic Effects of Long-Term Debt in Imperfect Competition." *Journal of Economic Theory* 62: 428–43.

Jensen, Michael C. 1986. "Agency Costs of Free Cash Flow, Corporate Finance, and Takeovers." *American Economic Review* 76: 323–9.

Jensen, Michael C., and William H. Meckling. 1976. "Theory of the Firm: Managerial Behavior, Agency Costs, and Ownership." *Journal of Financial Economics* 3: 305–60.

Joskow, Paul L. 2010. "Vertical Integration." *Antitrust Bulletin* 55: 545–586.

Katz, Michael L. 1991. "Game-Playing Agents: Unobservable Contracts as Precommitments." *RAND Journal of Economics* 22: 307–28.

Klein, Benjamin, Robert Crawford, and Armen A. Alchian. 1978. "Vertical Integration, Appropriable Rents, and the Competitive Contracting Process." *Journal of Law and Economics* 21: 297–326.

Lafontaine, Francine, and Margaret Slade. 2007. "Vertical Integration and Firm Boundaries: The Evidence." *Journal of Economic Literature* 45: 629–85.

Legros, Patrick, and Andrew F. Newman. 1996. "Wealth Effects, Distribution, and the Theory of Organization." *Journal of Economic Theory* 70: 312–41.

Legros, Patrick, and Andrew F. Newman. 2004. "Competing for Ownership." Technical Report DP 148, Boston University, IED.

Legros, Patrick, and Andrew F. Newman. 2008. "Competing for Ownership." *Journal of the European Economic Association* 6: 1279–308.

Legros, Patrick, and Andrew F. Newman. 2013. "A Price Theory of Vertical and Lateral Integration." *Quarterly Journal of Economics* 128: 725–70.

Legros, Patrick, Andrew F. Newman, and Eugenio Proto. 2014. "Smithian Growth through Creative Organization." *Review of Economics and Statistics* 96 (5): 796–811.

Lyandres, Evgeny. 2006. "Capital Structure and Interaction among Firms in Output Markets: Theory and Evidence." *Journal of Business* 79: 2381–421.

Machlup, Fritz. 1967. "Theories of the Firm: Marginalist, Behavioral, Managerial." *American Economic Review* 57: 1–33.

Marx, Leslie M., and Greg Shaffer. 2004. "Opportunism in Multilateral Vertical Contracting: Nondiscrimination, Exclusivity, and Uniformity: Comment." *American Economic Review* 94: 796–801.

McAfee, R. Preston, John McMillan, and Michael D. Whinston. 1989. "Multiproduct Monopoly, Commodity Bundling, and Correlation of Values." *Quarterly Journal of Economics* 104: 371–83.

McLaren, John. 2000. "'Globalization' and Vertical Structure." *American Economic Review* 90: 1239–54.

Milgrom, Paul Robert. 1987. "Employment Contracts, Influence Activities and Efficient Organization Design." *Journal of Political Economy* 96: 42–60.

Nalebuff, Barry J., and Joseph E. Stiglitz. 1983a. "Information, Competition, and Markets." *American Economic Review* 73: 278–83.

Nalebuff, Barry J., and Joseph E. Stiglitz. 1983b. "Prizes and Incentives: Towards a General Theory of Compensation and Competition." *Bell Journal of Economics* 14: 21–43.

Nickell, Stephen J., Daphne Nicolitsas, and Neil Alistair Dryden. 1997. "What Makes Firms Perform Well?" *European Economic Review* 41: 783–96.

O'Brien, Daniel P., and Greg Shaffer. 1992. "Vertical Control with Bilateral Contracts." *RAND Journal of Economics* 23: 299–308.

Ordover, Janusz A., Garth Saloner, and Steven C. Salop. 1990. "Equilibrium Vertical Foreclosure." *American Economic Review* 80: 127–42.

Perelman, Michael. 2011. "Retrospectives: X-Efficiency." *Journal of Economic Perspectives* 25: 211–22.

Povel, Paul, and Michael Raith. 2004. "Financial Constraints and Product Market Competition: Ex Ante vs. Ex Post Incentives." *International Journal of Industrial Organization* 22: 917–49.

Prendergast, Canice. 2002. "The Tenuous Trade-Off between Risk and Incentives." *Journal of Political Economy* 110: 1071–102.

Raith, Michael. 2003. "Competition, Risk, and Managerial Incentives." *American Economic Review* 93: 1425–36.

Reitman, David. 1993. "Stock Options and the Strategic Use of Managerial Incentives." *American Economic Review* 83: 513–24.

Scharfstein, David. 1988. "Product-Market Competition and Managerial Slack." *RAND Journal of Economics* 19: 147–55.

Scherer, F. M. 1980. *Industrial Market Structure and Economic Performance*. 2nd ed. Boston: Houghton Mifflin.

Schmidt, Klaus. 1997. "Managerial Incentives and Product Market Competition." *Review of Economic Studies* 64: 191–213.

Schmitz, Patrick W., and Dirk Sliwka. 2001. "On Synergies and Vertical Integration." *International Journal of Industrial Organization* 19: 1281–95.

Segal, I. 1999. "Contracting with Externalities." *Quarterly Journal of Economics* 114: 337–88.

Segal, I. 2003. "Collusion, Exclusion, and Inclusion in Random-Order Bargaining." *Review of Economic Studies* 70: 439–60.

Showalter, Dean M. 1995. "Oligopoly and Financial Structure: Comment." *American Economic Review* 85: 647–53.

Sklivas, S. D. 1987. "The Strategic Choice of Managerial Incentives." *RAND Journal of Economics* 18 (3): 418–52.

Spagnolo, Giancarlo. 2000. "Stock-Related Compensation and Product-Market Competition." *RAND Journal of Economics* 31: 22–42.

Syverson, Chad. 2011. "What Determines Productivity?" *Journal of Economic Literature* 49: 326–65.

Tadelis, Steven. 2002. "Complexity, Flexibility, and the Make-or-Buy Decision." *American Economic Review* 92: 433–37.

Vickers, John. 1985. "Delegation and the Theory of the Firm." *Economic Journal* 95: 138–47.

Vives, Xavier. 2000. "Corporate Governance: Does It Matter?" In Xavier Vives (ed.) *Corporate Governance: Theoretical and Empirical Perspectives*, 1–21. Cambridge: Cambridge University Press.

Wickelgren, Abraham L. 2005. "Managerial Incentives and the Price Effects of Mergers." *Journal of Industrial Economics* 53: 327–53.

Williamson, Oliver E. 1971. "The Vertical Integration of Production: Market Failure Considerations." *American Economic Review* 61: 112–23.

Williamson, Oliver E. 1975. *Markets and Hierarchies: Analysis and Antitrust Implications*. New York: Free Press.

Williamson, Oliver E. 1985. *The Economic Institutions of Capitalism: Firms, Markets, Relational Contracting*. New York: Free Press.

Williamson, Oliver E. 1990. "Mergers, Acquisitions and Leveraged Buyouts: An Efficiency Argument." In Lucian A. Bebchuk (ed.) *Corporate Law and Economic Analysis*, 7–26. Cambridge: Cambridge University Press.

19

Discussion of "Contracts, Ownership, and Industrial Organization: Past and Future," by Patrick Legros and Andrew Newman

MATHIAS DEWATRIPONT

I am of course very happy to be here, to celebrate the 25th anniversary of the famous Grossman-Hart paper, which has led to the "GHM paradigm." I am also very happy to be able to comment on this interesting paper by Patrick and Andy (Legros and Newman 2014).

As is by now very clear, the influence of Grossman and Hart (1986) is really very significant and very wide-ranging in a number of fields. This being said, here is a territory where it could grow further. There is indeed a contrast between other fields, like corporate finance, where one can say that the situation has been "revolutionized" by Grossman-Hart, and industrial organization, where it has not been the case to the same extent. This paper by Patrick and Andy convincingly argues that much progress could be made in this respect, in that the incomplete contract paradigm has a lot to offer that has not been "discovered" yet.

Indeed, it is true that traditional industrial organization textbooks, including the celebrated Tirole (1988) text—a very impressive piece of work which has stood the test of time well—start with a chapter that explains that what happens inside firms is rich and complex, and then move to an analysis of markets that takes the firm as a profit-maximizing black box.

There are admittedly some exceptions, discussed in the paper by Patrick and Andy, like contracts as a barrier to entry or vertical integration as a foreclosure strategy. Since the other discussant of this session is Kai-Uwe Kühn, now chief competition economist for the European Union, I will let him discuss the strategic role of contracts and focus on the relation between incomplete contracting, firm organization, and competitive markets (see chapter 20). Here, there is clearly much more to do.

Earlier on in this book (see chapter 2), Bengt Holmström has, somewhat facetiously, said that Grossman-Hart is maybe more a theory of markets than a theory of the firm. It is in fact true in the sense that the extent of market pressures may influence the relative efficiency of various organizational structures that Grossman and Hart study, as well as the need to adopt them despite transitional costs. In this respect, it makes a lot of sense, as argued by Patrick and Andy, to look at the mutual interaction between market developments and organizational developments.

In a sense, a precursor of this approach, discussed in Patrick and Andy's paper, concerns the impact of the intensity of market competition on firm performance. It is only a partial approach, looking at only one direction: how market pressures influence organizational efficiency. And it is a "pre-Grossman-Hart" literature in the sense that the firm here is a simple principal-agent pair where asset ownership and control are given: the principal owns the machine, and the agent controls it.

Interestingly, as is often the case, Oliver was a pioneer in this literature, thanks to his highly cited 1983 paper (Hart 1983). A very nice follow-up paper is by Klaus Schmidt (1997), which highlights a fundamental trade-off: on the one hand, more competition and the fear of bankruptcy can lead the agent to work harder for a given incentive scheme; on the other hand, more competition may weaken the incentive given by the principal to the agent to work hard: if the agent's effort is a fixed cost (that has to be paid for in the end by the principal) and its reward a cut in the firm's marginal cost, the more competition the smaller the size of the firm and the lower the gain from lower marginal cost.

Introducing a Grossman-Hart perspective into such a problem means looking at how changes in control rights will affect the outcome. If one thinks of "effort" as a "noncontractable action," this may just be "who takes the effort," or "what is the objective function of those who take the effort." Together with Philippe Aghion and Patrick Rey, we have followed the latter, more reduced-form approach (see Aghion et al. 1997, 1999). Specifically, stressing the same type of trade-off as Schmidt, we analyze an endogenous growth model and compare owner-controlled, profit-maximizing firms with manager-controlled, satisficing firms, which are assumed to be ready to expend the effort necessary to engineer cost-reducing process innovations only to avoid bankruptcy.

This model delivers interesting predictions on the link between "corporate governance" on the one hand and the desirability of competition policy or industrial policy—meaning innovation subsidies here—on the other hand. Indeed, owner-controlled, profit-maximizing firms will tend to innovate more if they receive innovation subsidies, but they will innovate less if competition policy means more, and therefore smaller, firms in a market and therefore a lower incentive to expend the fixed cost of innovation to cut marginal production costs. Instead, if managers control the firm, they will respond to competition pressures by innovating faster, and instead they will use the "breathing space" of innovation subsidies by "buying time" and innovating later.

We therefore see that corporate governance, that is, who de facto controls firms, has very significant implications on the desired innovation and growth policies: a "Schumpeterian" policy is optimal under profit-maximizing firms, and instead a "Darwinian" policy under manager-controlled firms.

As I said already, this analysis only takes a reduced-form approach to firm control. It does not involve an endogenization of control structures as a function of market forces, a feature that, as stressed by Patrick and Andy, would clearly be very desirable, and which they detail in their paper. They look at cases where organization structure changes in function of the nature of market competition, and then there is a feedback effect on market competition.

Let me illustrate Patrick and Andy's key point in a manner that will properly suit Oliver's research approach. In fact, there is a distinctive feature of Oliver that, surprisingly, has not been stressed so far in this conference: the fact that he is a quantitative economist, in the sense that he likes to write papers based on numerical examples!

In his honor, let me consider the following instructive numerical example. Consider two individuals, A and B, who have the opportunity of working together. Assume transferable utility. If A and B choose to work together in an "integrated fashion," with A as "the boss," A obtains a utility level of 20, and B a utility level of 5. If instead they work under nonintegration mode, assume they each get a utility of 10. Since 20 + 5 is bigger that 10 + 10, integration is in principle a good idea. On the other hand, a key question is whether A has the financial resources to convince B to "be integrated." The more financial resources A has (or has access to), the more she can induce B to accept integration. Specifically, B will need to receive at least 5 for integration to take place. Indeed, as first pointed out by Philippe Aghion and Patrick Bolton (1992) in their famous paper on debt as a contingent control mechanism, organization structure and the allocation of control rights will depend on available financial resources.

The point made by Patrick and Andy is that beyond access to financial resources, market competition matters too. Indeed, add now another individual, A', who competes with A for potentially working with B (who, by assumption, is "unique"). Assume that A' is equivalent to A in that A' and B can also generate

20 + 5 if A′ integrates B and 10 + 10 if she does not. On the other hand, the unmatched individual, whether A or A′, receives zero utility.

We have now introduced competition for working with B. This will unsurprisingly help B out, to the detriment of A and A′ compared to the situation where they would be alone facing B. More interestingly, the equilibrium production mode may be affected too, even if: (1) integration remains the efficient production mode, and (2) A still has access to more than 5 in financial resources to compensate B for being integrated. In fact, and this is surprising at first, it is when A′ *also* has significant financial resources that the inefficient nonintegrated production mode can be the equilibrium one here!

To see this, assume A has 10 in financial resources, and A′ has less than that. If in fact A′ has less than 5, the earlier outcome, with A integrating B and paying him at least 5, remains an equilibrium, since A′ cannot compete against such an offer. However, if A′ has more than 5, for example 7, A will remain the one working with B but now in an unintegrated fashion! Indeed, going for integration will not work for A: by assumption, A cannot offer B more than 10 in financial resources, which would give B a utility of 5 + 10 under integration; but A′ could counter such an outcome by offering B to work under nonintegration while paying him 7. This gives B 10 + 7 while A′ can still enjoy a net gain of 10 − 7. The only equilibrium is therefore for A to simply "outcompete" A′ by replicating this outcome, that is, offer B an amount of 7 plus ε arbitrarily small. In this case, B enjoys 10 + 7 + ε and A enjoys 10 − 7 − ε.

This example shows that very interesting things can happen if one starts taking into account market conditions and matching patterns, and Patrick and Andy discuss real-life examples, like the trucking industry, where these types of things have been taking place. They also discuss an application building on the Hart and Holmström (2010) paper looking at firm scope where, again, significant things can happen.

And another natural area of application is R&D, where organization design and the allocation of control rights is also very relevant. With Philippe Aghion and Jeremy Stein (Aghion et al. 2008), we have for example analyzed the relative merits of academic and private-sector research using a control-right perspective. Specifically, we focus on academic freedom as the key dimension of academic research and investigate the trade-off between the two types of research in a world where academics are ready to accept lower wages in return for academic freedom (a feature that seems to match wage structures). We consider a world where research funders are interested in maximizing the return on research, and where an innovation requires stepwise discoveries (think, for example, of biotech). We make the assumption that academic freedom raises the risk of "failure" because the researcher may decide to explore a research direction that is not economically profitable. We still show endogenously the optimality of academic research early on in the discovery process, because at that stage the advantage of lower academic wages outweighs the higher risk of failure. This is not the case any more as one gets closer to the final discovery: intuitively, one does not want to risk lowering the probability of obtaining the final go-ahead for a multibillion-dollar drug! Like the other topics discussed here, this one would very nicely benefit from endogenizing the supply of potential research topics, the number of researchers, and financial resources/investors.

To conclude this short discussion, let me stress how inspiring I find this paper by Patrick and Andy. Indeed, it demonstrates that, while the Grossman-Hart-Moore paradigm has already generated a wealth of very diverse and very valuable economic insights, many very promising topics remain to be investigated, in particular by explicitly considering these links between organization structure and the market environment: the "GHM gospel" is alive and well!

References

Aghion, P., and P. Bolton. 1992. "An Incomplete Contracts Approach to Financial Contracting." *Review of Economic Studies* 59: 473–94.

Aghion, P., M. Dewatripont, and P. Rey. 1997. "Corporate Governance, Competition Policy and Industrial Policy." *European Economic Review* 41: 797–805.

Aghion, P., M. Dewatripont, and P. Rey. 1999. "Competition, Financial Discipline and Growth." *Review of Economic Studies* 66: 825–52.

Aghion, P., M. Dewatripont, and J. Stein. 2008. "Academic Freedom, Private-Sector Focus, and the Process of Innovation." *RAND Journal of Economics* 39: 617–35.

Grossman, S., and O. Hart. 1986. "The Costs and Benefits of Ownership: A Theory of Vertical and Lateral Integration." *Journal of Political Economy* 94: 691–719.

Hart, O. 1983. "The Market Mechanism as an Incentive Scheme." *Bell Journal of Economics* 14: 366–82.

Hart, O., and B. Holmström. 2010. "A Theory of Firm Scope." *Quarterly Journal of Economics* 125: 483–513.

Legros, P., and A. F. Newman. 2014. "Contracts, Ownership, and Industrial Organization: Past and Future." *Journal of Law, Economics, and Organization* 30(suppl. 1): i82–117. Reprinted in this volume as chapter 1.

Schmidt, K. 1997. "Managerial Incentives and Product Market Competition." *Review of Economic Studies* 64: 191–213.

Tirole, J. 1988. *The Theory of Industrial Organization.* Cambridge, MA: MIT Press.

20

Discussion of "Contracts, Ownership, and Industrial Organization: Past and Future," by Patrick Legros and Andrew Newman

KAI-UWE KÜHN

When I saw the first couple of examples that Patrick Legros gave about the demand for different theories, I realized that after two months as chief economist at the European Commission, I was in fact in demand. So let me build my comments around how these theories could be potentially useful for competition policy and the sorts of problems that may arise in the practical use of these theories.

There are really three parts in this paper (Legros and Newman 2014): one is about the impact of competition on the internal organization of the firm; the second is the other way around, about the impact of the internal organization on how firms compete; and the third is trying to put these two aspects together into an equilibrium framework and ask whether more interesting comparative static results can be obtained in this equilibrium framework. This is the novel part, where the authors are pushing the theory, as they also do in their other papers.

How Does Competition Affect the Internal Organization of the Firm?

Much of that literature is ultimately concerned about the relationship between competition and productivity, their link to internal incentive schemes, and the extent to which the right incentives and the optimal organization of the firm can increase productivity and reduce costs.

We know from this literature that there are countervailing effects, and there is often a U-shaped relationship. A little bit of competition is normally good for incentives in R&D, or at least for other incentive schemes, but the endogeneity of the incentive schemes gives us a trade-off. This means that very often, we are not going to be able to say much about whether a certain policy is going to affect productivity in one direction or in another direction.

There are two main insights from this literature: incentive schemes are endogenously driven by market conditions, and the cost of integration is also going to depend on market conditions. Both have been very important for the empirical study of incentive schemes, and the key challenge is to find instruments to control for them.

Can this help us design effective proposals for policy interventions? This approach has helped practitioners of competition policy quite a bit in making arguments. One leading example is the interaction between antitrust policy and intellectual property rights. There, if we have very concentrated markets with large dominant firms, the theories together with the empirical evidence give us some comfort that we should not be afraid to intervene to restore competition. We are also comforted in ignoring in the process some of the arguments that firms will almost always make, that any intervention will depress their R&D decisions. This argument has been deployed in practically every antitrust case since the Microsoft case.

The approach we are describing may also be useful for other policies, like state aid policy in the European Union, where we query the effects on R&D activities, or the productivity of subsidies to different firms, effectively creating a more or a less balanced competitive environment.

Beyond the role of internal organization for productivity, another important element for productivity is the selection that comes through the entry and exit of firms. There is a strong logic for controlling aid and subsidies, so as not to interfere with the process of selection. This also raises the question of whether organizational structure may not also be a subject of selection in many cases. There is a lot of trial and error in organizational structure, and experimentation may be an important explanation for heterogeneity in productivity among firms. It may also mean that in bad times, there is selection against poor organizational structures and therefore, more homogeneity in the types of organizational forms that we find after a crisis, for example.

How Does Organizational Structure Affect Market Behavior?

The second part of the paper is about something that industrial organization economists have been thinking about a little bit more: how organization structures may affect market behavior. The paper reviews the large literature on the possibility to commit to incentive schemes. The literature that relied on observability of the contracts has luckily died. Typically, we do not have observability; we do not observe what the incentive contracts are for managers. That insight is important and may prove crucial given our greater and greater reliance in a lot of merger cases on merger simulations.

What we do in merger simulations is to decide whether it's a homogeneous goods market or not. We always do Cournot because we know that's the right thing for homogeneous goods markets, and when it's differentiated goods markets, we know it's differentiated good Bertrand. That is the standard. Then you have the unfortunate cases in which you're actually getting the realized costs and you see that neither Cournot nor differentiated goods Bertrand actually work. There may be many reasons for which these theories do not work, but one of the reasons is internal incentive structures of the firms. So I think that once you realize that, you realize that for a lot of the empirical work where you are trying to evaluate something like a merger simulation, we just don't have the information about behavior to actually make good predictions about how our prices might be, and we have to question how much we can do with those types of instruments.

A big success of the theory in industrial organization and in antitrust, at least among economists and among consultants probably, is the use of the theory in foreclosure, in particular the works of Hart and Tirole and of Bolton and Winston on vertical integration. There are many papers that are more contractual but also rely on incompleteness of markets to show foreclosure effects. This has really become the staple of trying to construct a theory of harm to bring antitrust foreclosure for their cases. In Europe the Microsoft case is probably the first time such a theory of harm has been tried.

At the same time, our efficiency stories for many vertical restraints often rely on incomplete contracts stories of noncontractabilities. For both the foreclosure and the efficiency views based on incomplete contracting ideas, there is a practical problem since the literature has not been out there so widely that economists and lawyers actually understand it. Whenever you make an argument on that type of basis, a typical answer will be "Oh, you should be able to do this through some other contract that doesn't have the potential anticompetitive effects." I was reminded of this when we were told the Grossman and Hart views before they wrote their paper (1986). You see this type of reaction a lot in practice.

Equilibrium Determination of Organizational Structure

First, I think one has to be a little careful with these models when one asks if we are explaining heterogeneity here. While endogenous heterogeneity is attractive, I think a lot of the heterogeneity that we are finding in organizations really comes from the heterogeneity of the people who are in these organizations. There will be very different behavior as these people are changing, and the types of skills that people have are very different from organization to organization. So if you get changes in leadership, you tend to get changes in the types of people who want to work there and you get changes in what they are emphasizing relative to one another, so I think that heterogeneity is already there. The interesting question is how you classify this type of heterogeneity in these organizations and how the organizations change as you bring in people with different characteristics. I think that this is a more important question than asking what happens with completely homogeneous people.

What I do like about this whole research program is actually the possibility of answering some of the most basic questions that one asks when dealing with mergers and antitrust cases: how have we come to this point? Why have these practices been adopted? Why does this merger come now? What the literature does not really give us is the comparative static that we should be looking for what triggered this change in the market. Understanding that is often the key to understanding what is going on in the market so as to differentiate whether there is something anticompetitive going on or whether it is something that is efficiency enhancing. This ability to answer these basic questions is going to be really important in practice.

References

Grossman, S., and O. Hart. 1986. "The Costs and Benefits of Ownership: A Theory of Vertical and Lateral Integration." *Journal of Political Economy* 94: 691–719.

Legros, P., and A. F. Newman. 2014. "Contracts, Ownership, and Industrial Organization: Past and Future." *Journal of Law, Economics, and Organization* 30(suppl. 1): i82–117.

PART 7

INCOMPLETE CONTRACTS
AND INTERNATIONAL TRADE

21

Grossman-Hart (1986) Goes Global: Incomplete Contracts, Property Rights, and the International Organization of Production

POL ANTRÀS

In 1986, the year of publication of Sandy Grossman and Oliver Hart's seminal paper on the boundaries of the firm, the state of the art mobile phone, the Motorola DynaTAC 8000x, resembled a large brick, weighed close to two pounds, and was sold at $3,995 a piece (or a whopping $8,235 in current U.S. dollars). That same year, IBM released its first laptop computer, the 13-pound IBM PC Convertible, featuring an Intel 80C88 CPU that ran at 4.77 MHz, 256 kb of RAM, and a narrow 10-inch LCD screen, all for just $2,000 (or the equivalent of $3,820 today).

The past 25 years have witnessed an information and communication technology (ICT) revolution that has transformed the world economy. The exponential growth in the processing power and memory capacity of computers (as exemplified by Moore's law) and the equally exponential growth in the network capacity of optical fiber have led to a dramatic fall in the cost of processing and transmitting information at long distances. One of the manifestations of this ICT revolution has been the gradual disintegration of production processes (or "slicing of the value chain") across borders. More and more firms now

This survey was prepared for the "Grossman and Hart at 25" conference held in Brussels on June 24–26, 2011. I am grateful to Lucia Antras, Davin Chor, Arnaud Costinot, Oliver Hart, and an anonymous referee for very helpful comments and to Elhanan Helpman for many conversations on this topic over the years. I am also grateful to Davin Chor, Federico Díez, Nathan Nunn, Heiwai Tang, and Dan Trefler for kindly sharing their data with me, and to Ruiqing Cao for excellent research assistance.

organize production on a global scale and choose to offshore parts, components, or services to producers in foreign and often distant countries.

Although this trend is significant enough to be salient in aggregate statistics, it is often best illustrated through particular examples.[1] Apple's iPad 2 tablet is a case in point. Its slim and sleek exterior hides a complex manufacturing process combining components provided by multiple suppliers located in various countries. Apple does not disclose information on its input providers, but teardown reports (such as those published by isuppli.com and ifixit.com) have shed light on the global nature of the iPad 2 production process. The tablet itself is assembled in China (and by the end of 2011 also in Brazil) by Taiwan-based Foxconn. The displays are believed to be manufactured by LG Display and, more recently, by Samsung, both of which are based in South Korea. The distinctive touch panel is produced by Wintek, a Taiwan-based company that also owns plants in China, India, and Vietnam, while the case is provided by another Taiwanese company, Catcher Technologies, with operations in Taiwan and China. A third important component, the battery pack, also originates in Taiwan and is sold by Simplo Technologies and Dynapack International. Apart from these easily identifiable parts, the iPad 2 incorporates a variety of chips and other small technical components provided by various firms with R&D centers in developed economies and manufacturing plants (under various organizational structures) worldwide. A nonexhaustive list includes (again) Korea's Samsung, which is believed to manufacture the main processor (designed by Apple) and possibly the flash memory, Japan's Elpida contributing the SDRAM, Germany's Infineon and U.S. Qualcomm both supplying 3G modules, and Italo-French STMicroelectronics, Japan's AKM Superconductors, and U.S. TAOS each contributing key sensors.

When designing their global sourcing strategies, one of the key organizational decisions faced by firms concerns the extent of control they want to exert over their foreign production processes. Ownership of foreign assets is one of the key methods to enhance such control as exemplified by Intel's decision in 1997 to offshore a significant part of its worldwide production of microprocessors to a $300 million wholly owned manufacturing plant in Costa Rica. Other firms, such as Nike or Apple, also rely heavily on offshore manufacturing, but choose to subcontract production to nonaffiliated producers around the world, while keeping within firm boundaries only the design and marketing stages of production.

Why do some firms find it optimal to exert a tight control over their foreign production operations while others choose not to do so? Or paraphrasing

---

[1] For aggregate evidence on the increase in vertical fragmentation, see Feenstra and Hanson (1996), Campa and Goldberg (1997), Hummels, Ishii, and Yi (2001), and Yeats (2001). This trend also featured prominently in the WTO's 2008 *World Trade Report*.

the opening sentences of Grossman and Hart's 1986 article (GH), "what is a multinational firm? And what are the determinants of how vertically or laterally integrated the activities of the multinational firm are?" The purpose of this paper is to provide an overview of recent literature in international trade that has attempted to provide answers to these questions by applying some of the insights of the influential property rights theory first exposited in GH and further developed in Hart and Moore (1990) and Hart (1995).

The relevance of incomplete contracting theories of integration is not particularly difficult to motivate in international environments in which goods or services are exchanged across borders. Global production networks necessarily entail contracting relationships between agents located in countries with heterogeneous legal systems and contracting institutions.[2] A natural difficulty in contract disputes involving international transactions is determining which country's laws are applicable to the contract being signed. Even when they are competent (in a legal sense), local courts may be reluctant to enforce a contract involving residents of foreign countries, especially if such enforcement would entail an unfavorable outcome for local residents. Although there have been coordinated attempts to reduce the contractual uncertainties and ambiguities associated with international transactions, such as the signing of the United Nations Convention on Contracts for the International Sale of Goods (CISG), many countries have opted out of these agreements (most notably, the United Kingdom). Other forms of arbitration, such as those provided by the International Chamber of Commerce in Paris, are also available but are rarely used in practice. The limited amount of repeated interactions and lack of collective punishment mechanisms often associated with international transactions also makes implicit contracts less sustainable in those environments. As summarized by Rodrik (2000) "ultimately, [international] contracts are often neither explicit nor implicit; they simply remain incomplete."

The detrimental effects of imperfect contract enforcement on international trade flows are particularly acute in transactions involving intermediate inputs, as those tend to be associated with longer time lags between the time the order is placed (and the contract is signed) and the time the goods or services are delivered (and the contract executed), and they also often entail significant relationship-specific investments and other sources of lock-in on the part of both buyers and suppliers. For instance, suppliers often tailor their manufacturing production to the needs of particular buyers and have difficulty placing those goods in world markets should the buyer decide not to abide by the terms of the contract. Similarly, buyers undertake significant investments whose

---

[2] As an example, Djankov et al. (2003) document that the total duration of a legal procedure aimed at collecting a bounced check ranges from 7 days in Tunisia to 1,003 in Slovenia.

value can be severely diminished by incompatibilities, production line delays, or quality debasements associated with suppliers not following through with their contractual obligations.

In *Poorly Made in China*, Paul Midler describes his misadventures as an offshoring consultant in China, where his command of Chinese made him a valuable asset for U.S. companies seeking suppliers in that country. Midler describes numerous last-minute pricing maneuvers and clever manipulations of quality undertaken by Chinese suppliers, attempting to extract more surplus from the Western buyers they transact with.[3] As Midler puts it, "'Price go up!' was the resounding chorus heard across the manufacturing sector" (p.184) which is very much reminiscent of the classical hold-up problem modeled in GH. Furthermore, Midler illustrates how potential solutions to this hold-up problem tend to be ineffective in China. For instance, relational contracting does not appear to diminish the frustrations of Western companies, and if anything, tends to increase them, something he labels the "reverse frequent flyer" effect. Furthermore, and consistently with one of the fundamental assumptions in GH, ownership of Chinese suppliers does not eliminate opportunistic behavior on the part of these producers, or as he puts it, there is no "joint venture panacea."

The remainder of the paper is divided into three sections and a final section with concluding remarks. In section 1, I develop a variant of the partial equilibrium framework in GH, along the lines of Antràs (2003), which has served as the basis for most applications of the property rights in international environments. Although the literature has generally assumed particular functional forms to derive results on the key determinants of the integration decision, I show that some of the key predictions of the model are robust to more general assumptions on preferences and technology. Later in the section, I outline several extensions of this framework that have been developed in the literature, including the introduction of liquidity constraints, multiple suppliers, partial contractibility and productivity heterogeneity across firms.

In section 2, I summarize different ways in which this partial-equilibrium property rights model has been adapted in general-equilibrium, open-economy environments. Even restricting oneself to partial-equilibrium environments, considering the location of different parts of the production process significantly complicates the organizational decisions of firms. It is thus natural that the literature has largely focused on simple environments with either a limited number of countries (often two) or with particularly convenient symmetry assumptions across firms and countries. As a payoff to these simplifications,

---

[3] The lack of enforceability of contracts is illustrated by the Chinese saying that "signing a contract is simply a first step in negotiations."

these frameworks deliver sharp implications for how the organizational deci-sions of firms aggregate up to easily observable statistics, such as the intrafirm component of international trade across sectors and countries. I argue, however, that future contributions should incorporate more realistic features, particularly when the goal is to develop theoretical frameworks that guide empirical analysis using *firm-level data*.

The empirical implementation of open-economy property rights frameworks is precisely the focus of section 3. Empirically validating the property rights the-ory poses at least two important challenges. First, the theory's predictions are associated with subtle characteristics of marginal returns to investments that are generally unobservable in the data (see Whinston 2003). Second, data on the integration decisions of firms are not readily available. Admittedly, the inter-national trade literature has not made an awful lot of progress addressing the first concern (although it has not ignored it). Conversely, data on international transactions are particularly accessible due to the existence of official records of goods crossing borders. Furthermore, some countries collect detailed data on whether international trade flows involve related parties or nonrelated parties, thus generating hundreds of thousands of observations *per year* describing the relative prevalence of integration across products and countries. In section 3, I describe the rich variation observed in U.S. intrafirm import data and explicitly discuss the pros and cons of using this source of data to test the property rights theory. I also review several papers in the empirical literature on intrafirm trade by graphically illustrating their key findings and how they have been interpreted in light of the GH framework. Finally, I briefly discuss a few recent contributions using international firm-level data sources and suggest some avenues for future research.

In section 4, I offer some concluding remarks and outline the broader influence of GH in the field of international trade.

Before proceeding any further, it is important to mention some topics that are omitted in this survey. First, it should be emphasized that GH's property rights approach has not been the only theory of the firm applied to understand mul-tinational firm boundaries. The literature has understood since Hymer's (1960, 1976) seminal Ph.D. thesis that the issue of control is essential to understand-ing the nature of the multinational firm, and several early contributions adopted the transaction cost approach of Coase (1937) and Williamson (1975, 1985) to shed light on some of the key determinants of the boundaries of the multi-national firm.[4] The first general equilibrium implementation of the transaction cost approach is due to Ethier (1986), with important subsequent contributions by Ethier and Markusen (1996), McLaren (2000), and Grossman and Helpman

---

[4] See, among others, Casson (1979), Dunning (1981), or Rugman (1981).

(2002, 2003).[5] Second, the international trade literature has also concerned itself with other organizational decisions of multinational firms, such as the allocation of decision rights among employees and the optimal compensation of worker effort. For instance, Marin and Verdier (2009) and Puga and Trefler (2010) have applied the Aghion and Tirole (1997) authority framework in general equilibrium, open-economy environments, while Grossman and Helpman (2004) have studied how optimal incentive schemes interact with multinational firm boundaries. Reviewing these contributions in detail is outside the scope of this paper, though I will touch on them toward the end of section 2.[6] Similarly, I will refrain from delving into the foundations of incomplete contracting frameworks since this is not more of an issue in open-economy environments than it is in closed-economy ones, and since it has been discussed in depth elsewhere in the literature (see, for instance, the articles in the 1999 symposium in the *Review of Economic Studies*).

1. A Property Rights Model

In this section, I develop a simple variant of GH along the lines of Antràs (2003).

1.1 Model Set-up

Environment Consider a situation in which only the manager of a firm F has access to a technology for converting a specialized intermediate input or component m into a differentiated final good. The manager F is also in charge of providing headquarter services h, which raise the marginal product of m. Given an amount m of components and an amount h of headquarter services, sale revenue is given by $R(h, m)$ with $R_h > 0$, $R_m > 0$, $R_{hm} > 0$, $R_{hh} < 0$, $R_{mm} < 0$, and $R(h, 0) = R(0, m) = 0$. The manager F needs to contract with an operator of a manufacturing plant (denoted by M) for the provision of m. Production of h and m require investments on the part of F and M, respectively. F obtains $1/c_h$ units of h for each unit of investment, while M obtains $1/c_m$ units of m for each unit of investment. Investments are made simultaneously at some date $t = 1$ and the inputs are obtained at a later date $t = 2$. The inputs are tailored specifically to the other party in the transaction and are useless or incompatible in alternative

---

[5] See also Qiu and Spencer (2002) and Chen and Feenstra (2008) for related frameworks. As a curiosity, Ethier's (1986) article cites a 1984 working paper version of GH, and thus appears to be the first published paper in international trade to cite GH.

[6] These topics have been treated in some detail in surveys by Markusen (1995), Spencer (2005), Helpman (2006), and Antràs and Rossi-Hansberg (2009), as well as in the classic book by Caves (1996).

production processes.[7] Finally, F converts inputs h and m into the final good at a final date $t = 3$. For simplicity, agents do not discount the future between $t = 1$ and $t = 3$.

Contracting The managers F and M get together at some initial stage $t = 0$ to negotiate a contract. As in GH, before investments in h and m are made, the only contractibles are the allocation of residual rights (i.e., the ownership structure) and a lump-sum transfer between the two parties.[8] I will consider later more general environments in which contracts on a wider set of variables are enforceable. Without a binding contract detailing the terms of exchange, parties are left to negotiate these terms (i.e., a payment by F to M for the provision of m) after these inputs have been produced at stage $t = 2$. As in GH, it is assumed that this ex post agreement *is* fully enforceable, that F and M have symmetric information at that stage, and that the negotiation outcome can be approximated by the symmetric Nash bargaining solution. The significance and ramifications of these assumptions have been discussed at length in the literature, and although they remain controversial, they continue to be standard in the literature.[9]

Property Rights and Bargaining Power Following GH's property rights approach to the theory of the firm, and contrary to the Coase-Williamson approach, it is assumed that the space of contracts and the nature of the ex post negotiations between F and M are independent of the ownership structure decision at stage $t = 0$. The ex post distribution of surplus is, however, sensitive to the chosen organizational structure. To see this, notice that given our assumptions, when F and M remain unaffiliated entities, a case I refer to throughout as *outsourcing*, a contractual termination leaves both agents with a zero pay-off because the inputs are useless unless combined together. In this framework the same would be true if M were to integrate F because F's human capital has been assumed essential for the production of the final good. For this reason, and because it does not appear to feature prominently in the data, I hereafter abstract from considering the possibility of (forward) integration of F by M. The case of

---

[7] Of course, partial relationship specificity would suffice for the results. Furthermore, in the presence of search frictions or time-to-build constraints, a lock-in effect might arise even in the absence of customization of inputs, as producers might be unable to costlessly combine their inputs with those of other producers.

[8] In practice, contractual disputes are often triggered by concerns about substandard quality of inputs or incompatibilities of these inputs with other parts of the production process, both of which are seldom verifiable by third parties. Furthermore, the particular nature of the required investments in h and m might be difficult to specify in a comprehensive contract.

[9] Following GH, I assume that both agents have symmetric primitive bargaining in the ex post negotiations. The international trade literature has for the most part considered the generalized Nash bargaining solution.

backward integration, which I refer to throughout simply as *integration*, is more consequential. This is because when F integrates the production of m, it effectively purchases the residual rights of control over this input. As a result, if M refuses to trade after these inputs have been produced, F now has the option of selectively firing M and seizing the amount of m already produced. To ensure positive ex post gains from trade, it is assumed, however, that F cannot use the input without M as effectively as it can with the cooperation of M, so firing M results in a loss of a fraction $1 - \delta$ in sale revenue.

Discussion At this point, it may be useful to compare the assumptions I have made with those in GH. First, note that the above framework is more general than GH in two respects: it allows investments to be complementary in creating surplus and it also considers the possibility that one agent's investments might affect the other agent's disagreement payoffs, thereby avoiding the need to narrowly interpret investments as being human capital investments. As pointed out by Whinston (2003), these features are indispensable to be able to comfortably use the model to interpret integration decisions in the real world.

Despite these generalizations, it should be clear that the above framework is more restrictive than GH in at least three dimensions. First, ownership of physical assets (buildings, machines) has been associated above with ownership of the inputs that are produced with those assets. This is a narrow interpretation of the role of asset ownership, but it is a useful assumption to make when one is trying to simplify the exposition of the partial equilibrium side of the model. Second, although in principle the parties could agree at $t = 0$ on the allocation of ownership rights over two assets (h and m), as pointed out above it is never optimal to allocate ownership rights over h to M. Again, this is largely an expositional assumption that draws attention away from situations that do not appear essential in general equilibrium, open-economy applications of the GH framework. Third, the model above places much more structure on how investments affect inside and outside options than the original GH framework does. To be more precise, given the assumptions, the payoffs obtained by F and M in the ex post bargaining are proportional to a common aggregator of h and m, with the ownership structure decision simply affecting the shares obtained by each agent. In particular, F obtains a fraction β_k of revenue $R(h, m)$ and M obtains the remaining $1 - \beta_k$, where

$$
\beta_k = \begin{cases} \beta_O = \dfrac{1}{2} & \text{if } F \text{ outsources to } M \\[2mm] \beta_V = \delta + \dfrac{1}{2}(1 - \delta) & \text{if } F \text{ integrates } M \end{cases} \tag{1}
$$

Obviously, this is a significant point of departure from GH, but as I shortly demonstrate, it will deliver a particularly sharp representation of one of the key insights from the property rights theory, while sidestepping Whinston's (2003) criticism about the robustness of GH's insights to the presence of complementary investments.

Formulation of the Problem Having discussed our assumptions, I next offer a succinct formulation of the "organizational problem" solved by F and M. Notice that given the existence of ex ante transfers, firms will agree at $t = 0$ on the ownership structure (outsourcing or integration) that maximizes the joint payoff of F and M. This surplus is of course affected by the investments in h and m undertaken by F and M; these investments are chosen simultaneously and non-cooperatively by these two agents at $t = 1$ with the aim of maximizing their ex post payoffs at $t = 2$. In sum, the key organizational decision $k \in \{V, O\}$—V for vertical integration and O for outsourcing—solves

$$\max_{k \in \{V, O\}} \pi_k = R\left(h_k, m_k\right) - c_h \cdot h_k - c_m \cdot m_k$$

$$\text{s.t.} \quad h_k = \arg\max_{h} \{\beta_k R\left(h, m_k\right) - c_h \cdot h\} \tag{P1}$$

$$m_k = \arg\max_{m} \{(1 - \beta_k) R\left(h_k, m\right) - c_m \cdot m\},$$

where β_k is given in (1).

1.2 Characterization

Notice that program (P1) boils down to choosing a value of $\beta \in \{\beta_V, \beta_O\}$ to maximize joint profits. As suggested by Antràs and Helpman (2004, 2008), a pedagogically useful way to characterize the optimal choice of ownership structure is to consider the hypothetical case in which F and M could freely choose β from the continuum of values in $[0, 1]$. Intuitively, integration will tend to be more attractive in situations in which the joint profit maximizing share of surplus accruing to F is large, while outsourcing will tend to be preferred when this share is low.

Straightforward differentiation of the objective function in (P1) delivers

$$\frac{d\pi_k}{d\beta} = (R_h - c_h) \frac{dh}{d\beta} + (R_m - c_m) \frac{dm}{d\beta}, \tag{2}$$

which, plugging the first-order condition associated with the constraints in (P1) and setting $d\pi_k/d\beta = 0$, delivers the following joint profit maximizing division of surplus β^*:

$$\frac{\beta^*}{1 - \beta^*} = \frac{\eta_{R,h} \cdot \xi_{h,\beta}}{\eta_{R,m} \cdot (-\xi_{m,\beta})}, \tag{3}$$

where $\eta_{R,j} \equiv jR_j/R$ is the elasticity of surplus to investments in input $j = h, m$ and $\xi_{j,\beta} \equiv \frac{dj}{d\beta}\frac{\beta}{j}$ is the elasticity of investment in j to changes in the distribution of surplus β. In words, equation (3) implies that:[10]

Proposition 1 The (hypothetical) optimal share of revenue allocated to an agent is increasing in the elasticity of revenue with respect to that agent's investment and in the elasticity of that agent's investment with respect to changes in the distribution of surplus.

Because in the property rights theory the only way to shift surplus between agents is via the allocation of ownership rights, the first result above is reminiscent of one of the key results in GH, namely, that ex ante efficiency dictates that ownership of assets, and thus residual rights of control, should be assigned to the party whose investment contributes relatively more to the value of the relationship. The relative importance of an agent's investment is captured here by the elasticity of revenue with respect to that agent's investment.

Equation (3) highlights, however, that the responsiveness of investments to changes in bargaining power is also an important determinant of the ownership decision. What determines this responsiveness? One might worry that if this elasticity depends on the division of surplus β and on features of the revenue function, the overall effects of the revenue elasticities $\eta_{R,h}$ and $\eta_{R,m}$ might be less clear-cut than as suggested in equation (3). Totally differentiating the first-order conditions associated with the constraints in program (P1) we indeed find that

$$\xi_{h,\beta} = \frac{-R_h\left(1 - \beta\right)R_{mm} - R_m\beta R_{hm}}{\left(1 - \beta\right)h\left(R_{hh}R_{mm} - \left(R_{hm}\right)^2\right)}; \tag{4}$$

$$\xi_{m,\beta} = \frac{\beta R_m R_{hh} + R_h\left(1 - \beta\right)R_{hm}}{\left(1 - \beta\right)m\left(R_{hh}R_{mm} - \left(R_{hm}\right)^2\right)}. \tag{5}$$

These equations indicate that the optimal division of surplus, and thus the optimal allocation of ownership rights, depends on subtle properties of the revenue function $R(h, m)$, not just on its partial derivatives.[11] Although as pointed out above the assumptions we have made about how investments affect inside and

---

[10] I choose to represent equation (3) in terms of elasticities rather than in terms of marginal returns and marginal effects on investment, that is, $\frac{\beta^*}{1-\beta^*} = \frac{R_h\cdot(dh/d\beta)}{R_m\cdot(-dm/d\beta)}$, to facilitate a comparison with previous results derived in the literature and discussed later.

[11] Note that even the effect of β on investments is of ambiguous sign. The denominator in (4) and (5) is necessarily positive if the second-order conditions for the choice of h and m in a complete contracting environment are to be met, but the sign of the numerators is shaped by the relative concavity and complementarity of $R(h, m)$.

outside options are rather restrictive, these results resonate with those exposited by Whinston (2003).

To make some progress, the literature has typically assumed particular functional forms for the revenue function $R(h, m)$. A particularly widely used formulation, starting with the work of Antràs (2003), is to assume

$$R(h, m) = Ah^{\eta_h} m^{\eta_m}, \tag{6}$$

with $A > 0, 0 < \eta_h < 1, 0 < \eta_m < 1$, and $\eta_h + \eta_m < 1$. This specification may seem ad hoc, but it follows directly from two assumptions that are fairly common in modern international trade models, namely, that preferences feature a constant elasticity of substitution across varieties within an industry (see Dixit and Stiglitz 1977) and that inputs are combined in production according to a Cobb-Douglas technology (see section 2 for more details). It may be argued that the Cobb-Douglas assumption is particularly restrictive, so I address this concern later. In any case, with the revenue function in (6), the revenue elasticities $\eta_{R,h}$ and $\eta_{R,m}$ are pinned down by the parameters η_h and η_m, respectively, and the ratio of elasticities $\xi_{h,\beta}/\xi_{m,\beta}$ turns out to depend only on these parameters as well. Equation (3) then takes a particularly simple form:

$$\frac{\beta^*}{1 - \beta^*} = \sqrt{\frac{\eta_h/(1 - \eta_h)}{\eta_m/(1 - \eta_m)}}. \tag{7}$$

I will associate throughout the parameters η_h and η_m with the terms *headquarter intensity* and *component intensity*, respectively. It is then clear from equation (7) that the joint profit maximizing share of revenue assigned to an agent is increasing in the relative importance of that agent's investment, as measured by the elasticity of revenue to that investment. In terms of the choice of ownership structure, this isoelastic example delivers the following sharp result (see, for instance, Antràs and Helpman, 2008, for a proof):

Proposition 2 Let firm revenues be given by (6) and let $\eta_h = \alpha v$ and $\eta_m = \alpha(1 - v)$, with $0 < \alpha < 1$ and $0 < v < 1$. Then there exists a unique threshold $\hat{v} \in (0, 1)$ such that for all $v > \hat{v}$, integration dominates outsourcing (or $k^* = V$), while for $v < \hat{v}$, outsourcing dominates integration (or $k^* = O$). Furthermore, the threshold $\hat{v}$ is independent of the cost parameters c_h and c_m.

Hence, integration is optimal for headquarter intensities above (or component intensities below) a given threshold, while outsourcing is chosen for headquarter intensities below (or component intensities above) that threshold.

Even though the specification in (6) has been widely used in the literature, one might still be concerned that the results in Proposition 2 heavily rely on the Cobb-Douglas assumption implicit in (6). It can be shown, however, that the result readily generalizes to the case in which the revenue function is a general homogeneous of degree $\alpha \in (0, 1)$ in h and m.[12] In the Appendix, it is shown that in that case, equation (3) simplifies to:

$$\frac{\beta^*}{1 - \beta^*} = \sqrt{\frac{\eta_{R,h} \; \alpha \, (1 - \eta_{R,m}) + (1 - \alpha) \, (\sigma_{h,m} - 1) \, \eta_{R,m}}{\eta_{R,m} \; \alpha \, (1 - \eta_{R,h}) + (1 - \alpha) \, (\sigma_{h,m} - 1) \, \eta_{R,h}}}, \tag{8}$$

where $\eta_{R,h}$ and $\eta_{R,m}$ again denote the revenue elasticities of headquarter services and components, respectively, and $\sigma_{h,m}$ is the elasticity of substitution between headquarter services h and the input m in revenue. Simple differentiation then confirms that for any constant $\sigma_{h,m} > 0$, β^* continues to be increasing in $\eta_{R,h}$ and decreasing in $\eta_{R,m}$, and as a result it continues to be efficient to allocate residual rights of control and thus "power" to the party whose investment has a relatively larger impact on surplus.[13] In other words, the prediction of the model that integration is more attractive in headquarter-intensive sectors than in component-intensive sectors appears robust.

1.3 Extensions

Before discussing the open-economy implementation of the model, I briefly describe some of the extensions of the benchmark model above that have been considered in the literature. These extensions have been developed in open-economy, general equilibrium environments, but it is more convenient to discuss them here and refer back to them in section 2. For simplicity, I develop these extensions one at a time, though they could be readily incorporated in a unified framework. Also, I focus throughout on revenue functions akin to equation (6), which implicitly assume that F faces a demand schedule with a constant price elasticity and that headquarter services and the bundle of supplier inputs feature a unit elasticity of substitution. Presumably, the results I am about to discuss would still hold under more general environments (such as those discussed at the end of the previous section), but I will not attempt to verify this here.

Financial Constraints

Following GH, I have assumed so far that the choice of organizational form is always ex ante efficient, in the sense that, at $t = 0$, both parties can freely exchange lump-sum transfers and this ensures that a joint profit maximizing ownership

---

[12] This would the case, for instance, if the inverse demand faced by the final good producer is homogeneous of degree $\alpha_r - 1 < 0$ in output – as with Dixit-Stiglitz preferences – and the production function combining h and m is homogeneous of degree $\alpha_q \in (0, 1]$. In such a case, we would have $\alpha = \alpha_r \alpha_q$.

[13] It should be noted that if the revenue function does not feature a constant elasticity of substitution between h and m, then $\sigma_{h,m}$ will of course be endogenous to the parameters of the model.

structure is chosen. In practice, however, it is not clear that firms can easily resort to nondistortionary transfers in their initial negotiations. For instance, some firms might be financially constrained and might have difficulties raising the amount of cash that would be needed to compensate their counterparty for choosing a particular ownership structure, and this may lead to an inefficient choice of organizational form. I next build on Basco (2010) to illustrate how financial constraints shape the choice of ownership structure within the version of GH. A more complete treatment of how liquidity constraints shape organizational choices in other variants of the GH model can be found in Aghion and Tirole (1994), Legros and Newman (2008), and Carluccio and Fally (2012).

In anticipation of the market structure discussed in section 2, I focus on situations in which F has full bargaining power ex ante (that is, F makes a take-it-or-leave-it offer to M) and the initial contract calls for a positive transfer from M to F. The key new feature is that M is now assumed to only be able to pledge to external financiers at most a share ϕ of the income it receives from transacting with F, which remember is given by $(1 - \beta_k) R (h_k, m_k) - c_m \cdot m_k$ under organizational mode $k \in \{V, O\}$.[14] When financial constraints bind, the optimal ownership structure from the point of view of F now solves program (P1) but with the objective function now given by

$$\pi_k = \beta_k R (h_k, m_k) - c_h h_k + \phi [(1 - \beta_k) R (h, m) - c_m m_k]. \tag{9}$$

Following the same steps as in section (1.2), we find that the (hypothetical) profit-maximizing division of surplus β^* for F is given by

$$\frac{\beta^*}{1 - \beta^*} = \phi \frac{\eta_{R,h} \cdot \xi_{h,\beta}}{\eta_{R,m} \cdot (-\xi_{m,\beta})} + (1 - \phi) \frac{\beta^*}{1 - \beta^*} \frac{1}{\eta_{R,m} \cdot (-\xi_{m,\beta})},$$

which naturally reduces to (3) when $\phi = 1$ and financial constraints disappear. When the revenue function further has the isoelastic form in (6), we can use equations (4) and (5) to obtain:

$$\frac{\beta^*}{1 - \beta^*} = \phi \frac{\eta_h}{\eta_m} \frac{(1 - \beta^*) - \eta_m}{\beta^* - \eta_h} + (1 - \phi) \left(\frac{\eta_h}{\eta_m} \frac{(1 - \beta^*) - \eta_m}{\beta^* - \eta_h} + \frac{1 - \eta_m}{\eta_m} \right). \tag{10}$$

A few things are worth highlighting about equation (10). First, and quite obviously, we have that when $\phi = 1$, financial constraints disappear and (10)

---

[14] For consistency with the other parts of the model, one should not interpret this financial contract as a revenue-sharing agreement, because sale revenues are assumed to be noncontractible. A typical way to rationalize this formulation of credit constraints is to introduce limited commitment on the part of the supplier; if the supplier can default on external investors and still retain a share of sale revenue, then the size of the initial loan will indeed be proportional to expected revenue.

simplifies to (7). Second, note that the right-hand side is a weighted sum of two decreasing functions of β^*, with the weights being ϕ and $1 - \phi$, and with the second term being necessarily higher than the first one. This immediately implies that β^* is necessarily higher the lower is ϕ. In words, the desired division of surplus is more tilted toward F, the tighter are financial constraints, reflecting the fact that F now uses integration not only to balance incentives but also to extract surplus from M. Third, and in a related manner, the optimal share of ex post surplus accruing to F is positive even when headquarter intensity is negligible, that is, $\beta^* = (1 - \eta_m) (1 - \phi) / (1 - \phi (1 - \eta_m)) > 0$ when $\eta_h = 0$. Finally, it is easily verified that the positive effect of η_h and negative effect of η_m on the profit-maximizing value division of surplus β^* continues to hold for any value of $\phi \in (0, 1]$.[15]

As in the model without financial constraints, one can show that there continues to exist a headquarter-intensity cutoff $\hat{\eta}_h \in [0, 1)$ such that for all $\eta_h > \hat{\eta}_h$, integration dominates outsourcing (or $k^* = V$), while outsourcing dominates integration (or $k^* = O$) for $\eta_h < \hat{\eta}_h$ whenever $\hat{\eta}_h > 0$. The key new features brought about by financial constraints are (see the Appendix for a proof):

Proposition 3 The cutoff $\hat{\eta}_h$ is lower the larger is ϕ, implying that integration is more prevalent the tighter the financial constraints. Furthermore, for large enough ϕ, integration may be optimal for any value of $\eta_h \in (0, 1)$, that is, $\hat{\eta}_h = 0$.

As in the model without financial frictions, I show in the Appendix that $\hat{\eta}_h$ is decreasing in η_m, and thus integration continues to be more prevalent, the less important are supplier investments.

Multiple Suppliers

So far, I have focused on situations in which F is concerned only with the provision of one input. Acemoglu et al. (2007) consider a more realistic environment in which production requires multiple intermediate inputs. Although their framework does not allow for headquarter services it is straightforward to incorporate them into the analysis. With that in mind, suppose that the environment is as before, but F's production process now entails the combination

---

[15] Only in the limiting case $\phi \rightarrow 0$, when M has no ability to transfer cash to F at stage 0, we have that $\beta^* \rightarrow 1 - \eta_m$, and the effect of headquarter intensity vanishes. The intuition behind this result is that when $\phi = 0$, the objective function of F coincides with that in the first constraint of program (P1). Hence, the effect of changes in η_h working through the choice of input h have no first-order effect on F's choice of ownership structure. Of course, η_h could still affect F's profits via its effects on M's choice of input m, but the latter effect turns out to be zero with the isoelastic revenue function in (6).

of headquarter services and a unit measure of components, each provided by a different manager. Denote by $\mathbf{m} \equiv \{m(i)\}_{i \in [0,1]}$ the (infinitely dimensional) vector of investments by suppliers. I impose the following functional form, which will serve to illustrate the role of input substitutability on the integration decision:

$$R(h, \mathbf{m}) = Ah^{\eta_h} \left(\int_0^1 m(i)^\rho di \right)^{\frac{\eta_m}{\rho}}. \tag{11}$$

A few comments are in order. First, equation (11) is a direct generalization of the specification in (6), with m being now replaced by a constant elasticity of substitution (CES) aggregator of the continuum of inputs. Second, the new parameter $\rho \in (0, 1)$ governs the substitutability of the different inputs provided by suppliers; when $\rho \to 1$, these inputs become perfect substitutes, while when $\rho \to 0$, they are all essential in production. Third, equation (11) imposes complete symmetry across production stages, in terms of both substitutability patterns and the importance of these suppliers' investments in production. It would be interesting to incorporate asymmetries into the framework, but I shall not attempt to do so here.

As before, the initial contract between F and its suppliers only includes an organizational structure (that is, which suppliers are integrated and which are not) and a set of lump-sum transfers across agents, on which I place no constraints in this section. Without a binding contract governing the ex post trade in inputs, the agents in the model are left to (multilaterally) bargain over the division of surplus at $t = 2$, when the inputs have been produced. Despite being infinitesimally small, individual suppliers can use the threat of withholding their respective inputs from F to extract surplus. Acemoglu et al. (2007) follow Hart and Moore (1990) in using the Shapley value to determine the division of ex post surplus between F and its suppliers.[16] It can be verified that in a symmetric equilibrium in which no supplier is integrated, a particular supplier's i payoff in the ex post bargaining is given by (see the Appendix):

$$s_O(h, m(-j), m(j)) = \frac{\eta_m}{\eta_m + \rho} Ah^{\eta_h} m(-i)^{\eta_m} \left(\frac{m(i)}{m(-i)} \right)^\rho = \frac{\eta_m}{\eta_m + \rho} R(h, \mathbf{m}), \tag{12}$$

where $m(-i)$ represents the (symmetric) investments of all suppliers other than i and where in the second equality we have used the fact that supplier investments will be symmetric in equilibrium. The final good manager F then captures

---

[16] A complication arises from the fact that we now have a continuum of agents bargaining over surplus. Acemoglu et al. (2007) resolve this issue by considering a discrete player version of the game and computing the *asymptotic* Shapley value of Aumann and Shapley (1974).

the residual share $\rho / (\eta_m + \rho)$ of revenue. Notice that the more substitutable are inputs in production (the higher is ρ), the lower is the share of revenues that accrues to suppliers, as their ability to hold up F is lower in that case.

Consider next the polar case in which all suppliers are integrated by F. Assume that in such a case, suppliers cannot withhold the full value of their marginal contribution to revenue, but only a share $1 - \delta$, as in our benchmark model above.[17] This results in $t = 2$ payoffs for suppliers equal to

$$s_V\left[h, m(-i), m(i)\right] = \frac{\eta_m(1-\delta)}{\eta_m + \rho} Ah^{\eta_h} m(-i)^{\eta_m} \left(\frac{m(i)}{m(-i)}\right)^{\rho} = \frac{\eta_m(1-\delta)}{\eta_m + \rho} R(h, m),$$

(13)

leaving F with the residual share $(\eta_m\delta + \rho) / (\eta_m + \rho)$ of revenue.

Solving for all suppliers' production levels as well as F's provision of head-quarter services, one can obtain joint profits of F and all suppliers in terms of the parameters of the model, including η_h, η_m, and ρ, and the ownership structure decision as captured by δ. Even in the presence of multiple suppliers, it can be shown again that the ratio of joint profits under integration relative to those under outsourcing continue to be increasing in the relative importance of headquarter services as captured by η_h, and thus integration is again predicted to be more prevalent in headquarter intensive sectors.[18] The main new result that emerges from the modeling of multiple suppliers is the following role of input substitutability in shaping the integration decisions of F (see the Appendix for a proof):

Proposition 4 There exists a unique threshold $\hat{\rho} \in (0, 1)$ such that for all $\rho < \hat{\rho}$, integration of all suppliers dominates outsourcing, whereas for $\rho > \hat{\rho}$, outsourcing dominates integration. Hence, integration is more prevalent the higher the complementarity (or the lower the substitutability) across supplier inputs.

The intuition behind this result is as follows. When there is a high degree of technological complementarity across inputs, the ex-post payoff of F under outsourcing tends to be relatively low (note, in particular, that F's payoff under outsourcing is 0 when $\rho \to 0$) and the choice of headquarter

---

[17] Acemoglu et al. (2007) consider an alternative formulation in which suppliers withhold a share $1 - \delta$ of their intermediate input. This generates analogous predictions for how input substitutability shapes the integration decision, but the proofs are much more cumbersome in that case.

[18] Conversely, the effect of η_m on the relative profitability of integration and outsourcing is less clear-cut. The reason for this is that as η_m goes down, the relative importance of suppliers' investment goes down, but their bargaining strength is also diminished, thereby aggravating the hold-up problem. It can be shown, however, that in the neighborhood of $\eta_m \to 0$, integration is necessarily more profitable than outsourcing.

services is particularly distorted. In such cases, vertical integration is particularly attractive because it helps restore the incentives of F to provide these headquarter services. Conversely, when ρ is high, suppliers face a particularly acute hold-up problem since their inputs are highly substitutable with each other; in those situations, strengthening the bargaining power of suppliers via an outsourcing contract constitutes the profit-maximizing organizational mode.

The variant of the model with multiple suppliers that I have developed assumes that all stages of production are performed simultaneously and that F negotiates with all suppliers also simultaneously. Antràs and Chor (2011) consider the case in which the production process is sequential in nature and the relationship-specific investments made by suppliers in upstream stages can affect the incentives of parties involved in later downstream stages. As a result, they show that F might have differential incentives to integrate suppliers along the value chain, and might end up outsourcing some inputs and integrating others, even when the production function treats these inputs symmetrically as in (11). In other words, the "downstreamness" of an input becomes a determinant of the ownership structure decisions related to that input. Whether upstream stages are more or less likely to be integrated than downstream stages turns out to depend critically on the relative size of the parameters η_m and ρ. When inputs are sufficiently close complements ($\rho < \eta_m$), the optimal choice involves the outsourcing of upstream stages and the integration of downstream stages, while the converse is true when inputs are sufficiently close substitutes ($\rho > \eta_m$).[19]

Partial Contractibility

The models have assumed that none of the aspects of production, except the allocation of ownership rights and a lump-sum transfer, are contractible before productive investments have taken place. This is obviously an unrealistic assumption even in the international environments we will be considering shortly, so it is important to discuss the implications of relaxing it. For that purpose, and to simplify matters, let us go back to the case in which there is a unique supplier with whom F contracts and revenue is given by the simpler function in (6). Following Acemoglu et al. (2007) and Antràs and Helpman (2008), we now allow the inputs h and m to be produced by combining a set of input-specific

---

[19] Intuitively, outsourcing elicits high levels of investment from upstream suppliers. The complementarity of upstream with downstream inputs in the case $\rho < \eta_m$ in turn alleviates the underinvestment problem for downstream suppliers, and the firm introduces fewer distortions by integrating downstream to retain a larger share of the realized output and enhance the investments in headquarter services.

components or services $\{x_j(i)\}_{i \in [0,1]}$ for $j = h, m$, each at a marginal cost c_j, according to

$$j = \exp\left[\int_0^1 \log x_j(i)\, di\right], \quad j = h, m. \tag{14}$$

To capture partial contractibility, assume that the components related to input j in the range $[0, \mu_j]$, $0 \leq \mu_j \leq 1$, $j = h, m$, are now contractible in the sense that the characteristics of these activities can be fully specified in advance in an *enforceable* ex ante contract (though these investments take place at $t = 2$, simultaneously with the noncontractible ones). Notice that the parameters μ_h and μ_m capture the level of contractibility of headquarter services and components, respectively. Because the terms of exchange of some of the inputs are not determined by the initial contract, F and M will again negotiate the price of those exchanges at $t = 2$. Even though each party is bound to provide the contractually stipulated levels for the contractible components, they can threaten to withhold part of the noncontractible ones, which in light of the specification in (14) can significantly impact revenue. Following GH and in analogy with the benchmark model above, assume that suppliers can entirely withhold those noncontractible components in case of a contractual breach when F outsources the production of m to M. Conversely, in the case of integration, F can selectively fire M in case of a contractual disagreement and use the components in production (since it has ownership rights over them), but as in the benchmark model we continue to assume that this entails an efficiency loss of a fraction $1 - \delta$ of revenue.

Given the symmetry in the model it is straightforward to verify that in equilibrium there will be symmetric investments x_{jn} in all noncontractible activities and x_{jc} in all contractible activities for $j = h, m$. This allows writing the revenue function as

$$R(h, m) = A x_{hc}^{\mu_h \eta_h} x_{mc}^{\mu_m \eta_m} x_{hn}^{(1-\mu_h)\eta_h} x_{mn}^{(1-\mu_m)\eta_m} = \tilde{A} x_{hn}^{(1-\mu_h)\eta_h} x_{mn}^{(1-\mu_m)\eta_m}.$$

Clearly, this revenue function is identical to (6) except that the revenue shifter A is now replaced by $\tilde{A} = A (x_{hc})^{\mu_h \eta_h} (x_{mc})^{\mu_m \eta_m}$, and η_h and η_m are now replaced by $(1 - \mu_h)\,\eta_h$ and $(1 - \mu_m)\,\eta_m$, respectively. From the analysis above, it is then clear that the integration decision now depends on the relative magnitude of the terms $(1 - \mu_h)\,\eta_h$ and $(1 - \mu_m)\,\eta_m$, that is, on the relative intensity of the noncontractible inputs provided by F and M, respectively. Furthermore, from equation (7), the (hypothetical) share of revenue that would optimally be allocated to F is given by

$$\frac{\beta^*}{1 - \beta^*} = \sqrt{\frac{(1 - \mu_h)\,\eta_h / (1 - (1 - \mu_h)\,\eta_h)}{(1 - \mu_m)\,\eta_m / (1 - (1 - \mu_m)\,\eta_m)}}, \tag{15}$$

and is increasing in η_h and μ_m, and decreasing in η_m and μ_h.[20] As Antràs and Helpman (2008), one can show the following sharper result:

Proposition 5 There exists a unique headquarter intensity cutoff $\hat{\eta}_h \in (0,1)$ such that profits are higher under outsourcing for $\eta_h < \hat{\eta}_h$ and higher under integration for $\eta_h > \hat{\eta}_h$. Furthermore, the cutoff η_{hc} is higher the larger μ_h is and the smaller μ_m is.

This result highlights that with partial contractibility, the integration decision depends not only on the level of headquarter intensity but also on the degrees of contractibility of the different inputs, with distinct effects for different types of inputs. An improvement in contracting possibilities for components enhances integration (since F is less dependent on the incentive effects of outsourcing to elicit investments from M), while an improvement on the contractibility of headquarter services has the opposite effect and makes integration less attractive.

Organizational Fixed Costs and Producer Heterogeneity

The frameworks we have considered so far treat the decisions of F and its suppliers independently of the decisions of other firms in F's industry. In reality, firms within industries tend to face similar demand conditions and tend to operate with similar production technologies. Yet even within narrowly defined industries, we observe significant variation in the organizational decisions of firms, including the location of their production stages but also the extent of control they want to exert over those processes. What explains these differences? I next follow Antràs and Helpman (2004) in showing how the mere existence of either heterogeneity in the (Hicks-neutral) productivity level or in the demand level faced by firms can give rise to heterogeneous organizational decisions among firms sharing a common headquarter intensity level. A useful implication of generating such heterogeneity is that the key parameters of the model not only affect the incentives of firms to integrate or not particular production processes (something that is rarely observed in the data), but they now also lead to smooth changes in the set of firms choosing different organizational modes, thus generating comparative static predictions for how changes in these parameters affect *aggregate* measures of the prevalence of integration in particular sectors.

---

[20] It may seem surprising that we do not need to concern ourselves with solving for the level of contractible investments and computing overall profits to determine the optimal bargaining share in (15). Note, however, that the level of contractible investments is irrelevant for the choice of β^* because these investments are set at $t = 0$ to maximize joint surplus and thus the envelope theorem washes out these terms in the first-order condition in (2).

To illustrate these features, I consider two simple modifications of the above framework. First, the revenue function now includes a productivity (or demand shifter) θ,

$$R(h, m) = A\theta h^{\eta_h} m^{\eta_m}, \tag{16}$$

so that firms with higher values of θ generate larger amounts of revenue for a given size of investments in h and m, perhaps because they combine these inputs more efficiently or perhaps because consumers are particularly keen on the manner in which these inputs are combined. Let θ be distributed across firms according to the cumulative density function $G(\theta)$. The second new feature is the presence of organizational fixed costs f_k, $k = V, O$, that vary by ownership structure. Following Antràs and Helpman (2004, 2008), I focus on the plausible case in which integration entails higher fixed costs than outsourcing, $f_V > f_O$, though most of the results discussed in this survey only require that these organizational fixed costs be distinct from each other.[21] With these assumptions it is straightforward to verify the following result (see Antràs and Helpman 2004, 2008, for a proof):

Proposition 6 There exists a unique headquarter intensity cutoff $\hat{\eta}_h \in (0, 1)$ and a unique productivity level $\hat{\theta}$, such that if $\eta_h < \hat{\eta}_h$ all firms outsource the production of m, while if $\eta_h > \hat{\eta}_h$, all firms with $\theta < \hat{\theta}$ outsource the production of m, while all firms with $\theta > \hat{\theta}$ firm integrate it. In the latter case, the share of firms integrating the production of m is increasing in the level of headquarter intensity and decreasing in the level of component intensity.

Intuitively, even though integration might be the organizational mode that maximizes operating profits whenever $\eta_h > \hat{\eta}_h$, firms with relatively low revenue levels might not be able to amortize the relatively high fixed costs associated with integration and are thus left to obtain input m via outsourcing contracts.

2. The Boundaries of Multinational Firms

In this section, I overview how the property rights theory has been used to draw multinational firm boundaries and thereby shed light on important aspects of the international economy. I first discuss how the benchmark partial equilibrium

---

[21] There is an obvious tension between this assumption and the spirit of GH's approach which associates different ownerships structures only with different allocations of assets, while holding technology and contracting constant. Still, differences in these organizational fixed costs are likely to be relevant in practice so the literature has incorporated them into the analysis.

model developed above is modified by the possibility of international trade across borders and later discuss how the framework can be embedded in industry equilibrium and general equilibrium. The bulk of the section is devoted to describing the novel results that emerge from such an analysis.

We begin by considering an N-country version of the benchmark model in the previous section, but now allow F to locate different parts of the production process in different countries. The production process we described above entails three stages (production of h, m, and the final good), thus giving rise to several potential locational decisions. Let us denote by L the set of possible locational decisions and by $\ell \in L$ a particular one. For example, ℓ could entail production of headquarter services and of the final good in F's home country and production of m in a foreign country. Notice that different location choices will in general entail different values for the key parameters of the model. In particular, trade barriers (technological or manmade), and cross-country differences in production costs and in institutions imply that different locational choices can be associated with different values for the parameters c_h, c_m, f_V, f_O, and β_V, as well as for the revenue function $R(h, m)$. How do these generalizations affect the way firms organize production? In analogy with (P1), the optimal ownership structure k^* and the optimal locational choice ℓ^* now solve the following program:

$$\max_{k \in \{V, O\}, \ell \in L} \quad \pi_k^\ell = R^\ell\left(h_k^\ell, m_k^\ell\right) - c_h^\ell \cdot h_k^\ell - c_m^\ell \cdot m_k^\ell - f_k^\ell$$

$$s.t. \quad h_k^\ell = \arg\max_h \left\{ \beta_k^\ell R\left(h, m_k^\ell\right) - c_h^\ell \cdot h \right\} \qquad \text{(P2)}$$

$$m_k^\ell = \arg\max_m \left\{ \left(1 - \beta_k^\ell\right) R\left(h_k^\ell, m\right) - c_m^\ell \cdot m \right\}.$$

Notice that even in this stylized model the cardinality of the firms' choice set can be very large. There are three potential production stages, two possible ownership structures, and N countries, thus giving rise to at least $2N^3$ possible organizational modes.[22] For $N = 5$, this generates 250 possible combinations, whereas for $N = 100$, there are two million combinations. To reduce the dimensionality of the problem, the literature has typically followed one of two approaches. One of them involves imposing symmetry across countries in most parameters of the model, and the other one entails focusing on two-country environments. Below I sketch an example of each of these two approaches.

---

[22] This assumes that headquarter services and final good production are always integrated (which is consistent with the property rights theory since F is essential for those stages), and that the production of m takes place in only one country. Relaxing these assumptions would only increase the complexity of the firm problem.

2.1 Headquarter Intensity and Comparative Advantage

Antràs (2003) considers a general equilibrium model of trade in which consumers in N countries have identical preferences and spend a constant share of their income on a continuum of differentiated varieties in two sectors Y and Z. The set-up is similar to the transaction cost model in Grossman and Helpman (2002). Identical Dixit-Stiglitz subutility functions in each sector give rise to a demand function for a particular variety ω in sector s of the form

$$q_s(\omega) = \frac{\mu_s E}{\int_0^{n_s} p_s(\omega)^{-\alpha/(1-\alpha)} dj} p_s(\omega)^{-1/(1-\alpha)} = A_s p_s(\omega)^{-1/(1-\alpha)}, \qquad (17)$$

where μ_s is the share of aggregate spending E spent in sector s, n_s is the measure of varieties available to consumers, and α governs how substitutable varieties are within sectors. Because firms take their demand shifter as given, firm revenue can simply be expressed as $R_s(\omega) = A_s^{1-\alpha} q_s(\omega)^\alpha$ (see eq. (17)), where A_s is treated as a constant by firms. Production of differentiated varieties is as described in section 1, with final good production of each variety being controlled by a different manager F who is also in charge of providing headquarter services but needs to contract with a production plant manager M for the provision of input m. Production of inputs can be located in any of the N countries in the world. Antràs (2003) focuses on the case in which h and m produce output according to a constant returns to scale Cobb-Douglas production function, with the elasticity of output to headquarter services given by a sector-specific constant, which I denote by η_s. The production technology is identical for all firms within an industry. Notice that firm-level revenue takes the isoelastic form in (6).

To simplify the complexities inherent in the general problem (P2), Antràs (2003) considers the case in which countries differ *only* in their relative factor endowments and thus in their (autarky) factor costs. In particular, he rules out trade costs across countries, lets contract incompleteness and the efficiency loss parameter δ be identical in all countries, and assumes that organizational fixed costs are independent of ownership structure and feature the same factor intensity as variable costs (i.e., they combine h and m under the same Cobb-Douglas aggregator as these enter the firm's production function).

The combination of these assumptions makes the problem (P2) particularly easy to solve because the ownership structure and location decisions can be treated independent from each other. In particular, the ownership structure decision is characterized by Proposition 2 above with F managers *worldwide* choosing to integrate their suppliers if $\eta_s > \hat{\eta}$, and outsource to them if $\eta_s < \hat{\eta}$, the key being that $\hat{\eta}$ is independent of production costs (and thus factor prices). On the other hand, the location decision boils down to choosing the location of input production that minimizes the marginal cost of provision of inputs.

Antràs (2003) assumes that when F invests in h for a production plant located in country ℓ, it needs to hire local factors ℓ and thus faces the production costs in that country, thus implying that the location decision simply solves $\min_\ell \left\{ \left(c_h^\ell \right)^{\eta_s} \left(c_m^\ell \right)^{1-\eta_s} \right\}$.[23]

To complete the description of the general equilibrium of the world economy, one needs to specify the market structure in each industry as well as the factors of production that firms employ in producing inputs. Antràs (2003) considers a Helpman and Krugman (1985) model with monopolistic competition and free entry driving profits down to zero.[24] He assumes that inputs are produced with physical capital and labor and that the production of headquarter services is more capital intensive than that of components. The latter is the key assumption of the paper as it introduces a positive correlation between the abstract concept of headquarter intensity and an observable variable, namely, capital intensity. Antràs (2003) justifies this assumption on empirical grounds, arguing that cost-sharing practices of multinational firms in their relations with independent subcontractors tend to be associated with physical capital investments rather than with labor input choices. We come back to the plausibility of this assumption in section 3.

Given the positive association between headquarter intensity and capital intensity, Proposition 2 then implies a higher prevalence of integration in capital-intensive sectors. To complete the characterization of the equilibrium, one need only impose that factor markets clear country by country and that world income equals world spending. Antràs (2003) shows that if relative factor endowments are not too different across countries, free trade will equalize factor prices worldwide, but aggregate production patterns and bilateral trade flows across countries will be fully determined. For example, labor-abundant countries will end up with the same wage level as capital-abundant countries, but factor market clearing ensures that they will end up producing a disproportionate amount of the worldwide production inputs in the labor-intensive industry.

Antràs (2003) derives explicit formulas for overall bilateral trade flows as well as their intrafirm component and highlights two main predictions from

---

[23] The fact that technology involves increasing returns to scale ensures that, with free trade, each input will be produced in only one location.

[24] To ensure that no agent earns rents in equilibrium, Antràs (2003) allows F managers to make take-it-or-leave-it offers to M managers at $t = 0$. The ex ante transfer between F and M thus ensures that M managers end up with a zero net payoff. On the other hand, free entry by F managers implies that the expected operating profits from producing a differentiated variety in a given industry exactly cover the fixed organizational costs associated with that industry. An alternative approach is developed in Grossman and Helpman (2002), where a process of search is specified and free entry leads all agents to anticipate a zero net payoff *in expectation* despite the absence of ex ante transfers between agents.

the model. First, in a cross-section of industries, the share of intrafirm imports in total imports should be increasing in the capital intensity in production of the exporting industry.[25] Second, in a cross-section of countries, the share of intrafirm imports in total imports should be increasing in the aggregate capital-labor ratio of the exporting country, as labor-abundant countries tend to export small amounts of capital-intensive goods.

2.2 Heterogeneity and Global Sourcing

In the model in Antràs (2003), the organizational decisions of firms in the world economy and their implications for certain aggregate variables, such as the intrafirm component of trade across industries and countries, are easy to characterize due to the strong symmetry assumptions made regarding the nature of contracting across countries. These "tractability" assumptions are the bread and butter of applied theorists seeking to construct models to understand certain qualitative features of the world. Yet these same assumptions often result in models that are not particularly useful tools for empirical analysis. As an example, Antràs' (2003) model clarifies that a variable that is well known to be key in understanding the pattern of trade, namely, capital intensity, may also be a key determinant of the integration decision of multinational firms and of the intrafirm component of trade, but it does so by making assumptions that render the model unsuitable for empirical analyses of the global sourcing strategies of firms or for empirical studies of the *various* determinants of the share of intrafirm trade.

In this section, I briefly describe the frameworks in Antràs and Helpman (2004, 2008), which incorporate several sources of heterogeneity while keeping the analysis manageable by focusing on a particularly simple two-country, north-south model. The key elements of the model are as follows. Consumers in both countries demand the output of one homogeneous-good sector and J differentiated-good sectors. Preferences are quasilinear in the homogeneous good and feature a constant elasticity of substitution between differentiated varieties within a sector and also between varieties in different sectors (with the latter elasticity assumed higher). This preference structure delivers a demand function for a particular variety in industry j that is analogous to that in (17), but with a demand shifter that is only a function of the aggregate consumption in the sector.

Firm behavior is a variant of the general program (P2). It is assumed that all F managers reside in the north and that the final good and headquarter services

---

[25] Strictly speaking, the model predicts that this share should be 0 for all industries with capital intensity below $\hat{\eta}$ and 1 for all industries with capital intensity above this threshold.

are always produced in that country. The location decision thus reduces to the choice of where to produce m, that is, $\ell \in \{N, S\}$. Producers in each country face a perfectly elastic supply of a unique factor of production, labor. Wage rates are fixed in general equilibrium by the "outside" homogeneous good sector and technology in that sector is such that $w^N > w^S$. The final good is produced according to a Cobb-Douglas technology in h and m that features a productivity shifter θ. Given these assumptions, the revenue function is of the type introduced above in (16). The productivity parameter θ is firm specific and drawn from a Pareto distribution with shape z, that is, $G(\theta) = 1 - (b/\theta)^z$ for $\theta \geq b > 0$, while the elasticity of output with respect to h, denoted again by η, is common to all firms within a sector, but may vary across sectors. Production of intermediate inputs requires one unit of labor per unit of output in the country where they are produced. International trade in components is costly and τ units of m need to be shipped from the south for one unit to arrive to the north. Provided that this transport cost is low enough, these assumptions imply that $c_h^N = c_m^N = w^N > \tau w^S = c_m^S$.

Production also involves different types of fixed costs, which are all defined in terms of northern labor. First, F needs to incur a fixed cost f_E of entry, upon which the productivity parameter θ is revealed to him or her, as in Melitz (2003). If F decides to remain in the market, additional fixed organizational costs need to be incurred. As discussed already and in more detail in Antràs and Helpman (2004), these fixed organizational costs are likely to vary depending on whether m is sourced in the north or in the south, and on whether it is insourced or outsourced. In particular, a natural ranking of these fixed costs is

$$f_V^S > f_O^S > f_V^N > f_O^N.$$

In words, fixed organizational costs are higher when M is located in the south regardless of ownership structure, and given the location of M, the fixed organizational costs are higher when M is integrated than when it is not.

In terms of the contracting parameters, Antràs and Helpman (2004) consider environments in which no aspects of h and m are contractible regardless of where production takes place but there is cross-country variation in the efficiency loss parameter δ, with $\delta^N > \delta^S$, and thus $\beta_V^N > \beta_V^S$, reflecting better legal protection in the north. Antràs and Helpman (2008) extend the analysis to incorporate partial contractibility (along the lines of the model developed in section 1.3), and allow the degree of contractibility to be a function of both the type of input and the country where production takes place.

Given the assumptions of the model, the choice of an organizational form faces two types of tensions. In terms of the location decision, the south entails relatively lower variable costs, but relatively higher fixed costs. As in the work of Melitz (2003), it is clear that the firm-specific productivity parameter θ will crucially affect the firm's participation in foreign sourcing. In terms of the ownership structure decision, integration improves efficiency of variable production when the intensity of headquarter services is high (as implied by Proposition 2), but involves higher fixed costs. Hence, the integration decision will crucially depend on both η and θ.

Antràs and Helpman (2004) show that the model can easily generate equilibria featuring multiple organizational forms within an industry. In particular, in sufficiently headquarter-intensive sectors it is possible for the least productive firms to exit the market upon observing their productivity, and for four nonempty (and connected) subsets of the remaining firms to choose each of the four possible organizational forms. The most productive firms in the north engage in foreign insourcing (or FDI in the south), the next most productive firms undertake foreign outsourcing, the next subset insource domestically, and the least productive firms among the surviving ones outsource domestically. This pattern is illustrated in Figure 21.1.

Antràs and Helpman (2004) also use the model to study the various determinants of the relative prevalence of these different organizational forms. As hinted already, the predictions of their model move well beyond those derived in Antràs (2003) and have served as the springboard for empirical studies of the determinants of the global sourcing strategies of firms. In particular, the model predicts that in a cross-section of industries, the share of intrafirm imports of components in total imports of components should be higher in industries with higher headquarter intensity (higher η), higher productivity dispersion (lower z), and higher transport costs or import tariffs (higher τ). Furthermore, these parameters shape the relative prevalence of domestic insourcing and domestic outsourcing in the same manner (even for the case of trade frictions τ).

When extending the model to allow for partial contractibility, Antràs and Helpman (2008) find that an improvement in contractual institutions in south raises the share of firms engaged in offshoring in that country, but it can reduce the relative prevalence of either FDI or offshore outsourcing if it affects disproportionately the contractibility of headquarter services or components,

Figure 21.1 Sorting in a Headquarter Intensive Sector (Antràs and Helpman 2004, 2008)

respectively. This result relates to our previous Proposition 5, which highlighted that the relative prevalence of alternative organizational forms crucially depends on the degree to which contractual incompleteness affects the inputs controlled by the final good producer or by his or her suppliers.

2.3 Brief Overview of Other Contributions

Before discussing the empirical implementation of the property rights theory of multinational firm boundaries, I briefly overview other significant contributions to the literature and later identify what I view as important gaps in the literature.

In section 1.3, I discussed the effects of financial or liquidity constraints on the integration decision. Naturally, the results derived there have implications for how firm boundaries are pinned down in open-economy environments. For instance, Basco (2010) and Carluccio and Fally (2012) develop general equilibrium, open-economy models in which, consistently with Proposition 3, multinationals are more likely to integrate suppliers located in countries with poor financial institutions. Furthermore, both papers predict that the effect of financial development should be especially large when trade involves complex goods, and both provide independent empirical evidence supporting this prediction.

As emphasized by Legros and Newman (2008), in the presence of financial constraints, equilibrium firm boundaries will also depend on the relative ex ante bargaining power of each party and their ability to exchange lump-sum transfers. This idea has been fruitfully applied in open-economy environments by Conconi et al. (2012) and Alfaro et al. (2010), who show that vertical integration should be relatively more prevalent in industries in which (relative) prices are high, perhaps due to import-protecting trade policies. Intuitively, in their set-up, which builds on Hart and Holmström (2010) and Legros and Newman (2009), ownership decisions are not ex ante optimal but instead trade off the pecuniary benefits of coordinating production achieved under integration and the managers' private benefits of operating in their preferred ways associated with nonintegration. Consequently, the higher the industry price, the higher the monetary benefits of integration and thus the more attractive this option is. Alfaro et al. (2010) provide evidence of a positive association between import tariffs and domestic integration decisions. Díez (2010) finds similar evidence in a cross-section of U.S. industries when looking at intrafirm trade flows, but interprets the result in light of the Antràs and Helpman (2004, 2008) models, which as mentioned already, also predicts a positive effect of imports tariffs on foreign integration. I illustrate his empirical results in section 3.

The insights of the property rights theory have also been applied to dynamic, general equilibrium models of international trade with the goal of understanding how ownership decisions vary along the life cycle of a product or input. Antràs (2005), for instance, develops a model in which the incomplete nature of contracts governing international transactions limits the extent to which the production process can be fragmented across borders, thereby generating the emergence of Vernon-type product cycles, with new goods being initially manufactured in the north (where product development takes place), and only later (when the goods are mature) is manufacturing carried out in the south. Antràs (2005) also draws the boundaries of multinational firms and shows that the model gives rise to a new version of the product cycle in which, consistently with empirical evidence, manufacturing is shifted to the south first within firm boundaries, and only at a later stage to independent firms in the south.[26]

Throughout this section, I have restricted myself to reviewing papers that can be considered "direct offspring" of GH in the sense that they adopt variants of the property rights approach to drawing firm boundaries in open-economy environments. As I will spell out in more detail in the conclusion, the incomplete contracting framework of GH has had a much broader impact in the international trade field via the influence of other theoretical frameworks that are themselves direct offspring of GH. For instance, in the presence of incomplete contracts, another important organizational decision of firms concerns the allocation of decision rights among employees. In particular, in the presence of noncontractible effort decisions by workers, managers face a trade-off between granting decision rights to workers or keeping these to themselves. The former option has the benefit of providing workers with "initiative," which may lead to higher effort, but delegation may result in decisions that are not necessarily optimal from the point of view of the manager. Avoiding delegation (i.e., exerting "authority") tends to inhibit the initiative of workers but entails more control over the course of production. This trade-off was first formalized by Aghion and Tirole (1997) and has been applied to general equilibrium frameworks by Marin and Verdier (2009) and Puga and Trefler (2010).

2.4 The Road Ahead

In 2036, we will be celebrating the 50th anniversary of Grossman and Hart's article. How will GH shape the field of international trade in the next 25 years? As I will try to convey in the next section, there are good reasons to believe that the bulk of new work on multinational firm boundaries will be empirical in nature. I believe, however, that the theoretical frameworks that have been developed

---

[26] Despite the dynamic nature of the model, Antràs (2005) assumes that the game played by managers can be treated as a static one and thus abstracts from an analysis of reputational equilibria. Corcos (2006) studies such dynamic contracts by applying the relational contract approach of Baker, Gibbons, and Murphy (2002).

to date are still too rudimentary to be taken to the data in their current form. To a large extent this is due to the fact that these models were designed to guide empirical work based on industry-level data, whereas future work is more likely to make use of firm-level data sets. The theoretical frameworks in Antràs and Helpman (2004, 2008) generate a rich set of predictions, but they are fairly low-dimensional (featuring one supplier per firm and only two countries) and impose substantial symmetry in order to highlight a few key industry-level predictions. For example, the assumption that headquarter intensity varies across industries but not across firms within an industry is clearly counterfactual (see Corcos et al. 2013 for French evidence). Future models should also incorporate multiple inputs and suppliers as in the model developed in section 1.3, while allowing for some heterogeneity among these inputs.[27] Introducing such new sources of heterogeneity into the sort of partial equilibrium models that we started with in section 1.1 is relatively straightforward. The challenge for future theoretical work is to introduce these features in a way that still permits characterizing the open-economy general equilibrium of such models, a feature that might be particularly relevant for performing counterfactual exercises when one is estimating these models structurally.

Another potentially fruitful area for future research relates to the study of the effects of the nonexcludable nature of knowledge on the internalization decision. Following GH, existing work has arguably focused too much on the distortionary effect of contractual incompleteness on ex ante investments. In practice ex post inefficiencies, including the possibility of technological expropriation by suppliers or licensees. are often highlighted as being key to the internalization decisions of multinational firms. Previous attempts to incorporate a notion of nonexcludable knowledge into general equilibrium models of the multinational firm have adopted a transaction cost approach and thus shed little light on how foreign integration circumvents the dissipation of knowledge to local producers. A more satisfactory approach would entail the application of the property rights approach and of the notion of "access" developed by Rajan and Zingales (2001).[28]

3. Taking the Property Rights Theory to International Data

As I argued in the introduction, the growing importance of international production networks, involving transactions both within and across multinational

---

[27] The recent papers by Antràs and Chor (2011), van Biesebroeck and Zhang (2011), and Schwarz and Suedekum (2011) constitute first steps in that direction.

[28] See Chen, Horstmann, and Markusen (2008) and Ponzetto (2009) for early attempts along these lines.

firms, is a key factor in understanding the recent impact of the property rights theory in the field of international trade. Although the trigger for the development of new theoretical models was empirical in nature, it is fair to say that this branch of the literature has yet not come full circle in providing definitive empirical tests of these models. Several well-crafted papers have offered different pieces of evidence that are consistent with the property rights theory, but the power of such tests remains fairly low.

In great part, these limitations are due to the fact that empirically validating the property rights theory poses at least two important challenges. First, data on the integration decisions of firms are not readily available, and thus researchers are often left to test these theories with industry- or product-level data, which do not always allow one to appropriately control for unobservable characteristics of firms that might be driving the patterns observed in the data. Second, the predictions from the property rights theory are associated with subtle features of the environment (such as the relative value of the marginal return to noncontractible, relationship-specific investments) that, by their own nature, are generally unobservable in the data (see Whinston 2003).

Admittedly, the contributions in the international trade literature have not made too much progress regarding this second hurdle, though the issue has not been completely ignored, as I highlight later in this section. With regard to the first challenge on data availability, however, an advantage of researchers in our field is that data on international transactions are particularly accessible due to the widespread existence of official records of goods and services crossing borders. For instance, there exist fairly detailed data on U.S. intrafirm trade at the six-digit Harmonized System classification of the product shipped (of which there are over 5,000 categories) and at the origin/destination country level. This amounts to hundreds of thousands of observations *per year* on the relative prevalence of integration versus nonintegration. In the next section, I discuss some of the pros and cons to using these data to test the property rights theory and will also graphically illustrate some of the empirical patterns that emerge from the data and how they relate to the models we discussed here.

Beyond these product-level data sets from official statistics, a few researchers have made use of firm-level data sets (with different levels of representativeness) that contain detailed information on the sourcing strategies of firms in different countries. In the second part of this section, I provide more details on these data sets and on how they have been used to test the property rights theory of the multinational firm. I conclude this section by offering some thoughts on future avenues for empirical research in the area.

3.1 Tests with Product-Level Intrafirm Trade Data

A significant share of empirical tests of the property rights theory of the multinational firm have used data from official import and export merchandise trade statistics, which in some countries identify whether transactions involve related or nonrelated parties. Most tests use the "U.S. Related Party Trade" data collected by the U.S. Bureau of Customs and Border Protection, so I focus on discussing some of the advantages and disadvantages associated with using this data source. Later, I briefly discuss some special features of a similar data set compiled by the Customs General Administration of the People's Republic of China, which has also been used in the literature.

Pros and Cons of Product-Level Sources

Several features of these official statistics make them particularly attractive to empirical researchers. First, for some countries, notably the United States, intrafirm trade data are publicly available and easily downloadable from government websites.[29] Second, the data are of high quality and are not subject to sampling error, since several quality assurance procedures are performed, and the data offer a complete picture of the sourcing strategies of firms in a country. Third, there is a large amount of variation in the data: the share of U.S. intrafirm imports over total U.S. imports varies widely across products and origin countries, and there also exists significant variation in that share across products within exporting countries and across exporting countries within narrowly defined products. This is an important feature of the data so I will document it below. Fourth, by including information on all industrial sectors, these data make it easier to spot certain *fundamental* factors that appear to shape whether international transactions are internalized or not independently of the sector one studies. A fifth advantage of using these comprehensive datasets is that by covering a wide range of sectors, countries and time periods, they offer the potential to exploit exogenous changes in sector characteristics (due perhaps to technological change) or in institutional characteristics of exporting or importing countries (due, for instance, to institutional reforms) to better identify some of effects predicted by the property rights theory.

---

[29] The U.S. data are publicly available at http://sasweb.ssd.census.gov/relatedparty/. This website permits downloading the data at the six-digit NAICS level. The finer six-digit Harmonized System (HS) data are available from the U.S. Census Bureau for a fee. Other researchers (e.g., Zeile 1997; Antràs 2003) have constructed intrafirm trade using direct investment data from the U.S. Bureau of Economic Analysis or BEA (see http://www.bea.gov/iTable/index_MNC.cfm), but the publicly available data do not feature a fine industry disaggregation. The underlying firm-level data used to construct this data set are available only to researchers affiliated with the BEA and have not been used to test the property rights theory.

It is important, however, to also be up front about some of the limitations of using this type of data. First, there is an obvious tension in using product-level data, which aggregate the decisions of various firms, to test the validity of theories of firm boundaries. Although some of the available data are sufficiently disaggregated to ensure that each observation aggregates the transactions of only a handful of firms (or perhaps even just one firm), the inability to control for idiosyncratic firm-level characteristics remains problematic. Second, the data are reported based on the sector or industry category of the good being transacted and do not contain information on the sector that is purchasing the good or on whether the good is an intermediate inputs or a final good (though the level of disaggregation of the data often allows to make informed choices about whether the goods are inputs). Third, in related party transactions, the data do not typically report which firm is owned by whom, that is, whether integration is backward or forward, and also do not provide information on the extent of control (or ownership share) of the parent company.[30] A fourth and final concern in using these data to study the global sourcing strategies of firms based in a given country (say the United States) is that this country's trade statistics will only capture those sourcing decisions that entail goods being shipped back to that country, while in practice some large firms have production networks in which parts and components are shipped across foreign locations (within and across firm boundaries) and then only shipped back to the home country after being assembled abroad (as is the case of the iPad 2). For this reason, U.S. intrafirm imports generally underrepresent the involvement of U.S. multinational firms in global sourcing strategies, though it is not obvious how this phenomenon biases the results of empirical studies using these data.

Some Features of U.S. Intrafirm Trade Data

Before I discuss in detail how U.S. intrafirm trade data have been employed to test the property rights theory, it is worth providing some brief descriptive statistics that demonstrate the empirical relevance of intrafirm trade and illustrate how the share of intrafirm trade varies across products and countries.

---

[30] The U.S. data define related party trade as including import transactions between parties with various types of relationships including "any person directly or indirectly, owning, controlling or holding power to vote, 6 percent of the outstanding voting stock or shares of any organization." In practice, extracts from the confidential direct investment data set collected by the BEA suggest that intrafirm trade is generally associated with one of the entities having a controlling stake in the other entity. Furthermore, the same source indicates that about two-thirds of total U.S. intrafirm imports are accounted for by imports shipped by overseas affiliates to their U.S. parents, rather than by imports shipped U.S. affliates by their foreign parent group. Nunn and Trefler (2008) use information from this same data set to restrict the sample to countries for which at least two-thirds of intrafirm U.S. imports from the country are imported by U.S. parents.

Throughout the section, I focus on data on U.S. imports of goods for 2010, except when using the more disaggregated six-digit Harmonized System data, for which the most recent year available (to me) is 2005.

In 2010, intrafirm imports of goods totaled $922 billion and constituted a remarkable 48.6% of total U.S. imports of goods ($1,899 billion), thus indicating the importance of multinational firms for U.S. trade. The share of U.S. intrafirm imports varies widely across countries. On the one end, intrafirm imports equal 0 for 13 countries and territories (including Cuba and North Korea), which all record very low volumes of exports to the United States, while the share of intrafirm trade reaches a record level of 98.9% for U.S. imports from Mauritius. Leaving aside communist dictatorships and tropical islands and focusing on the 50 largest exporters to the United States, Figure 21.2 illustrates that the share of intrafirm trade still varies significantly across countries, ranging from a mere 2.7% for Bangladesh to 83.6% for Costa Rica.

Similarly, the share of intrafirm trade varies widely depending on the type of product being imported. Again, the raw data contain infrequently traded goods with shares close to 0 and 100, but even when focusing on the top 25 six-digit NAICS industries by importing volume, one observes in Figure 21.3 significant variation in the share of intrafirm trade, ranging from shares under 8% for U.S. imports of women's and girls' blouses, shirts and other outerwear to over 95% for imports of finished autos and light duty vehicles as well as of finished heavy duty trucks.

The very high intrafirm trade share of these finished vehicle industries (which are associated with exports from foreign manufacturing plants to U.S. wholesale affiliates) highlights one of the potential limitations of the data, namely, the fact that it combines data on both intermediate input sectors and final good sectors. It is important to emphasize, however, that the question of why finished vehicles are rarely imported at arm's length is one of tracing firm boundaries (though applying in manufacturer-distributor relationships rather than in supplier-manufacturer relationships), and thus it is not obvious that one would want to discard these type of observations when testing the property rights theory of multinational firms. In any case, the deeper the level of disaggregation in the data, the easier it is to distinguish the nature of the products being imported.

I illustrate this point by moving from the publicly available six-digit NAICS classification (with around 450 distinct industry categories) to the six-digit Harmonized System classification (which contains over 5,000 distinct products).[31] Continuing to focus on the case of vehicle imports, in Figure 21.4

[31] I thank Nathan Nunn and Dan Trefler for allowing me to use their data to illustrate the rich variation in the data. The empirical results in the rest of the paper use the publicly available six-digit NAICS data.

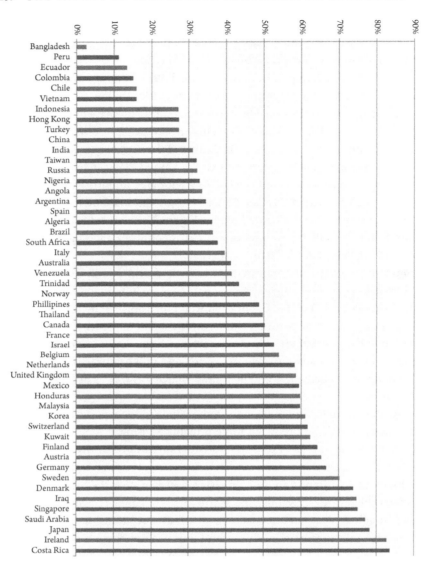

Figure 21.2 Share of U.S. Intrafirm Imports for Largest 50 U.S. Exporters in 2010

I report the share of intrafirm trade for the 76 six-digit subcategories of the two-digit HS industry 87 ("Vehicles other than railway or tramway rolling-stock, and parts and accessories thereof"). Again, the variation in the share of intrafirm trade within the sector is obvious to the eye and again essentially ranges from 0 to 100%.[32]

---

[32] A verbal description of these industry codes is available from the following website: http://www.foreign-trade.com/reference/hscode.htm

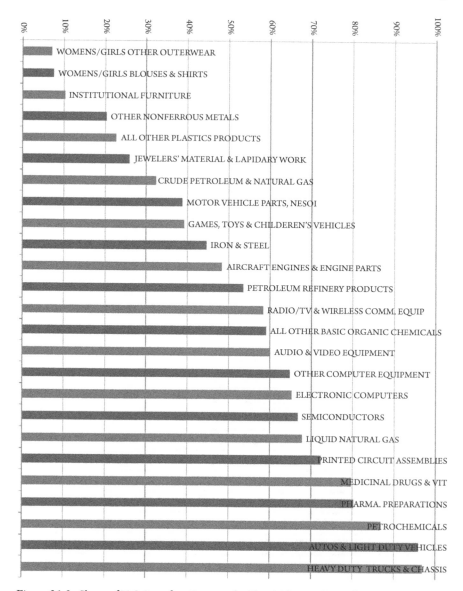

Figure 21.3 Share of U.S. Intrafirm Imports for Top 25 Importing Industries (NAICS6) in 2010

In Figure 21.5, I restrict the sample to a subset of these 76 subcategories, namely, those that fall under the four-digit sector 8708 ("Parts and accessories of motor vehicles") thereby focusing on intermediate input imports. Though the share of intrafirm trade now only ranges from 34.4% for "road wheels and parts" to 78.7% for "gear boxes for motor vehicles," it is clear that firms based

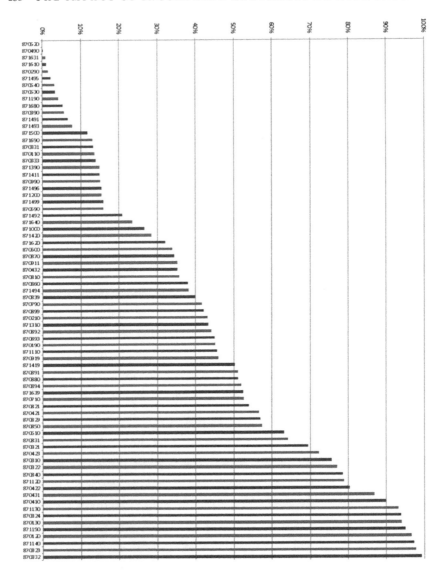

Figure 21.4 Variation in the Share of Intrafirm Trade within HS 87 (Vehicles, exc. Railways, and Parts) in 2005

in the United States seem to source different auto parts under quite different ownership structures.

As a final illustration of the richness and variation in the data, in Figure 21.6 I take one of the six-digit HS industries depicted in Figure 21.5, namely HS 870810 ("Bumpers and parts thereof for motor vehicles"), and report the share of intrafirm trade for all 42 countries with positive exports to the

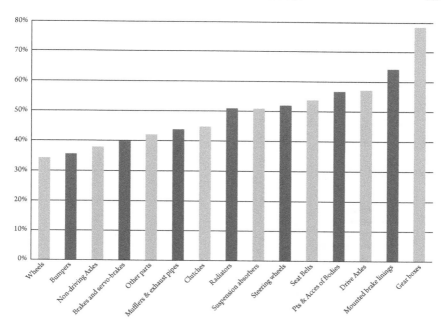

Figure 21.5 Variation in the Share of Intrafirm Trade within HS Sector 8708 (Auto Parts) in 2005

United States in that sector. As is clear from the graph, even when focusing on a narrowly defined component, a similar pattern to that in Figure 21.2 emerges, with U.S.-based firms appearing to source particular inputs quite differently depending on the location from which these products are bought. Imports from 12 of the 42 countries are exclusively transacted at arm's length, whereas two countries (Slovakia and Hungary) sell bumpers to the United States exclusively within multinational firm boundaries. The remaining 28 countries feature shares of intrafirm trade fairly uniformly distributed between 0 and 100%.

Intrafirm Trade and the Property Rights Theory: Empirical Strategies and Findings

Having described some of the basic sources of variation in intrafirm data, I now turn to describing how researchers have attempted to use the data to assess the empirical validity of the property rights theory of the firm. The key robust implication I have highlighted in sections 1 and 2 is that the relative prevalence of integration should be higher in relationships that feature high headquarter intensity, that is, when noncontractible, relationship-specific investments carried out by headquarters are disproportionately more important than those undertaken by suppliers. A key question is then: how do we measure headquarter intensity in the data?

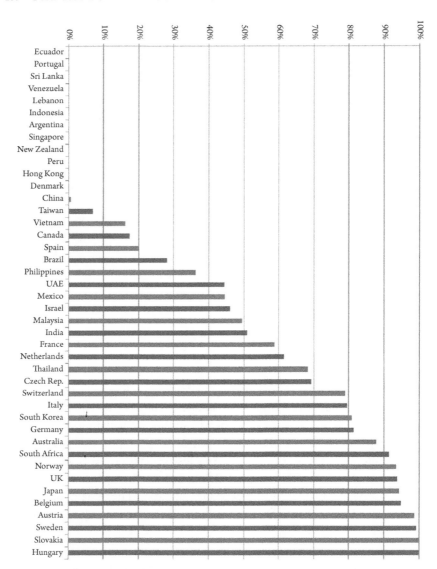

Figure 21.6 Variation in the Share of U.S. Intrafirm Imports within HS 870810 (Bumpers) in 2005

A first attempt at dealing with this issue was offered by Antràs (2003). As mentioned, his property rights theory of the multinational firm assumed that the investments provided by headquarters are more physical capital intensive than those provided by suppliers. In his framework, all investments are noncontractible and fully relationship specific and thus the model generates a positive correlation between the *unobservable* headquarter intensity and physical capital intensity. The assumptions needed to make that connection are strong, so I work on relaxing them below. Even when making these assumptions, however, one is still faced with some open questions. First, which capital intensity matters for the integration decision? And second, how does one measure it in the data?

As pointed out already, intrafirm trade data do not identify the industry or sector purchasing the imported goods, and thus one cannot easily construct a measure of capital intensity based on the relative investments of the importing sector and those of the exporting sector. Following Antràs (2003), most researchers using intrafirm trade data have associated headquarter intensity with the capital intensity *of the product being imported*. This is because in Antràs's (2003) general equilibrium model, factors of production are internationally immobile so the headquarter's capital investments are undertaken in the location of the supplier division or firm, thus implying that these investments will be embodied in the intermediate input being shipped back to the headquarter's home country. With that strict interpretation, using the imported good sector's capital intensity is justified, yet it is important to bear in mind that in the real world, headquarters often undertake other noncontractible relationship-specific investments that may not be embodied in the good being imported. I return to this point later.

Now even when settling on the use of the capital intensity of the product being imported as a proxy of headquarter intensity, one still needs to measure it in the data. Ideally, one would construct measures of capital intensity (such as the ratio of physical capital expenditures to labor input expenditures) at the same level of disaggregation at which intrafirm trade data are available, namely, at the product and country-of-origin level. Unfortunately, this is typically infeasible because industry-level data on capital intensity at an acceptable level of disaggregation are only available for a handful of countries. It should be emphasized that this limitation is not specific to the use of intrafirm trade data and also applies to certain empirical tests of the Heckscher-Ohlin model of trade (see, for instance, Romalis 2004). A standard solution to this problem is to work with data from just one country, typically the United States for reasons of availability and data quality, and to impose the same capital intensity to all countries exporting a particular good. This assumption is typically justified by appealing to the absence of capital intensity reversals.

In sum, a typical proxy for the headquarter intensity associated with U.S. imports in a given good or sector is the physical capital intensity (i.e., the ratio of physical capital to employment) in that good or sector in the United States. It may be argued that Antràs's (2003) assumption that headquarters and suppliers' investments differ *only* in their capital intensity is too restrictive. With that in mind, the literature has offered alternative measures of headquarter intensity based on other measures of factor intensity, such as skill intensity (the ratio of nonproduction workers to production workers) or R&D intensity (the ratio of R&D expenditures to sales). The idea behind these proxies is that headquarters are particularly likely to be involved in investments related to skilled workers (e.g., training) or to R&D outlays.

Having described the measurement of headquarter intensity, I next turn to discuss some of the key findings in the literature. Rather than simply enumerating the results in previous papers, I attempt to illustrate some of the key ones with scatter plots.

Antràs (2003) begins his paper by showing that in a cross-section of manufacturing sectors, there exists a striking positive correlation between the share of intrafirm trade in that sector and its physical capital intensity in the United States (see Figure 21.7). The data in Antràs (2003) include, however, only 23 fairly aggregated industries, and thus one might be skeptical of the robustness of such correlation.[33] This concern is addressed in Figure 21.8, in which

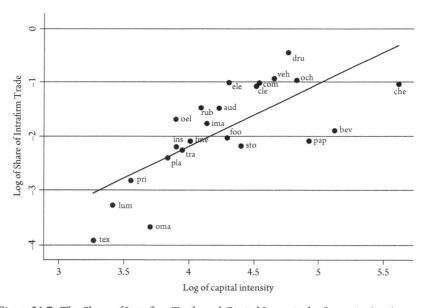

Figure 21.7　The Share of Intrafirm Trade and Capital Intensity by Sector in Antràs (2003)

---

[33] Antràs's (2003) data are coarse because he used public extracts from the direct investment dataset collected by the U.S. Bureau of Economic Analysis (BEA). Yeaple (2006) performs similar tests using the confidential BEA data set, which increases the number of sectors from 23 to 51 and allows him to perform the analysis for different sets of countries. He finds that the effect of capital intensity is robust to the finer disaggregation of the data though it appears much stronger when focusing on less developed and emerging economies than when restricting the sample to developed countries. His empirical analysis as well as Antràs's have now been superseded by a new wave of empirical work using the much more disaggregated U.S. customs intrafirm trade data.

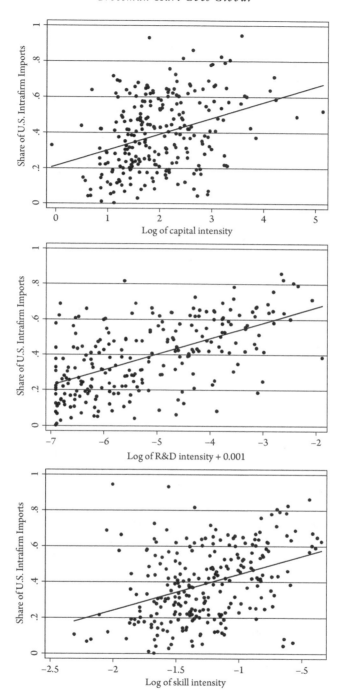

Figure 21.8 The Effect of Headquarter Intensity on the Share of U.S. Intrafirm Imports

I correlate the share of intrafirm trade with the three measures of headquarter intensity mentioned above (capital intensity, R&D intensity and skill intensity), while using the much more disaggregated U.S. customs data on intrafirm trade described above (which have only become available in recent years). The intrafirm trade shares are computed for imports from all exporting countries in a given six-digit NAICS, while the headquarter intensity measures are computed using data from the U.S. Census of Manufactures (in the case of capital and skill intensity) and from Orbis (in the case of R&D intensity).[34] All variables are averaged over the period 2000–2005. As is clear from the left panel of Figure 21.8, the positive correlation between the share of intrafirm trade and capital intensity is robust to the use of this much more detailed data set. The fit is not as good as in the case of Antràs (2003), but the relationship is highly statistically significant. Furthermore, as documented by Nunn and Trefler (2011) and Bernard et al. (2010), this relationship is robust to the inclusion of various industry controls and to the addition of country fixed effects in regressions that exploit both the industry as well as the exporting country variation in the data.

The remaining two panels of Figure 21.8 show the correlations between the share of intrafirm trade and R&D and skill intensity. The positive correlation between these variables is also strongly statistically significant and visible to the naked eye, and as in the case of capital intensity, the effect of these variables continues to hold conditional on a wide set of industry covariates and is also robust to the inclusion of fixed effects in specifications exploiting the cross-country dimension of the data.

There are various reasons one should be cautious in interpreting these results as empirically validating the property rights theory of multinational firm boundaries. First, U.S. physical capital, skill, and R&D intensity measures are imperfect proxies for headquarter intensity as they only capture imperfectly the relative importance of the noncontractible, relationship-specific investments carried out by headquarters and their suppliers. Nunn and Trefler (2011) point out, for instance, that standard measures of capital intensity embody several investments that are fairly easy to contract on or that are not particularly relationship-specific. If the property rights theory is correct, one would then expect investments in specialized equipment to be much more relevant for the integration decision than investments in structures or in nonspecialized equipment (such as automobiles or computers), which tend to lose little value when not used in the intended production process. As found by Nunn and Trefler (2011), Figures 21.9 and 21.10 confirm that this is indeed what one observes in the data

---

[34] I am grateful to Davin Chor, Nathan Nunn, Dan Trefler, and Heiwai Tang for making their data available to me. I add 0.001 to the measure of (log) R&D intensity to avoid throwing away a large number of observations with zero R&D outlays.

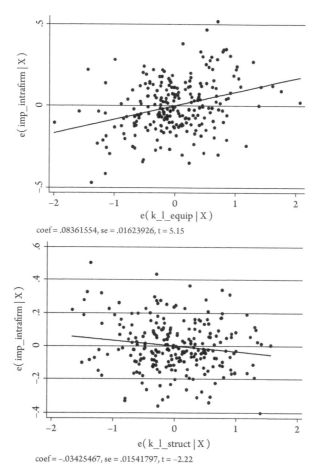

Figure 21.9 The Effect of Capital Intensity and Its Components on the Share of U.S. Intrafirm Imports

when using disaggregated measures of capital intensity from the U.S. Census of Manufactures. In particular, the two panels of Figure 21.9 depicts the partial effect of capital equipment intensity (i.e., the ratio of capital equipment expenditures to worker wages) and of capital structures intensity (i.e., the ratio of expenditures on capital structures to worker wages) in cross-industry regressions that also control for skill intensity and R&D intensity. As is clear from the figure, the positive effect of capital equipment intensity on the share of intrafirm trade is highly statistically significant, while the effect of capital structures intensity appears to be negative (and also statistically significant). Figure 21.10 further breaks down the effect of capital equipment intensity into three components and shows that the effect observed in the left panel of Figure 21.9

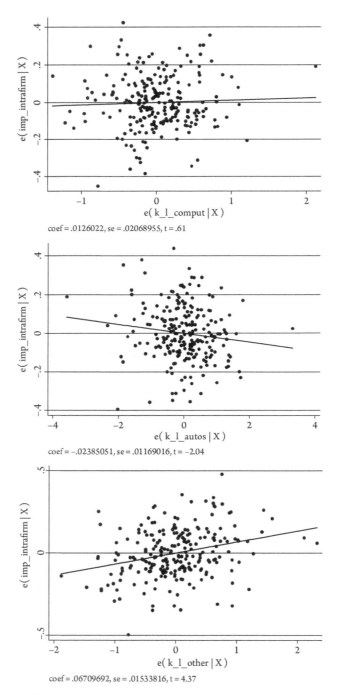

Figure 21.10 The Effect of Equipment Capital Intensity and Its Components on the Share of U.S. Intrafirm Imports

is not driven by expenditures on computers and data processing equipment or on automobiles and trucks, which would be problematic for the theory. In fact, the effect of expenditures on automobiles and trucks appears to have a statistically significant *negative* effect on the share of intrafirm trade, which resonates with the results in Antràs and Helpman (2008) and section 1.3 indicating a negative effect of headquarter services contractibility on the integration decision.[35]

A second reason to be cautious about the findings discussed above relates to the relatively low statistical power of these tests of the property rights theory. In other words, the patterns one observes in the data are consistent with the property rights theory, but they are not necessarily inconsistent with alternative theories of firm boundaries. For instance, the significance of R&D intensity for the integration decision of multinational firms could be viewed as a validation of transaction cost theories that emphasize the importance of the nonexcludable nature of knowledge in shaping multinational firm boundaries (see, for instance, Ethier and Markusen 1996).

To alleviate this concern, the literature has attempted to provide more elaborate tests of the theory that relate to the richer set of implications that arise in the property rights theory of the multinational firm with intraindustry heterogeneity developed by Antràs and Helpman (2004, 2008). Remember, for instance, that these frameworks predict that the share of intrafirm imports should not only increase in headquarter intensity but also be positively affected by trade frictions and by the degree of productivity dispersion within industries. Figure 21.11 confirms the empirical validity of these predictions. In the left panel of the figure, I graphically summarize the results in Díez (2010), who unveils a positive association between the share of intrafirm trade and U.S. tariffs in a cross-section of industries. In particular, the figure sorts industries into bins according to their tariff value (with the first bin containing all industries for which U.S. tariffs are 0, and the remaining industries sorted into quartiles) and reports the median share of intrafirm trade in those industries.[36] The right panel of Figure 21.11 depicts

---

[35] Another reason that standard proxies for headquarter intensity are problematic is the fact that they use only information on the capital, skill, or R&D intensity of the "selling" industry, that is, of the good or sector being imported. Antràs and Chor (2011) acknowledge this limitation and use U.S. input-output data to build measures of headquarter intensity that reflect the capital intensity of the "average buying" industry rather than of the selling one. This has only a minor effect on the estimates, though admittedly this might have to do with the fact that data limitations (i.e., insufficient disaggregation) prevent one from satisfactorily identifying the precise buying industry associated with different U.S. import purchases. For the same reason, alternative tests using measures of capital, skill, or R&D intensity of both the buying and selling industry, as developed for instance in Acemoglu et al. (2010), are typically infeasible using U.S. intrafirm import data.

[36] Díez (2010) performs a more complete empirical analysis at the country and industry level that confirms the positive association between the prevalence of intrafirm trade and U.S. tariffs. He also

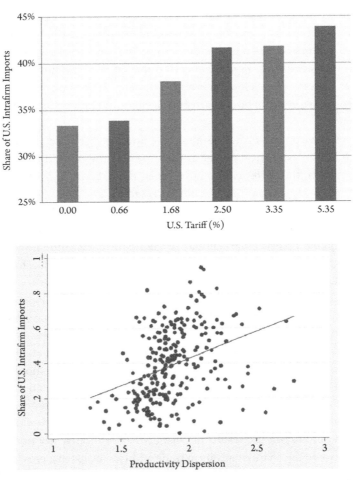

Figure 21.11 The Implications of Heterogeneity for the Determinants of Intrafirm Imports

a positive correlation between the share of intrafirm trade and productivity dispersion, as measured by Nunn and Trefler (2008), who also show that the effect of productivity dispersion is higher the higher the quintile of headquarter intensity, a prediction that is again consistent with the property rights framework in Antràs and Helpman (2004, 2008).[37]

finds a negative correlation between U.S. intrafirm imports and foreign tariffs and shows that it can be reconciled with a variant of the Antràs and Helpman (2004) framework.

[37] The Nunn and Trefler (2008) measure of productivity dispersion corresponds to the standard deviation of log exports reported by the U.S. Department of Commerce for each of the constituent HS10 products from each U.S. location to each destination country in 2000.

A particularly promising way to discriminate the property rights theory of the multinational firm against alternative theories of firm boundaries consists of exploiting the implications of the theory for the effect of contractibility on the share of intrafirm trade. As discussed already, the work of Antràs and Helpman (2008) highlights that the effect of contractibility on the prevalence of integration depends crucially on the degree to which contractual incompleteness stems from noncontractibilities in the inputs controlled by the final good producer or by his or her suppliers. If production processes in certain sectors are particularly noncontractible because of the nature of the investments carried out by headquarters, then the theory would predict that the share of intrafirm trade should be negatively affected by the level of these sectors' contractibility. Conversely, if the source of noncontractibilities stems from the nature of the supplier's activities, the theory may instead predict a positive correlation between the share of intrafirm trade and contractibility, a result that is hard to reconcile with transaction cost theories of multinational firm boundaries.[38] Though the theory generates sharp predictions for how the source of noncontractibilities affects the share of intrafirm trade, a natural challenge for empiricists is to find appropriate proxies for these different sources of contractual frictions. Figure 21.12 depicts the correlation between two proposed measures of contractibility and the share of intrafirm trade. The left panel uses the measure of contractibility proposed by Bernard et al. (2010), which is a weighted average of the wholesale employment share of firms importing goods in a particular sector, the idea being that contracting is likely to be easier for products passing through intermediaries such as wholesalers. The right panel uses Nunn's (2007) measure of contractibility (see Nunn and Trefler 2008), which corresponds to the proportion of each sector's intermediate inputs that are not traded on organized exchanges and are thus more susceptible to potential contracting problems. Both panels suggest a negative correlation between the share of intrafirm trade and contractibility, which is broadly in line with what one would expect from transaction cost models of firm boundaries, but can also be rationalized within the property rights theory, provided that the lack of contractibility emanates from investments carried out by headquarter services (and possibly embodied in the good transacted across borders). Other findings in the literature, however, appear to be harder to rationalize in transaction cost models, while they continue to be consistent with the property rights approach. For instance, Nunn and Trefler (2008) and Bernard et al. (2010) find that Nunn's measure of contractibility has a positive effect on the share of intrafirm trade in regressions that

---

[38] The qualifier "may" in the previous sentence comes from the fact that improvements in contractibility also affect the participation of firms in international trade and may reduce the share of intrafirm trade on that account. See Antràs and Helpman (2008) for details.

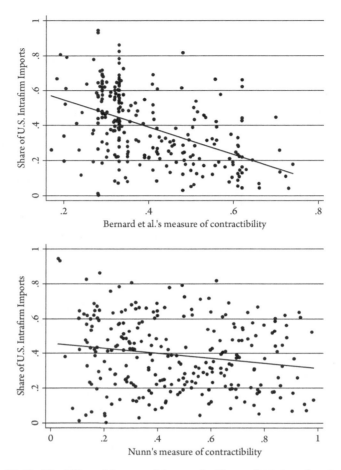

Figure 21.12 The Effect of Contractibility on the Share of U.S. Intrafirm Imports

incorporate the cross-country variation in the data, suggesting that the correlation in the right panel in Figure 21.12 might simply reflect that the U.S. imports highly contractible goods from countries that export to the United States mostly at arm's length (perhaps for other reasons). In any case, future work should be directed at better identifying different sources of variation in contractibility so as to better discriminate among alternative models of multinational firm boundaries.

Throughout this section, I have focused on discussing empirical tests based on the cross-sectoral implications of the property rights theory. The cross-national nature of intrafirm trade data naturally also permits an analysis of some of the cross-country implications of the framework. For instance, the Antràs (2003) framework predicts that the share of intrafirm imports in total imports should be increasing in the aggregate capital-labor ratio of the exporting country,[39] and the framework in Antràs and Helpman (2008) might suggest that the quality of a country's contracting institutions might well have a positive impact on the share of intrafirm trade, a counterintuitive result from the point of view of transaction cost theories. Consistently with the findings of Antràs (2003), Nunn and Trefler (2008), and Bernard et al. (2010), the two panels in Figure 21.13 confirm the existence of these correlations in the data. Nevertheless, the standard concerns associated with cross-country regressions (omitted variable biases, endogeneity, etc.) apply here as well, so one should be cautious in interpreting these correlations as formal validations of the theory. Nunn and Trefler (2008) and Bernard et al. (2010) also experiment with the addition of controls that interact country and industry variables, but it is not always easy to map these results to the simple models that have been developed so far.[40]

Due to data availability, the bulk of work using product-level data to test the property rights theory has employed U.S. intrafirm import data. Feenstra and Hanson (2005) and Fernandes and Tang (2010) are two notable exceptions that instead use Chinese data (see also Feenstra 2011 for an overview). In particular, product-level export data from the Customs General Administration of the People's Republic of China contain detailed information on whether the exporter is a foreign-owned plant. It is not clear that foreign-owned plants will necessarily export their output to affiliated parties (thus generating intrafirm

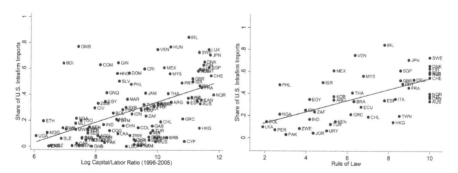

Figure 21.13 Cross-Country Determinants of the Share of U.S. Intrafirm Imports

---

[39] The Antràs and Helpman (2004) framework would also generate the same prediction if wages in the exporting country are positively affected by that country's aggregate capital-labor ratio.

[40] For instance, Bernard et al. (2010) find that the share of intrafirm trade is increasing in the interaction of physical capital abundance and physical capital intensity, whereas in Antràs (2003), conditional on capital intensity, the incentive to integrate suppliers is independent of factor prices (and thus of physical capital abundance).

trade), but regardless the data are suitable for an analysis of the determinants of foreign ownership of suppliers in China. Both sets of authors also make use of the fact that the data distinguish between different types of customs regimes (pure assembly or import and assembly), depending on whether the plant in China is in charge of importing inputs or that responsibility falls to a foreign producer. This motivates the development of rich variants of the property rights theory, which appear to be able to successfully account for the patterns observed in the data.

3.2 Tests with Firm-Level Data

The property rights theory is a theory of firm boundaries, and thus firm-level data would appear to be the ideal laboratory to use in testing it. An obvious limitation, however, is that this type of data are not readily available. Recent studies have, however, unveiled the existence of a few firm-level data sets that can help shed some light on the empirical relevance of the property rights theory. In this section, I focus on describing four of these firm-level data sets (those that I am aware of), while discussing both their main advantages and limitations, and outlining some of the results that have been obtained when exploiting them.

The first paper to use firm-level data to assess the validity of the property rights theory of multinational firm boundaries is Tomiura (2007), who uses data from the Basic Survey of Commercial and Manufacturing Structure and Activity in Japan. The survey covers 118,300 Japanese manufacturing firms and according to the author, "is regarded as an accurate overall representation of the whole of manufacturing in Japan," though unfortunately it was carried out only in one year, 1998. The survey contains various data on the operations of firms (sales, employment, capital expenditures, exports, foreign direct investment) and crucially also asks firms whether they "contract out manufacturing or processing tasks to other firms overseas." Hence, the survey can be used to explicitly distinguish firms that are engaged in foreign outsourcing versus those engaged in foreign direct investment. A key limitation of the data is that they do not appear to contain information on the volumes (i.e., the intensive margin) of foreign insourcing and outsourcing. Tomiura (2007) uses the data set to show that, consistently with the sorting predicted by the Antràs and Helpman (2004) model, firms that are engaged in FDI are distinctively more productive than firms that are engaged in foreign outsourcing, which in turn are more productive than domestic firms. No other predictions from the model are tested. An interesting feature of the data is that most firms are neither "pure FDI" firms nor "pure outsourcing" firms, which suggests that current models are too stylized to capture the rich organizational decisions of firms.

A second line of papers, most notably Defever and Toubal (2007), Corcos et al. (2013), and Carluccio and Fally (2012) have used French data from the EIIG (Échanges Internationaux Intra-Groupe), a survey conducted in 1999 by the SESSI (Service des Études Statistiques Industrielles), which documents the sourcing mode (through independent suppliers or through affiliates) of each firm's yearly imports of intermediate inputs by origin country and by four-digit HS product codes in 1999. The survey includes all French firms that trade more than €1 million and that are owned by manufacturing groups that control at least 50% of the equity capital of an affiliate based outside France. Though not all firms responded to the survey, the 4,305 responding firms represent more than 80% of total exports and imports of French multinationals in 1999.[41] A key limitation of the EEIG data set is the potential for sample selection biases arising from including only firms with at least one affiliate outside France. Corcos et al. (2013) acknowledge this problem and complement the data set with data coming from the French Customs Office, documenting the universe of yearly imports and exports flows in 1999 at the firm, origin country and product level, allowing them to offer a more representative picture of the foreign outsourcing operations of French firms. The goals and scope of the papers using the EEIG data set are somewhat different, but they all find supportive evidence of a positive correlation between headquarter intensity and the relative importance of intrafirm trade, with the measures of headquarter intensity in Corcos et al. (2013) being a *firm-level* measure (namely, capital intensity, skill intensity, and the ratio of value added over sales of the importing firm). Another conclusion that emerges from these studies is that selection bias identified by Corcos et al. (2013) appears to be important in the sense that the productivity advantage of FDI firms over foreign outsourcers predicted by the theory (see Figure 21.1) arises only when including firms that only engage in outsourcing into the analysis.

More recently, the property rights theory of the multinational firm has been tested using firm-level data from Spain provided by the Fundación SEPI. In particular, Kohler and Smolka (2009) make use of the ESEE (Encuesta sobre Estrategias Empresariales), which surveys approximately 2,000 Spanish firms with at least 10 employees on a yearly basis since 1990 and provides information on their income and balance sheet statistics, as well as a variety of more specific organizational variables. A notable characteristic of the ESEE is its representativeness, which is ensured by the careful statistical criteria used in

---

[41] This data source can in turn be matched with another SESSI database, the EAE (Enquête Annuelle Entreprise), which provides balance sheet data on manufacturing firms with at least 20 employees.

the initial year of the sample and the special attention that has been given to account for entry and exit of firms of different sizes in subsequent years. For the purposes of testing the property rights theory, a particularly relevant feature of the data is that they allow one to compute the overall spending on intermediate inputs by firms and their breakup into (1) domestic purchases from independent suppliers, (2) domestic purchases from affiliated parties, (3) imports from foreign independent suppliers, and (4) imports from foreign affiliates. Hence, one can easily map some of the variables of the survey into the key equilibrium variables in existing models, such as the Antràs and Helpman (2004, 2008) frameworks with intraindustry heterogeneity. An important disadvantage of this Spanish data set is that it only distinguishes between domestic and foreign input purchases, with the latter not being disaggregated by country of origin. Kohler and Smolka (2009) use the ESEE dataset and find evidence supportive of the productivity sorting of firms into organizational forms predicted by the Antràs and Helpman (2004, 2008) models (see Figure 21.1). In particular, conditional on the location of sourcing (domestic or foreign), integrating firms appear to be more productive than nonintegrating ones, and they also provide evidence that firms outsourcing abroad appear to be slightly more productive than firms integrating in Spain. Furthermore, Kohler and Smolka (2009) find that higher levels of firm-level capital intensity and skill intensity are associated with higher intrafirm shares in both domestic and foreign intermediate input purchases, and also that the effect of productivity on the choice between integration and outsourcing, both at home and abroad, is observed only at high capital intensity levels, again consistently with the predictions in Antràs and Helpman (2004, 2008).

A final international firm-level data set that has been used to shed light on the property rights theory is Dun & Bradstreet's WorldBase database, which contains public and private plant-level observations in more than 200 countries and territories. The data set does not contain an awful lot of operational data related to these plants, but as pointed out by Alfaro et al. (2010), it does offer a comprehensive picture of firm boundaries across borders. In particular, it contains detailed information on the location, ownership (e.g., its domestic or global parent) and industry classification for hundreds of thousands of plants worldwide. Alfaro et al. (2010) use these data to document a positive association between higher tariffs on final products (as measured by MFN tariffs at the four-digit SIC industry level for all WTO members) and an index of domestic vertical integration constructed with the ownership information in the Dun & Bradstreet's WorldBase database and input-output tables. The empirical exercise exploits both cross-section and time-series variation in trade policy, as well as a more significant trade liberalization episode, namely, China's entry into the WTO in 2001. The authors take these results as empirically validating the model of organizational design in Legros and Newman (2009) and Conconi et al. (2012), but they are also consistent with the findings in Antràs and Helpman (2004, 2008).

3.3 Road Ahead

The findings of the studies I have described in this section are interesting and offer broad support for some of the key predictions of the property rights theory of multinational firm boundaries. Nevertheless, the evidence is far from conclusive because for the most part, the tests that have been performed up to now have relatively low statistical power. In my view, successful testing of the theory will need to follow one of the two following approaches.

A first possibility is to better exploit the large variation in the relative prevalence of integration retrievable from intrafirm trade data, and most notably, from U.S. intrafirm import data. In particular, the cross-industry studies that I have described above are interesting and informative, but they cannot convincingly identify a causal effect of headquarter intensity (even when appropriately measured) on the share of intrafirm trade. A potential avenue for future research is to use narrower slices of the data, perhaps focusing on the patterns in a single industry, but exploiting exogenous changes in sector characteristics driven by technological or demand-driven shocks, in the spirit of Baker and Hubbard (2003), or perhaps performing analyses exploiting within-country variation stemming from changes in the institutional characteristics of countries, such as observable changes in the quality of institutions or in restrictions on foreign ownership in those countries.

A second, and maybe even more fruitful area of future research, entails a more structural use of the available firm-level data sets. At present, little work has been devoted to structurally estimating the models I have discussed in this survey. This is partly due to the stylized nature of some of these frameworks, and partly due to the under-utilization of this type of empirical techniques in the international trade field. Yet as I have argued in section 2.4, future theoretical developments are likely to provide much richer property rights frameworks that will be more amenable for structural work. Part of the appeal of using this set of techniques is that this might permit an evaluation of the quantitative importance of multinational firm boundaries for firm-level performance, a question that so far has not been sufficiently explored in the literature.[42]

---

[42] The work of Guadalupe, Kuzmina, and Thomas (forthcoming) is a first promising step in that direction.

4. Concluding Remarks

In this paper, I surveyed the influence of Grossman and Hart's (1986) seminal paper for the study of the international organization of production. I discussed the implementation of the theory in open-economy environments and its implications for the structure of international trade flows and multinational activity. I also reviewed empirical work suggestive of the empirical relevance of the property rights theory. Along the way, I developed novel theoretical results and have also outlined some of the key limitations of existing contributions.

I want to conclude by briefly discussing the broader impact of GH in the field of international trade. First, as emphasized earlier, GH has been an inspiration for the development of various complementary theories of the organization of production, some of which have also been put to work both theoretically and empirically in open-economy environments (see, for instance, the references described at the end of section 2.3). These papers may not be direct offspring of GH, but they clearly carry some of GH's traits.

Perhaps more significant, soon after the development of property rights theories of multinational firm boundaries, the literature acknowledged that incomplete contracting of the type introduced by GH could shape not only the ownership structure of firms but also their geographical location. In other words, contracting institutions are not only important for understand vertical integration decisions, they also constitute a source of comparative advantage. The literature on trade and institutions has exploded in the past few years, with work studying both theoretically as well as empirically the effects of contracting, financial and labor market institutions on trade patterns, multinational activity, and more broadly the impact of these institutions on the workings of general equilibrium models.[43] The main ideas behind these papers can all be traced back in some form or other to the seminal work of GH.

Finally, by formalizing the idea of power in market and nonmarket economic transactions, the ideas in GH have been shown to have new and interesting implications for how the process of globalization affects different agents in society (depending on their endowments of assets or information), and also for how the effects of trade policies are transmitted across countries, with implications for the efficacy of the rules that currently govern negotiations at the World Trade Organization (see, among others, Antràs and Costinot 2011; Antràs and Staiger 2012).

---

[43] See, among many others, Acemoglu et al. (2007), Levchenko (2007), Nunn (2007) on contracting institutions; Antràs and Caballero (2007), Antràs et al. (2009), and Manova (2010) on financial institutions; and Helpman et al. (2010) on labor market institutions.

Appendix

Derivation of Equation (8) Due to $R(h, m)$ being homogeneous of degree α, we can write

$$hR_h + mR_m = \alpha R$$

$$hR_{hh} + mR_{hm} = (\alpha - 1) R_h$$

$$hR_{hm} + mR_{mm} = (\alpha - 1) R_m,$$

while the formula for the elasticity of substitution between h and m is given by

$$\sigma_{h,m} = \frac{-R_h R_m \left(hR_h + mR_m \right)}{hm \left(R_{hh} \left(R_m \right)^2 + R_{mm} \left(R_h \right)^2 - 2R_{hm} R_h R_m \right)}.$$

Denoting by

$$\eta_{R,h} = \frac{hR_h}{R}; \; \eta_{R,m} = \frac{mR_m}{R},$$

we can use the formulas above (together with $\eta_{R,h} + \eta_{R,m} = \alpha$) to obtain:

$$\frac{R_{hh}}{R} = -\frac{\left(\sigma_{h,m} \left(1 - \alpha \right) \eta_{R,h} + \eta_{R,m} \right) \eta_{R,h}}{\alpha h^2 \sigma_{h,m}}$$

$$\frac{R_{mm}}{R} = -\frac{\left(\sigma_{h,m} \left(1 - \alpha \right) \eta_{R,m} + \eta_{R,h} \right) \eta_{R,m}}{\alpha m^2 \sigma_{h,m}}$$

$$\frac{R_{hm}}{R} = \frac{\left(1 - \sigma_{h,m} \left(1 - \alpha \right) \right) \eta_{R,h} \eta_{R,m}}{\alpha hm \sigma_{h,m}}.$$

Now plugging these expressions into (3) using (4) and (5) delivers

$$\frac{\beta^*}{1 - \beta^*} = \frac{\eta_{R,h}}{\eta_{R,m}} \frac{\sigma_{h,m} \left(1 - \alpha \right) \eta_{R,m} + \eta_{R,h} - \alpha \beta^*}{\alpha \beta^* - \eta_{R,h} + \sigma_{h,m} \eta_{R,h} \left(1 - \alpha \right)},$$

which in turn simplifies to (8), or

$$\frac{\beta^*}{1 - \beta^*} = \sqrt{\frac{\eta_{R,h}}{\eta_{R,m}} \frac{\alpha \left(1 - \eta_{R,m} \right) + \left(1 - \alpha \right) \left(\sigma_{h,m} - 1 \right) \eta_{R,m}}{\alpha \left(1 - \eta_{R,h} \right) + \left(1 - \alpha \right) \left(\sigma_{h,m} - 1 \right) \eta_{R,h}}}.$$

Straightforward differentiation confirms that β^* is increasing in $\eta_{R,h}$ and decreasing in $\eta_{R,m}$ for any $\sigma_{h,m} > 0$ (remember that $\eta_{R,h} > 0$, $\eta_{R,m} > 0$ and $\eta_{R,h} + \eta_{R,m} = \alpha$).

Proof of Proposition 3 Following the algebra in Antràs and Helpman (2008), it can easily be verified that when F obtains a share of revenue β_k in the ex post bargaining, the equilibrium level of revenues is given by

$$R = A^{1/(1-\eta_h-\eta_m)} \left(\frac{\beta_k \eta_h}{c_h} \right)^{\eta_h/(1-\eta_m-\eta_h)} \left(\frac{(1-\beta_k)\,\eta_m}{c_m} \right)^{(1-\eta_h)/(1-\eta_m-\eta_h)},$$

while input choices satisfy

$$c_h h = \beta_k \eta_h R$$
$$c_m m = (1-\beta_k)\,\eta_m R.$$

Using equations (1) and (9), the relative profits obtained by F under integration versus outsourcing are then given by

$$\frac{\pi_V}{\pi_O} = \frac{(1+\delta)\,(1-\eta_h) + \phi\,(1-\delta)\,(1-\eta_m)}{(1-\eta_h) + \phi\,(1-\eta_m)} \left((1+\delta)^{\eta_h}\,(1-\delta)^{\eta_m} \right)^{1/(1-\eta_h-\eta_m)}.$$

To characterize the effects of the different parameters on this ratio of profits, it is simplest to work with the following monotonic transformation of π_V/π_O:

$$\Theta\,(\eta_h, \eta_m, \phi, \delta) = (1-\eta_h-\eta_m)\ln\left(\frac{\pi_V}{\pi_O} \right)$$

$$= (1-\eta_h-\eta_m)\ln\left(\frac{(1+\delta)\,(1-\eta_h) + \phi\,(1-\delta)\,(1-\eta_m)}{(1-\eta_h) + \phi\,(1-\eta_m)} \right)$$

$$+ \eta_h \ln\,(1+\delta) + \eta_m \ln\,((1-\delta)).$$

Simple differentiation shows that $\Theta\,(\eta_h, \eta_m, \phi)$ is a decreasing function of ϕ, and thus the relative profitability of integration is higher, the tighter are financial constraints (i.e., the lower is ϕ). We next show that $\Theta\,(\eta_h, \eta_m, \phi)$ is also increasing in η_h and decreasing in η_m.

We begin by noting that

$$\frac{\partial^2 \Theta\,(\eta_h, \eta_m, \phi, \delta)}{\partial\,(\eta_h)^2}$$
$$= 4(1-\eta_m)\delta\phi \frac{\eta_m(1+\delta)(1-\eta_h) + \phi\,(1-\eta_m)\,(\eta_m\,(1-\phi) + \phi\,(1-\delta) + \eta_m\delta\phi + 1 - \eta_h)}{((1+\delta)\,(1-\eta_h) + \phi\,(1-\delta)\,(1-\eta_m))^2\,((1-\eta_h) + \phi(1-\eta_m))^2} > 0$$

and

$$\frac{\partial^2 \Theta\,(\eta_h, \eta_m, \phi, \delta)}{\partial\,(\eta_m)^2}$$
$$= -4\,(1-\eta_h)\,\delta\phi \frac{\phi^2\eta_h\,(1-\eta_m)\,(1-\delta) + \phi\,(1-\eta_h)\,(\eta_h + 1 - \eta_m) + (1-\eta_h)^2\,(1+\delta)}{((1+\delta)\,(1-\eta_h) + \phi\,(1-\delta)\,(1-\eta_m))^2\,((1-\eta_h) + \phi\,(1-\eta_m))^2} < 0,$$

so it suffices to show that $\partial\Theta\left(\eta_h, \eta_m, \phi\right)/\partial\eta_h \geq 0$ when $\eta_h = 0$ and $\partial\Theta\left(\eta_h, \eta_m, \phi\right)/\partial\eta_m \leq 0$ when $\eta_m = 0$.

One can verify, however, that

$$\left.\frac{\partial\Theta\left(\eta_h, \eta_m, \phi, \delta\right)}{\partial\eta_h}\right|_{\eta_h = 0} = \ln\left(1 + \delta\right) - \ln\left(\frac{1 + \delta + \phi\left(1 - \delta\right)\left(1 - \eta_m\right)}{1 + \phi\left(1 - \eta_m\right)}\right)$$

$$-\frac{2\delta\phi\left(1 - \eta_m\right)^2}{\left(1 + \phi\left(1 - \eta_m\right)\right)\left(1 + \delta + \phi\left(1 - \delta\right)\left(1 - \eta_m\right)\right)} \geq 0,$$

where the sign follows from the right-hand side being increasing in δ and equaling 0 when $\delta = 0$. Similarly, we have

$$\left.\frac{\partial\Theta\left(\eta_h, \eta_m, \phi, \delta\right)}{\partial\eta_m}\right|_{\eta_m = 0} = \ln\left(1 - \delta\right) - \ln\left(\frac{\phi(1 - \delta) + \left(1 + \delta\right)\left(1 - \eta_h\right)}{1 - \eta_h + \phi}\right)$$

$$+\frac{2\delta\phi\left(1 - \eta_h\right)^2}{\left(1 - \eta_h + \phi\right)\left(1 - \eta_h + \phi + \delta - \delta\phi - \delta\eta_h\right)} \leq 0,$$

where the sign follows now from the right-hand side being decreasing in δ (which can be verified via differentiation) and equaling 0 when $\delta = 0$.

Next note that for sufficiently high η_h, we must have $\Theta\left(\eta_h, \eta_m, \phi, \delta\right) > 0$. This can be verified analytically but it suffices to point out that this is true when $\phi = 1$ (see Proposition 2) and the function $\Theta\left(\cdot\right)$ is decreasing in ϕ. Conversely, for sufficiently low η_h, i.e., $\eta_h \to 0$, we have

$$\Theta\left(\eta_h, \eta_m, \phi, \delta\right) \to \left(1 - \eta_m\right)\ln\left(\frac{\left(1 + \delta\right) + \phi\left(1 - \delta\right)\left(1 - \eta_m\right)}{1 + \phi\left(1 - \eta_m\right)}\right) + \eta_m \ln\left(\left(1 - \delta\right)\right),$$

which is negative for sufficiently high η_m, but may be positive for sufficiently low η_m (this is easily verified by setting $\phi = 0$, for instance). In sum, given that π_V/π_O is increasing in η_h, we can conclude that there exists a headquarter intensity cutoff $\hat{\eta}_h \in [0, 1)$ such that for all $\eta_h > \hat{\eta}_h$, integration necessarily dominates outsourcing. When $\hat{\eta}_h > 0$, outsourcing dominates integration for all $\eta_h < \hat{\eta}_h$ but note that it is possible that $\hat{\eta}_h = 0$ and thus integration dominates outsourcing for all $\eta_h \in (0, 1)$. Finally, given the comparative statics discussed above, we can use the implicit function theorem to conclude that the cutoff $\hat{\eta}_h$ is lower the larger is ϕ and the smaller is η_m.

Proof of Proposition 4 We first derive the formulas for the ex post payoffs of the firm and the suppliers. To compute the Shapley value for supplier j, first note that the firm is an *essential* player in the bargaining game and thus a supplier's marginal contribution is equal to zero when a coalition does not include the firm. When it does include the firm and a measure n of suppliers, the marginal contribution of supplier j is equal to $m(j, n) = \partial R(h, \mathbf{m}, \mathbf{n}) / \partial n$, where $R(h, \mathbf{m}, \mathbf{n}) = Ah^{\eta_h} \left(\int_0^n m(i)^\rho di \right)^{\frac{\eta_m}{\rho}}$. This produces

$$m(j, n) = \frac{\eta_m}{\rho} Ah^{\eta_h} m(-i)^{\eta_m} \left(\frac{m(i)}{m(-i)} \right)^\rho n^{\frac{\eta_m - \rho}{\rho}},$$

where $m(-i)$ represents the (symmetric) investments of all suppliers other than i and where in the second equality we have used the fact that supplier investments will be symmetric in equilibrium.

The Shapley value of supplier j is the average of her marginal contributions to coalitions that consist of players ordered below her in all feasible orderings. A supplier that has a measure n of players ordered below her has a marginal contribution of $m(j, n)$ if the firm is ordered below her (probability n) and 0 otherwise (probability $1 - n$). Averaging over all possible orderings of the players and using the above formula for $m(j, n)$ we obtain:

$$s_O(h, m(-j), m(j)) = \int_0^1 nm(j, n)\, dn = \frac{\eta_m}{\eta_m + \rho} Ah^{\eta_h} m(-i)^{\eta_m} \left(\frac{m(i)}{m(-i)} \right)^\rho,$$

which corresponds to (12). In the case of vertical integration, the marginal contribution of a supplier is reduced by a factor $1 - \delta$ and so is her final payoff, thus resulting in (13).

Denote by γ_k the share of revenue accruing to the firm under the (symmetric) ownership structure $k \in \{V, O\}$, so $\gamma_O = \rho/(\eta_m + \rho)$ and $\gamma_V = (\eta_m \delta + \rho)/(\eta_m + \rho)$. From equations (12) and (13) and imposing symmetry, we have that equilibrium input choices satisfy

$$\gamma_k \eta_h A (h_k)^{\eta_h - 1} (m_k)^{\eta_m - 1} = c_h$$

$$(1 - \gamma_k) \rho A (h_k)^{\eta_h} (m_k)^{\eta_m - 1} = c_m,$$

Combining these equations, we have that joint profits are given by

$$\pi_k = (1 - \gamma_k \eta_h - (1 - \gamma_k) \rho) A^{1/(1 - \eta_m - \eta_h)} \left(\frac{\gamma_k \eta_h}{c_h} \right)^{\eta_h/(1 - \eta_m - \eta_h)} \left(\frac{(1 - \gamma_k)\rho}{c_m} \right)^{\eta_m/(1 - \eta_m - \eta_h)}.$$

Computing the ratio of profits under integration and outsourcing, taking logarithms, and multiplying by $1 - \eta_m - \eta_h > 0$, we can write

$$\Theta(\eta_h, \rho) = (1 - \eta_h - \eta_m) \ln \left(\frac{\pi_V}{\pi_O} \right)$$

$$= (1 - \eta_h - \eta_m) \ln \left(\frac{(\eta_m + \rho) - (\eta_m \delta + \rho) \eta_h - \eta_m (1 - \delta) \rho}{\eta_m (1 - \rho) + \rho (1 - \eta_h)} \right)$$

$$+ \eta_h \ln \left(\frac{(\eta_m \delta + \rho)}{\rho} \right) + \eta_m \ln (1 - \delta).$$

Straightforward differentiation delivers:

$$\frac{\partial^2\left(\Theta\left(\eta_h,\rho,\delta\right)\right)}{\partial\eta_h\partial\delta} = \frac{\left(\eta_m\delta + \delta\rho + 1 - \delta\right)\left(\eta_m + \rho\right)\left(1 - \rho\right)\left(\eta_m\right)^2}{\left(\left(\eta_m + \rho\right) - \left(\eta_m\delta + \rho\right)\eta_h - \eta_m\left(1 - \delta\right)\rho\right)^2\left(\rho + \eta_m\delta\right)} > 0,$$

while it is also easily verified that

$$\left.\frac{\partial\Theta\left(\eta_h,\rho\right)}{\partial\eta_h}\right|_{\delta=0} = 0.$$

This implies that $\frac{\partial\Theta(\eta_h,\eta_m,\rho)}{\partial\eta_h} \geq 0$ and the relative profitability of integration is increasing in η_h.

We next focus on the effect of ρ on the integration decision. Note first that

$$\lim_{\rho\to 0}\Theta\left(\eta_h,\rho\right)$$
$$= \left(1 - \eta_h - \eta_m\right)\ln\left(1 - \delta\eta_h\right) + \eta_h\lim_{\rho\to 0}\left(\ln\left(1 + \tfrac{\eta_m\delta}{\rho}\right)\right) + \eta_m\ln\left(1 - \delta\right) = +\infty,$$

and

$$\Theta\left(\eta_h, 1\right) = \left(1 - \eta_m\right)\ln\left(1 + \eta_m\delta\right) + \eta_m\ln\left(1 - \delta\right) < 0,$$

where the last expression is negative because it is decreasing in δ and equals 0 at $\delta = 0$. Hence, integration dominates outsourcing for sufficiently low ρ, and the converse is true for a high enough ρ. To demonstrate the existence of a unique threshold as stated in Proposition 4, note that

$$\frac{\partial\left(\Theta\left(\eta_h,\rho\right)\right)}{\partial\rho}$$
$$= \Delta\left[\rho^2 + \rho\frac{\left(\delta\eta_m\left(1 - \eta_h\right) - \eta_h\left(1 - \delta\right)\right)\left(1 - \eta_h - \eta_m\right) - \eta_h\left(1 - \eta_m\left(1 - \delta\right) - \eta_h\right)}{\left(1 - \eta_m - \eta_h\right)\left(1 - \delta\eta_h\right)} - \frac{\eta_m\eta_h}{\left(1 - \eta_m - \eta_h\right)}\right],$$

$$\tag{18}$$

with

$$\Delta = \frac{\left(\eta_m\right)^2\delta\left(1 - \eta_m - \eta_h\right)\left(1 - \delta\eta_h\right)}{\rho\left(\eta_m\delta + \rho\right)\left(\eta_m + \rho - \eta_h\left(\rho + \eta_m\delta\right) - \eta_m\rho\left(1 - \delta\right)\right)\left(\eta_m\left(1 - \rho\right) + \rho\left(1 - \eta_h\right)\right)} > 0.$$

Note that the term in brackets in (18) constitutes a quadratic equation in ρ of the form $\rho^2 + b\rho + c$, with $c < 0$. This implies, however, that it can only take a value of 0 at most once for $\rho > 0$. Together with the limiting values $\lim_{\rho\to 0}\Theta\left(\eta_h,\rho\right) = +\infty$ and $\Theta\left(\eta_h, 1\right) < 0$, we can thus conclude that $\Theta\left(\eta_h,\hat{\rho}\right) = 0$ for a unique value $\hat{\rho} \in (0, 1)$, as stated in the proposition.

References

Acemoglu, Daron, Philippe Aghion, Rachel Griffith, and Fabrizio Zilibotti. 2010. "Vertical Integration and Technology: Theory and Evidence." *Journal of the European Economic Association* 8: 1–45.

Acemoglu, Daron, Pol Antràs, and Elhanan Helpman. 2007. "Contracts and Technology Adoption." *American Economic Review* 97: 916–43.

Aghion, Philippe, and Jean Tirole. 1994. "The Management of Innovation." *Quarterly Journal of Economics* 109: 1185–209.

Aghion, Philippe, and Jean Tirole. 1997. "Formal and Real Authority in Organizations." *Journal of Political Economy* 105: 1–29.

Alfaro, Laura, Paola Conconi, Harald Fadinger, and Andrew F. Newman. 2010. "Trade Policy and Firm Boundaries." NBER Working Paper 16118.

Antràs, Pol. 2003. "Firms, Contracts, and Trade Structure." *Quarterly Journal of Economics* 118: 1375–418.

Antràs, Pol. 2005. "Incomplete Contracts and the Product Cycle." *American Economic Review* 95: 1054–73.

Antràs, Pol, and Ricardo J. Caballero. 2007. "Trade and Capital Flows: A Financial Frictions Perspective." *Journal of Political Economy* 117: 701–44.

Antràs, Pol, and Davin Chor. 2011. "Organizing the Global Value Chain." Working paper, Harvard University.

Antràs, Pol, and Arnaud Costinot. 2011. "Intermediated Trade." *Quarterly Journal of Economics* 126: 1319–74.

Antràs, Pol, Mihir Desai, and C. Fritz Foley. 2009. "Multinational Firms, FDI Flows and Imperfect Capital Markets." *Quarterly Journal of Economics* 124: 1171–219.

Antràs, Pol, and Elhanan Helpman. 2004. "Global Sourcing." *Journal of Political Economy* 112: 552–80.

Antràs, Pol, and Elhanan Helpman. 2008. "Contractual Frictions and Global Sourcing." In E. Helpman, D. Marin, and T. Verdier (eds.) *The Organization of Firms in a Global Economy.* Cambridge, MA: Harvard University Press.

Antràs, Pol, and Esteban Rossi-Hansberg. 2009. "Organizations and Trade," *Annual Review of Economics* 1: 43–64.

Antràs, Pol, and Robert W. Staiger. 2012. "Offshoring and the Role of Trade Agreements." *American Economic Review* 102(7): 3140–83.

Aumann, Robert J., and Lloyd S. Shapley. 1974. *Values of Non-Atomic Games.* Princeton, NJ: Princeton University Press.

Baker, George, Robert Gibbons, and Kevin J. Murphy. 2002. "Relational Contracts and the Theory of the Firm." *Quarterly Journal of Economics* 117: 39–84.

Baker, George P., and Thomas N. Hubbard. 2003. "Make Versus Buy in Trucking: Asset Ownership, Job Design, and Information." *American Economic Review* 93: 551–72.

Basco, Sergi. 2010. "Financial Development and the Product Cycle." Working paper, Universidad Carlos III.

Bernard, Andrew B., J. Bradford Jensen, Stephen Redding, and Peter K. Schott. 2010. "Intra-Firm Trade and Product Contractibility." *American Economic Review* 100: 444–48.

Campa, Jose M., and Linda S. Goldberg. 1997. "The Evolving External Orientation of Manufacturing: A Profile of Four Countries." *Federal Reserve Bank of New York Economic Policy Review* 3: 53–81.

Carluccio, Juan, and Thibault Fally. 2012. "Global Sourcing under Imperfect Capital Markets," *Review of Economics and Statistics* 94 (3): 740–63.

Casson, Mark. 1979. *Alternatives to the Multinational Enterprise.* London: Palgrave Macmillan.

Caves, Richard E. 1996. *Multinational Enterprise and Economic Analysis.* 2nd ed. Cambridge: Cambridge University Press.

Chen, Yongmin, and Robert C. Feenstra. 2008. "Buyer Investment, Export Variety and Intrafirm Trade." *European Economic Review* 52: 1313–37.

Chen, Yongmin, Ig Horstmann, and James Markusen. 2008. "Physical Capital, Knowledge Capital and the Choice between FDI and Outsourcing." *Canadian Journal of Economics* 45: 1–15.

Coase, Ronald H. 1937. "The Nature of the Firm." *Economica* 4: 386–405.

Conconi, Paola, Patrick Legros, and Andrew F. Newman. 2012. "Trade Liberalization and Organizational Change. "*Journal of International Economics* 86 (2): 197–208.

Corcos, Gregory. 2006. "Globalisation, Vertical Linkages, and Relational Contracts." Working paper, Paris School of Economics.

Corcos, Gregory, Delphine M. Irac, Giordano Mion, and Thierry Verdier. 2013. "The Determinants of Intra-Firm Trade." *Review of Economics and Statistics* 95(3): 825–38.

Defever, Fabrice, and Farid Toubal. 2007. "Productivity and the Sourcing Modes of Multinational Firms: Evidence from French Firm-Level Data." CEP Discussion Paper 842, London School of Economics and Political Science.

Díez, Federico J. 2010. "The Asymmetric Effects of Tariffs on Intra-Firm Trade and Offshoring Decisions." Working Paper 10–4, Federal Reserve Bank of Boston.

Dixit, Avinash K., and Joseph E. Stiglitz. 1977. "Monopolistic Competition and Optimum Product Diversity." *American Economic Review* 67: 297–308.

Djankov, Simeon, Rafael La Porta, Florencio Lopez-de-Silanes, and Andrei Shleifer. 2003. "Courts." *Quarterly Journal of Economics* 118: 453–517.

Dunning, John H. 1981. *International Production and the Multinational Enterprise*. London: Allen and Unwin.

Ethier, Wilfred J. 1986. "The Multinational Firm." *Quarterly Journal of Economics* 101: 805–33.

Ethier, Wilfred J., and James R. Markusen. 1996. "Multinational Firms, Technology Diffusion and Trade." *Journal of International Economics* 41: 1–28.

Feenstra, Robert C. 2011. "Offshoring to China: The Local and Global Impacts of Processing Trade." Lectures presented at the University of International Business and Economics, Beijing, April 18–20.

Feenstra, Robert C., and Gordon H. Hanson. 1996. "Globalization, Outsourcing, and Wage Inequality." *American Economic Review* 86: 240–5.

Feenstra, Robert C., and Gordon H. Hanson. 2005. "Ownership and Control in Outsourcing to China: Estimating the Property-Rights Theory of the Firm." *Quarterly Journal of Economics* 120: 729–61.

Fernandes, Ana P., and Heiwai Tang. 2010. "Determinants of Vertical Integration in Export Processing: Theory and Evidence from China." Working paper, Tufts University.

Grossman, Sanford J., and Oliver D. Hart. 1986. "The Costs and Benefits of Ownership: A Theory of Vertical and Lateral Integration." *Journal of Political Economy* 94: 691–719.

Grossman, Gene M., and Elhanan Helpman. 2002. "Integration vs. Outsourcing in Industry Equilibrium." *Quarterly Journal of Economics* 117: 85–120.

Grossman, Gene M., and Elhanan Helpman. 2003. "Outsourcing versus FDI in Industry Equilibrium." *Journal of the European Economic Association* 1: 317–27.

Grossman, Gene M., and Elhanan Helpman. 2004. "Managerial Incentives and the International Organization of Production." *Journal of International Economics* 63: 237–62.

Guadalupe, Maria, Olga Kuzmina, and Catherine Thomas. 2012. "Innovation and Foreign Ownership." *American Economic Review* 102 (7): 3594–627.

Hart, Oliver. 1995. *Firms, Contracts, and Financial Structure*. New York: Oxford University Press.

Hart, Oliver, and Bengt R. Holmström. 2010. "A Theory of Firm Scope." *Quarterly Journal of Economics* 125: 483–513.

Hart, Oliver, and John Moore. 1990. "Property Rights and the Nature of the Firm." *Journal of Political Economy* 98: 1119–58.

Helpman, Elhanan. 2006. "Trade, FDI and the Organization of Firms." *Journal of Economic Literature* 44: 589–630.

Helpman, Elhanan, Oleg Itskhoki, and Stephen Redding. 2010. "Inequality and Unemployment in a Global Economy." *Econometrica* 78: 1239–83.

Helpman, Elhanan, and Paul R. Krugman. 1985. "Single-Product Firms." In *Market Structure and Foreign Trade: Increasing Returns, Imperfect Competition, and the International Economy.* Cambridge, MA: MIT Press.

Hummels, David, Jun Ishii, and Kei-Mu Yi. 2001. "The Nature and Growth of Vertical Specialization in World Trade." *Journal of International Economics* 54: 75–96.

Hymer, Stephen H. 1960. "The International Operations of National Firms: A Study of Direct Foreign Investment." Ph.D diss., Massachusetts Institute of Technology.

Hymer, Stephen H. 1976. *The International Operations of National Firms: A Study of Direct Foreign Investment.* Cambridge, MA: MIT Press.

Kohler, Wilhelm, and Marcel Smolka. 2009. "Global Sourcing Decisions and Firm Productivity: Evidence from Spain." CESifo Working Paper 2903, CESifo Group, Munich.

Legros, Patrick, and Andrew F. Newman. 2008. "Competing for Ownership." *Journal of the European Economic Association* 6: 1279–308.

Legros, Patrick, and Andrew F. Newman. 2009. "A Price Theory of Vertical and Lateral Integration." CEPR Discussion Paper No. 7211, London.

Levchenko, Andrei. 2007. "Institutional Quality and International Trade." *Review of Economic Studies* 74: 791–819.

Manova, Kalina. 2010. "Credit Constraints, Heterogeneous Firms and International Trade. "Working paper, Stanford University.

Marin, Dalia, and Thierry Verdier. 2009. "Power in the Multinational Corporation in Industry Equilibrium." *Economic Theory* 38: 437–64.

Markusen, James R. 1995. "The Boundaries of Multinational Enterprises and the Theory of International Trade." *Journal of Economic Perspectives* 9: 169–89.

McLaren, John. 2000. "Globalization and Vertical Structure." *American Economic Review* 90: 1239–54.

Melitz, Marc J. 2003. "The Impact of Trade on Intra-Industry Reallocations and Aggregate Industry Productivity." *Econometrica* 71: 1695–725.

Midler, Paul. 2009. *Poorly Made in China.* Hoboken, NJ: Wiley.

Nunn, Nathan. 2007. "Relationship-Specificity, Incomplete Contracts, and the Pattern of Trade." *Quarterly Journal of Economics* 122: 569–600.

Nunn, Nathan, and Daniel Trefler. 2008. "The Boundaries of the Multinational Firm: An Empirical Analysis." In E. Helpman, D. Marin, and T. Verdier (eds.) *The Organization of Firms in a Global Economy.* Cambridge, MA: Harvard University Press.

Nunn, Nathan, and Daniel Trefler. 2011. "Incomplete Contracts and the Boundaries of the Multinational Firm. " Working paper, Harvard University.

Ponzetto, Giacomo. 2009. "Intellectual Property Rights and Efficient Firm Organization." Working paper, CREI-Universitat Pompeu Fabra.

Puga, Diego, and Daniel Trefler. 2010. "Wake Up and Smell the Ginseng: The Rise of Incremental Innovation in Low-Wage Countries." *Journal of Development Economics* 91: 64–76.

Qiu, Larry D., and Barbara Spencer. 2002. "Keiretsu and Relationship-Specific Investment: Implications for Market-Opening Trade Policy." *Journal of International Economics* 58: 49–79.

Rajan, Raghuram G., and Luigi Zingales. 2001. "The Firm as a Dedicated Hierarchy: A Theory of the Origins and Growth of Firms." *Quarterly Journal of Economics* 116: 805–52.

Rodrik, Dani. 2000. "How Far Will International Economic Integration Go?" *Journal of Economic Perspectives* 14: 177–86.

Romalis, John. 2004. "Factor Proportions and the Structure of Commodity Trade." *American Economic Review* 94: 67–97.

Rugman, Alan M. 1981. *Inside the Multinationals: The Economics of Internal Markets.* New York: Columbia University Press.

Schwarz, Christian, and Jens Suedekum. 2011. "Global Sourcing of Complex Production Processes." CESifo Working Paper 3559, Munich.

Spencer, Barbara. 2005. "International Outsourcing and Incomplete Contracts." *Canadian Journal of Economics* 38: 1107–135.

Tomiura, Eiichi. 2007. "Foreign Outsourcing, Exporting, and FDI: A Productivity Comparison at the Firm Level." *Journal of International Economics* 72: 113–27.

van Biesebroeck, Johannes, and Lijun Zhang. 2011. "Global Sourcing of a Complex Good." Working paper, K.U. Leuven.

Whinston, Michael D. 2003. "On the Transaction Cost Determinants of Vertical Integration." *Journal of Law, Economics, and Organization* 19: 1–23.

Williamson, Oliver E. 1975. *Markets and Hierarchies: Analysis and Antitrust Implications.* New York: Free Press.

Williamson, Oliver E. 1985. *The Economic Institutions of Capitalism.* New York: Free Press.

World Trade Organization. 2008. *World Trade Report 2008: Trade in a Globalizing World.* Geneva: World Trade Organization.

Yeaple, Stephen R. 2006. "Offshoring, Foreign Direct Investment, and the Structure of U.S. Trade." *Journal of the European Economic Association* 4: 602–11.

Yeats, Alexander J. 2001. "Just How Big Is Global Production Sharing?" In S. Arndt and H. Kierzkowski (eds.) *Fragmentation: New Production Patterns in the World Economy.* New York: Oxford University Press.

Zeile, William J. 1997. "U. S. Intrafirm Trade in Goods." *Survey of Current Business* 78: 23–38.

22

Comment on Pol Antràs: "Grossman-Hart (1986) Goes Global: Incomplete Contracts, Property Rights, and the International Organization of Production"

ELHANAN HELPMAN

Dunning (1977) developed the OLI approach to foreign direct investment (FDI), which dominated the profession's thinking about multinational corporations for many years. In this view, which was often described as an eclectic approach, a company needs to have advantages in three areas to form a subsidiary in a foreign country: ownership, location, and internalization (OLI). An ownership advantage is attained through the possession of specific assets, often related to technology or fixed costs. A locational advantage, which dictates where to acquire a subsidiary, can arise from low manufacturing costs, low servicing costs, or high demand conditions. An internalization advantage exists when controlling an operation in the foreign country internally is better than through an arm's-length arrangement. Under this broad roof one can accommodate a wide variety of specific factors in explaining patterns of foreign direct investment. Yet one can also argue that this framework is too broad, making it difficult to derive specific predictions that can be confronted with data.

In the 1980s scholars started to develop more detailed models of multinational corporations. Helpman (1984) developed a model of vertical FDI in which firms fragment the production process and locate parts of the value chain in a foreign country to save costs. And Markusen (1984) developed a model of horizontal FDI in which firms build an integrated facility in a foreign country to serve host country consumers. The latter decision trades of concentration for proximity; while concentration of production in the home country saves fixed costs, it entails variable trade costs that are saved through FDI. This two-pronged view of FDI dominated the literature for a long time, despite the fact that more complex integration strategies were evolving in the world economy. Yeaple (2003) provided the first formalization of a more nuanced view, in which horizontal and vertical FDI are interdependent, and they can reinforce each other (i.e., be complementary). Importantly, Helpman (1984), Markusen (1984), and Yeaple (2003) all assumed that whenever it is profitable to have production in a foreign country it also is profitable to own the foreign enterprise. In other words, they, like almost all the literature on multinational corporations, did not explicitly analyze the internalization decision. An exception was Ethier (1986), who analyzed the internalization decision. But his framework was not adopted by subsequent scholars.

Understanding the internalization decision is central to a satisfactory theory of multinational corporations. A company can source inputs from a foreign country under a variety of arrangements, for example, it can import them at arm's length, license a foreign producer, or engage in a joint venture with minority holding. So why do firms choose to own a foreign enterprise? Or have a large stake in a foreign company?

While scholars of international trade were aware of the need to have an understanding of this issue, for a long time they did not manage to develop an attractive framework for addressing it. International trade theory requires microeconomic foundations that can be embodied in multisectoral multicountry general equilibrium models, which require a delicate balance between complexity and tractability to make progress. Indeed, the past decade has witnessed a revolution in trade theory, as the right balance was found for incorporating firm heterogeneity and incomplete contracts into trade theory. While Melitz (2003) provided the building blocks for firm heterogeneity, Antràs (2003) provided the building blocks for incomplete contracts. These building blocks were then combined to develop a rich model of international trade that explains the relative prevalence of four major organizational forms: outsourcing at home, outsourcing abroad, integration at home, and integration abroad (FDI). In the Spanish data studied by Kohler and Smolka (2009), the fractions of firms who sourced inputs in one of these four forms is described in Table 22.1. About one third of these firms produced their own inputs in Spain, while 28% acquired inputs from their foreign subsidiaries. Ninety-one percent of the Spanish firms purchased inputs from unaffiliated Spanish suppliers, while 66% imported inputs from unaffiliated foreign firms. Moreover, there exist firms in these data who used multiple sourcing strategies, possibly for different inputs. This sort of data could not be explained by the trade theory that existed prior to 2003.

Table 22.1. **Fraction of Spanish firms in each organizational mode, 2007**

	Home	Offshore
Integration	0.34	0.28
Outsourcing	0.91	0.66

Note: These data are for firms with more than 200 employees.

Source: Kohler and Smolka (2009, Table 2).

Antràs provides in this paper an admirably clear exposition of the new trade theory with multinational corporations, and in the process develops extensions that pertain to the internalization decision. He shows clearly how this theory builds on Grossman and Hart (1986) and what its empirical implications are. Moreover, he reviews the evidence that builds on the theory, which mostly consists of correlations implied by the theory among observable variables. As he also makes clear, 2 none of the existing empirical studies tests the theory directly. Rather, what is tested is whether various implications of the theory are consistent with the data. A reader of this review who is not familiar with the literature will find it to be an excellent introduction to the subject. And a reader who is familiar with the literature will appreciate the clarity of exposition and the balanced coverage of this complex line of research.

References

Antràs, Pol. 2003. "Firms, Contracts, and Trade Structure." *Quarterly Journal of Economics* 118: 1375–418.

Dunning, John H. 1977. "Trade, Location of Economic Activity and the MNE: A Search for an Eclectic Approach." In B. Ohlin, P.-O. Hesselborn, and P.M. Wijkman (eds.) *The International Allocation of Economic Activity: Proceedings of a Nobel Symposium Held at Stockholm.* London: Macmillan.

Ethier, Wilfred J. 1986. The Multinational Firm." Quarterly Journal of Economics 101: 805–33.

Grossman, S., and O. Hart. 1986. "The Costs and Benefits of Ownership: A Theory of Vertical and Lateral Integration." *Journal of Political Economy* 94: 691–719.

Helpman, Elhanan. 1984. "A Simple Theory of International Trade with Multinational Corporations." *Journal of Political Economy* 92: 451–71.

Kohler, Wilhelm K. and Marcel Smolka. 2009. "Global Sourcing Decisions and Firm Productivity: Evidence from Spain." CESifo Working Paper No. 2903.

Markusen, James R. 1984. "Multinationals, Multi-Plant Economies and the Gain from Trade." *Journal of International Economics* 16: 205–16.

Melitz, Marc J. 2003. "The Impact of Trade on Intra-Industry Reallocations and Aggregate Industry Productivity." *Econometrica* 71: 1695–725.

Yeaple, Stephen R. 2003. "The Complex Integration Strategies of Multinationals and Cross Country Dependencies in the Structure of Foreign Direct Investment." *Journal of International Economics* 60: 293–314.

23

The Theory of the Firm Goes Global

DALIA MARIN

In chapter 21, Pol Antràs gives an excellent review of the influence that Grossman and Hart (1986) (GH) has had on recent developments in international trade. The "new new trade theory" brings "real firms" into international trade by incorporating firm heterogeneity and by opening the black box of the firm introducing organizational considerations into international trade and foreign direct investment (for an overview, see Helpman, Marin, and Verdier 2008). Similar to the development of the theory of the firm (see Bolton and Scharfstein 1998), the theory of international trade and organizations (ITO) has been developing in two directions. One approach focuses on the boundaries of the multinational corporation (see Grossman and Helpman 2002; Antràs 2003; Antràs and Helpman 2004, 2008; Nunn and Trefler 2008); the second approach focuses on the internal organization of national and multinational firms (Marin and Verdier 2003, 2008a,b, 2009, 2012, 2014; Puga and Trefler 2010; Antràs, Garicano, and Rossi-Hansberg 2006, 2007; Bloom, Sadun, and van Reenen 2010; Guadalupe and Wulf 2010; Caliendo and Rossi-Hansberg 2011;; Marin, Rousova, and Verdier 2012). In his paper, Pol mainly describes the literature on the boundaries of the multinational corporation of which he and Elhanan Helpman are the leading exponents. This is natural, because the theory of the international organization of production is a direct offspring of Grossman and Hart (1986) taken to the global economy. However, GH had an indirect influence on the theories of internal organizations, such as Aghion and Tirole (1997), which have been incorporated into trade models. Therefore, I use my discussion to talk about the second approach.

Why should we take the theory of the firm global? In the past two decades, the nature of international trade has been changing. Modern economic commerce involves movements across international boundaries—but often within the boundaries of the firm. It is often characterized by a "war for talent" rather than a "war for market shares." Firms engaged in international trade have met these challenges of the new features of world trade by organizing production in an international value chain, by decentralizing their system of command in flatter corporate hierarchies, by making human capital to the new stakeholder of the firm, and by compensating their CEOs with skyrocket earnings. Thus, we ask: have international trade and competition been the driving forces behind these observed changes in the corporation?[1]

In Marin and Verdier (2008a,b, 2012, 2014) we introduce internal hierarchies into models of international trade with imperfect competition to answer how international trade may lead to flatter corporate hierarchies, to decentralization of decision making in the firm, to a "war for talent," to a rise in CEO pay in rich countries, to organizational convergence across countries, and to heterogeneity across firms in the same industry. I will briefly discuss how international trade can give rise to each of these phenomena in turn.[2]

International Trade and Flatter Corporate Hierarchies

Theory

In Marin and Verdier (2008a, 2014) we introduce a variant of the Aghion and Tirole (1997) (AT) theory of the firm into a Dixit and Stiglitz (1977) model of monopolistic competition and into a Melitz and Ottaviano (2008) model of international trade to examine how international trade may affect corporate organization in similar countries (north-north trade).

In the AT theory of the firm, the owner (the principal) hires a manager (the agent) to bring new projects to the firm. Once the contract is signed both the principal and the agent may exert effort to find profitable projects for the firm. To make things interesting, we assume that there is a conflict of interest between the owner and the manager: the manager will suggest a high-cost project—a project that maximizes his private benefits (perks, career concerns) rather than a project which maximizes the profits of the firm. In the AT theory there is a trade-off between control and initiative in the firm. Having a boss—hierarchies—is bad, because it destroys the initiative of workers. However, if the owner decides not to look for projects, say, because of overload, and the manager searches

---

[1] As discussed by Pol, intrafirm trade—trade within the boundaries of the firm—accounts for about 40% of world trade. But among some of the European countries it may account for almost all trade between pairs of countries, such as between Austria and Hungary, see Marin (2006).

[2] I am not discussing the papers by Antràs, Garicano, and Rossi-Hansberg (2006, 2007), Caliendo and Rossi-Hansberg (2011), and Marin, Rousova, and Verdier (2012) here, because they are not based on incomplete contracting but rather on a theory of knowledge hierarchies that does not belong to the tradition of GH. Marin and Verdier (2009) and Puga and Trefler (2010) use Aghion and Tirole (1997) to explain the organization of multinational firms.

and proposes a project, it is profitable for the owner/principal to follow his suggestion. In this case, the manager has "real" rather than "formal" authority. Alternatively, the owner may decide to keep the manager's initiative alive and decentralize the decision to the manager. In this case the manager has formal authority.

In Marin and Verdier (2014) we bring the AT firm into a one-sector economy with monopolistic competition with differentiated goods à la Melitz and Ottaviano (2008) (MO). In each firm, a principal hires a manager to monitor projects and workers to produce. As in AT, the allocation of authority in these firms is governed by the trade-off between control and initiative. Consumers have linear demand across a continuum of varieties and price mark-ups become endogenous and a function of the toughness of competition in the market.

How is trade openness affecting the trade-off between control and initiative in the firm? With more trade, the market becomes larger and profits increase. When profits increase, the owner/principal monitors more, since there is more at stake. When the trade shock is sufficiently large, the stakes rise and owners in firms are monitoring so much that they destroy the initiative of their managers in the firm. To prevent this from happening, principals decide to delegate formal authority to their managers. At the same time, however, more trade means more foreign competition. Tougher competition, in turn, makes incentives between the owner and the manager less aligned. The conflict of interest between owner and manager rises and hence the owner monitors more. At some level of competition, the owner decides to delegate authority to the manager to encourage his initiative. Thus, with more trade, decentralization to the manager occurs, because under her formal authority the owner cannot otherwise keep the manager's initiative alive.

Incorporating AT into international trade brings two important insights. First, the trade-off between control and initiative of the AT model disappears in very weak and very tough trade environments. As a result, the relationship between international trade and the level of decentralization is nonmonotonic. Firms in a small market protected from foreign competition have small profits in which owners/principals monitor little and do not destroy the initiative of managers. In protected markets, there are no costs of control in the firm, because firms can keep the initiative of their managers alive even when principals have formal authority. Hence, the firm organization is centralized in trade-protected markets. Firms in large open markets face tough competition, but profits are unambiguously larger (the market size effect dominates the competition effect when trade is liberalized). Because the stakes are very large, principals in firms monitor and search so intensively that they destroy the initiative of their managers even when they decentralize and delegate formal authority to them. Hence, there are again no costs of control, since the principal cannot keep the enthusiasm of the manager alive even when she empowers him. The organization will again be centralized in markets very open to trade. It is only at intermediate levels of trade openness that there is a trade-off between control and initiative as described in the theory of the firm of AT. Principals decentralize power to their managers to keep their initiative alive.

Second, the conflict of interest between owners/principals and managers/agents (congruence in the parlance of AT) becomes endogenous and a function of the trade environment that firms face. In markets more open to trade, the conflict of interest between the owner and the manager increases. It matters more who runs the firm in a more competitive environment. When the manager has formal authority, he chooses the larger cost project (which maximizes his private benefit), which translates into more profit losses to the firm in a tougher trade environment. Profits decline more in firms run by the manager, because high-cost firms lose more sales and fight this loss by lowering their price mark-ups compared with low-cost firms run by principals.

Empirics

In Marin and Verdier (2014) we derive predictions from the theory and confront them with the data. We predict that in a cross-section of firms, firms will have more decentralized corporate hierarchies when they face tougher competition and they are more exposed to international trade. We predict further that organizational change toward less hierarchical firms is more likely to happen in firms more exposed to international trade. We test these predictions for a cross-section of 2,200 firms with novel data we collected among German and Austrian corporations. The data are generated from a full population survey of Austrian and German firms that invest in Eastern Europe, including Russia and Ukraine. Our data set provides detailed information on the internal organization of firms in the two countries. We measure delegation of authority by asking the CEO at the headquarters of the corporation: "Who decides in your company over the following decisions (listed in Figure 23.1), please rank between 1 taken at headquarters and 5 taken at the divisional level?" The figure reveals that firms in the smaller economy, Austria, are more centralized compared with firms in the larger economy, Germany. This finding is in accordance with the theory, since the theory predicts that in larger and more competitive markets firms are more likely to decentralize authority. The figure also reveals that corporate decisions for which the effort of the agent matters most—such as the decisions over R&D and the decision to introduce a new product—are jointly decided by headquarters and the divisional level, as is predicted by the theory.

We then rank each firm by its level of decentralization by averaging the hierarchical score of the 16 corporate decisions listed in Figure 23.1. Figure 23.2 shows

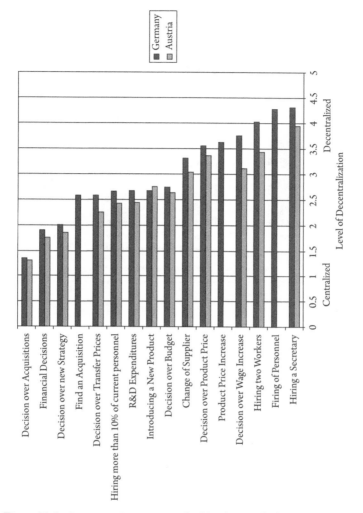

Figure 23.1 Corporate Decisions ranked by the Level of Decentralization

the correlation between the number of foreign competitors as perceived by firms and the level of decentralization in firms in Austria and Germany. In both countries firms with a larger number of foreign competitors tend to be more decentralized. Note also, that—as predicted by the theory—in the larger more competitive economy, Germany, firms recentralize authority when competition becomes very tough.

Two empirical papers by Bloom, Sadun, and Van Reenen (2010) and Guadalupe and Wolf (2010) also find—based on different data for different countries—that increased competition leads to more decentralization and to the removal of hierarchical layers in the corporation.

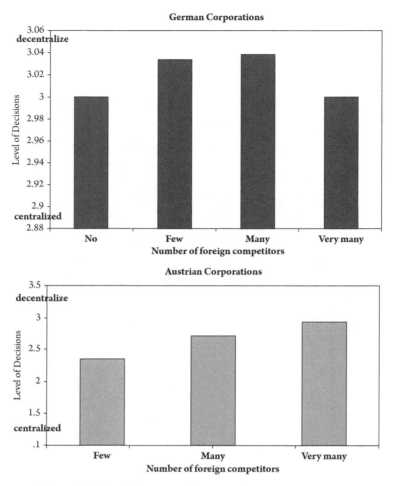

Figure 23.2   Level of Decentralization and Foreign Competition

International Trade and the "War for Talent"

In the previous section we examined the effect of north-north trade on the way firms organize. I turn now to how north-south trade may influence corporate organization in different countries. In Marin and Verdier (2003, 2012) we introduce a variant of the Aghion and Tirole (1997) theory of the firm into a Helpman and Krugman (1985) (HK) model of international trade in which countries differ in factor endowments. We consider a world economy consisting of two countries, the human capital–rich North, and the labor-rich South. In each country there are two sectors: the X-sector produces differentiated goods under monopolistic competition and the Y-sector produces homogeneous goods under perfect competition. In each firm in the X-sector a principal hires a skilled manager to run the firm. We assume that the X-sector is more skill intensive than the Y-sector. Consumers' preferences over the two goods Y and X are given by CES utility.

We gain several insights from putting the partial equilibrium theory of the firm of AT into the general equilibrium of trade of HK. First, the mode of organization that firms choose becomes a function of relative factor prices, and therefore, in equilibrium, of relative factor endowments of countries. In countries where skilled labor is relatively scarce, the wages of unskilled workers will tend to be low, whereas the start-up costs of a firm (which consist of the wages of skilled managers) will tend to be high, thus making entry more costly. These forces tend to make the ratio of profits to unskilled wages high in skill-scarce countries and low in skill-abundant countries. It follows that countries with very high or very low ratios of skilled managers to unskilled workers will tend to have firms in which principals keep formal authority, and in countries with intermediate ratios of skills the mode of organization in which authority is delegated to skilled managers might prevail.

Second, we find that in the general equilibrium of the closed economy, there exists a range of relative factor endowments for which there are multiple equilibria, with all principals in the monopolistically competitive X-sector either decentralizing or not decentralizing authority.

Third, we show in the Rybczynski theorem of firm organization that there also exists a range of factor endowments for which we get a unique mixed equilibrium, with some principals decentralizing formal authority and others not. For this range of factor endowments, factor prices are independent of factor endowments: factor market clearing comes about through a relocation of resources from one organizational mode to the other (in equilibrium, different organizational modes differ in their factor intensity). In this range of factor endowments, the mode of organization becomes a new source of comparative advantage.

How does international trade affect corporate organization in the skill-rich North? Suppose that the North is sufficiently skill-rich. Then in autarky, the start-up costs (the cost of a manager) in the North will be low relative to wages of low-skilled workers. Because the stakes are low, principals in firms monitor little and do not destroy the initiative of managers. Thus, in autarky, principals will keep formal authority and choose a centralized organization. When the skill-rich North opens up to trade, it specializes more in the skill-intensive monitoring activity, resulting in a fall in the relative wage for low-skilled workers and an increase in profits. When profits increase, firms want to enter the market. Because firms can enter and run a firm only by hiring a skilled manager, market entry is constrained by the pool of available managers in the country.

Firms compete for the limited number of skilled managers available in the economy, pushing up the relative wage for skilled managers. Thus, with more trade, manager talent has more opportunities outside the firm and managers become more mobile, resulting in a "war for talent" triggered by trade liberalization. With the rise in start-up costs of firms, the stakes rise and principals start to monitor more, destroying the initiative of managers. When the trade shock is sufficiently large, principals decentralize formal authority to the skilled manager and the talent firm emerges in equilibrium.

International Trade and the Rise of Executive Pay

The compensation of executive board members in industrialized countries has become a highly controversial topic as CEO pay increased 6-fold from 1980 to 2005 in the United States and 3.5-fold from 1977 to 2008 in Germany.

Why is international trade a candidate to explain the rise of executive pay? Recent long-run time series evidence for the United States in the period 1936–2005 (Frydman and Saks 2010) and for Germany (Fabbri and Marin 2015) suggests that the available explanations for the surge in executive compensation receive only modest support from the data if at all. A proper understanding of the rise in executive pay requires integrating the theory of the firm into international trade theory. Most of the explanations on executive pay (except Gabaix and Landier 2008) have in common that they focus on failures in the internal control mechanism of firms, but they neglect the market environment in which firms operate, in particular the market for executives. In Marin and Verdier (2012) we examine both the incentives inside firms as well as how these incentives interact with the trade environment firms' face, allowing us to analyze how international trade affects executive pay.

One major prediction of our theory is that globalization is leading to a rise in executive pay above and beyond the typical trade-induced increases in the skill premium in skill-rich countries. The mechanism by which international trade may lead to a rise in CEO pay in the skill-rich North is that international trade puts pressure on the demand for managers for two novel reasons: the "war for talent," and an economy-wide shift to a more skill-intensive organization. As described before, in the "war for talent" new firms enter the market and compete with incumbent firms for the available manager talent in the North to start a firm, which pushes up the relative wage of skilled managers. The skill bias organizational change involves an economy-wide move from a low-skill intensive organization, in which the owner runs the firm, to a skill-intensive organization in which the skilled manager runs the firm.

Organizational Convergence

I am turning now to a further insight we gain from introducing the AT firm into international trade. In Marin and Verdier (2012, 2014) we show that international trade will lead to convergence in corporate cultures across countries. In Marin and Verdier 2014 we examine how international trade affects corporate organization in similar countries. We show that decentralizing authority to lower levels of the corporation and the move to less hierarchical organizations emerge in equilibrium when competition is neither too tough nor too weak. The model produces multiple equilibria that arise out of strategic complementarities among firms' organizational decisions. This way, two otherwise identical countries may have a different corporate organization in autarky. In this theory, international trade may result in convergence of corporate organization across countries. However, the organizational equilibrium to which the world economy converges remains undetermined.

In Marin and Verdier (2012) we allow countries to differ in factor endowments that enable us to predict to which organizational equilibrium the integrated world economy will converge. In the integrated world economy, we predict the emergence of firms with decentralized corporate hierarchies in which human capital becomes the new stakeholder of the firm.

How is convergence coming about? In the human capital–rich North, international trade leads to a stronger specialization in the skill-intensive monitoring activity, resulting in an increase in profits and more monitoring by principals. Eventually, principals decentralize authority to human capital to keep the initiative alive. In the labor-rich South, trade leads to a resource reallocation toward the labor-intensive sector and to a decline in profits, with some firms exiting the market, lowering the start-up cost of firms. Because there is less at stake, principals in southern firms care less about control and more about enhancing the initiative of middle managers and hence delegate authority to them. This results in a shift toward decentralization. Thus, in the integrated world economy, all principals in both countries decentralize authority to human capital—the emergence of the talent firm—even when no principal in either of the countries was decentralizing in autarky.

We give conditions under which an organizational equilibrium with decentralized firms is more likely to emerge in the integrated world economy that waits to be put to an empirical test. One main prediction from Marin and Verdier (2012) is that the more different the countries are in terms of relative factor endowments, the more they will trade with one another (controlling for country size) and thus the more likely is organizational convergence.

Firm Heterogeneity and Firm Organization

I turn now to the final insight we gain from incorporating AT into trade. Firm heterogeneity in size and productivity in the same industry has been widely documented in empirical firm-level studies (see Bernard et al. 2007). Melitz (2003) and Antràs and Helpman (2004) introduce firm heterogeneity into models of international trade by assuming an exogenous ex ante distribution of potential productivity levels. After entry, competition provides an endogenous mechanism for selection of the equilibrium distribution of productivity within an industry. Trade integration leads to a reallocation to high-productivity firms within a sector resulting in an increase in aggregate productivity.

But what determines differences in productivity and size across firms in the same industry in the first place? In Marin and Verdier (2008b) we focus on understanding the sources of firms' ex ante heterogeneity by asking: do firms differ in size and productivity in the same industry because they adopt different types of organizations? We introduce organizational choices in a Melitz and Ottaviano (2008) model of trade. Our model simultaneously determines firms' organizational choices and heterogeneity across firms in size and productivity.

References

Aghion, P., and J. Tirole 1997. "Formal and Real Authority in Organizations." *Journal of Political Economy* 105(1): 1–29.

Antràs, P. 2003. "Firms, Contracts, and Trade Structure." *Quarterly Journal of Economics* 118(4): 1375–418.

Antràs, P., L. Garicano, and E. Rossi-Hansberg. 2006. "Offshoring in a Knowledge Economy." *Quarterly Journal of Economics* 121(1): 31–77.

Antràs, P., L. Garicano, and E. Rossi-Hansberg. 2007. "Organizing Offshoring: Middle Managers and Communication Costs." In E. Helpman, D. Marin, and T. Verdier (eds.), *The Organization of Firms in a Global Economy*, pp. 55–83. Cambridge, MA: Harvard University Press.

Antràs, P., and E. Helpman. 2004. "Global Sourcing." *Journal of Political Economy* 112(3): 552–80.

Antràs, P., and E. Helpman. 2008. "Contractual Frictions and Global Sourcing." In E. Helpman, D. Marin, and T. Verdier (eds.) *The Organization of Firms in a Global Economy*. Cambridge, MA: Harvard University Press.

Bernard, J.B. Jensen, St. Redding and P. Schott (2007), [3]Firms in International Trade[2], Journal of Economic Perspectives, Vol 21/3, pp 105–130.

Bloom, N., J. Van Reenen, and R. Sadun. 2010. "Does Product Market Competition Lead Firms to Decentralize?" *American Economic Review* 100 (2): 434–38.

Bolton, P., and D. S. Scharfstein. 1998. "Corporate Finance, the Theory of the Firm, and Organizations." *Journal of Economic Perspectives* 12(4): 95–114.

Caliendo, L., and E. Rossi-Hansberg. 2011. "The Impact of Trade on Organization and Productivity." CEPR Discussion Paper 8535.

Dixit, A. K., and J. E. Stiglitz. 1977. "Monopolistic Competition and Optimum Product Diversity." *American Economic Review* 67(3): 297–308.

Fabbri, F. and D. Marin (2015), "What Explains the Rise of Executive Pay in Germany?". *Scandinavian Journal of Economics*, forthcoming.

Frydman, C. and R.E. Saks (2010), "Executive Compensation: A View from a Long-Term Perspective, 1936–2005," *Review of Financial Studies*, 23, 2099–2138.

Gabaix, X., and A. Landier. 2008. "Why Has CEO Pay Increased So Much?" *Quarterly Journal of Economics* 123 (1): 49–100.

Grossman, S. J., and O. D. Hart. 1986. "The Costs and Benefits of Ownership: A Theory of Vertical and Lateral Integration." *Journal of Political Economy* 94(4): 691–719.

Grossman, G. M., and E. Helpman. 2002. "Integration versus Outsourcing in Industry Equilibrium." *Quarterly Journal of Economics* 117 (1): 85–120.

Guadalupe, M., and J. Wulf. 2010. "The Flattening Firm and Product Market Competition: The Effect of Trade Liberalization on Corporate Hierarchies." *American Economic Journal: Applied Economics* 2(4): 105–27.

Helpman, E., and P.R. Krugman. 1985. *Market Structure and Foreign Trade: Increasing Returns, Imperfect Competition, and the International Economy*. Cambridge, MA: MIT Press.

Helpman, E., D. Marin, and T. Verdier es.). 2008. *The Organization of Firms in a Global Economy*, Cambridge, MA: Harvard University Press.

Marin, D. 2006. "A New International Division of Labor in Europe: Outsourcing and Offshoring to Eastern Europe," *Journal of the European Economic Association* 4 (2–3): 612–622.

Marin, D., L. Rousov,á and T. Verdier. 2012. "Do Multinationals Transplant their Business Model?" University of Munich, mimeo.

Marin, D., and T. Verdier. 2003. "Globalization and the New Enterprise," *Journal of the European Economic Association* 1 (2–3): 337–44.

Marin, D., and T. Verdier. 2008a. "Power Inside the Firm and the Market: A General Equilibrium Approach." *Journal of the European Economic Association* 6(4): 752–88.

Marin, D., and T. Verdier. 2008b. "Competing in Organizations: Firm Heterogeneity and International Trade." In E. Helpman, D. Marin and T. Verdier (eds.) *The Organization of Firms in a Global Economy*, pp. 142–72, Cambridge, MA: Harvard University Press.

Marin, D., and T. Verdier. 2009. "Power in the Multinational Corporation in Industry Equilibrium,." *Economic Theory* 38(3): 437–64.

Marin, D., and T. Verdier. 2012. "Globalization and the Empowerment of Talent." *Journal of International Economics* 86(2): 209–23.

Marin, D., and T. Verdier. 2014. "Corporate Hierarchies and International Trade: Theory and Evidence." *Journal of International Economics* 94(2): 295–310.

Melitz, M. 2003. "The Impact of Trade on Aggregate Industry Productivity and Intra-industry Reallocations." *Econometrica* 71(6): 1695–725.

Melitz, M. J., and G. I. P. Ottaviano. 2008. "Market Size, Trade, and Productivity." *Review of Economic Studies* 75(1): 295–316.

Nunn, N., and D. Trefler. 2008. "The Boundaries of the Multinational Firm: An Empirical Analysis." In E. Helpman, D. Marin, and T. Verdier (eds.) *The Organization of Firms in a Global Economy*, pp. 55–83. Cambridge, MA: Harvard University Press.

Puga, D., and D. Trefler. 2010. "Wake Up and Smell the Ginseng: International Trade and the Rise of Incremental Innovation in Low-Wage Countries." *Journal of Development Economics* 91(1): 64–76.

PART 8

INCOMPLETE CONTRACTS
AND PUBLIC OWNERSHIP

24

Incomplete Contracts and Not-for-Profit Firms

PAUL A. GROUT

I'm really pleased to be at the conference and delighted to be talking in the panel session on "Incomplete Contracts, Public Ownership and Cooperatives." Today, I want to make a point in the talk, which I'm not actually quite sure I'm allowed to make since I will talk about some empirical work where the predictions of the incomplete contract literature aren't found in the data. To do this, let me start off by discussing yet another Hart paper.

These days it is difficult to talk about the interface of public and private sectors without mentioning the Hart, Shleifer, and Vishny (1997) paper (HSV) on the proper scope of government. The paper clarifies in a very simple way what the issues are. It is a great paper in that it is relatively straightforward, can be taught to basic students, and gets right to the "heart" of the question. To cut to the main point, private ownership is very good at lowering costs, as you would expect, but has the big disadvantage that because of the contractual incompleteness, the private sector is able to ignore delivering what we can generically called quality. We will come back to this in a moment. The private sector is good at reducing cost, but noncontractible quality, broadly defined, will be "too" low because quality is expensive to deliver and hence higher quality means lower profit. As a result there is a potential advantage arising from nonprofits. I emphasize here, because it fits into the theme of the session, that I'm thinking of cooperatives, not-for-profits, and the public sector as one. That is, the distinction I wish to draw is really between private, meaning "for profit" in this context, and nonprofit, which means either not-for-profits or the public sector.

The critical point in HSV concerning ownership sitting with the public sector is that there is a potential for improvement in quality, that is, whatever the nonprofit sector is concerned about will be taken into account. Therefore it is less likely that there will be excessive cost reduction, but at the same time, for various reasons (depending on how you set the model up), it is harder to motivate the agents. So there is a trade-off. HSV gives a good answer to the question, "What should be in the private sector and what should be in the public sector?" Activities that will not sit well in the private sector are those where the rush to reduce the cost causes tremendous damage, for example, unregulated brain surgery with free entry into the market would not be right for private provision. At the least, one will need some form of regulation. But in other areas the problems of and correcting for low quality is less of a problem. As an example, consider when somebody comes and empties your trash. If they get it slightly wrong and the rubbish is on the floor for a while, then that doesn't matter so much. This is a classic activity that can gain from not being in the public sector. Bins can be successfully emptied with private agents doing it on long contracts, and indeed this activity has been privatized quite extensively in the past 30 years. The HSV paper has been very influential. It is a good, clear bringing together of the relevant opposing forces.

What I wish to talk about today is a very special case of this, namely, a significant section of the "not-for-profits" literature. I think it started with Arrow (1963) who talked about trust signals. Henry Hansmann (see chapter 25 and, e.g., Hansmann (1980)) has done a lot of work. More recently, the person who got me interested in the area, Patrick Francois, has had a series of papers on this topic. Essentially the definition of quality in a significant part of the not-for-profit literature is prosocial motivation. You may wish to call it donated labor. The idea can be cast in a world of incompleteness. Francois's work is the clearest in this regard. Loosely, the idea is that if an activity is in the private sector then, because of the nature of the residual claimant and incomplete contracts, whenever people have prosocial motivation, it is not possible to stop the extra effort being diverted into higher profit rather than the things the person wanted it diverted into, which would presumably be better quality output. This story is very squarely an incomplete contracts model. So one can interpret at least some of this literature as a special case of HSV.

If you wish to have a practical example of how you might think of the forces, imagine that there is a nursing home or a small hospital. The staff working there, the nurses, care about the patients; imagine they all get together as a team and say, "What will happen from now on is that no one will ever leave a shift unless there is somebody to take over. This is a decision that we make because we care about the patients." However, if the nursing home is a for-profit activity, then in the presence of incomplete contracts, the profit-maximizing response from the for-profit owners would be to cut back on the workforce because they don't have to worry that the end of the shift might come and there is no one to take over. The owners are less exposed to legal damages arising from shortages of staff and lack of professional cover because all the workers have agreed that they won't actually leave until there is someone to take over. So in a for-profit organization, the donated labor will not actually have the beneficial effects but will simply increase profit. However, because employees already realize that this will happen, they would never make the agreement to "go the extra mile" in the first place. In contrast in a nonprofit environment, whether it's public sector or not-for-profit, because of the nondistribution constraints, what should happen (at least in theory) is that the extra commitment arising from the employees' donated labor would transfer itself into an improved product. There is no residual claimant that can take advantage of the workforce accordingly. This is a simple incomplete contract story with a clear prediction—willingness to donate labor should depend on the institutional structure.

What I wish to talk about today is an empirical test of this prediction. It is based on a study with colleagues at the University of Bristol, some of which is to be published in the *Journal of Public Economics* (now published as Gregg, Grout, Ratcliffe, Smith and Windmeijer (2011)). It is a study on British households, based on the British Household Panel Survey from 1993 to 2000. We use unpaid overtime as a measure of prosocial behavior, using employees who work more than 30 hours a week. We exclude the self-employed and those who work in the armed forces, forestry, and agriculture. We identify for-profit and nonprofit employers. Note that nonprofit includes not-for-profit and the public sector. The main reason for this is that there are far fewer not-for-profit observations than the public sector or for-profit sector in the data set. For each employee we categorize their employment as being either in for-profit or nonprofit and also denote whether they are working in caring services (which we define as health, education, and social care services).

Initially, consider simple regressions that pool all the data and use the four groups (caring for-profit, noncaring for-profit, noncaring nonprofit, and caring nonprofit) to explain unpaid overtime. There are 24,135 observations in the sample. Omitting for-profit caring, we find that the coefficient on nonprofit caring is 0.174 and significant at 1%, on nonprofit noncaring is –0.062 and significant at 5%, and is not significant on for-profit noncaring. Of course, unpaid overtime depends on many factors including, for example, career concerns. If we repeat the exercise using a wide array of controls, we find that the coefficient on nonprofit caring is 0.123 and significant at 1%, on nonprofit caring is –0.148 and significant at 1%, and on for-profit noncaring is –0.118 and significant at 1%. The prediction of the literature is if one is in nonprofit caring, then you will be more likely to engage in prosocial activities (i.e., donating labor) than in the other sectors, and this appears to be confirmed in this analysis, that is, the nonprofit caring has higher levels of this measure of donated labor.

However, in such regressions we are not using the benefits of the panel. Specifically, we are not allowing for individual fixed effects. Using individual fixed effects really tests what is happening as individuals change the institutional environment. The question we most would like to answer is whether as some-body moves do they do more donated labor as the institutional framework in which they work changes. If we repeat the exercise discussed above but intro-duce individual fixed effects, then the results change dramatically. Omitting for-profit caring we find that the coefficient on nonprofit caring is 0.000, on non-profit noncaring is –0.042, and on for-profit noncaring is –0.015. None of these are significant. Thus the distinction between for-profit and nonprofit in caring occupations falls to zero. The results are very similar using the full array of con-trols. The coefficient on nonprofit caring rises a little to 0.002, which is still very close to zero and remains insignificant. So the prediction that the institutional structure will allow employees to donate labor is not confirmed in the data.

Finally, I will briefly say something about the characteristics of the people who move. The number of movers between the groups is small, so one has to be careful in reading too much into the results. Looking at the difference between the people in the sectors who move we find that somebody who is in the car-ing nonprofit sector and chooses to move out is typically doing less donated labor than the people that remain. Similarly, if someone is in the for-profit caring sector and donating labor and moves into the nonprofit, then they are typically engaging in more donated labor than the sector that they came from.

So the research suggests—although I should call it the initial view since more work needs to be done—that the incomplete contract implications do not hold up in the data, that is, it looks like it is not the organizational structure that makes any difference to the donated labor in an incomplete contract framework. The results could be taken to suggest that the Besley and Ghatak (see, e.g., Besley and Ghatak, 2005) approach of the mission matching rather than the conventional incomplete contracts approach may have some traction, although the approach does not deal with mission matching directly, so one shouldn't read too much into this.

I would like to conclude by first thanking the organizers for setting up an excellent conference and second suggesting that the topic of this session is indeed important and that it would be good to see a lot more empirical work in this area.

References

Arrow, K.J., 'Uncertainty and the Medical Economics of Medical Care', *American Economic Review*, 1963, 53 (5), 941–973.

Besley, T.J. and M. Ghatak, 'Competition and Incentives with Motivated Agents', *American Economic Review*, 2005, 95 (3), 616–636.

Hansmann, H.B., 'The Role of Nonprofit Entreprise', *Yale Law Review*, 89, 835–901.

Hart, O.D., A. Shleifer and R.W. Vishny, 'The Proper Scope of Government: Theory and Application to Prisons, *Quarterly Journal of Economics*, 1997, 112 (4), 1127–1161.

Gregg, P., P.A. Grout, A. Ratcliffe, S. Smith and F. Windmeijer, 'How Important is Pro-Social Behaviour in the Delivery of Public Services?, *Journal of Public Economics*, 2011, 95 (7–8), 758–766.

25

Firm Ownership: The Legacy
of Grossman and Hart

HENRY HANSMANN

This brief paper was presented as part of a session titled "Incomplete Contracts, Public Ownership, and Cooperatives." That title suggests that the session was intended to focus on a relatively small group of idiosyncratic organizations that are structured differently from the investor-owned firms that are the productive mainstay of modern economies. Yet when viewed from the perspective of the modern theory of the firm—and particularly with an eye to Grossman and Hart's contribution to that theory—we see that nearly all organizations that produce goods and services in developed market economies, including publicly traded business corporations and even governments, are organized as cooperatives. We are simply in the habit of using the term "cooperative" to describe a rather arbitrary subset of collectively owned productive enterprise. But if we fail to recognize the real ubiquity of the cooperative form, we risk failing to appreciate important economic factors that govern the structure of ownership in general.

The logic of this view is well illuminated by the analysis of ownership presented in the classic Grossman and Hart (1986) paper that the conference celebrated. That paper, to be sure, focuses more on what a firm owns than on who owns the firm. In particular, with one exception we will come to, neither that paper nor most of the subsequent work on the relationship between ownership and incomplete contracting produced by Grossman, Hart, and Moore has focused on explaining the ownership structure of firms with a large class of owners, such as the conventional widely held business corporation.[1] Nonetheless, if we take the license to apply the Grossman-Hart model metaphorically rather

---

[1] An important exception is Hart and Moore (1996), discussed below.

than literally,[2] it provides an extremely helpful starting point for understanding the ownership of enterprise in general.

All Firms Are Cooperatives

A firm is, in essence, the common party to a group of contracts. Some of those contracts are with suppliers of inputs, some with employees, some with vendors of capital, and some with customers. We conventionally use the term "cooperative" to refer to firms that are owned by some subset of the firm's contractual counterparties other than vendors of capital. Thus, a firm that is owned by its customers is called a consumer cooperative, a firm that is owned by its suppliers is called a producer cooperative, and a firm that is owned by its employees is called a worker cooperative. In contrast, firms that are owned by suppliers of capital are called business corporations or joint stock companies or capitalist enterprise, as if they were a completely different type of animal. But in fact they're just a particular form of producer cooperative—a lenders' cooperative, or capital cooperative—owned by (a subset of) the persons who supply the firm with one important factor of production: financial capital.

The economic logic for forming a firm as a capital cooperative, moreover, is very much the same as the logic for forming a firm as a consumer cooperative, a worker cooperative, or a (noncapital) producer cooperative. (We'll deal with governments below.) To see this, we begin with the observation that all of the contracts that a firm has with other persons—customers, suppliers, or whatever—are incomplete to a greater or lesser extent. As a consequence, either the firm is exposed to opportunistic behavior by its contractual counterparties or, conversely, the firm's counterparties are exposed to opportunistic behavior by the firm—or both. For any given counterparty, the incentive for such opportunism, and hence its costs, can potentially be reduced by putting the firm and the counterparty under common ownership—that is, by integrating vertically.

One approach to integration is to have the firm own the counterparty. But for the reasons illustrated by the Grossman and Hart article that we're celebrating, the result of this form of vertical integration may be to weaken incentives for the counterparty to manage efficiently the assets that are under its control. If the costs that result from these weakened incentives exceed the costs of having the firm and its counterparty contract with each other as independent actors, then it will be inefficient for the firm to own the counterparty. We can then say that

---

[2] As do Grossman and Hart themselves in using, as the principal example in their article, a scenario involving a client list for insurance policies that conforms more to the spirit of their model than to its particular assumptions.

the firm's contractual counterparty, rather than the firm itself, is the "Grossman-Hart (G-H) efficient" owner of the assets that the counterparty manages.

There is, however, an alternative form of vertical integration to be considered. Rather than having the firm own the counterparty, the counterparty can own the firm. Moreover, if the firm contracts with a large number of counterparties that are similarly situated, the efficient approach may be to have those counterparties own the firm collectively—that is, to organize the firm as, in effect, a cooperative. In fact, this is the standard form of organization for large-scale enterprise of all types.

An Unusual But Clear Example: Franchising

The considerations involved, and the clarity with which they can be seen in Grossman-Hart terms, is perhaps best illustrated by a generally neglected example—namely, retail franchising. In a typical arrangement, as is familiar, the franchisor owns the system's trademark(s), provides general advertising, supplies important inputs to the retail stores, and maintains a coordinating network. The retail stores are independently owned by their managers, who have long-term contracts with the franchisor that give the franchisee the right to use the franchisor's trademark and other services. To forestall individual franchisees from providing poor customer service and consequently damaging the reputation of the franchisor's entire system, the franchisor generally retains substantial discretion to terminate contracts with franchisees that fail to meet the franchisor's standards. At the same time, the franchisee must make sizable franchise-specific investments, such as building a specially designed store, advertising locally, and training personnel. These investments give the franchisee an incentive to keep its contractual commitments to meet system standards. At the same time, these franchise-specific investments, together with the franchisor's discretion to terminate individual franchisees, exposes the franchisees to opportunism on the part of the franchisor. In short, franchise systems face a well-known dilemma of double moral hazard: adjusting the terms of the contract to reduce franchisor opportunism threatens to increase the scope for franchisee opportunism, and vice versa.[3]

The incentives for opportunistic behavior by both the franchisor and the franchisee could be mitigated if the franchisor owned the franchisee—that is, if the system were vertically integrated rather than being structured as a franchise. But the local retail store is typically an asset that is more efficiently owned and controlled by the store's local manager than it is by the franchisor, whose

---

[3] See generally Blair and LaFontaine (2005).

information about the store is inferior to the manager's. That is, the manager of the local retail store is the G-H efficient owner of that store. It is of course precisely because the G-H efficiencies of having the individual stores owned by their local managers are so large that franchise retailing is so common, accounting for roughly half of all U.S. retail sales.[4]

These G-H efficiencies can be maintained, however, while the incentives for franchisor opportunism are substantially reduced by taking an alternative approach to vertical integration: instead of having the franchisor own the retail stores, the retail stores can collectively own the franchisor. That is, the shares in ownership of the franchisor can be distributed pro rata among the retail store franchisees.[5] A number of franchise systems are organized in this fashion, as were many others in the past. For most of their existence, for example, both the Visa and MasterCard credit card systems were organized this way, with the central franchise collectively owned by the thousands of individual banks that sold cards and extended credit under a franchise from the system. Other examples with familiar brand names have included Ace Hardware, Allied Van Lines, and Associated Press (see generally Hansmann 1996).

Other Cooperatives

In essence, franchisors that are collectively owned by their franchisees are consumer cooperatives, and the logic just invoked to explain those franchise systems explains consumer cooperatives of all types. Consider, for example, a cooperative apartment building. The G-H efficient owner of an individual apartment is often the family that occupies it, given the incentives for maintenance and renovation that are involved. But if the occupants own their individual apartments, while the common elements of the building—elevators, hallways, lobby, and so on—are owned by a separate person, that person can charge the apartment occupants monopoly prices for access to the common elements or scrimp

---

[4] The U.S. Department of Commerce, in a posting on a conference on franchising, has noted that "Franchising accounts for 50% of all U.S. retail sales (just over $1 trillion annually)." See   http://export.gov/industry/franchising/index.asp?EventID=30,937&InputType=EVENT (accessed November 28, 2011).

[5] To be sure, what is most clearly removed through such a system of franchisee ownership is the franchisor's incentive to exploit its franchisees as a group—for example, by charging them all monopolistic fees where the franchisor has market power. The incentive to exploit individual franchisees may remain if the majority of franchisees choose to exploit the minority. In practice this seems to be an uncommon problem, because strong norms of equality of treatment among owners commonly arise to solve collective choice problems where the owners all have roughly equal ownership shares. See Hansmann (1996, 157–59).

on their maintenance. The solution is a housing cooperative or condominium, in which the apartment owners collectively own the building's common elements.

Similar reasoning explains producer cooperatives. For example, purchasers of staple grain crops, such as wheat and corn, have substantial market power. To avoid exploitation of that market power vis-à-vis the numerous farmers from whom the grain is bought, large grain dealers (or major end purchasers such as General Mills) might integrate[6] upstream and own the farms where the grain is grown. But individual farmers are the G-H efficient owners of the land they tend—as more than a century of failed efforts at industrial farming has amply proved.[7] Exploitation of monopsony power has, however, been avoided by instead making the farmers the collective owners of the major grain marketers, in the form of the huge farmer-owned agricultural marketing cooperatives that handle 40% of the nation's annual grain production.

Investor-Owned Firms

The story is the same for the type of producer cooperative that dominates the industrial sector of all developed market economies: the capital cooperative. Industrial firms could in principle obtain all of the capital they need in the form of debt and leave ownership in the hands of customers, employees, or other suppliers. But this would expose the firm's creditors to the potential for serious opportunism on the part of the firm via asset substitution, excessive distributions, and self-dealing. This problem might be solved by having firms own the institutions that lend them capital—as when an investment bank acquires a commercial bank. That won't work with individual investors, however, who are clearly the G-H efficient owners of their own persons, and generally of the property they use (such as automobiles and houses) as well. And in any case, for reasons of G-H inefficiency and other reasons besides, slavery is illegal. A more feasible approach to vertical integration might be to merge finance-hungry firms with other firms that are cash cows. In fact there exist some successful diversified conglomerates organized as worker cooperatives.[8] In general, however, the bloom is off the rose these days for conglomerates as internal capital markets, essentially on the grounds that they are usually G-H inefficient.

---

[6] "Understanding Cooperatives: Agricultural Marketing Cooperatives, Department of Agriculture, Rural Development, Cooperative Information Report 45," Section 15, available at http://www.rurdev.usda.gov/rbs/pub/CIR%2045_15.pdf. ("Cooperatives account for 86% of total farm value of all milk marketed in the United States; 41% of the cotton; 40% of the grains and oilseeds; and 20% of the farm value of all fruits and vegetables.")

[7] See Allen and Lueck (2003).

[8] The worker-owned conglomerate of industrial firms in Mondragon, Spain, is the most conspicuous example.

Incentives are better aligned if, rather than having the firm own its suppliers of capital, the suppliers of capital own the firm. The latter arrangement, like the former, reduces the firm's incentive to exploit the incompleteness of its contracts with the suppliers of capital, yet lets those suppliers remain independently owned, as required for G-H efficiency. So it is that most firms in market economies, though by no means all of them, are owned by their suppliers of capital.

Governments

Much the same analysis applies to governments. In essence, a government—or at least a democratic government—is a territorial consumer cooperative. This characterization is most transparent in the case of municipalities. Municipal corporations provide services—such as roads, police, firefighters, and primary education—that are effectively local monopolies. When a family buys a house within the territory of a municipality, they are making a transaction-specific investment with respect to the package of services provided by the municipality. It isn't possible to write a long-term contract between the homeowner and the municipality that will effectively bind the municipality to providing services of optimal price and quality. As elsewhere, vertical integration can help solve that problem. One approach is to have the municipality own the residential housing and lease it to the residents. That in fact is done in some company towns, as Oliver Williamson (1985, 35–38) has noted. But owner occupancy is generally the G-H efficient approach to home ownership, particularly for detached dwellings. Consequently, municipalities take the opposite approach to vertical integration by, in effect, having the residents collectively own the municipality.

Other Determinants of Ownership

Of course, considerations other than G-H efficiency are important in determining patterns of firm ownership. G-H efficiency helps us understand why the entire economy is not just one big firm—that is, why a firm transacts with many of its suppliers and customers by contract rather than integrating them into the firm itself. When it comes to determining which of a firm's counterparties will be given ownership of the firm, G-H efficiency is still generally relevant, but less directly helpful. Because all of a firm's contracts are incomplete to a greater or lesser degree, the logic we have been exploring here suggests that there could be efficiencies from giving ownership of the firm to any group of the firm's contractual counterparties—or perhaps to all of them together, including suppliers, customers, employees, and lenders of capital. Yet some classes of a firm's counterparties are better situated than others to be effective owners of the firm, owing to considerations such as their homogeneity of interest, knowledge of the firm, ease of organization, and ability to bear risk. We are just beginning to understand the costs and benefits of such considerations, and hence the relative efficiency of alternative forms of collective ownership—or, put differently, we are just beginning to understand the considerations that make it more efficient to organize a firm as one kind of cooperative rather than another.[9]

Grossman and Hart's famous article, as we said at the beginning, does not focus much on this question of who it is that owns the firm, as opposed to helping us understand what the firm owns and (particularly) what the firm *doesn't* own. In a later coauthorship, however, Hart and Moore (1996) have given us a simple model of the problem of firm ownership, focusing on whether stock exchanges are more efficiently owned (as they often have been) by the stock-brokers who trade on them, making them effectively consumer cooperatives, or in contrast are most efficiently owned by pure investors of capital (as they increasingly are), making them producer cooperatives of the capitalist type. The competing considerations reflected in the model are, on one hand, the distortions from monopoly pricing that will come with investor ownership (owing to the economies of scale in providing liquidity) and, on the other hand, the governance distortions that will come with broker ownership owing to diversity of preferences among brokers, which is modeled as a divergence between the interests of the mean and the median brokers.

Conclusion

In short, Grossman and Hart show clearly why the problems of incomplete contracting that routinely appear in transactions between the firm and its contractual counterparties are not always solved by having the firm acquire ownership of the counterparty. This, in turn, helps us understand why problems of incomplete contracting are instead commonly—indeed, almost universally—addressed by giving ownership of the firm to a subset of its contractual counterparties, effectively making the firm a producer or consumer cooperative, such as the business corporations (capital cooperatives) that dominate our economy, and the governments (residential cooperatives) that regulate them.

References

Allen, Douglas, and Dean Lueck. 2003. *The Nature of the Farm: Contracts, Risk, and Organization in Agriculture*. Cambridge, MA: MIT Press.

Blair, Roger, and Francine LaFontaine. 2005. *The Economics of Franchising*. Cambridge: Cambridge University Press.

---

[9] These issues are a principal focus of Hansmann (1996).

Grossman, Sanford, and Oliver Hart. 1986. "The Costs and Benefits of Ownership: A Theory of Vertical and Lateral Integration." *Journal of Political Economy* 94: 691–719.

Hansmann, Henry. 1996. *The Ownership of Enterprise*. Cambridge, MA: Harvard University Press.

Hart, Oliver, and John Moore. 1996. "The Governance of Exchanges: Members' Cooperatives versus Outside Ownership." *Oxford Review of Economic Policy* 12(4): 53–69.

Williamson, Oliver. 1985. *The Economic Institutions of Capitalism*. New York: Free Press.

26

Ex Ante Anonymity and Government
Allocation of Property Rights

ROHAN PITCHFORD

Since people were reminiscing about their first encounters with incomplete contracts theory, I thought this would be a rare opportunity to relate my own humble first experience. Incomplete contracts and renegotiation were the "big ideas" in theory when I entered MIT as a fresh graduate student in 1989. The theory was exciting because it offered to explain puzzles which agency and implementation theory had trouble with: why do firms have boundaries? What determines the structure of ownership? When should we contract out versus produce in-house? Oliver's leadership in this area was enhanced by the fact of his recognition of the importance of backing up theory with real-world examples— ownership of client lists and the insurance industry, ownership of a car-body company by General Motors, and so on. The potential appeal to empirical verification struck me as very important and somewhat neglected in modern theory. So I was very excited to hear that Oliver was going to present a seminar on his latest work (with John Moore) on the nature of the firm. This was to be a generalization of Grossman and Hart (1986), the paper that began it all. I sat in the lecture theater with bated breath, waiting for the next installment of theoretical rigor founded on institutional and empirical pertinence... "Consider," began Oliver, "an asset, a boat—if you will. There is an agent, a skipper, who has the common skills necessary to operate the boat. There is also a chef who can invest in the culinary skills of a ship's cook. And there is a tycoon who demands culinary cruises. Ask yourselves: who should own the boat?" I immediately recognized Oliver's empirical example. He was talking about *Gilligan's Island*,[1] a childhood favorite TV sitcom. Nailed it again, Oliver...

[1] See http://en.wikipedia.org/wiki/Gilligan%27s_Island.

Returning to the topic at had, instead of the exact topic of public versus private ownership (or residual rights of control) over assets, I wanted to make an observation about a perhaps neglected source of contractual incompleteness and explore how this source may necessitate government or court intervention in the allocation of property rights. This source of incompleteness derives from situations where parties may have some economic interaction with each other in the future, but who are anonymous to each other ex ante. Specifically, they are anonymous to each other at a time when investments or other important decisions are being made that might affect the future economic interaction.

This is a different source of incomplete contracts to usual one: we typically think of incompleteness as deriving from difficulties in specifying all contingencies in a contract ex ante. Our "new" source stems from it being difficult for the first guy to arrive on the scene to know who might interact with them in the future, because there are so many possible parties who might be "neighbors" in the future. This is particularly important in the case of bilateral externalities, the problem made famous in Coase (1960).

An example helps fix ideas. Suppose party A sets up a plant that has the potential to pollute a river, but there are no current downstream users of the river who might be affected by this. Party A knows that at some later date, one party, B, out of a set $\{B_i\}$, $i = 1, \ldots, N$, may establish itself downstream. A does not know which of these will emerge: N is very large, reflecting the idea that the second mover is anonymous to A when she sets up the plant. It is too costly for A to negotiate contingent contracts with all potential second movers in $\{B_i\}$. The upshot is that even if A and B can negotiate costlessly over all variables ex post, that is, at the time when A's pollution is affecting B, they cannot negotiate over the size or type of plant that A built in the past. In Pitchford and Snyder (2003) we analyze the bilateral externality problem under this assumption, and refer to this source of incompleteness as "ex ante anonymity."

Ex ante anonymity would appear to be a pervasive source of contractual incompleteness in many problems in law and economics and urban economics and one that I feel could do with more explicit recognition. We have given an example that overlaps both these areas. The economic analysis of tort law examines situations where accidents may arise between previously anonymous parties. There are no doubt examples in other fields where this source of incompleteness is a key feature.

The example of the polluting firm clearly represents a departure from the assumption made in the first part of Coase (1960), where all variables can be contracted on at zero cost. With ex ante anonymity, A can influence its capacity to generate the by-product pollution through its choice of plant without this being part of a contract with B. And, depending on the allocation of property rights over pollution, A has an incentive to distort its ex ante investment so as to favorably influence its ex post payoff from negotiation over pollution. Unlike the "Coase theorem," the allocation of property rights to either the first mover A or the second mover B has welfare implications. Since the parties can neither negotiate nor bid for pollution rights before A's investment decision, the government has a role in deciding the kind of rights A and B should be allocated.

Ex ante anonymity in the bilateral externality problem gives us an incomplete contracts–founded reason that government is needed. Interestingly, this feature also leads to the overturning of two important items of conventional wisdom in environmental economics. The first wisdom is that allocating land ownership to one of the parties gives rise to an optimal level of pollution, because the owner will internalize externalities. Our example can be used to illustrate where this goes wrong. Ownership by A of the land on which B will locate in the future effectively gives party A an exclusion right, that is, A can entirely prevent B from setting up its resort. This is a powerful form of right, because it reduces B's threat point in ex post negotiations over the externality to its outside opportunity, and increases A's threat point to its stand-alone surplus evaluated at its favored level of the externality. Following the usual assumptions on ex post bargaining, A gets a weighted average of the joint surplus from ex post negotiation and her own threat point surplus. Anticipating this before B arrives on the scene, owner A will overinvest in the plant. Thus, land ownership does not yield the efficient outcome, resulting instead in excessive investment in the polluting plant.

The second conventional wisdom we can challenge is the idea that the identity of the generator of an externality is irrelevant—see Pitchford and Snyder (2007). The wisdom is that we could equally say that party B is the generator, since B can impose an externality on A if it has the right to choose the cleanliness of the water. We adopt the following intuitive definitions of a generator and a recipient of an externality: a generator is a party whose preferred choice of the externality varies with her choice of investment, whereas a recipient is a party whose preferred level is zero regardless of her choice of investment. Thus, our factory will want to pollute at different levels depending on how big her plant is, but the resort, regardless of its size, wants zero pollution. It is clear that the generator can affect her threat point through investment, but the recipient cannot harm the generator any more than threatening zero pollution. Leaving the details to our published work, this asymmetry leads us to want to condition the allocation of rights on the identity of the generator.

As a final comment on our running example, it is worth noting that a very rich set of property rights emerges from the analysis. We discussed ownership of land—an exclusion right. But we are also able to analyze first and second party injunctions and damages rights, along with more exotic forms, such as exclusion damage rights, and so on. We can also rank property rights according to social welfare, and we can use this framework to analyze a swathe of different kinds of problems.

To sum up, I hope I have convinced you of two things. One is that ex ante anonymity is a theoretically and hopefully empirically interesting and important form of contractual incompleteness that can provide an impetus for government intervention. The second is how powerful incomplete contracts ideas—leading to the allocation of rights affecting bargaining outcomes and thus ex ante investments—can be in areas beyond the traditional theory of the firm examples. I think there is a huge range of things like this waiting to be applied in law and economics. I am indebted to Oliver Hart and Sandy Grossman for providing the inspiration, through their seminal work, to think about broad application of incomplete contracts ideas.

References

Coase, R. H. 1960. "The Problem of Social Cost." *Journal of Law and Economics* 3: 1–44.

Grossman, Sanford, and Oliver Hart. 1986. "The Costs and Benefits of Ownership: A Theory of Vertical and Lateral Integration." *Journal of Political Economy* 94: 691–719.

Pitchford, R., and C. M. Snyder. 2003. "Coming to the Nuisance: An Economic Analysis from an Incomplete Contracts Perspective." *Journal of Law, Economics and Organization* 19: 491–516.

Pitchford, R., and C. M. Snyder. 2007. "The Identity of the Generator in the Problem of Social Cost." *Journal of Environmental Economics and Management* 54: 49–67.

PART 9

INCOMPLETE CONTRACTS
AND POLITICAL ECONOMY

27

Political Treaties as Incomplete Contracts

BÅRD HARSTAD

The Government As a Firm

What is a firm? This was the opening question in the seminal paper by Grossman and Hart (1986), but their answer and analysis have had implications far beyond the initial question. Incomplete contracts and hold-up problems are now familiar concepts also in the field of political economy. This may not be very surprising, since a leading candidate to the initial question is "a governance structure." The firm is a governing institution, and as such it shares many features with public and political governments. The issue of "how to organize the firm" has the analogous "how to organize political institutions."

Personally, I learned this analogy the hard way. I was a visiting student at Harvard, and Oliver Hart had kindly agreed to be my host. I guess this made him feel that he had to chat with me from time to time, even though I kept on talking about politics and political institutions rather than Oliver's theory of the firm. Our somewhat different interests required some tactic. To catch his attention, it did not suffice to depart from existing theory and intuition and apply them in another area. Nor was it sufficient to depart from the particular details of political institutions and let this guide new extensions. Either one of these approaches were unlikely draw more attention than Oliver's window or ceiling. Instead, the solution was to show how political lessons could illuminate aspects that were important but overlooked in the traditional theory of the firm. This chapter surveys some of the (preliminary) fruits of my (ongoing) effort to impress Oliver.

To satisfy space constraints, I do not formally present any model. Instead, the claims that follow should be interpreted as possibilities which hold under certain assumptions. The details of sufficient assumptions and proofs can be found in the papers I draw on (Harstad 2005, 2012, 2015).

The next section starts by allowing for many agents (you may call them districts or countries). It then studies how a voting rule affects the hold-up problem and the incentives to invest in collective projects. The main message of this section is that the hold-up problem can be solved by carefully selecting the voting rule. The following section permits dynamics and an infinite time horizon. This allows us to analyze how the hold-up problem is influenced by the duration and the terms of the contract and also discuss how these aspects of the contract should be designed to reduce the cost of the hold-up problem. I also discuss renegotiation design (and how this can implement the first-best outcome) before I conclude.

Multiple Agents and Majority Requirements

Most papers on the hold-up problem assume that there are two agents (an exception is Hart and Moore 1990). In legislatures or international politics, however, there are typically many more than two agents. Furthermore, they may take decisions by voting rather than simply bargaining. This changes the hold-up problems in several ways.

Consider a setting where a number of districts first invest in a public project. An example can be liberalization of agricultural policies within the European Union. The more a country invests (by modernizing its sector), the more it benefits (and the more competitive it will be) if the public project is implemented. After the countries have invested, preference shocks may distort the country-specific as well as the aggregate value of the public project. Once the realized values can be observed, the countries determine whether to implement the public project or instead stick to the status quo.

At the bargaining stage, it is both transparent and useful to separate two processes. First, the coalition is formed. One may assume that one of the representatives are randomly drawn to propose a coalition: with a continuum of agents, the outcome is the unique core at this stage of the game. Second, the coalition members negotiate two aspects of the policy: whether to implement the final decision and a set of side transfers among all the countries. Assume that the bargaining outcome at this stage is characterized by the Nash bargaining solution. This ensures that every coalition member receives the same utility relative to the status quo. This assumption can be relaxed and replaced by noncooperative bargaining if unanimity is required within the coalition (in particular, one could assume that a randomly drawn coalition member can make a take-it-or-leave-it offer to the other members). Finally, the countries vote. The negotiated proposal passes if it is approved by the required majority. In addition, one may require that no country should prefer to exit the union, that is, one cannot transfer an unlimited amount of side payments from other countries, even if they do not belong in the majority coalition.

In equilibrium, the countries that are not in the coalition will be taxed up to the point where their participation constraints bind. Therefore, the majority coalition is able to extract the entire surplus when contemplating to implement the public project. The coalition will thus implement the public project if and only if it raises total surplus: the Coase theorem holds and the voting rule is irrelevant.

Proposition 1. The project is implemented if and only if it increases total surplus, regardless of what the majority requirement is.

This result is in stark contrast to the traditional view (as in Grossman and Hart 1988; Aghion and Bolton 2003), where transaction costs ensure that the voting rule will affect the selection of projects.

Although the coalition will make the decision that maximizes social surplus, the distribution of side transfers within the coalition is not necessarily even. Instead, transfers will go from those countries inside the coalition which have a high value of the project to those countries that benefit less. We may say that countries with low valuation has more bargaining power. This is the standard hold-up problem.

Since we are solving the game by backward induction, consider next the coalition formation stage. The size of the coalition will, in equilibrium, be equal to the majority requirement. That is, this model predicts a minimum winning coalition, as did Riker (1962). More interesting is to study the identity of the coalition members: in equilibrium, the coalition will consist of those countries that value the project the most. These countries do not need to be compensated to vote in favor of the project, and instead they are ready to compensate others. Thus, a country has more political power, in the sense that it is more likely a member of the majority coalition, if it has invested a lot in the public project.

Proposition 2. A country that values the project more has less bargaining power but more political power.

At the investment stage, the countries anticipate all this, and they know that more investments will reduce their bargaining power but raise their chances of being included in the majority coalition. But what is the value of political power? Well, that depends on the majority requirement. If the majority requirement is large, perhaps close to unanimity, then political power has a low value: most countries will, in any case, be a member of the coalition, and few can be exploited and taxed. In equilibrium, countries will invest little since the concern for their future bargaining power is more important than the value of gaining political power. If, instead, the majority requirement is small, then political power has a much larger value: a large minority can then be taxed and the total surplus is distributed on relatively few coalition members. In this situation, a country will be motivated to invest a lot since that raises the chance of gaining political power. The concern for bargaining power will play a less important role.

Proposition 3. If the majority requirement is large, the hold-up problem dominates and countries invest little. If the majority requirement is small, the concern for political power is more important and countries may invest more than is socially optimal.

To summarize, the majority requirement is not affecting the collective decision, given the realized valuations of the project, but it does affect how much a country is willing to invest and raise their expected value of the project. Hence, one should select the majority requirement such that the incentives to invest are just right.

Proposition 4. When the voting rule is optimally chosen, the concern for political power cancel with the hold-up problem and investments are first-best.

In Harstad (2005), I show how the optimal majority requirement can be derived as a function of the other parameters in the model: the expected value of the project, the heterogeneity among the countries, and the variance of the preference shocks. The paper further argues that the predictions regarding the optimal voting rules are consistent with the actual voting rules of the European Union.

Although the model above is motivated by political decision making, the argument can be applied also to firms. Martinelli and Sicotte (2011) have developed such a voting model for legal cartels and empirically documented that the model can rationalize the empirical pattern of voting rules in U.S. cartels.

Dynamics and Duration

In many international settings, unanimity is always required. There is currently no hope of forcing through a climate agreement, for example, without the consent of every participating country. The climate application also reminds us that it can be important to capture the dynamic nature of the problem. Following the

Kyoto Protocol, the countries negotiated the vector of emission reductions for a five-year period (2008–12), but investments in the complementary technology (such as abatement technology or renewable energy sources) were left to each individual country to decide.

The setting above will now therefore be modified in the following ways (for details, see Harstad 2012 and 2015). There is an infinite time horizon and the stages where countries invest and the stages where they contribute to the public good are sequentially alternating. They may also negotiate and sign binding contracts/treaties or agreements—specifying every country's contribution (i.e., abatement level) to the public good. In contrast to the foregoing setting, we allow for a nonbinary public project and each country's individual contribution is up for negotiations. Again, we can let the Nash bargaining solution characterize the outcome.

Once the contributions (i.e., the emission quotas) have been negotiated, each country can top its consumption of fossil fuels by investment in renewable energy sources. Alternatively, it can reduce the cost of its emission reduction by investing in modern abatement technology. Such investments are more beneficial under (and thus complementary to) a tough and demanding treaty which allows for little emissions.

In the next bargaining round, the countries with the best technology will find it cheapest to contribute. The other countries will hold them up and require that the technology-leading countries contribute the most in the contract. This is, again, the hold-up problem, and when countries anticipate to be held up at the investment stage, they will certainly invest too little. The discouraging effect of the hold-up problem will be at the largest when the next round of negotiations is near.

Proposition 5. The shorter the duration of the contract, the lower the equilibrium investment levels.

In fact, the countries may invest less in a setting with short-term agreements than they would if there were no bargaining game coming up (this possibility was first observed by Buchholz and Konrad 1994). The explanation is that when future negotiations are anticipated, the countries do not find it necessary to take a prompt and unilateral action already today. The problem will in any case be "solved," to a certain extent, by the upcoming negotiations, and costly investments in green technology can wait. If investments are important (i.e., if they are relatively cheap such that they should have been relied on to a larger extent), then the reduced investments associated with short-term agreements can lower payoffs relative to a noncooperative situation with no agreement at all.

Proposition 6. A short-term agreement can be strictly worse than no treaty.

To avoid this hold-up problem and motivate more investments, the countries are better off negotiating a more long-lasting agreement. That is, they may contract on the contributed quantities not only for this period but for several periods ahead. This certainly reduces the hold-up problem, and investments increase. The raise in investments is particularly desirable if the hold-up problem is large, that is, when investments are sensitive to the hold-up problem or if there are technological spillovers (i.e., positive externalities) when countries invest. The cost of such a long-lasting agreement may be that it is hard to guess today on the optimal contribution levels for the future when one cannot contract on the realization of future preference shocks. That is, we do not yet know how severe the climate change problem is in 80 years. By comparing the cost and the benefit of more long-term commitments, we can conclude that the contract duration should be longer if the hold-up problem is severe.

Proposition 7. The larger the hold-up problem, the more long-lasting the agreement should be.

If the technological spillovers are large, for example, the agreement should be more long-lasting. I derive an explicit formula for the optimal duration in Harstad (2015).

Terms and Toughness

A more long-lasting agreement is not the only way of motivating investments. The "depth" of the contract will also matter. In particular, if the quantities (which each country must abate or contribute to the public good) are large, then a country will find it necessary to invest to reduce the cost of complying to the contract. That is, if a country is committed to abate a large fraction of its pollution (or if it is facing a low emission quota), then it must instead invest more in renewable energy sources so as to be able to consume a desirable amount of energy without relying on consuming fossil fuels. The larger the required abatement quantities (of public good provision), the larger the equilibrium investment levels.

Combined, this suggests that a "tough" contract (with low emission quotas or large required quantities of public good provisions) is particularly important when the duration of the contract is short, since that is when the hold-up problem would otherwise severely reduce the incentives to invest.

Proposition 8. The shorter is the duration of the contract, the tougher it should be.

Harstad (2012) lays out the assumptions and the proofs backing up these results.

One problem is that although any fixed-term contract may look like a long-term contract at the time of ratification, once the expiration date is approached, it tends to look more and more like a short-term contract—given the short time that remains before the contract expires. Once the expiration date is approached, the countries become more concerned with how their investments will deteriorate their bargaining power once a new treaty is to be negotiated. To encourage countries to invest also at this stage, the required abatement quantities must increase and the contract should thus become tougher to satisfy toward the end.

Proposition 9. The contract should be tougher to satisfy toward its end.

We can apply similar logic when countries have heterogeneous investment costs. Since equilibrium investments will be larger when the contract is tough, it is particularly important to impose tough requirements on those countries that have the largest potential to invest. That is, countries that face relatively small investment costs should face smaller emission quotas than countries with high investment costs.

Proposition 10. The contract should be tougher to satisfy for countries with low investment costs.

In Harstad (2012), I allow for heterogeneous investment costs and show that the technology leaders should and will, in equilibrium, consume less energy than countries with high investment costs. This result may at first appear counterintuitive, but the explanation is that such differentiation is necessary to give the various countries the right incentive to invest.

Renegotiation Design

The contract outlined in the previous section is not "renegotiation-proof": to ensure that countries had sufficiently large incentives to invest, the optimal contract had to be tougher than what were likely going to be optimal ex post, particularly if the contract duration were relatively short. Once the investments are sunk, this implies that the countries can gain by relaxing the initial contract and allow each other to pollute a little bit more. If such renegotiation cannot be prevented and is anticipated, would it then be harder to design an agreement which encouraged the countries to invest?

The answer is no—quite the contrary. If renegotiation is possible, the first-best can be implemented. To understand this result, suppose the timing of the game is the following. First, the countries negotiate contribution levels for the future. Next, they noncooperatively decide how much to invest in complementary technologies. Then, before the commitments are carried out, they renegotiate the initial contract.

When the renegotiation game is without transaction costs (i.e., side transfers are permitted), then a Coasian argument suggests that the contribution levels will indeed be first-best, conditional on the existing levels of technology. The initial contract, negotiated at the beginning, does not change this fact. Instead, the initial contract will influence the incentives to invest. If the initial contract is very tough, then a country has to invest quite a lot to avoid being "desperate" when the initial contract is up for renegotiation. A country that instead invests little at this stage will be in severe trouble if the initial contract is eventually enforced. Such a country's willingness to pay to renegotiate the contract is then large and the other countries can take advantage of this.

Note that the hold-up problem is now going in the opposite direction : with no initial agreement, investing more reduces a country's bargaining power. With a tough initial agreement, instead, investing more makes the country comfortable with the status quo and it will get an upper hand in the negotiations.

Proposition 11. Renegotiation ensures that the contribution levels are ex post optimal. The initial contract only affects the incentives to invest.

By fine-tuning the initial contract, the incentives to invest can be just right. The initial contract is then ensuring that the incentives to invest are socially optimal, while the renegotiation stage ensures that the contribution levels will be optimal. Just as before, the initial contract should be relatively tough to ensure that countries are motivated to invest. That is, the contract should be tougher (by requiring larger contributions to the public good) than what is expected to be socially optimal ex post—and this difference is larger if the duration of the agreement is short.

Proposition 12. In equilibrium, the countries make ambitious promises to reduce pollution in the future, but once the future arrives, the commitments are renegotiated and relaxed. This procedure implements the first-best outcome.

The above results hold whether the initial contract lasts a single period or any (finite) number of periods. Sufficient assumptions and proofs are presented in Harstad (2012). As many readers may recognize, the reasoning draws on the lessons from renegotiation design as analyzed by Aghion et al. (1994), Edlin and Reichelstein (1996), and Segal and Whinston (2002), among others. However, these papers consider a relatively static situation (Guriev and Kvasov 2005 is an exception) and a situation with only two agents. For political situations, it is important to know how renegotiation design can work when the situation is much more complex.

Coalition Size and the Benefits of Contract Incompleteness

When countries can decide between participating in the negotiations or opt our and free-ride, then countries have a strong incentive to free-ride and the equilibrium coalition tends to be very small. That prediction changes radically when contracts are incomplete, however: in fact, the equilibrium coalition can be much larger when contracts are incomplete, and this can make an incomplete contracting environment welfare-improving compared to a complete contracting environment. This finding may rationalize why climate agreements tend to be incomplete (by letting technology investments be unspecified).

To understand this result (proven in Battaglini and Harstad, 2016), suppose there is an equilibrium coalition size m^*. Consider a country that will participate in equilibrium, but who is tempted to free-ride. By participating, the coalition of size m^* will sign a long-lasting agreement to mitigate the hold-up problem. By free-riding, instead, the coalition size will be m^*-1 and that remaining coalition must decide between a long-lasting agreement of size m^*-1 or a short-lasting agreement, expecting the one-shot deviator to return to the coalition at the next opportunity. Unless m^* is too large, the coalition will prefer the latter option. The short-term agreement, however, implies that every country will invest little as long as the deviator free-rides; this is harmful also for the deviating country. Facing this credible threat, the temptation to free ride is relatively small, and a large coalition size m^* can be sustained. If the contract were complete (specifying investments, as well), then investments would not collapse if one deviation motivated a short-term agreement, and the incentive to free-ride would thus be larger (and, hence, the equilibrium coalition would be smaller).

Proposition 13. If the contract is incomplete, rather than complete, then the equilibrium coalition size is larger, and so is efficiency. The hold-up problem is a credible out-of-equilibrium threat which disciplines countries and motivates participation.

Conclusions

This chapter shows that the hold-up problem is important in politics as well as in business. Districts decide on how much to invest or prepare for federal policies and, internationally, countries decide on how much to invest in green technology before negotiating climate treaties.

The focus on politics makes it natural to permit more than two investing entities. This, in turn, makes it reasonable to consider voting instead of negotiations requiring unanimity. The majority requirement will then be crucial for the magnitude of the hold-up problem. In fact, selecting the appropriate voting rule can mitigate the hold-up problem.

The focus on international treaties makes it natural to introduce dynamics and multiple periods. It then becomes evident that the hold-up problem is particularly severe when the treaty is close to its expiration date. Short-term treaties may thus be very costly, and it is possible that no agreement is better than short-lasting ones. At the same time, investments may be encouraged by designing a tougher agreement, where each country is required to contribute more to the public good (or less to pollution). Consequently, the treaty should be tougher if it is short-lasting, close to the expiration date, or if investments are considered to be fundamentally important as a solution to the public good problem.

If countries can decide between participating in the coalition and free-riding, then free-riding may induce the remaining coalition to sign a short-term agreement while it waits for the deviator to return to the table. The short-term agreement generates a costly hold-up problem if the contract is incomplete; and the temptation to free-ride is then smaller. Hence, incomplete contracts may be beneficial since they lead to larger coalitions.

Most of the results hold no matter whether the initial contract can be renegotiated. If renegotiation is possible, the single purpose of the initial contract is to set the stage and motivate the countries to invest. Thereafter, the renegotiation stage ensures that the contribution levels will be socially optimal. Combined, a careful renegotiation design can ensure that the first-best outcome is implemented, even in a political environment that is much more complex than simpler models with only two players and two stages. This way, politics can motivate extensions that are important although overlooked in the traditional theory of the firm.

References

Aghion, P., and P. Bolton. 2003. "Incomplete Social Contracts." *Journal of the European Economic Association* 1: 38–67.

Aghion, P., M. Dewatripont, and P. Rey. 1994. "Renegotiation Design with Unverifiable Information." *Econometrica* 62: 257–82.

Battaglini, M., and B. Harstad (2016). "Participation and Duration of Environmental Agreements." *Journal of Political Economy*, forthcoming.

Buchholz, W., and K. Konrad. 1994. "Global Environmental Problems and the Strategic Choice of Technology." *Journal of Economics* 60: 299–321.

Edlin, A. S., and S. Reichelstein. 1996. "Hold-ups, Standard Breach Remedies, and Optimal Investment." *American Economic Review* 86: 478–501.

Grossman, S., and O. Hart. 1986. "The Costs and Benefits of Ownership: A Theory of Vertical and Lateral Integration." *Journal of Political Economy* 94: 691–719.

Grossman, S., and O. Hart. 1988. "One Share-One Vote and the Market for Corporate Control." *Journal of Financial Economics* 20: 175–202.

Guriev, S., and D. Kvasov. 2005. "Contracting on Time." *American Economic Review* 95: 1269–385.

Harstad, B. 2005. "Majority Rules and Incentives." *Quarterly Journal of Economics* 120: 535–68.

Harstad, B. 2012. "Climate Contracts: A Game of Emissions, Investments, Negotiations, and Renegotiations." *Review of Economic Studies* 79(4): 1527–57.

Harstad, B. 2015. "The Dynamics of Climate Agreements." *Journal of the European Economic Association*, forthcoming.

Hart, O., and J. Moore. 1990. "Property Rights and the Nature of the Firm." *Journal of Political Economy* 98(6): 1119–58.

Martinelli, C., and R. Sicotte. 2011. "Voting and Incentives in Cartels." Working paper.

Riker, W. H. 1962. *The Theory of Political Coalitions*. New Haven, CT: Yale University Press.

Segal, I., and M. D. Whinston. 2002. "Design with Renegotiation." *Econometrica* 70: 1–45.

28

Incomplete Contracts and Political Economy

GERARD ROLAND

It may seem puzzling to have a panel on political economics at a conference cele-brating the 25 years of the Grossman and Hart paper. The links between political economics and incomplete contracts may at first glance seem very distant, but they are closer than one might think.

The links between political economics and incomplete contract theory may seem distant because important parts of the field of political economics are not at all about contracts. They are about fundamental issues of politics, such as democratic representation, political accountability, and selection of politicians. How do you translate votes into seats? How does political competition work, and how does it vary with changes in electoral rules? What kind of predictions can we make about the effect of political competition, selection of politicians, and constitutional rules in general? These questions and other related ones are specific to the field and define its scope. As such, this seems remote from incomplete contract theory.

On the other hand, incomplete contracts and political economics can be argued to be very close because, as was already emphasized by John Moore (see chapter 1), residual rights of control—in short, power—are at the heart of both incomplete contracts and political economics. Allocation of powers is at the heart of real-world constitutions and also of political economics as it has developed in the past 20 years. Constitutions do not define what actions political agents should take in various types of contingencies, nor do they define incen-tive contracts leading political agents to take such actions. Instead, they define the powers of the various branches of government (the executive, legislative, and judiciary body) and rules that constrain these powers or regulate its exercise. If incomplete contracts is about power, then political economics can indeed be considered the heart of incomplete contracts.

More generally, a large part of the field of political economics can be viewed through the lens of contracts and agency. Groups of voters, possibly organized in interest groups, can be seen as the principals and politicians can be seen as the agents of the voters or of the interest groups.[1]

The incomplete contract approach provides a natural lens of analysis for the comparative analysis of institutions. In a world of incomplete contracts, and also in a non-Pigovian world where the government and politicians are not assumed to be maximizing social welfare, politicians can abuse their power when in office, between two elections. In a nutshell, they can do things or divert resources in a way that is utility-maximizing for them but hurts the interests of voters. The big question in such an incomplete contract view of politics is then how to limit these abuses of powers and how to align the interests of politicians with those of voters—in other words, how to make politicians accountable.

Elections and Separation of Powers

Elections in a democracy help create accountability given the possibility of abuse of power by office-holding politicians. This is a first-order effect of democracy relative to nondemocratic regimes, since in nondemocratic regimes political leaders cannot be made accountable to voters.

Elections are nevertheless a limited tool to make politicians accountable because they can abuse their powers between elections. It is easy to see this in the spirit of incomplete contract theory. The only constraints to abuses of powers are judicial constraints, that is, laws impeding politicians from taking specific actions. Judicial constraints are often limited because abuses of powers must be proved illegal and must thus be verified, which is never an easy task and fails to be done in many cases. It is thus no wonder that abuses of power are universal. Only their extent is variable across countries and across institutions.

Why are elections a limited tool of accountability? Setting aside judicial constraints, a politician will be indifferent between wholly abusing powers while in office and limiting abuse voluntarily so as to be reelected. This means that voters should not be too strict in denying politicians possibilities of abuse of powers, because otherwise politicians would prefer to fully abuse their powers during one term in office rather than restrain themselves. In the end, voters must allow politicians abuse of power that is in net present value equivalent to full abuse of

---

[1] There is another literature that looks at politicians as the principals and bureaucrats as agents, but it is closer to organization theory and to standard incentive theory so I will not mention it. There is also a large literature applying tools of complete contract theory to issues in political economics. For example, there is the book by the Laffont (2001) that also addresses issues of constitutional design but within the complete contract framework.

power during one term in office. Voters cannot do better to keep politicians on their toes. The stronger the possibility of abuse of power, the longer the period between two elections, the more rents inevitably must be conceded by voters to a politician in power. Asking for more would unambiguously lead to a lower welfare level for voters because abuse of powers would be maximal between two elections. Because of the incomplete contract nature of political power, elections are thus limited as a tool to discipline politicians.

The question is then: how does one constrain the powers of the executive? This is the classical question of separation of powers between branches of government and of checks and balances between these various branches. It goes back to Montesquieu, to the Federalist Papers in the United States, and to other important writers. The question of separation of powers is thus a very important part of our democratic intellectual inheritance.

I have done work with Torsten Persson and Guido Tabellini (1997, 2000) on that issue, and it is also very well explained in the graduate textbook on political economics by Persson and Tabellini (2000). The main idea is that electoral accountability plus separation of powers with checks and balances can help limit abuses of power and to a large extent align incentives of politicians with the interests of voters. Checks and balances are key to limit abuses of powers because they not only limit the scope for abuse of powers but create a conflict between different branches of government or different decision makers so that in equilibrium very little abuse of powers takes place.

Two key principles are important here. First, it is good to give decision-making powers to political agents so as not make them residual claimants on rents that can be generated from those decisions. This aligns their interests with the interests of voters since they benefit less from rents and can be disciplined by voters in their reelection decisions. Second, decisions of the different decision makers must be interdependent, not independent. This makes it possible, by creating a conflict of interest between decision makers, to design a decision-making process that is on the whole aligned with the interests of voters. Combined with electoral accountability, separation of powers and checks and balances can be designed in such a way to strongly improve accountability of elected office-holders.

From that point of view, the incomplete contract approach helps focus directly on the allocation of powers between various branches of government within government. The questions it asks are: who has rights to propose what? Who has rights to veto what kind of decisions? Who votes on what kinds of proposals? Who is pivotal? Who has rights to make what decisions?

One of the important insights that comes out of this research program is that not only is the specific allocation of powers important, so is also the particular sequence of decision making as well as the nature of interdependencies between the decisions. These things together—the allocation of power together with the sequence and the interdependencies—are fundamentally at the heart of checks and balances.

This is all quite abstract, and there are many ways in which separation of powers may be ill-designed and many ways things may go wrong if the principles are neglected. The following example will illustrate this. If the different ministries and agencies in a democratic government have independent and partially unmonitored spending powers, this can create what is called the fiscal common pool problem with overspending. Each agency spends independently out of the common pool of resources without internalizing (or only internalizing to a partial extent) the opportunity cost of spending. There is a large literature on budget processes. Given recent events in Greece with the Eurozone crisis, that literature is certainly very relevant. Even when one has formal spending limits, even with constitutionally designed spending limits, the common pool problem may not be overcome ex post because of weak ex ante barriers to spending. The common pool arises from the wrong type of separation of powers because independent decision makers make spending decisions without checks on their decision-making powers from other decision makers. This illustrates the importance of *interdependent* decision making in correctly designed separation of powers.

Another example, positive this time, shows how one can have a form of separation of powers designed in such a way that rents by politicians can be limited. This will be the case if one branch, say, the treasury or the executive, has proposal rights over the size of the budget, for example, but no residual rights of control on the allocation of the budget. The legislature, on the other hand, controls the decisions on the allocation of the budget but has absolutely no influence on the determination of the size of the budget. In this way, the decision maker over the size of the budget will not make his or her decision in view of rents he or she can receive but will have an incentive to follow the interests of voters. Voters will also be more demanding in their reelection decision because they know that the decision maker has the ability to act in their interests.

This institutionalized conflict of interest is really what checks and balances are about. Checks and balances between the executive and the legislative branch of government can limit rents and force different agents in power and different branches of government to jointly make decisions that are in the interests of voters, because a disagreement would induce punishment by voters.

Comparative Constitutional Analysis

The essential features of specific constitutions can be modeled via specific extensive forms in games, and equilibrium outcomes under different constitutional arrangements can be compared. Contrary to other fields of economics, where the choice of a particular extensive form game, or a particular order of play in a game, can often be seen as arbitrary, but may affect the equilibrium outcome in a substantial way, in the case of political economics and the analysis of constitutions, the extensive form of the game can be directly modeled after the written constitutional rules, albeit in a simplified way. In that sense, noncooperative game theory can be used very fruitfully to analyze equilibrium outcomes of particular sets of constitutional rules.

While the incomplete contract approach in political economics shares the basic premises of incomplete contract theory with its focus on power and allocation of powers, incomplete contract models of political economics do not share the standard features of incomplete contract models. These standard features are generally bilateral contractual relations, investment by one or more of the parties, and ex post bargaining. In political economics, there are usually more than two players and agenda-setting plays a bigger role than Nash bargaining since particular constitutional rules give proposal powers to particular powers, which are usually well captured by agenda-setting models.

Possibly another difference with the standard incomplete contract literature is that political economics has a strong focus on models of real-world political institutions with an eye on empirical testing. Given the shift of the profession toward more empirical work in recent years, researchers put a strong emphasis on writing models that can be brought to the data. The Persson and Tabellini (2003) book on the effects of political constitutions was a first important step in that direction. Comparative analysis of political institutions is not an easy task if one wants to do rigorous empirical analysis; institutions are not random, and it is very difficult to find good instrumental variables satisfying the exclusion restriction. Nevertheless, researchers are coming up with ingenious identification and research design. When it is not easy to disentangle specific effects of institutions, it is often possible to do laboratory experiments. The advantage is that these experiments can be more controlled and designed to be closer to the model being tested. The difficulty, as always with laboratory experiments, is the quality of the experiment, issues of framing, and external validity.

Substantial Progress in the Field

Overall, there has been much progress in political economics in the past 25 years. Before that, the standard Downsian model was the main tool used by economists interested in analyzing the interaction between economics and politics. As we know, the median voter model, while still very useful to understand general issues of redistribution, is limited in its analytical possibilities.

Models of abuse of power by politicians in the public choice tradition were rarely game-theoretic, and models of lobbying were usually between one lobbyist and one politician. Here is not the place to survey in detail all the progress made on that front, but our toolbox has greatly expanded. First, we have a bigger diversity of voting models such as probabilistic voting or models of partisan politicians with no platform commitment that allow to deal in a flexible way with multidimensionality in politics and deliver predictions that are different from median voter models. Lobbying models have been enriched with common agency models, embedding multiple interest groups simultaneously making contributions, and also with cheap talk models that deal with informational lobbying (on all this, see Grossman and Helpman 2001). Models of comparative politics go beyond the first-generation public choice models by incorporating noncooperative games between different players in the political process (voters, legislature, executive, lobbyists) that reflect the constitutional rules in place in a given country. Models in recent years have also combined electoral processes (with specific electoral rules) or lobbying processes with particular legislative processes, which represents great progress over previous models that were confined either only to electoral processes, legislative bargaining, or lobbying.

To summarize, political economics has its own agenda and new advances in economic theory give new tools to analyze questions of the field. In conclusion, it is worth noting that the field has gone in a somewhat different direction in recent years. The comparative politics agenda I outlined here is confined to the comparison of political institutions in democracies. Since the turn of the millennium, researchers have taken a larger view of politics to encompass the study of all political regimes. After all, democracy is historically a relatively recent phenomenon, and the major political divide in the world is still mainly between democracy and autocracy. There has thus been an interest in theories of democratization (Acemoglu and Robinson 2006), in the comparison of different forms of autocracy (Egorov and Sonin 2005, 2011; Myerson 2008; Acemoglu et al. 2008), in institutions, state capacity, and development (Besley and Persson 2012), in interactions between culture and civil society on one hand and political institutions on the other hand (see, e.g., Tabellini 2008 and the references therein or Gorodnichenko and Roland 2012). This has brought political economics closer to development and economic history. Models have relied less on technical innovations, as was the case before 2000, but they have nevertheless generated new insights while broadening the scope of inquiry and taking a more long-run view of things. Moreover, the empirical content of research has become stronger, in line with the evolution of the profession. Despite all that, power and the allocation of power in political systems remains a central topic, and in that sense stays connected to the spirit of incomplete contract theory.

References

Acemoglu, D., G. Egorov, and K. Sonin. 2008. "Coalition Formation in Non Democracies." *Review of Economic Studies* 75(4): 987–1009.

Acemoglu, D., and J. Robinson. 2006. *Economic Origins of Democracy and Dictatorship*. Cambridge: Cambridge University Press.

Besley, T., and T. Persson. 2012. *Pillars of Prosperity: The Political Economics of Development Clusters*. Princeton, NJ: Princeton University Press.

Egorov, G., and K. Sonin. 2005. "The Killing Game: Reputation and Knowon-Democratic Succession." CEPR Discussion Paper No. 5092.

Egorov, G., and K. Sonin. 2011. "Dictators and Their Viziers: Endogenizing the Loyalty-Competence Trade-Off." *Journal of the European Economic Association* 9(5): 903–33.

Gorodnichenko, Y., and G. Roland. 2012. "Culture, Institutions and Democratization." UC Berkeley, mimeo.

Grossman, G., and E. Helpman. 2001. *Special Interest Politics*. Cambridge, MA: MIT Press.

Laffont, J.-J. 2001. *Incentives and Political Economy*. Oxford: Oxford University Press.

Myerson, R. 2008. "Moral Hazard in High Office and the Dynamics of Aristocracy." University of Chicago, mimeo.

Persson, T., G. Roland, and G. Tabellini. 1997. "Separation of Powers and Political Accountability." *Quarterly Journal of Economics* 112(4): 1163–202.

Persson, T., G. Roland, and G. Tabellini. 2000. "Comparative Politics and Public Finance." *Journal of Political Economy* 108(6): 1121–61.

Persson, T. and G. Tabellini. 2000. *Political Economics*. Cambridge, MA: MIT Press.

Persson, T., and G. Tabellini. 2003. *The Economic Effect of Constitutions*. Cambridge, MA: MIT Press.

Tabellini, G. 2008. "Institutions and Culture." *Journal of the European Economic Association* 6(2–3): 255–94.

29

Incomplete Contracting and the Design of Constitutions

GUIDO TABELLINI

I am a consumer of the literature on incomplete contracts more than a producer. As Gerard Roland said (chapter 28), we have been applying some of the key ideas on incomplete contracts to another domain, namely, the governance of public policy, where the constitution is viewed as an incomplete contract. The constitution is modeled as an allocation of control rights (proposal or veto rights) over specific policy areas to specific offices and with specific decision-making procedures. The questions asked are both positive and normative. For instance, how do observed constitutions (i.e., allocation of control rights) shape specific policies? Can we say something about why constitutions look the way they do? Why are specific control rights given to specific offices? And what are the relevant trade-offs in alternative assignments of control rights over public policy?

I want to talk about two examples of this literature. One compares presidential versus parliamentary government, and Gerard has anticipated some of the insights. The second is the distinction between bureaucrats and politicians. The first line of research is joint with Gerard Roland and Torsten Persson.[1] The second one is joint with Alberto Alesina.[2]

In the work with Gerard Roland and Torsten Persson, we analyze the features of presidential versus parliamentary government, identifying the key distinction between these constitutional types in the following way. In presidential government, you have several offices which are assigned throughout the legislatures: the president, Congress, congressional committees. Each of these offices has specific prerogatives, such as proposal or veto rights. These prerogatives

[1] See Roland, Persson, and Tabellini (1997, 2000) and Persson and Tabellini (2003).
[2] See Alesina and Tabellini (2007, 2008).

are designed so that you typically have separations of powers and check and balances, and there are shifting majorities. In other words, whoever has the proposal power can build a majority in different ways over different policy dimensions. This is a consequence of the fact that control rights are assigned throughout the legislature, irrespective of which majority coalition approves specific policy proposals. In a parliamentary democracy instead, the proposal power sits with the cabinets in government, but the holders of these proposal powers would be reshuffled in the event of a government crisis. Thus, the key distinction between presidential and parliamentary regimes is having fixed control rights assigned at the beginning of the legislature, versus having control rights that can be reshuffled in the event of disagreement.

What are the implications of this distinction? In a parliamentary regime, because control rights will be reshuffled in the event of disagreement, there are strong incentives to hold together the coalition that currently holds these valuable control rights. So when you look at the policies that get implemented, they are more inclusive and you tend to see a larger amount of public good provision. To the extent that there is redistribution, it favors the majority. In a presidential system, you have more checks and balances. So there is better control of the political agency problem, and to the extent that there is redistribution it favors powerful minorities rather than an inclusive maturity.

Empirically, these results imply that that the overall size of government is larger in a parliamentary democracy. From a normative perspective, however, there is a trade-off, because public group provision is also larger in parliamentary democracies. These predictions are consistent with the evidence.

An open question is why some counties choose one system versus the other. Of course the normative trade-off could go some way toward answering this question, but that is not the only possible answer, and it is still an open issue.

Let me then talk about a second application of these ideas to the distinction between politicians and bureaucrats. Elu von Tadden remarked that the European Union could be viewed as an instance of an incomplete contract or an application of this idea. This is in effect how we started thinking with Alberto Alesina about these issues. The mode of integration in the European Union has always been bureaucratic delegation. You have a technocracy, and you give more tasks to these bureaucrats in a centralized setting. A widespread opinion is that if we move on to additional integration, for instance, in foreign policy or in fiscal policy, we need to change mode. We need to think about political integration, not just bureaucratic integration. That led us thinking about the distinction between how to hold politicians accountable versus how to hold bureaucrats accountable. That is the perspective that we take in distinguishing between bureaucrats or politicians.

A politician is typically held accountable by voters, and he doesn't have a specific contract. He is held accountable on the basis of a general indicator of performance, overall social welfare as perceived by voters or groups of voters. And you don't need to define ex ante what is the relevant notion of performance when you hold the politician accountable.

A bureaucrat instead is typically held accountable by peers, and you have to give him a specific mission. It is difficult to imagine how you can hold a bureaucrat accountable unless you have a well-defined mission defined ex ante. This is what we try to model in a career concern model.

Of course, the immediate implication is that contract incompleteness becomes an important issue for the bureaucrats, but not for the politicians. Suppose that the mission you assigned to a bureaucrat is incomplete in some relevant dimension. Then you can hold him accountable, but there is a distortion, because he's not going to be able to redirect his policy priorities for the contingencies that were not incorporated in his mission. A politician, instead, is more flexible. You don't need to tell him in advance what to do.

So there is a trade-off between credibility or flexibility. You prefer bureaucratic delegation in policy tasks where credibility is important. Monetary policy is an obvious instance. A politician instead should be delegated policy tasks where flexibility is important, such as foreign policy.

A second difference between bureaucrats and politicians concerns redistributive policies. Typically, a politician will try to build a majority in support of his policy decisions, because he is elected by majorities. So a politician has a strong incentives to compensate losers, at least to some extent, and to provide risk sharing in a way that benefits the majority of the population. A bureaucrat instead will typically not care about the redistributive consequences of his decisions, unless this is explicitly stated in his mission—which may be hard to do ex ante.

Turning to European integration, in light of this analysis it is not surprising that bureaucratic delegation worked well in technical policy areas such as competition policy or monetary policy, where a policy mission can be stated ex ante in terms of economic efficiency. Achieving European integration of foreign or fiscal policy, however, may require designing institutions for political accountability, and this would entail deeper changes to the European constitution.

In applying the notion of incomplete contracts to political constitutions, this literature asked about the positive implications of specific alternative constitutional forms and the key normative trade-offs in the allocation of control rights to alternative offices. But most contributions have refrained from asking about the optimal mechanism for choosing policies. There are a few exceptions, Jean Jacques Laffont being one, but the literature has not asked what is the optimal constitution and how it depends on specific features of the external environment. One may wonder whether this approach of comparing alternative and specific constitutional forms is appropriate. The answer I would give is that we observe specific features of constitutions, so a natural starting point is to try to understand the implications of these observed features and why they come about.

Nevertheless, this approach leaves me uncomfortable for two reasons. First, there is some unavoidable ambiguity in modeling what you observe. So you wonder whether you have really captured the key features of observed constitutions. Second, the source of incompleteness is assumed to be exogenous, which makes it more difficult to explain the observed allocation control rights.

An exception to this approach, which goes in the direction of trying to make the incompleteness endogenous, is the work on international trade institutions by Horn, Maggi, and Staiger (2010) that builds on Battigalli and Maggi (2002). These authors are explicit about the cost of incorporating contingencies in international trade agreements. And then they seek to explain the features of the World Trade Organization as an optimal endogenous incomplete contract, given the assumptions on the cost of these contingencies. They make some headway toward explaining some of the features of the World Trade Organization. This is an example that might be fruitfully applied also to domestic political constitutions.

Finally, I close with a question that I don't have time to address, but perhaps we can return to it in the discussion section. A key distinction between constitutional economics and organizational economics is that in constitutional economics we don't have third-party enforcement. So the issue of enforcement is a key issue. To the extent that there is enforcement, it must be part of the equilibrium. In other words, ultimately a constitution must be self-enforcing. But it is still not clear what are the political and social mechanism that make this self-enforcement possible and reliable.

References

Alesina, A., and G. Tabellini. 2007. "Bureaucrats or Politicians? Part I: A Single Task." *American Economic Review* 97(1): 169–79.

Alesina, A., and G. Tabellini. 2008. Bureaucrats or Politicians? Part II: Multiple Tasks." *Journal of Public Economics* 92(3–4): 426–47.

Battigalli, P., and G. Maggi. 2002. "Rigidity, Discretion and the Costs of Writing Contracts." *American Economic Review* 92(4): 798–817.

Horn, H., G. Maggi, and R. Staiger. 2010. "Trade Agreements as Endogenously Incomplete Contracts." *American Economic Review* 100(1): 394–419.

Persson, T., and G. Tabellini. 2003. *The Economic Effects of Constitutions.* Cambridge, MA: MIT Press.

Roland, G., T. Persson, and G. Tabellini. 1997. "Separation of Powers and Political Accountability." *Quarterly Journal of Economics* 112(4): 1163–202.

Roland, G., T. Persson, and G. Tabellini. 2000. "Comparative Politics and Public Finance." *Journal of Political Economy* 108(6): 1121–61.

PART 10

INCOMPLETE CONTRACTS, MECHANISM DESIGN, AND COMPLEXITY

30

Comments on the Foundations
of Incomplete Contracts

ERIC MASKIN

I am very happy to participate in this conference—not just because Oliver and Sandy are old friends but also because their paper is such a great piece of theory. The conference concentrates mostly on the many applications of Grossman and Hart (1986), and that is only right: these applications have been very important. But quite apart from the way it has been applied, the paper makes a pure theoretical contribution of landmark significance—in particular, its formalization of the concept of ownership as the residual rights of control has been deeply influential.

That said, I think it is fair to suggest that the theoretical *foundations* for incomplete contracts remain incomplete, and I'd like to outline why developing them has proved so elusive.

The incomplete contracts literature, starting from Grossman and Hart (1986), studies how assigning ownership rights for productive assets affects the efficiency of contractual outcomes. But from the Coase theorem, we know that there must be *constraints* on contracting for this issue to be interesting. Specifically, for there to be any departure at all from first-best efficiency, contracts cannot be as fully contingent on the state of the world as the parties would want.

Roughly speaking, there have been two major approaches to explaining a possible lack of contingency. One approach (see Bolton and Dewatripont 2005) assumes pervasive moral hazard: it posits that if a party to a contract controls an asset, nobody else can observe what he does with it. Such an assumption guarantees that ownership *must* matter; since a contract cannot specify *how* the asset is used, the best it can do is to specify *who* gets to use it, that is, who the "owner" is. However, this assumption of nonobservability is very strong and doesn't apply to many situations of interest.

Thus, a common alternative assumption is to suppose that the set of possible states of the world is so vast that it cannot be foreseen or described in advance. For example, imagine the parties to a contract plan to trade some good in the future, but at the time of contracting, they do not yet know the good's characteristics. Assume, furthermore, that the number of possibilities is far too big to enumerate. Then, seemingly, the contract will necessarily be incomplete.

Nevertheless, the so-called irrelevance theorem (as developed, in Maskin and Tirole 1999) challenges this conclusion. The theorem asserts that if parties are risk averse and can assign a probability distribution to their future payoffs, then under certain conditions they can achieve the same expected payoffs as with optimal fully contingent contracts (even though they cannot describe the possible states in advance). In other words, the fact that contracts are incomplete does *not* constrain parties' welfare possibilities.

Let me give a sketch of the ideas in the proof. The first idea is to make a contract's outcome contingent on the payoff possibilities (which can be described ex ante) associated with a given state of the world, rather than on the state itself (which cannot be described). Then, once the state is realized, its remaining details can be "filled in" (since the state is observable to the parties ex post).

The potential hitch in this scheme is that filling in the details must be done by the parties themselves; they are, after all, the only ones who know the state ex post (if a third party, e.g., a judge, could also observe it, then making the contract fully state-contingent would be easy: the judge himself could be made responsible for providing the details). But how can we be sure they will be willing to reveal the states truthfully?

This is where the second idea comes in. Provided that parties have different preferences in each possible state (this is a critical condition for the theorem to go through), mechanism design theory can be enlisted to construct a mechanism g that makes the truthful revelation of states incentive compatible. The mechanism g becomes part of the contract.

Let's pursue this line of reasoning and consider a bilateral contract in which, in mechanism g, the two parties are supposed to play strategies (s_1, s_2) in state θ, that is, (s_1, s_2) is the equilibrium of g in state θ, and $g(s_1, s_2)$ is the outcome that an optimal fully contingent contract would attain in that state. If party 1 instead played s'_1, then he must be "punished"; otherwise, (s_1, s_2) won't be an equilibrium. But imagine that strategies (s'_1, s'_2) constitute an equilibrium in state θ'. Then, if (s'_1, s_2) are the strategies actually played, it may not be clear to a judge whether it was party 1 who deviated in state θ or party 2 who deviated in state θ' (remember that the state is unobservable to anyone but the parties themselves). A way out of this difficulty is to punish *both* parties. That is, the mechanism could assign a "punishment" outcome a to (s'_1, s_2) (i.e., $a =$

$g\left(s'_1, s_2\right)$) such that party 1 doesn't prefer a to $g\left(s_1, s_2\right)$ in state θ, and party 2 doesn't prefer a to $g\left(s'_1, s'_2\right)$ in state θ'.

Now, if parties get such punishment payoffs from outcome a (in states θ and θ'), then a would appear to be a successful punishment. But there's a potential problem: what if parties can renegotiate the outcome a ex post? This issue would not arise were the judge able to prevent renegotiation. But what if the parties can replace the original contract with a renegotiated one without this being detected by the judge? Then the parties need not settle for a, and if a is Pareto inefficient in state θ, they won't settle: they will renegotiate the contract ex post so that the resulting outcome a' is Pareto optimal.

Such renegotiation can limit the effectiveness of punishments, and to see how limiting it can be, suppose that the two parties are risk neutral. In this case, the Pareto frontier (in payoff space) is linear for any state, and so if one party strictly prefers $g\left(s_1, s_2\right)$ to a' in state θ, the other must strictly prefer a' to $g\left(s_1, s_2\right)$—it is not possible to strictly punish both players provided they can renegotiate. Indeed, this constraint on punishment underlies the results in Segal (1999) and Hart and Moore (1999). Those papers give conditions under which renegotiation imposes such severe limitations that mechanisms are completely useless.

If, however, parties are risk-averse, then the Pareto frontier becomes strictly concave (for such concavity, it suffices to have one risk-neutral and one risk-averse party). This is where the third idea comes in: if a mechanism randomizes between two Pareto-optimal points, it will generate a point that is strictly below the frontier. In other words, by allowing a to be a random outcome, a mechanism can punish both parties after all.

Why isn't this randomization itself renegotiated away? The key reason is that the randomization occurs only out of equilibrium. Ex ante, parties have no incentive to renegotiate, because they forecast equilibrium outcome $g\left(s_1, s_2\right)$ in state θ, not a. Indeed they have an incentive not to renegotiate, since renegotiation would interfere with getting to that equilibrium. And renegotiation ex post can be ruled out by designing the randomizing device so that the randomization is realized as soon as a party deviates from equilibrium. In other words, there is no time to renegotiate before the outcome of the randomization is known. Finally, since that outcome is itself Pareto optimal, there is no scope for renegotiation afterward.

Thus, I have outlined a way that parties can achieve the payoffs of a first-best fully contingent contract without being able to foresee states. The elements of story are (1) payoff-contingent contracts, (2) mechanisms that implement the desired outcomes in each state, and (3) random out-of-equilibrium outcomes.

This suggests that we do not yet have a fully satisfactory foundation for second-best incomplete contracts. But this should not be cause for discouragement. The history of economic thought is replete with seminal ideas for which rigorous foundations were found only later. I have no doubt that Sandy and Oliver's ideas are in this category.

Note

This work was supported by the NSF and the Rilin Fund at Harvard University.

References

Bolton, P., and M. Dewatripont. 2005. *Contract Theory*. Cambridge, MA: MIT Press.

Grossman, S., and O. Hart. 1986. "The Costs and Benefits of Ownership: A Theory of Vertical and Lateral Integration." *Journal of Political Economy* 94(4): 691–719.

Hart, O., and J. Moore. 1999. "Foundations of Incomplete Contracts." *Review of Economic Studies* 66(1): 115–38.

Maskin, E., and J. Tirole. 1999. "Unforeseen Contingencies and Incomplete Contracts." *Review of Economic Studies* 66(1): 83–114.

Segal, I. 1999. "Complexity and Renegotiation: A Foundation for Incomplete Contracts." *Review of Economic Studies* 66(1): 57–82.

31

Comments on the Foundations
of Incomplete Contracts

JOHN MOORE

A session on the (lack of) foundations of contractual incompleteness might usefully be shaped around the question I raised in my introductory remarks: Grossman-Hart (1986) may work in practice, but does it work in theory?

The lack of firm foundations in our field means that we need someone to be the arbiter of good taste. As we all recognize—and are entirely happy with the fact—our arbiter is Oliver Hart. But who is going to take over the role when he's gone? Be reassured that Oliver's father lived until he was 106 and was still doing serious research until he was 104. It's quite a thought: with advances in modern medicine, we're probably going to have Oliver around for at least another 50 years. So my most important suggestion is that you all book into your diaries the fiftieth anniversary of Grossman-Hart (1986) and—let me do the math—the seventy-fifth too. The hundredth? Well, I guess that depends on those advances in medicine.

As a vehicle for discussing some of the recent history of research in the field, consider the following example. A buyer and seller, both risk–neutral, meet and contract at date 0, ex ante. At an interim date $\frac{1}{2}$, the seller has a choice whether to invest; the investment is private and costs her $i > 0$. At date 1, ex post, the parties may or may not trade. Assuming they do trade, the buyer's value from it is $v = \bar{v}$ if the seller has invested, but only $v = \underline{v} < \bar{v}$ if she hasn't. (Note this is quite different from model I used in my introductory remarks. Here we have a direct externality: the seller's investment affects the buyer's benefit.) If there is trade at date 1, it costs the seller $c > 0$. Assume $c < \underline{v}$, so that first-best entails trade at date 1 even if the seller hasn't invested at date $\frac{1}{2}$. Further assume:

$$\frac{1}{2}(\bar{v} - \underline{v}) < i < (\bar{v} - \underline{v}). \tag{1}$$

Because of the right-hand inequality in (1), the seller should invest in first-best. A social planner would want the seller to bestow the external benefit onto the buyer.

In the absence of a contract, if we assume the parties divide surplus equally at date 1, the trade price p, say, will end up being the average of c and v, whatever v is. With that in view, and given the left-hand inequality in (1), the seller will not invest because she faces hold-up: for every dollar she generates, 50 cents are stolen by the buyer at date 1. The point is that if her investment cost, i, is close enough to $(\bar{v}-\underline{v})$—above half way—then the seller won't want to invest because her return won't cover the cost.

The contractual solution is easy: write a contingent contract, specifying that the trade price p equals $\bar{v}$ if the date 1 state of nature is $v = \bar{v}$, and equals $\underline{v}$ in the state $v = \underline{v}$. That is, give the seller all the ex post surplus. Then she will make the investment at date $\frac{1}{2}$: although she fully bears the cost i, she fully internalizes the gain $(\bar{v} - \underline{v})$ in the buyer's value.

(Note that there is no exogenous uncertainty in this example, because, unlike a classic moral hazard problem, the mapping from investment to value is deterministic. So when we speak of the date 1 "state of nature", it is endogenous: the state hinges on whether or not the seller invested at date $\frac{1}{2}$.)

A contingent contract might not be feasible, though. Let us suppose that the seller's investment choice, and hence the buyer's value v, are observable to the two of them, but not to a judge. Then a statement of the form "p equals $\bar{v}$ if $v = \bar{v}$, and equals $\underline{v}$ if $v = \underline{v}$" cannot be enforced—because the judge cannot tell what v equals. In short, we invoke a mantra much used in incomplete contract theory: the state is observable (to the buyer and seller, who are insiders) but not verifiable (by outsiders).

At this point we should make use of implementation theory. The best person to turn to is Eric Maskin, who wrote the Nobel Prize–winning article on Nash implementation. According to this theory, the buyer and seller should design and play a game that elicits the state of nature. The game is specified in the date 0 contract. The contract says that the buyer and seller must—on pain of death if they don't—play the following game at date 1:

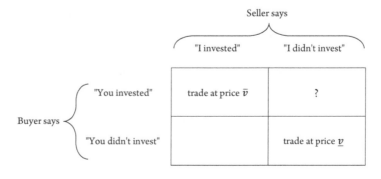

Everything in this 2-by-2 outcome matrix is written into the contract at date 0. In the game, the buyer plays the rows, saying either "You invested" or "You didn't invest". The seller plays the columns, saying either "I invested" or "I didn't invest". The game is designed so that if the seller has invested (state $v = \bar{v}$), then both parties will truthfully say this, and from the top left box of the matrix we can read trade at price $p = \bar{v}$. But if the seller hasn't invested (state $v = \underline{v}$), then they will both say as much, and from the bottom right box emerges trade at price $p = \underline{v}$. The job of the implementation theorist is to design the game so that those diagonal entries are the *unique* equilibria. To satisfy the uniqueness requirement, it's not enough to shoot the parties if they stray off the diagonal.

We know from Maskin's paper that in this example there is no game that delivers the desired outcomes as unique Nash equilibria. The problem lies with what entry ? to put into the top right box of the outcome matrix. On the one hand, the entry ? must not perturb bottom right from being a Nash equilibrium in state $v = \underline{v}$. That is, entry ? must be: (a) trade at a price not less than $\underline{v}$; or (b) no-trade (and with no payment from the seller to the buyer); or (c) a lottery of the two. Otherwise the buyer would deviate. On the other hand, entry ? must eliminate bottom right from being a Nash equilibrium in state $v = \bar{v}$. (Because the seller's preferences are constant across the states, we cannot hope for bottom left to eliminate bottom right from being a Nash equilibrium in state $v = \bar{v}$: it would be eliminated in state $v = \underline{v}$ too, when it should be an equilibrium.) But then entry ? cannot be (a), (b) or (c)!

The reason there is no game that Nash implements our desired outcomes— our so-called choice rule—is that, although our example is very simple, the choice rule we're trying to implement is not Maskin monotonic. And we know from Maskin (1977, 1999) that a choice rule has to be Maskin monotonic in order to be Nash implementable.

Turn next to a couple of Maskin's henchmen, Moore and Repullo, and ask them to design a game. They would recommend using games with stages, since the additional constraint of subgame perfection can knock out unwanted Nash equilibria. In particular, given that the difficulty with Nash implementation was filling the top right box, let's forget about it and construct a two-stage game, with something interesting in the bottom left box:

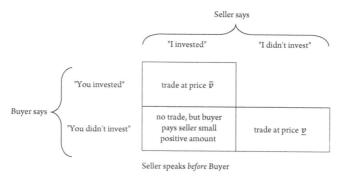

Seller speaks *before* Buyer

Crucially, in this game the seller moves first. If she says "I didn't invest", the game ends with trade at price $\underline{v}$. (In the matrix, we represent this by offering the buyer no choice but to agree with her that she didn't invest: the bottom right box. There is no top right box.) If the seller says "I invested", then the buyer has a choice: either to agree with her, and there is then trade at price $\bar{v}$; or to disagree with her, and there is then no trade but the buyer pays the seller some amount $\varepsilon > 0$.

Armed with subgame perfection, it is straightforward to confirm that, for ε not too large, this two-stage mechanism succeeds in implementing the desired outcome. In state $v = \bar{v}$, the seller says the truth ("I invested"), then the buyer agrees and there is trade at $p = \bar{v}$. In state $v = \underline{v}$, the seller again says the truth ("I didn't invest") and there is trade at $p = \underline{v}$. Anticipating that she will receive all the surplus at date 1, the seller invests at date $\frac{1}{2}$. Well done, Moore and Repullo (1988), for implementing the first-best. (Actually, this mechanism is an ε-variant on a standard mechanism in which the seller is given the right to make a take-it-or-leave-it offer to the buyer: that mechanism, too, succeeds in achieving first-best.)

But whose side are we on here? Should we be endlessly trying to find clever mechanisms that implement first-best, or should we be more interested in second-best analysis and, in particular, the economics of power and control? At this point, I have to put on my other hat and admit that I don't want mechanism design to be quite so successful.

To this cause, renegotiation is a useful weapon. At first sight paradoxically, the possibility of renegotiation makes the challenge of mechanism design *harder*. The idea is that, ex ante, the contractual parties may be unable to commit not to renegotiate the outcome of their mechanism ex post. The prospect of renegotiation typically skews the way the mechanism is played, and as a result the mechanism can be robbed of its effectiveness.

Consider the above two-stage mechanism. Off the equilibrium path, in the bottom left box, there is a blatant inefficiency: the mechanism specifies no trade, and yet there are always gains from trade. If the parties cannot commit not to renegotiate, the mechanism fails. Indeed, in this example renegotiation is such a constraint on the problem, it turns out that the parties can do no better with a contract than without. With renegotiation, there is no contractual solution to the hold-up problem: because of the left-hand inequality in (1), the seller won't invest. See Che-Hausch (1999); and also Maskin-Moore (1999). Let me now give some intuition as to why this is the case.

We need to trim our ambition. Instead of trying to implement date 1 trade prices $\bar{v}$ and $\underline{v}$ respectively in states $v = \bar{v}$ and $v = \underline{v}$ so as to give *all* of the ex post surplus to the seller, let's give her only *some* of the surplus. Let's aim to implement, say, prices $\bar{p}$ and $\underline{p}$ respectively, trying to make the price difference $(\bar{p} - \underline{p})$ as great as possible—because maximizing $(\bar{p} - \underline{p})$ serves to maximize the seller's incentive to invest at date $1/2$. With renegotiation, it turns out that our real challenge becomes: what entry ?? should we put into the bottom left box of our two-stage game:

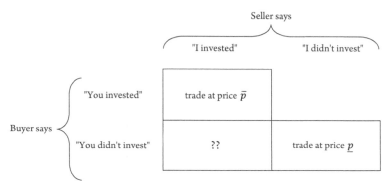

Seller speaks *before* Buyer

The most general entry ?? would be a lottery: trade with probability q; no trade with probability $1 - q$; and the buyer pays an amount p to the seller before the lottery wheel is spun. (Since the parties are risk–neutral, it actually makes no difference when the buyer makes this payment, or whether the amount of the payment is conditioned on the outcome of the lottery. But with risk aversion, this would not be true; see below for further discussion.)

In either state, $v = \bar{v}$ or $\underline{v}$, if the game ends up in the bottom left box, and the lottery wheel delivers (with probability $1 - q$) no-trade as the outcome, then the parties would renegotiate—dividing the surplus equally—and trade at price $\frac{1}{2}(v + c)$. If the outcome of the lottery (with probability q) is trade, there is nothing to renegotiate. Overall, then, the buyer and seller's payoffs from the bottom left box, net of the contractually-specified payment p, are respectively,

$$v - \tfrac{1}{2}(1 - q)(v + c) - p \quad \text{and} \quad p + \tfrac{1}{2}(1 - q)(v + c) - c.$$

We have two goals, which are in tension with each other. On the one hand, in state $v = \bar{v}$ we want to implement trade at price $\bar{p}$—i.e. we want top left to be the equilibrium. In particular, the buyer mustn't want to lie (to say "You didn't invest"). So $\bar{p}$ must satisfy

$$\bar{v} - \bar{p} \geq \bar{v} - \tfrac{1}{2}(1 - q)(\bar{v} + c) - p. \tag{2}$$

On the other hand, in state $v = \underline{v}$ we want to implement trade at price $\underline{p}$—i.e. we want bottom right to be the equilibrium. In particular, the seller mustn't want to lie (to say "I invested"). So $\underline{p}$ must satisfy

$$\underline{p} - c \geq p + \tfrac{1}{2} (1 - q) (\underline{v} + c) - c. \tag{3}$$

(Given $\bar{p} > \underline{p}$, it cannot be that the buyer would agree "You invested", otherwise the seller certainly wants to lie.)

Adding inequalities (2) and (3), we find that the price difference, $(\bar{p} - \underline{p})$, has an upper bound of $\tfrac{1}{2}(1 - q) (\bar{v} - \underline{v})$. Remember we're trying to maximize $(\bar{p} - \underline{p})$. The upper bound can be relaxed by choosing $q = 0$, but even then we reach the conclusion that $(\bar{p} - \underline{p})$ cannot exceed $\tfrac{1}{2}(\bar{v} - \underline{v})$.

This means that, in terms of giving the seller maximal incentive to invest, with renegotiation the parties can do no better with a contract that without, and will typically do strictly worse. (As has already been pointed out, without a contract they will negotiate a trade price of $\tfrac{1}{2}(v + c)$, and the price gap across the two states $v = \bar{v}$ and $v = \underline{v}$ will also be $\tfrac{1}{2}(\bar{v} - \underline{v})$. From the left-hand inequality in (1), we know that the seller won't invest.) Given that "no contract" is an incomplete contract par excellence, we have a model of contractual incompleteness.

The notion that renegotiation may lead to contractual incompleteness, first developed in Hart-Moore (1988), was part of a much richer program of research that Ilya Segal embarked upon in his doctoral research. His aim was bold: to demonstrate the counterintuitive idea that the richer the environment, the simpler the contract. We learn from Segal (1999) that, with renegotiation, contracts—simple or otherwise—may achieve very little in complex environments.

(Usually, it never helps to make a model more complex—the answer is merely made more complicated too. But there are telling counterexamples. In addition to Segal (1999), my favourite is Holmström and Milgrom's powerful insight that, in a dynamic context, a principal's optimal incentive scheme becomes simpler—in fact, linear—as the agent's set of actions becomes richer, because richness in action choice allows the agent to circumvent highly non-linear schemes. See Holmström and Milgrom (1987). See also Hellwig and Schmidt (2002) who, importantly, provide discrete-time underpinnings for Holmström and Milgrom's continuous-time result.)

Inspired by Segal's work, Oliver and I took a generalisation of the above buyer-seller example—where the parties have an item (a "special widget") that they plan to trade—and dropped it in a sea of irrelevant alternative items ("generic widgets"). The presence of these generic widgets, whose benefits and costs are scattered around those of the special widget, serves to make mechanism design massively more challenging. Maintaining the assumption of risk neutrality, we found that contracts don't help at all; see Hart-Moore (1999). That is, every contract performs as poorly as if the parties had written no contract.

This may be an even stronger basis for modeling contractual incompleteness than the model of Che-Hausch (1999), where contracts typically do affect welfare—albeit adversely, given that, as we have seen, writing no contract is best. In Hart-Moore (1999), because of the rich confusion created by the many irrelevant alternative widgets, all contracts are equivalent to each other, and, a fortiori, equivalent to having no contract.

There is an important caveat to these results. They rely on risk neutrality. If the parties are risk–averse, then "lottery" contracts can be used to great effect, as Maskin and Tirole (1999) have shown; see also Maskin-Moore (1999).

To understand how, consider again the first of the two-stage mechanisms we looked at above, with "no trade, but buyer pays seller small positive amount" as the outcome in the bottom left box. The role of this off-the-equilibrium-path outcome, reached if the buyer disagrees with the seller's first-stage announcement, is to discipline the seller into revealing the truth. The outcome is used to screen the two states: to be less (more) attractive to the buyer than trade at price $\bar{v}$ in state $v = \bar{v}$ (in state $v = \underline{v}$). But, in order to work as a discipline device, the outcome also has to be less attractive to the seller than trade at $\underline{v}$. To fulfill all these roles, it helps greatly that the outcome is *inefficient*; i.e. that it specifies no trade (as we have seen, renegotiation can make it impossible to find any outcome that works).

This is the point where we can exploit risk aversion, to build some inefficiency into a mechanism. In the presence of risk aversion, a lottery over the transfer achieves inefficiency, *and*, if the timing is chosen cleverly, the lottery wheel may have been spun before the parties have a chance to renegotiate—thus wriggling around the renegotiation constraint.

Specifically, the bottom left box can say "trade at a random price p, drawn from a distribution $F(.)$, where the draw happens at exactly the moment the buyer picks this box". By suitably designing $F(.)$ in the date 0 contract, the box can be made to look (through the eyes of the risk–averse parties at date 1) as inefficient as needed. But, off the equilibrium path, if the box were to end up as the final outcome of the game, there would be no scope for renegotiation.

Lotteries appear to have rescued mechanism design from the clutches of the renegotiation constraint: the first-best can typically be implemented. From a welfare perspective, there appears to be a major discontinuity at the boundary of risk neutrality. I'm not sure how this debate, caricatured as fought between the risk–neutrals and the risk–averse, should end. I remember giving a seminar about the use of lotteries in mechanism design. Ed Green was in the audience. He took me for dinner afterwards, plied me with drinks, and then gently told me he found it hard to think that the grandeur of Grossman-Hart (1986) had descended into an arcane debate about lotteries. I had another beer. I fear Ed may have been right.

To end a little grandly: Surely it is true that in contracting as in architecture, less is more. To put it the other way round: More is less (careful how many o's there are here). But why? That, to my mind, is the key question. I see a rough parallel with the old debate about decentralization versus centralization: markets versus planning. Because anything that can be achieved through a decentralized market can in principle be replicated by a central planner, planning can never be beaten by the market. Likewise, because anything that can be achieved by (say) simple asset ownership can in principle be replicated by a mechanism written into a contract, mechanism design, in all its complexity, can never be beaten by simple asset ownership. What is needed is a *cost* of complex contracts—of contracts with baroque mechanisms. We need an insight akin to that provided by Grossman and Hart (1986) about the costs of moving from the market (dispersed ownership of assets) to the firm (concentrated asset ownership).

In an attempt to nail down such a cost, Oliver and I published in 2008 a paper on contracts as reference points. For a mechanism designer, there are no doubt aspects of that paper that aren't entirely convincing. But I'm confident that the distinction we draw between consummate and perfunctory performance is a sensible starting point. Consider again the outcome matrices in the games above. Behind the seemingly innocuous edict "trade at price $\bar{v}$", or "trade at price $\underline{v}$", lurk some critical issues: How well will the seller behave; might she shade her performance and deliver a widget worth less than v to the buyer? Might the buyer behave badly and somehow raise the seller's cost above c? These things may be beyond the reach of the law—beyond the reach of mechanism design—in that a judge wouldn't be able to adjudicate between consummate performance (trading a widget that, indeed, costs c and is worth v) versus perfunctory performance (sticking to the letter of the contract, but not the spirit).

From this starting point, we attempt to explain what may be wrong with writing complex mechanisms into a contract. If the mechanism has many possible outcomes, the buyer may believe he is entitled to one particular outcome, and the seller may believe she is entitled to another. Necessarily, one party (perhaps both) will end up feeling aggrieved that the play of the mechanism isn't going their way, and, as a result, may shade their performance so as to hurt the other. Our argument is that these ex post inefficiencies stem from the complexity of the mechanism, and may be avoided by writing a simpler contract.

In case the psychological apparatus that's being adduced here isn't compelling enough, I believe it might be substituted by things that are rather more classical to economic theory: haggling costs, influence activities, rent seeking, and so on.

Just as Grossman and Hart (1986) gave us a theory of what's wrong with central planning, it would be good to articulate some theory along their lines to explain the costs of using a fictitious planner (a judge) to adjudicate the play of mechanisms, i.e., to rationalize the assumption of contractual incompleteness. I think we'd be unwise to spend the next twenty five years battling against mechanism design—with or without renegotiation, risk aversion, asymmetric information, communication costs—rather than thinking more deeply about what's wrong with complicated contracts in the first place.

References

Che, Y-K., and D. Hausch. 1999. "Cooperative Investments and the Value of Contracting." *American Economic Review* 89: 125–47.

Grossman, S., and O. Hart. 1986. "The Costs and Benefits of Ownership: A Theory of Vertical and Lateral Integration." *Journal of Political Economy* 94: 691–719.

Hart, O., and J. Moore. 1988. "Incomplete Contracts and Renegotiation." *Econometrica* 56: 755–85.

Hart, O., and J. Moore. 1999. "Foundations of Incomplete Contracts." *Review of Economic Studies* 66: 115–38.

Hart, O., and J. Moore. 2008. "Contracts as Reference Points." *Quarterly Journal of Economics* 123: 1–48.

Hellwig, M., and K. Schmidt. 2002. "Discrete-Time Approximations of the Holmstrom-Milgrom Brownian Motion Model of Intertemporal Incentive Provision." *Econometrica* 70: 2225–64.

Holmström, B., and P. Milgrom. 1987. "Aggregation and Linearity in the Provision of Intertemporal Incentives." *Econometrica* 55: 303–28.

Maskin, E. 1977, 1999. "Nash Equilibrium and Welfare Optimality." *Review of Economic Studies* 66: 23–38.

Maskin, E., and J. Moore. 1999. "Implementation and Renegotiation." *Review of Economic Studies* 66: 39–56.

Maskin, E., and J. Tirole. 1999. "Unforeseen Contingencies and Incomplete Contracts." *Review of Economic Studies* 6: 83–114.

Moore, J., and R. Repullo. 1988. "Subgame Perfect Implementation." *Econometrica* 56: 1191–220.

Segal, I. 1999. "Complexity and Renegotiation: A Foundation for Incomplete Contracts." *Review of Economic Studies* 6: 57–82.

32

Incomplete Contracts and Mechanism Design

RICHARD HOLDEN

Thank you very much to the organizers of this event for inviting me to speak. It's a great pleasure to do so. This room has been pretty hot, and after the intellectual force of the two previous speakers it seems to have gotten a little hotter, so I'll try and remedy that.

We have just been hearing about the so-called Maskin-Tirole critique—or the mechanism critique—of foundations of incomplete contracts. One reaction, the first reaction one might have, is: "these things are nuts, we never seem them in the world so let's not bother about it." But that's not really an excuse to leave things out of our models, as people have said. At least we want to understand why we don't see these things in the world. If we don't see them there must be some reason that's the case—so let's try and understand it. So the key point that Maskin and Tirole make, using a Moore-Repullo mechanism, is that this distinction between "observable" and "verifiable" is a bit dicey. Something that's observable can be made verifiable by using one of these clever mechanisms.

If you think about it for a little longer and get into the details, they are actually saying something somewhat stronger than that. They are saying that something that is common knowledge can be made verifiable. See, in the example that John gave, it is common knowledge whether the investment was made, and you might ask yourself, "Does that matter? Is that important for the mechanism?" Or if we perturbed things a little bit away—it's not quite common knowledge— does everything still go through? That's the question I have addressed with Philippe and other coauthors in recent work, and that's going to be the notion of robustness I want to consider here. Let's take an arbitrarily small deviation from common knowledge—so instead of you know, and I know, and you know that I know, and so on ad infinitum, it's going to be that you know with probability p very close to 1 and I know with probability p very close to 1, and you know with probability p that I know with probability p that you know with probability p, and so on ad infinitum. We want to ask: let's go from p equals 1 to p just a little bit less than 1—what happens?

In work with Philippe, Drew Fudenberg, Takashi Kunimoto, and Olivier Tercieux, we provide two main results. We take this class of mechanisms that John and Rafael developed, he gave an example of one there, but they are actually much more general than that. They have a remarkable result that says you can implement any social choice function—Maskin monotonic or not—as the unique equilibrium of one of their suitably designed mechanisms. Since they are the classic type of mechanisms that have been used in these sorts of problems, we take that as our starting point, and we ask what happens if we perturb the environment a little bit away from strict common knowledge. The answer is that the good equilibrium that you wanted to implement disappears, and in fact, a bad equilibrium always exists. So it says that if one wants to insist on this notion of robustness, that strict common knowledge seems like the parties are sort of borderline clairvoyant, we don't think in practice that it is going to be the case, if we insist on that notion of robustness, these mechanisms are actually not going to do the trick, as they do under strict common knowledge.

As we developed this work we discovered, much to my surprise, that almost every economist is a budding mechanism designer. So we'd say "Look, here's the result" and so on, and almost everyone would say "Ah, I've got a mechanism. They've only got three stages, I'm going to try one with four." Or, "I'm going to try Nash with a three-stage mechanism attached and a twist of lime." They would try all sorts of things. So frankly, it was just too time-consuming to keep checking all of these mechanisms. We wanted to understand what we could say about the class of all mechanisms.

Now that is a very broad class—that's essentially the set of all extensive-form games. So that's a hard thing to write down. Here is the line of attack we took. Suppose you want to implement a nonmonotonic social choice function and you find me some extensive-form mechanism that does so in a common-knowledge environment. We now perturb that environment just as we did before, from strict common knowledge to common p-belief for p arbitrarily close to one. What happens? The answer is that at the very least one of the bad equilibria— one of the Nash equilibria that you were using this extensive-form mechanism to knock out—it comes back. It rears its ugly head. In other words, one of those non–subgame-perfect equilibria can be sustained as a sequential equilibrium in the perturbed environment.

Put another way, or to give you a little intuition for it, once we perturb the environment even slightly, the set of Kreps-Wilson consistent beliefs expands a great deal and that allows us to sustain these undesirable equilibria. So one take on that is that we are back to Nash implementation. We're just back to the multiplicity problem that stems from using Nash implementation. That is obviously a bit of an issue, to have these bad equilibria, otherwise we could have been using these mechanisms that ask: "Did you invest, or not? If you disagree, we'll shoot you both." We probably do not want to be in a situation with an equilibrium in which, to avoid being shot, both players lie about whether the investment was made.

In work with Philippe, Ernst Fehr, and Tom Wilkening (who's at Melbourne University) we took this into a laboratory setting to see if there were, if you like, something to this. What we found basically is that if you run one of these mechanisms in the lab in a setting that amounts to common knowledge, that is, in a complete information environment and you look at whether people lie, it starts out with some lies, but as they play over time, after about 10 rounds or so, the lies are becoming de minimis. Then we do something where you have a small amount of asymmetric information. You're getting a 95% accurate signal about the true state of the world, but it's a conditionally independent private signal. That is a way of implementing common p-belief. We find that people start out lying and keep on lying. In that setting there is a significant difference, both economically and statistically, between the outcomes in the common knowledge environment and the p-belief environment.

So one reaction to that is: "Well, that's sort of a critique of a critique." We know that asymmetric information has large effects on bargaining, and Jean alluded to this yesterday, a fair horse race between assets and mechanisms is to consider an environment with asymmetric information and give both a fair shake. Allow for assets or outside options, and allow for mechanisms as well.

So here is a simple way you can do that. There's a buyer and a seller who trade a widget, and there's just one-sided asymmetric information. The buyer knows her valuation, but the seller does not. Just as in John's example, we'll have the seller invest to increase the probability of its being higher valuation. Start out with asset ownership where the seller owns the widget. It turns out that that setting, allowing the seller to make an offer, achieves a strictly more efficient outcome than any contract or mechanism can achieve. In that setting, a fairly simple setting, one might imagine richer contracting settings, but in that simple setting asset ownership, or if you like outside options as implemented through asset ownership, one can do something that mechanisms can't do. They can do strictly better. A rough intuition for that is that there are incentive compatibility constraints here. Once we move into an environment with asymmetric information, outside options and assets have the ability to relax those in ways that mechanisms or contracts do not.

I should say very briefly that you might ask whether we are asking too much to implement this social choice function exactly. We're trying to get it dead on. What about if we implement some nearby social choice function?

Wouldn't that be all right? And we know from the now classic work of Abreu and Matsushima, which has become known as virtual implementation, that those sorts of approaches are going to be robust to these p-belief perturbations. So you might say: "Well, OK, I'm comfortable with a nearby social choice function. That will get me almost the first-best investment and then we are back to where we started." But of course, there are three issues with virtual implementation, the first two of which are closely related. The first is that you can wind up implementing an arbitrarily bad outcome with positive probability, and somewhat as a consequence of that, they are not renegotiation proof. The third is that—and Matt Jackson has pointed this out more than once—virtual implementation takes the expected utility hypothesis very literally. That is, if utility is not strictly linear in the probabilities, then all hell breaks loose. And those things are definitely drawbacks of virtual implementation.

So in thinking about where we go from here and what more we can learn from this debate on foundations and mechanisms, let me be slightly philosophical for my last remark. I think that since Grossman-Hart, we all typically assumed ex post symmetric information—and with good reason, to make use of the Nash bargaining solution—and that's been a very fruitful approach. I remember walking into Oliver's office in my first year as a graduate student and saying "could we get ex post inefficiencies and maybe foundations by having asymmetric information?" And he said, "No, no, no, that's a complete mess. Don't do that." It is sort of a mess, but maybe it's not as big a mess as we thought in these sorts of settings. The one I just described there, it's not too big of a mess. In our recent *Journal of Economic Perspectives* paper, Philippe and I very briefly sketched how these sorts of very simple asymmetric information models can be useful, and it may address this point of ex post inefficiencies rather than simply ex ante inefficiencies as well.

References

Aghion, Philippe, Drew Fudenberg, Richard Holden Takashi Kunimoto and Olivier Tercieux "Subgame Perfect Implementation under Value Perturbations", Quarterly Journal of Economics, 127(4), 2012, 1843–1881.

Maskin, Eric., and Jean. Tirole, "Unforeseen Contingencies and Incomplete Contracts," Review of Economic Studies, 66 (1999a), 83–114.

33

Complexity and Undescribability

NABIL I. AL-NAJJAR, LUCA ANDERLINI, AND LEONARDO FELLI

1. Motivation

In the well-known case of *Jacobellis v. Ohio*,[1] Supreme Court Justice Potter Stewart argued that only "hard-core" pornography could be banned, but conceded:

> "I shall not today attempt to further define the kind of materials I understand to be embraced within the shorthand definition; and perhaps I could never succeed in doing so," Stewart had said. "But I know it when I see it." (Woodward and Armstrong, 1979, 94)

The describability problem faced by Justice Stewart exemplifies well the type of circumstances we focus on. These are events, objects, or activities that are well known and understood to all the parties involved but that are impossible to describe in an exhaustive manner.

Another example is the one of "academic tenure." Academic institutions routinely decide whether to grant tenure to junior faculty members. An ex ante contingent tenure rule would spell out in advance a detailed set of conditions under which tenure would be granted as a function of a candidate's performance. Formulating such a rule would entail considerable gains, such as reducing uncertainty, cutting down on the effort and resources spent in committee work, and reducing the potential for allegations of inequity, bias, and so on. Despite this, to our knowledge no research-oriented department in the United States has

The results we prove in this chapter were presented in the panel discussion on the "Foundation of Incomplete Contracts" of the conference "Grossman and Hart at 25." We are grateful to the panel chair, Sönje Reiche, for very helpful comments.

[1] *Jacobellis v. Ohio*, 378 U. S. 184 (1964).

set forth such a rule. Instead, decisions are usually made using a lengthy case-by-case process that often suffers from the drawbacks mentioned above. The issue is that the underlying event, "the candidate has a tenurable vita," is well understood by most of us but inherently hard to describe ex ante in its full details.

Finally, closer to home, when we first heard and learned of Grossman and Hart's key insight on the effects of contractual incompleteness, we all anticipated the revolutionary effect of such an insight on our understanding of ownership rights and the inner working of some key economic institutions. However, had we been asked 25 years ago to describe in detail such an impact, the task would clearly have been impossibe.

It is exactly this type of events or actions that are well understood and yet impossible to describe that are the core of contractual incompleteness.

> A basic assumption of the model is that the production decisions are sufficiently complex that they cannot be specified completely in an initial contract between the firms. We have in mind a situation in which it is prohibitively difficult to think about and describe unambiguously in advance how all the potentially relevant aspects of the production allocation should be chosen as a function of the many states of the world. (Grossman and Hart 1986, 696)

Of course, the description above could refer to an event that is simply unforeseen, a surprise to all parties involved. However, as Oliver Hart clarifies, these fully unforeseen events cannot be the reason behind the contractual incompleteness assumed in Grossman and Hart (1986).

> it is essential that, even though the agents are not capable of writing a contract that avoids hold-up problems, they are clever enough to understand (at least roughly) the consequences of their inability to do this. (Hart 1990, 699)

Here we identify the necessary conditions for a model that admits complex events that are understood by the parties to the economic transaction, in the sense that they are able to assess the probability associated with these events and hence compute their expected utility, and yet cannot be described at an ex ante stage in a nontrivial sense of the word. Indeed, consider the tenure example above: it is easy to write simple, clear-cut rules like "grant tenure if and only if the candidate publishes x or more papers in journal y." The problem is that such a rule is too coarse to capture the subtle ways in which membership in the event "the candidate has a tenurable vita" is determined as a function of observable characteristics of a candidate's record.

In the model proposed below *all* rules are feasible, provided only they are *finite* in a well-defined sense. Moreover, an event is complex if any feasible rule envisioned by the parties will leave a "positive measure" of exceptions. We label these events "undescribable."[2]

In Al-Najjar, Anderlini, and Felli (2006) we construct a model that allows for undescribable events and show in a simple co-insurance setting that risk-averse contracting parties facing such an event would optimally choose to write no contract at all and face the uncertainty of the environment. Here, instead, we identify the necessary conditions that every model of undescribable events needs to satisfy. Obviously the example in Al-Najjar, Anderlini, and Felli (2006) satisfies such conditions.

These necessary conditions correspond to two critical nonstandard features of the type of models we propose. The first is the use of a probability distribution over states of nature that is finitely additive, but *fails* countable additivity.[3] The second is a state space that is a "small" subset of the set of all possible potential states (the set of all possible infinite strings of 0s and 1s).

In other words, we here show that the two key features of the model in Al-Najjar, Anderlini, and Felli (2006) are what it takes to get a formal notion of undescribable events. There is a sense in which a rejection of the nonstandard ingredients that we highlight here is equivalent to saying that the formal notion of a event that is undescribable because it is "too complex" rather than because the parties do not have a sufficiently "rich language" is unattainable.

2. Ingredients

Our aim is to identify the properties that a model of undescribable events needs to satisfy. We start from a state space S with typical element s. The state space S needs to allow for a nontrivial event denoted $Z \subset S$ that is undescribable. In other words, all parties involved are able to foresee the event Z but are not able to describe such an event.

To define formally what can or cannot be described, we start from the language available to the parties. Since we are aiming at an event that is *too complex* to describe rather than at a language that is too simple to handle the event we are interested in, we allow for a *rich enough language*. In other words, we only restrict parties to use finite descriptions. Formally, the language is then an algebra $\mathcal{A}$ of subsets of S.

---

[2] The more commonly used English term would be "indescribable." However, we decided here to use the less common term "undescribable" to highlight the fact that the event we are referring to cannot be described by the parties involved *but* can be exactly foreseen by them. The only rationale we can provide for such a choice is that this is what you get when three non-native English speakers select the more suitable English term.

[3] See also Al-Najjar (2009).

Let μ be a finitely additive probability measure defined on $(\mathcal{S}, \mathcal{A})$ and $\sigma(\mathcal{A})$ the sigma algebra generated by $\mathcal{A}$. Denote μ^* any extension of μ to the sigma algebra $\sigma(\mathcal{A})$.

We now formally specify what we mean when we label the event $\mathcal{Z}$ as undescribable. In the first place all parties are able to foresee the event in question. We take this to mean that the parties can assess the probability of $\mathcal{Z}$. In other words, we restrict ourselves to events $\mathcal{Z} \in \sigma(\mathcal{A})$ for which $\mu^*(\mathcal{Z})$ is well defined.

Moreover, the parties cannot describe the event $\mathcal{Z}$ given the language $\mathcal{A}$. We take an event $\mathcal{Z} \in \sigma(\mathcal{A})$ to be describable if either $\mathcal{Z} \in \mathcal{A}$ or $\mathcal{Z}$ can be approximated using the language $\mathcal{A}$. We obviously first need to specify what we mean by approximating an event in a probability space.

Definition 1 *Approximation* An event $\mathcal{Z} \in \sigma(\mathcal{A})$ can be approximated using the language $\mathcal{A}$ if for every real number $\varepsilon > 0$ there exists a set $A \in \mathcal{A}$ such that $\mu^*(\mathcal{Z} \triangle A) < \varepsilon$.[4]

3. Results

Our main challenge here is that the most obvious model that comes to mind when attempting to formalize undescribable events is such that a general approximation result holds (Anderlini and Felli 1994). Let us first define what we mean by the term "approximation result."

Definition 2 *General Approximation Result* Let any set $\mathcal{S}$ be given, and $\mathcal{A}$ an algebra of subsets of $\mathcal{S}$. Let also μ be a finitely additive probability measure on $(\mathcal{S}, \mathcal{A})$ (not necessarily countably additive). Let μ^* be any extension of μ to the sigma algebra $\sigma(\mathcal{A})$.

We say that a general approximation result holds for the model $(\mathcal{S}, \mathcal{A}, \mu)$ if and only if every $\mathcal{Z} \in \sigma(\mathcal{A})$ can be approximated as in Definition 1.

Clearly, if the approximation result holds for a space $(\mathcal{S}, \mathcal{A}, \mu)$, then *no set* $\mathcal{Z} \in \sigma(\mathcal{A})$ will be undescribable. In other words, our aim here is to identify the properties of a model $(\mathcal{S}, \mu, \mathcal{A})$ for which the approximation result fails.

We first show that any model $(\mathcal{S}, \mu, \mathcal{A})$ that delivers a set $\mathcal{Z} \in \sigma(\mathcal{A})$ that cannot be approximated in the sense of Definition 1 must involve a measure μ that fails to be countably additive.

---

[4] Throughout the rest of the paper we use the standard notation $C \triangle D$ to indicate the symmetric difference between the two sets C and D. In other words we define $C \triangle D = [C - (C \cap D)] \cup [D - (D \cap C)]$.

Proposition 1 *Finitely Additive Measures* Let a space (S, A, μ) as in Definition 2 be given, and assume that μ is countably additive on A.

Then the approximation result holds for the space (S, A, μ).

The intuition behind Proposition 1 is not hard to outline. Roughly speaking, since μ is countably additive on the algebra A it has, by Carathéodory's extension theorem,[5] a *unique* countably additive extension μ^* to the sigma algebra $\sigma(A)$. Consider now a sequence of sets $\{A_n\}$ in A such that the symmetric difference $A_n \Delta Z \downarrow \emptyset$. Then, by countable additivity $\mu^*(A_n \Delta Z)$ converges to 0 and hence the approximation result holds.

We next focus on an event Z for which the approximation result fails in a *strong sense*. We take this to mean that Z cannot be approximated at all (Z is *independent* of all $A \in A$), and the approximation result fails *uniformly* over the entire state space S. These two features of our model imply that not only must μ fail countable additivity, but it must fail to be countably additive in the *strongest* possible way.

Definition 3 *Strong Undescribabilty* We say that $Z \subseteq S$ cannot be approximated in a strong sense if and only if for every $A \in A$ with $\mu(A) > 0$,

$$0 < \mu(Z|A) = \mu(Z) < 1. \tag{1}$$

So, the density of Z is the same conditional on all finitely definable sets that have positive measure under μ and Z is a not trivial subset of S: $Z \neq S$, and $Z \neq \emptyset$.

In other words, Z cannot be approximated in a strong sense if, knowing that s belongs to any finitely definable subset of S does not help us "predict" better whether it belongs to Z or to its complement.

We can now move to a complete characterization of the properties of a model (S, μ, A) that allows for an event $Z \in \sigma(A)$ that cannot be approximated in the strong sense of Definition 3. The following is a standard result that will enable us to derive this characterization.[6]

Remark 1 *Decomposition Theorem* Let any set S be given, and A an algebra of subsets of S. Let also μ be a finitely additive probability measure on (S, A) (not necessarily countably additive).

---

[5] See, for instance, Royden (1988, chap. 12.2.)

[6] Many of the results we quote and use in our arguments below are well known in the mathematical literature. A measure that fails countable additivity is known as a "charge." The most comprehensive reference of which we are aware in this field is Bhaskara Rao and Bhaskara Rao (1983).

Then μ can be written in the form $\mu = \mu^{CA} + \mu^{FA}$, where μ^{CA} is a countably additive measure, and μ^{FA} is purely finitely additive in the sense that there does not exist a nonzero countably additive measure ν on $(\mathcal{S}, \mathcal{A})$ such that $\nu \leq \mu^{FA}$.

Moreover, the decomposition of μ into $\mu^{CA} + \mu^{FA}$ is unique.[7]

We are now ready to prove that the strong failure of the approximation result as in Definition 3, corresponds to a μ that is purely finitely additive in the sense of Remark 1.[8]

Proposition 2 *Pure Finite Additivity* Let any set $\mathcal{S}$ be given, and $\mathcal{A}$ an algebra of subsets of $\mathcal{S}$. Let also μ be a finitely additive probability measure on $(\mathcal{S}, \mathcal{A})$.

Assume now that there exists a set $\mathcal{Z} \in \sigma(\mathcal{A})$ that cannot be approximated in the strong sense of Definition 3. Then the unique decomposition of μ into $\mu^{FA} + \mu^{CA}$ (as in Remark 1) is such that $\mu^{FA} = \mu$, and μ^{CA} is identically equal to zero.

Intuitively, if the countably additive component of μ is not identically equal to zero then, from Proposition 1, we can approximate, at least in part, any event in the sigma algebra $\sigma(\mathcal{A})$. This contradicts the presence of a set like $\mathcal{Z}$ that cannot be approximated in the strong sense of Definition 3.

Once we know that μ is purely finitely additive, it is easy to see that there cannot be a state s in $\mathcal{S}$ that has point mass. So another necessary feature of a

---

[7] The proof of this claim can be found for instance in Bhaskara Rao and Bhaskara Rao (1983, theorem 10.2.1). Notice that the standard name for a purely finitely additive measure like μ^{FA} is that of a "pure charge."

[8] A probability measure that is finitely additive and fails countable additivity, in the terminology of Bhaskara Rao and Bhaskara Rao (1983), is known as a *pure charge*. These measures do address the frustrations associated with countable additivity, as clearly and strongly stated by De Finetti:

Suppose we are given a countable partition into events E_i, and let us put ourselves into the subjectivistic position. An individual wishes to evaluate the $p_i = \mathbf{P}(E_i)$; he is free to choose them as he pleases, except that, if he wants to be coherent, he must be careful not to inadvertently violate the conditions of coherence.

Someone tells him that in order to be coherent he can choose the p_i in any way he likes, so long as the sum = 1 (it is the same thing as in the finite case, anyway!).

The same thing?!!! You must be joking, the other will answer. In the finite case, this condition allowed me to choose the probabilities to be all equal, or slightly different, or very different; in short, I could express any opinion whatsoever. Here, on the other hand, the *content* of my judgements enter in the picture: I am allowed to express them only if they are unbalanced to the extent illustrated [above]. Otherwise, even if I think they are equally probable [...] I am obliged to pick 'at random' a convergent series which, however I choose it, is in absolute contrast to what I think. If not, you call me *incoherent*! In leaving the finite domain, is it I who has ceased to understand anything, or is it you who has gone mad? (De Finetti 1974, 123)

model that delivers events $\mathcal{Z}$ that are undescribable in a strong way is that the measure μ is "diffuse" in a well-defined sense.[9]

Proposition 3 *Diffuse Probabilities* Let any set $\mathcal{S}$ be given, and $\mathcal{A}$ an algebra of subsets of $\mathcal{S}$. Let also μ be a finitely additive probability measure on $(\mathcal{S}, \mathcal{A})$.

Then if μ is purely finitely additive as in Proposition 2 there cannot be a state in $\mathcal{S}$ that has point mass in the following sense. There exists no $s \in \mathcal{S}$ and $\varepsilon > 0$ such that $s \in A$ implies $\mu(A) \geq \varepsilon$ for every $A \in \mathcal{A}$.[10]

Let $\mathcal{C} = \{0, 1\}^{\mathbb{N}}$, the set of all infinite strings of 0s and 1s, be the ambient set of $\mathcal{S}$, $\mathcal{S} \subset \mathcal{C}$. Of course $\mathcal{C}$ has the cardinality of the continuum. We show next that the state space $\mathcal{S}$ of a model $(\mathcal{S}, \mu, \mathcal{A})$ that delivers complex undescribable events is "small" relative to $\mathcal{C}$. In other words, the fact that $\mathcal{S}$ must be a "small" subset of $\mathcal{C}$, is also a consequence of the fact that the model admits a set $\mathcal{Z}$ that is undescribable in a strong sense.

Clearly if $\mathcal{S} \subset \mathcal{C}$ then each state of nature s_n is an infinite sequence $\{s_n^1, \ldots, s_n^i, \ldots\}$ of 0's and 1's where $s_n^i \in \{0, 1\}$ indicate the value of the ith digit of s_n. Define also

$$A(i, j) = \{s_n \in \mathcal{S} \quad \text{such that} \quad s_n^i = j\} \tag{2}$$

so that $A(i, j)$ is the set of states that have the ith digit equal to $j \in \{0, 1\}$. These are the elementary statements of the underlying language $\mathcal{A}$. We are now ready to define the finitely definable subsets of $\mathcal{S}$. These are the sets that can be described in the available language.

Definition 4 *Finitely Definable Sets* Consider the algebra of subsets of $\mathcal{S}$ generated by the collection of sets of the type $A(i, j)$ defined in equation (2). Let this algebra be denoted by $\mathcal{A}$. We refer to any $A \in \mathcal{A}$ as a finitely definable set.

Elements of $\mathcal{A}$ can be obtained by complements and/or finite intersections and/or finite unions of the sets $A(i, j)$. Hence every element of $\mathcal{A}$ can be defined by finitely many elementary statements about the digits of the states of nature that it contains.

Let λ denote the "uniform" distribution on $\mathcal{C}$. By this we mean the (unique, countably additive) probability distribution on $\mathcal{C}$ obtained as the product distribution on each of the digits and under which $\lambda(A(i, 0)) = \lambda(A(i, 1)) = 1/2$ for

---

[9] We refrain from using the term "nonatomic" here since a whole host of technical problems arise if one attempts to define this term in a general way for a measure μ that fails countable additivity. Bhaskara Rao and Bhaskara Rao (1983, chap. 5) devote an entire chapter to the subject.

[10] Obviously, if $\{s\} \in \mathcal{A}$, then Proposition 3 tells us that it cannot be that $\mu(s) > 0$.

every feature i. Note that this may be viewed as the translation of the Lebesgue measure on C.[11]

Proposition 4 *Zero Lebesgue Measure* Let S be any subset of $C = \{0, 1\}^{\mathbb{N}}$, and let A be the algebra of finitely definable sets of Definition 4.

Suppose that μ is such that the space (S, A, μ) admits a set $Z \in \sigma(A)$ that is undescribale in the strong sense of Definition 3. Assume also that $\mu(A) > 0$ for every $A \in A$.[12] Then $\lambda(S) = 0$.

Broadly speaking, Proposition 4 is a consequence of the fact that μ must be purely finitely additive, which in turn of course is a consequence of strong undescribability.

Intuitively, it is easiest to think of Proposition 4 in the following way. Suppose that we equip the set C with the algebra of finitely definable sets A and we place a *finitely* additive measure, say ν, on this pair. Then, by a theorem of Kolmogorov we know that ν must necessarily be *countably additive* as well.[13] It is then clear that we could not have our state space S equal to C, since to deliver strong undescribablity we need a measure that is purely finitely additive, as Proposition 2 shows.

Could it then be that S contains at least a subset of C which, conditional on say the first m "features" (digits of the binary expansion of an elementary state) being equal to a given sequence of 0s and 1s, contains all elements of C (a whole "cylinder")? The answer to this question is no. Roughly speaking, we could then apply the same theorem to this subset of C to obtain at least a "portion" of ν that is countably additive. But this is impossible if the measure is to be purely finitely additive, as Proposition 2 asserts that it must be if we are to obtain strong undescribability. It follows that the state space of a model of undescribable events must have a state space that is a "small" subset of C as in Proposition 4.

---

[11] To see this, embed the interval $[0, 1]$ in the real line as a subset of C, denoted C_1, by identifying each point in $[0, 1]$ with its binary expansion. This assignment is unique except for a countable number of points in $[0, 1]$ that have two possible binary expansions. For these points, we choose a unique point in C. Then the restriction of λ to C coincides with the Lebesgue measure on $[0, 1]$.

The measure λ is defined formally in Definition A.1 in the Appendix. Remarks A.4 and A.5 formalize the relationship between C and the interval $[0, 1]$ that we have just sketched out.

[12] Note that we make the assumption that $\mu(A) > 0$ for every $A \in A$ purely for the sake of simplicity. Without it we would need to take care separately of any possible "superfluous" portion of C. By this we mean that, for instance, μ could assign a mass of zero to the set of all states in S that have, say, feature 1 equal to 1. In this case it is possible that this entire cylinder in C is included in S. Since this part of μ is identically equal to 0, it would be purely finitely additive in the sense of Remark 1 since *both* its countably additive component and its purely finitely additive components are identically equal to 0.

[13] See for instance Billingsley (1995 theorem 2.3) or Doob (1994, theorem V.6).

4. Conclusions

In Al-Najjar, Anderlini, and Felli (2006) we showed that it is possible to construct a contracting environment in which some events have the following properties. Their probabilities and consequences are understood by all concerned, and all agents involved use this information to compute expected utilities arising from any possible finite ex ante contract. Yet these events are undescribable in the sense that any attempt to describe them in a finite ex ante agreement must fail. The contracting parties cannot describe these events to any degree that will improve their expected utilities relative to an agreement that ignores them altogether. This is so notwithstanding the fact that the contracting parties' language can in fact distinguish between any two states.

We have shown here that two key properties of the model presented in Al-Najjar, Anderlini, and Felli (2006) are *necessary* to capture the intuitive notion of an undescribable event. In particular, we proved that the probability measure that captures the parties' ability to predict the undescribable event need to be finitely additive and fail countable additivity. Moreover, the state space of any model that exhibits a strong failure of the approximation result needs to be small in a well-defined sense.

In our view, it is this subtle but intuitive notion of undescribable event that is at the foundation of the seminal insight of Grossman and Hart (1986) on the theory of ownership and institutions.

Appendix

Proof of Proposition 1 Since μ is countably additive on $\mathcal{A}$ by Catahéodory's extension theorem there exists a unique extension μ^* of μ to $\sigma(\mathcal{A})$. Since $\mathcal{Z} \in \sigma(\mathcal{A})$, we must then have that $\mu^*(\mathcal{Z})$ is equal to the outer measure of $\mathcal{Z}$ induced by μ. In other words it must be that

$$\mu^*(\mathcal{Z}) = \inf \sum_n \mu(O_n), \tag{A.1}$$

where the infimum extends over all finite and infinite sequences $\{O_n\}$ that satisfy

$$O_n \in \mathcal{A} \ \forall n \quad \text{and} \quad \mathcal{Z} \subseteq \bigcup_n O_n. \tag{A.2}$$

Hence, for any real number $\xi > 0$ there exists a sequence $\{O_n\}$ satisfying (A.2) and

$$\sum_n \mu(O_n) - \mu^*(\mathcal{Z}) < \xi. \tag{A.3}$$

Since the first term in (A.3) is a convergent series, for any real number $\eta > 0$ there exists a finite m such that

$$\sum_n \mu(O_n) - \sum_{n=1}^m \mu(O_n) < \eta, \qquad (A.4)$$

Notice next that (A.3) implies that

$$\mu^* \left(\bigcup_n O_n \right) - \mu^*(\mathcal{Z}) < \xi. \qquad (A.5)$$

Since the sequence $\{O_n\}$ satisfies (A.2), the inequality in (A.5) implies

$$\mu^* \left(\mathcal{Z} \triangle \bigcup_n O_n \right) < \xi. \qquad (A.6)$$

From (A.4) we deduce

$$\sum_{n>m} \mu(O_n) < \eta, \qquad (A.7)$$

and hence

$$\mu^* \left(\bigcup_{n>m} O_n \right) < \eta. \qquad (A.8)$$

From this it follows immediately that

$$\mu^* \left(\bigcup_n O_n \triangle \bigcup_{n=m}^m O_n \right) < \eta. \qquad (A.9)$$

It is straightforward to verify that the operator $\mu^*(\cdot \triangle \cdot)$ is in fact a pseudometric on the sigma algebra of sets $\sigma(\mathcal{A})$. Hence it satisfies the triangular inequality. Therefore

$$\mu^* \left(\mathcal{Z} \triangle \bigcup_{n=1}^m O_n \right) \le \mu^* \left(\mathcal{Z} \triangle \bigcup_n O_n \right) + \mu^* \left(\bigcup_n O_n \triangle \bigcup_{n=m}^m O_n \right). \qquad (A.10)$$

Using (A.6) and (A.9), (A.10) yields

$$\mu^* \left(\mathcal{Z} \triangle \bigcup_{n=1}^m O_n \right) \le \xi + \eta. \qquad (A.11)$$

Finally, since ξ and η are both arbitrary, and the finite union $\bigcup_{n=1}^{m} O_n$ is clearly an element of $\mathcal{A}$, (A.11) is obviously enough to prove the claim.

We will use the following result in the proof of Proposition 2. We state it here without proof for completeness. For the proof see Bhaskara Rao and Bhaskara Rao (1983, theorem 10.3.1).

Remark A.1 Fix an $\mathcal{S}$, and an algebra of subsets $\mathcal{A}$. Let also μ be a finitely additive probability measure on $(\mathcal{S}, \mathcal{A})$ (not necessarily countably additive).

Then μ is purely finitely additive if and only if for every countably additive measure ν on $(\mathcal{S}, \mathcal{A})$, every $A \in \mathcal{A}$, and every $\eta > 0$ there exists a set $M \in \mathcal{A}$ such that $M \subseteq A$

$$\nu(M) < \eta \quad \text{and} \quad \mu(A) - \mu(M) < \eta. \tag{A.12}$$

Remark A.2 Let any set $\mathcal{S}$ be given, and $\mathcal{A}$ an algebra of subsets of $\mathcal{S}$. Let also μ be a finitely additive probability measure on $(\mathcal{S}, \mathcal{A})$ (not necessarily countably additive), and consider its (unique decomposition) into $\mu^{CA} + \mu^{FA}$ as in Remark 1.

Then for every $\eta > 0$ there exists a set $B \in \mathcal{A}$ such that

$$\mu^{CA}(B) > \mu^{CA}(\mathcal{S}) - \eta \quad \text{and} \quad \mu^{FA}(B) < \eta. \tag{A.13}$$

Proof The claim is a straightforward consequence of Remark A.1.

Since μ^{CA} is countably additive and μ^{FA} is purely finitely additive, in Remark A.1 we can set $\mu = \mu^{FA}$ and $\nu = \mu^{CA}$. Hence, setting $A = \mathcal{S}$, Remark A.1 now tells us that for every $\eta > 0$ there exists a set $M \in \mathcal{A}$ such that

$$\mu^{CA}(M) < \eta \quad \text{and} \quad \mu^{FA}(\mathcal{S}) - \mu^{FA}(M) < \eta. \tag{A.14}$$

Next, set $B = \overline{M}$. We then note that $\mu^{CA}(M) = \mu^{CA}(\mathcal{S}) - \mu^{CA}(B)$ and $\mu^{FA}(M) = \mu^{FA}(\mathcal{S}) - \mu^{FA}(B)$. Substituting these equalities in (A.14) now immediately yields that for every $\eta > 0$ there exists a set $B \in \mathcal{A}$ such that

$$\mu^{CA}(\mathcal{S}) - \mu^{CA}(B) < \eta \quad \text{and} \quad \mu^{FA}(\mathcal{S}) - \mu^{FA}(\mathcal{S}) + \mu^{FA}(B) < \eta. \tag{A.15}$$

Rearranging (A.15) then immediately gives the result.

Proof of Proposition 2 Use Remark 1 to write $\mu = \mu^{CA} + \mu^{FA}$. From Proposition 1 we know that $\mu^{CA}(\mathcal{S}) < 1$. Assume now that the Proposition is false. Then it must also be the case that $\mu^{CA}(\mathcal{S}) > 0$.

Using Remark A.2 we know that for every $\eta > 0$ there exists a set $B \in \mathcal{A}$ such that

$$\mu^{CA}(B) > \mu^{CA}(\mathcal{S}) - \eta \quad \text{and} \quad \mu^{FA}(B) < \eta. \tag{A.16}$$

Since by assumption $\mu(\mathcal{Z}) \in (0, 1)$, we can choose η in (A.16) to satisfy

$$\eta < \mu^{CA}(\mathcal{S}) \frac{\mu(\mathcal{Z}) - \mu(\mathcal{Z})^2}{2 + \mu(\mathcal{Z}) + \mu(\mathcal{Z})^2}. \tag{A.17}$$

Notice next that since we know that $\mu^{CA}(\mathcal{S}) > 0$ (the contradiction hypothesis), and by assumption $\mu(\mathcal{Z}) \in (0, 1)$, the inequalities in (A.16) and (A.17) guarantee that $\mu(B) \geq \mu^{CA}(B) > 0$. Therefore, we can define the restrictions of μ and μ^{CA} to $B \in \mathcal{A}$ as $\mu_B = \mu/\mu(B)$ and $\mu_B^{CA} = \mu^{CA}/\mu^{CA}(B)$. Further, define μ_B^{FA} to be identically equal to 0 if $\mu^{FA}(B) = 0$, and $\mu_B^{FA} = \mu^{FA}/\mu^{FA}(B)$ if $\mu^{FA}(B) > 0$. Therefore,

$$\mu_B = \alpha \, \mu_B^{CA} + (1 - \alpha) \, \mu_B^{FA}, \tag{A.18}$$

where $\alpha = \mu^{CA}(B)/\mu(B)$. Notice that since $\mu^{CA}(\mathcal{S}) \geq \mu^{CA}(B)$, we can use (A.16) and (A.17) to conclude that

$$\alpha = \frac{\mu^{CA}(B)}{\mu^{CA}(B) + \mu^{FA}(B)} > \frac{\mu^{CA}(\mathcal{S}) - \eta}{\mu^{CA}(\mathcal{S}) + \eta} > \frac{1 + \mu(\mathcal{Z})^2}{1 + \mu(\mathcal{Z})}. \tag{A.19}$$

Next, define $\mathcal{Z}_B = \mathcal{Z} \cap B$, and notice that since $\mathcal{Z}$ is strongly undescribable then so is $\mathcal{Z}_B$ with respect to the restriction μ_B. In other words whenever $A \in \mathcal{A}$ and $A \subseteq B$ we must have that $\mu_B(\mathcal{Z}_B | A) = \mu_B(\mathcal{Z}_B)$, with the latter, of course, also equal to $\mu(\mathcal{Z})$.

Clearly, μ_B^{CA} is countably additive. Applying Proposition 1, for every real number $\xi > 0$ there exists $Q_\xi \in \mathcal{A}$ such that

$$\mu_B^{CA}(\mathcal{Z}_B | \overline{Q}_\xi) < \xi \quad \text{and} \quad \left| \mu_B^{CA}(Q_\xi) - \mu_B^{CA}(\mathcal{Z}_B) \right| < \xi. \tag{A.20}$$

Therefore

$$\mu_B\left(\mathcal{Z}_B | \overline{Q}_\xi\right) = \frac{\alpha \, \mu_B^{CA}\left(\mathcal{Z}_B | \overline{Q}_\xi\right) \, \mu_B^{CA}\left(\overline{Q}_\xi\right) + (1 - \alpha) \, \mu_B^{FA}\left(\mathcal{Z}_B | \overline{Q}_\xi\right) \, \mu_B^{FA}\left(\overline{Q}_\xi\right)}{\alpha \, \mu_B^{CA}\left(\overline{Q}_\xi\right) + (1 - \alpha) \, \mu_B^{CA}\left(\overline{Q}_\xi\right)}$$

$$< \frac{\xi + (1 - \alpha) \, \mu_B^{FA}\left(\mathcal{Z}_B | \overline{Q}_\xi\right) \, \mu_B^{FA}\left(\overline{Q}_\xi\right)}{\alpha \, \mu_B^{CA}\left(\overline{Q}_\xi\right) + (1 - \alpha) \, \mu_B^{CA}\left(\overline{Q}_\xi\right)}$$

$$< \frac{\xi + 1 - \alpha}{\alpha \, \mu_B^{CA}\left(\overline{Q}_\xi\right)}. \tag{A.21}$$

In other words, using the fact that $\mathcal{Z}$ is strongly undescribable with respect to μ_B, we can now write

$$\alpha \, \mu_B(\mathcal{Z}_B)(1 - \mu_B^{CA}(Q_\xi)) < \xi + 1 - \alpha. \tag{A.22}$$

Since $\mu_B(\mathcal{Z}_B) \geq \alpha\mu_B^{CA}(\mathcal{Z}_B)$, we use (A.20) to rewrite (A.22) as

$$\alpha < \frac{1 + \xi + \mu_B(\mathcal{Z}_B)^2}{1 + \mu_B(\mathcal{Z}_B)\,(1 - \xi)}. \tag{A.23}$$

Since $\mu_B(\mathcal{Z}_B) = \mu(\mathcal{Z})$, for ξ sufficiently small (A.23) implies that

$$\alpha < \frac{1 + \mu(\mathcal{Z})^2}{1 + \mu(\mathcal{Z})}. \tag{A.24}$$

However, since (A.24) directly contradicts (A.19), this is clearly enough to prove our claim.

Proof of Proposition 3 Since μ is purely finitely additive, from Remark 1 we know that μ^{CA} is identically equal to 0. Hence from Theorem 10.2.2 of Bhaskara Rao and Bhaskara Rao (1983) we can conclude that

$$0 = \inf\left\{ \sum_n \mu(A_n) \right\}, \tag{A.25}$$

where the infimum extends over all (finite or infinite) sequences of disjoint sets $\{A_n\}$ such that $A_n \in \mathcal{A}$ for every n, and $\bigcup_n A_n = \mathcal{S}$.

Suppose, by way of contradiction, that the statement of the proposition is false. Then there exists an $s \in \mathcal{S}$ such that $\mu(A) \geq \varepsilon$ whenever A contains s. Since for any sequence $\{A_n\}$ as above we must have that $s \in A_n$ for some n, this implies that the infimum in (A.25) is at least ε. This contradiction is enough to establish the result.

We will use the following result in the proof of Lemma A.1. We state it here without proof for completeness. For the proof see Billingsley (1995, theorem 2.3) or Doob (1994, theorem V.6).

Remark A.3 Consider the set $\mathcal{C} = \{0, 1\}^{\mathbb{N}}$, and any subset $\mathcal{S}$ of $\mathcal{C}$. Assume that $\mathcal{S}$ is equipped with the algebra $\mathcal{A}$ of finitely definable sets, and equip $\mathcal{C}$ with the algebra $\tilde{\mathcal{A}}$ corresponding to the algebra of finitely definable sets as follows.

For each $c \in \mathcal{C}$ let $\{c^i\}_{i\in\mathbb{N}}$ be the sequence of digits in $\{0, 1\}$ that define c, and for every $i \in \mathbb{N}$ and $j \in \{0, 1\}$ let

$$\tilde{A}(i, j) = \{c \in \mathcal{C} \quad \text{such that} \quad c^i = j\}, \tag{A.26}$$

and let $\tilde{\mathcal{A}}$ be the algebra of subsets of $\mathcal{C}$ generated by the collection of sets of the type $\tilde{A}(i,j)$. Notice that in this way, using (2), we obviously have that for every $\tilde{A} \in \tilde{\mathcal{A}}$ it must be that $\tilde{A} \cap S = A \in \mathcal{A}$.

Let μ be any finitely additive measure on $(\mathcal{A}, S)$ (not necessarily countably additive). Then there exists a unique countably additive measure $\tilde{\mu}$ on $(\sigma(\tilde{\mathcal{A}}), \mathcal{C})$ that satisfies $\tilde{\mu}(\tilde{A}) = \mu(A)$ whenever $\tilde{A} \cap S = A$.[14]

Lemma A.1 Let any $S \subset \mathcal{C}$ be given, and consider a purely finitely additive measure μ on $(S, \mathcal{A})$. Let $\tilde{\mu}$ be the extension of μ to $(\sigma(\tilde{\mathcal{A}}), \mathcal{C})$ as in Remark A.3.

Then, for every real number $\varepsilon > 0$ there exists $\tilde{A}_\varepsilon \in \sigma(\tilde{\mathcal{A}})$ such that $S \subseteq \tilde{A}_\varepsilon$ and $\tilde{\mu}(\tilde{A}_\varepsilon) < \varepsilon$.

Proof Since μ is purely finitely additive, appealing again to theorem 10.2.2 of Bhaskara Rao and Bhaskara Rao (1983) we can conclude that

$$0 = \inf \left\{ \sum_n \mu(A_n) \right\}, \tag{A.27}$$

where the infimum extends over all (finite or infinite) sequences of disjoint sets $\{A_n\}$ such that $A_n \in \mathcal{A}$ for every n, and $\bigcup_n A_n = S$. Hence, for every $\varepsilon > 0$ there exists a sequence of disjoint sets $\{A_{n,\varepsilon}\}$ such that $A_{n,\varepsilon} \in \mathcal{A}$ for every n, $\bigcup_n A_{n,\varepsilon} = S$ and

$$\sum_n \mu(A_{n,\varepsilon}) < \varepsilon. \tag{A.28}$$

Consider any sequence $\{A_{n,\varepsilon}\}$ as in (A.28) and the sequence $\{\tilde{A}_{n,\varepsilon}\}$ of subsets of $\mathcal{C}$ corresponding to it in the sense of Remark A.3, so that $\tilde{A}_{n,\varepsilon} \cap S = A_{n,\varepsilon}$ for every n. Let $\tilde{A}_\varepsilon = \bigcup_n \tilde{A}_{n,\varepsilon}$. Clearly, $\tilde{A}_\varepsilon \in \sigma(\tilde{\mathcal{A}})$.

Notice next that $\bigcup_n A_{n,\varepsilon} = S \cap \bigcup_n \tilde{A}_{n,\varepsilon}$. Hence $S = \tilde{A}_\varepsilon \cap S$, and therefore $S \subseteq \tilde{A}_\varepsilon$. Since $\tilde{\mu}$ is countably additive we now have that $\tilde{\mu}(\tilde{A}_\varepsilon) = \sum_n \tilde{\mu}(\tilde{A}_{n,\varepsilon})$. Since by construction we must have that $\tilde{\mu}(\tilde{A}_{n,\varepsilon}) = \mu(A_{n,\varepsilon})$ for every n we also know that

$$\tilde{\mu}(\tilde{A}_\varepsilon) = \sum_n \tilde{\mu}(\tilde{A}_{n,\varepsilon}) = \sum_n \mu(A_{n,\varepsilon}). \tag{A.29}$$

Using (A.28) and (A.29), it is immediate that $\tilde{\mu}(\tilde{A}_\varepsilon) < \varepsilon$, as required.

Lemma A.2 Let any $S \subset \mathcal{C}$ be given, and consider a purely finitely additive measure μ on $(S, \mathcal{A})$. Let $\tilde{\mu}$ be the extension of μ to $(\tilde{\mathcal{A}}, \mathcal{C})$ as in Remark A.3.
Then, there exists $\tilde{S} \in \sigma(\tilde{\mathcal{A}})$ such that $S \subseteq \tilde{S}$ and $\tilde{\mu}(\tilde{S}) = 0$.

---

[14] With a slight abuse of language we refer to $\tilde{\mu}$ as the *extension* of μ to $(\sigma(\tilde{\mathcal{A}}), \mathcal{C})$.

Proof From Lemma A.1 we know that, given any sequence $\varepsilon_m \to 0$ we can construct a corresponding sequence of sets $\{\tilde{A}_{\varepsilon_m}\}$ such that $S \subseteq \tilde{A}_{\varepsilon_m}$, $\tilde{\mu}(\tilde{A}_{\varepsilon_m}) < \varepsilon_m$, and $\tilde{A}_{\varepsilon_m} \in \sigma(\tilde{A})$ for every m. To prove the claim it is then sufficient to set $\tilde{S} = \bigcap_m \tilde{A}_{\varepsilon_m}$ and to notice that it must be the case that $\tilde{S} \in \sigma(\tilde{A})$.

Remark A.4 Each element c of $C = \{0, 1\}^{\mathbb{N}}$ can be interpreted as the binary expansion of a real number r in the interval $[0, 1]$ by taking the elements of the sequence c to be the digits of the binary expansion of r following a "0" and the "decimal" point.

This map assign a unique real in $[0, 1]$ to each element of C except for those that are of the form $\{c_1, \ldots, c_m, 1, 0, \ldots, 0, \ldots\}$ and $\{c_1, \ldots, c_m, 0, 1, \ldots, 1, \ldots\}$ which obviously correspond to the same real number r. Notice that there are countably many such pairs of elements of C.

In what follows we denote by C_0 the set of elements of C that are of the form $\{c_1, \ldots, c_m, 1, 0, \ldots, 0, \ldots\}$, excluding $\{0, \ldots, 0, \ldots\}$, and by C_1 the remainder of C so that $C_1 = C - C_0$.

From what we have just stated, it is clear that we can assign a unique real in $[0, 1]$ to each element of C_1 and a unique element of C_1 to every real in $[0, 1]$.

Finally, notice that if we define the sigma algebra $\sigma(\tilde{A}_1)$ of subsets of C_1 as consisting of the collection of sets $\tilde{A} \cap C_1$ for every $\tilde{A} \in \sigma(\tilde{A})$ we obtain that $\sigma(\tilde{A}_1)$ contains all the half-open intervals in $[0, 1]$ of the form $(a, b]$ where a and b are reals in $[0, 1]$.

Remark A.5 Consider the sigma algebra $\sigma(\tilde{A}_0)$ of subsets of C consisting of the collection of sets $\tilde{A} \cap C_0$ for every $\tilde{A} \in \sigma(\tilde{A})$. Consider also the sigma algebra $\sigma(\tilde{A}_1)$ of Remark A.4.

Then $\sigma(\tilde{A}) = \sigma(\tilde{A}_0) \cup \sigma(\tilde{A}_1)$.

Proof Since C_0 is a countable set it is enough to notice that every singleton set is already contained in $\sigma(\tilde{A})$. Hence $\sigma(\tilde{A}_0)$ consists of all subsets of C_0. The assertion is then immediate from the definition of $\sigma(\tilde{A}_0)$ and $\sigma(\tilde{A}_1)$. The details are omitted.

Definition A.1 Recall that from Remark A.5 we know that $\sigma(\tilde{A}) = \sigma(\tilde{A}_0) \cup \sigma(\tilde{A}_1)$. The Lebesgue measure λ on C is then defined as follows.

For every $\tilde{A}$ in $\sigma(\tilde{A})$, set $\lambda(\tilde{A}) = 0$ if $\tilde{A} \in \sigma(\tilde{A}_0)$, and $\lambda(\tilde{A}) = \mathcal{L}(\tilde{A})$ if $\tilde{A} \in \sigma(\tilde{A}_1)$ where $\mathcal{L}$ is the Lebesgue measure on the real interval $[0, 1]$ defined in the standard way.

Finally, as is standard, we take λ to be the completion of the measure we have just defined in the sense that it is defined and is equal to zero on all subsets of all measurable sets that have zero measure.[15]

---

[15] See for instance Billingsley (1995, 45).

Lemma A.3 Let $\tilde{\mu}$ be the extension of μ to $(\sigma(\tilde{\mathcal{A}}), \mathcal{C})$ as in Remark A.3, and assume that μ is such that $\mu(A) > 0$ for every $A \in \mathcal{A}$.

Then $\mathrm{supp}(\tilde{\mu}) = \mathcal{C}$, where $\mathrm{supp}(\cdot)$ indicates the support of a given measure.

Proof Suppose not. Then there is a nonempty open set O in $\mathcal{C}$ such that $\tilde{\mu}(O) = 0$. (We take O to be open in the product topology generated by the discrete topology on each coordinate of the elements of $\{0, 1\}^{\mathbb{N}}$.)

We will show that for every open set O we can find an $\tilde{A} \in \tilde{\mathcal{A}}$ that is contained in O. Since $\tilde{\mu}(\tilde{A}) = \mu(\tilde{A} \cap \mathcal{S})$ and the latter is, by assumption, positive this yields a contradiction and hence is sufficient to prove the claim.

Assume by way of contradiction that we can find a nonempty open $O \subseteq \mathcal{C}$ such that $\tilde{A} \not\subseteq O$ for every $\tilde{A} \in \tilde{\mathcal{A}}$.

Fix $c \in O$ and consider the nested sequence of sets $\{\tilde{A}_n\}$ where for every n, $\tilde{A}_n \in \tilde{\mathcal{A}}$ is the set (the "cylinder") of all those $\hat{c}$s that have the first n digits equal to the first n digits of c.

By our contradiction hypothesis it must be that $\tilde{A}_n \not\subseteq O$ for every n. Hence, for every n we must be able to find a $\hat{c}_n \in \tilde{A}_n$ and $\hat{c}_n \notin O$.

Clearly, the sequence $\{\hat{c}_n\}$ converges to c. But since $\hat{c}_n \notin O$ for every n, and $c \in O$, this contradicts the fact that O is open.

Proof of Proposition 4 Let $\tilde{\mu}$ be the extension of μ to $(\sigma(\tilde{\mathcal{A}}), \mathcal{C})$ as in Remark A.3 and λ be the Lebesgue measure on $\mathcal{C}$ as in Definition A.1.

By Lemma A.2 we know that there exists a set $\tilde{\mathcal{S}} \in \sigma(\tilde{\mathcal{A}})$ such that $\mathcal{S} \subseteq \tilde{\mathcal{S}}$ and $\tilde{\mu}(\tilde{\mathcal{S}}) = 0$, and by Lemma A.3 we know that $\mathrm{supp}(\tilde{\mu}) = \mathcal{C}$.

Since λ is, by definition, *complete* in the sense that it assigns measure zero to all subsets of any set in $\sigma(\tilde{\mathcal{A}})$ that have λ-measure zero, it is enough to show that $\lambda(\tilde{\mathcal{S}}) = 0$.[16] We proceed by contradiction. Hence suppose that $\lambda(\tilde{\mathcal{S}}) > 0$.

By the "Lebesgue Decomposition Theorem,"[17] we know that $\tilde{\mu}$ can be (uniquely) written as $\tilde{\mu} = \tilde{\mu}^C + \tilde{\mu}^S$ where $\tilde{\mu}^C$ is absolutely continuous with respect to λ, and $\tilde{\mu}^S$ is singular with respect to λ.

Let $Q^S = \mathrm{supp}(\tilde{\mu}^S)$ and $Q^C = \mathrm{supp}(\tilde{\mu}^C)$. Since $\mathrm{supp}(\tilde{\mu}) = \mathcal{C}$, we must have that $\mathcal{C} = Q^S \cup Q^C$. Hence $\tilde{\mathcal{S}} = [\tilde{\mathcal{S}} \cap Q^S] \cup [\tilde{\mathcal{S}} \cap Q^C]$.

Notice that since $\tilde{\mu}^S$ is singular with respect to λ, we immediately know that $\lambda(\tilde{\mathcal{S}} \cap Q^S) = 0$. Hence, by our contradiction hypothesis it must be that $\lambda(\tilde{\mathcal{S}} \cap Q^C) > 0$.

Now let f be the Radon-Nikodym derivative of $\tilde{\mu}^C$ with respect to λ, which of course we know exists because $\tilde{\mu}^C$ is absolutely continuous with respect to λ.

---

[16] See note 15.

[17] See for instance Royden (1988, theorem 11.24).

Notice that it must be the case that $f > 0$ except for a set of λ-measure zero on $\tilde{S} \cap Q^C$. Hence $\lambda(\tilde{S} \cap Q^C) > 0$ implies that

$$\tilde{\mu}^C(\tilde{S} \cap Q^C) = \int_{\tilde{S} \cap Q^C} f \, \mathrm{d}\lambda > 0. \qquad (A.30)$$

However, since $\tilde{\mu} = \tilde{\mu}^C + \tilde{\mu}^S$ and $\tilde{\mu}(\tilde{S}) = 0$, we must obviously have that $\tilde{\mu}^C(\tilde{S} \cap Q^C) = 0$. This contradiction is sufficient to prove the claim.

References

Al-Najjar, N. I. 2009. "Decision Makers as Statisticians: Diversity, Ambiguity and Learning." *Econometrica* 77: 1339–69.

Al-Najjar, N., L. Anderlini, and L. Felli. 2006. "Unforeseen Contingencies." *Review of Economic Studies* 73: 849–68.

Anderlini, L., and L. Felli. 1994. "Incomplete Written Contracts: Undescribable States of Nature." *Quarterly Journal of Economics* 109: 1085–124.

Bhaskara Rao, K. P. S., and M. Bhaskara Rao. 1983. *Theory of Charges.* New York: Academic Press.

Billingsley, P. 1995. *Probability and Measure.* 3rd ed. New York: Wiley.

De Finetti, B. 1974. *Theory of Probability.* Vol. 1. New York: Wiley.

Doob, J. L. 1994. *Measure Theory.* New York: Springer.

Grossman, S. J., and O. D. Hart. 1986. "The Costs and Benefits of Ownership: A Theory of Vertical and Lateral Integration." *Journal of Political Economy* 94: 691–719.

Hart, O. 1990. "Is 'Bounded Rationality' an Important Element of a Theory of Institutions?" *Journal of Institutional and Theoretical Economics* 146: 696–702.

Royden, H. L. 1988. *Real Analysis.* 3rd ed. New York: Macmillan.

Woodward, B., and S. Armstrong. 1979. *The Brethren: Inside the Supreme Court.* New York: Simon & Schuster.

PART 11

INCOMPLETE CONTRACTS, REFERENCE POINTS, AND COMMUNICATION

34

New Directions of Incomplete Contracts: Reference Points, Communication, and Renegotiation

CHRISTIAN ZEHNDER

This festschrift volume leaves no doubt that the property rights theory pioneered by Grossman and Hart (1986) and Hart and Moore (1990) is a tremendous success and has influenced a broad variety of fields in economics. The most important achievement of the property rights approach is probably that is has crucially improved economists' understanding of firm boundaries. However, while property rights theory has been useful for studying vertical integration and outsourcing, it has been less helpful for studying the internal organization of large firms. The reason is that the theory assumes that the trading parties always negotiate to an efficient outcome ex post so that the internal structure of the firm is largely irrelevant (see also Hart 2008 for a more detailed discussion). This is unsatisfying as authority, hierarchy, and delegation seem to be important topics in most organizations.

To broaden the approach, Hart and Moore (2008) propose a new theory that not only drops the assumption that Coasian renegotiation always leads to efficient ex post outcomes, but also introduces important behavioral elements. In particular, it is assumed that contracts not only define the parties' rights and obligation but also have psychological effects. The main idea is that ex ante contracts negotiated under relatively competitive conditions provide reference points for what the trading parties feel entitled to when they trade ex post. If a party feels that he didn't get what he was entitled to, the party is aggrieved and engages in performance shading, that is, he lowers his performance to hurt his trading partner. The combination of contractual reference points and partially contractible ex post trade leads to an interesting trade-off between contractual rigidity and flexibility: flexibility allows for ex post adjustments of contract terms, but provides room for diverging reference points and shading. Rigidity aligns reference points and avoids shading, but may prevent efficient ex post trade.

The new behavioral approach is interesting because the trade-off between contractual rigidity and flexibility has a number of important implications for the economics of organizations. Contractual reference points can explain employment contracts which fix wages in advance and leave task discretion to the employer (Hart and Moore 2008); indexation in contracts and the role of payoff uncertainty for vertical integration (Hart 2009); and firm scope, authority, and delegation (Hart and Holmström 2010).

The new theory rests, however, on strong behavioral assumptions. The organizational implications discussed above are therefore only of interest if the behavioral assumptions underlying the theory turn out to be of empirical relevance. To test these behavioral mechanisms Fehr et al. (2009, 2011, 2015) have conducted a series of controlled laboratory experiments. The results are favorable for the theory. The data not only confirm the existence of the trade-off between contractual rigidity and flexibility, but also shed light on the role of competition for the emergence of contractual reference points. In addition, the experiments demonstrate that contracts continue to be reference points in the presence of contract revision and identify circumstances in which a rigid contract that is renegotiated can achieve the benefits of flexibility without incurring its costs. Finally, the laboratory studies also identify important behavioral effects of contract revision. In particular, the evidence reveals that opportunistic renegotiations are perceived as unfair and trigger lots of shading.

The remainder of this article is structured as follows: Section 1 provides an intuitive discussion of the psychological mechanisms underlying the theory of contractual reference points and provides a short overview of the model's central implication for the theory of the firm. Section 2 summarizes the design and results of the experimental studies that have been conducted to test the psychological elements of the theory. Section 3 concludes.

1. Theory

In this section I outline the idea behind the theory of contracts as reference points and I briefly discuss the implication of the approach for organizational economics.

1.1 Contractual Reference Points

The theory proposed by Hart and Moore (2008) deviates in two important ways from the typical model in the incomplete contracting literature. First, it no longer assumes that ex post trade is perfectly contractible. The new view is that trade is only partially contractible, that is, the big things can be regulated in the contract, but there always remain details that cannot be specified in the contract. These unspecified details provide the trading parties with the discretion to engage in performance shading ex post. Second, to determine the conditions under which trading parties decide to lower their ex post performance, the new approach deviates from the self-interest hypothesis and introduces behavioral elements. In particular, Hart and Moore assume that trading parties compare the outcome of ex post trade to a reference point that defines what they feel entitled to. If a party obtains a lower payoff than he feels entitled to, the party is aggrieved. In line with the literature on negative reciprocity (see, e.g., Camerer 2003; Fehr and Schmidt 2003; Cooper and Kagel forthcoming), Hart and Moore assume that a party who feels shortchanged can offset his aggrievement, if he shades on performance and thereby hurts his trading partner. However, differently than in previous social preference models the reference point relative to which a trading party evaluates the fairness of an outcome does not follow from a simple distribution rule (see, e.g., Fehr and Schmidt 1999; Bolton and Ockenfels 2000), but is defined by the terms of the ex ante contract.[1] Specifically, it is assumed that each party is subject to a self-serving bias (see, e.g., Babcock and Loewenstein 1997) and hopes for the best outcome that the contract permits. This implies that if a contract allows for multiple outcomes, different parties may feel entitled to different outcomes. For example, if the ex ante contract specifies a range of possible prices from which the parties can pick the final price ex post, self-serving biases may imply that the seller hopes for a high price, while the buyer hopes for a low price. Hart and Moore argue that it is the combination of ex ante competition and ex post lock-in—what Williamson (1985) calls the "fundamental transformation"—that makes an initial contract a salient reference point. Competition provides objectivity to the contract terms, since market forces define what each party brings to the relationship, and market participants will therefore perceive the initial contract to be fair.

The most simple version of the model describes a situation in which a buyer and a seller have the possibility to trade a widget. Ex ante there is uncertainty about the seller's cost and the buyer's value. Ex post trade is voluntary, that is, if trade does not take place the court cannot determine whose fault it is and therefore the parties cannot be punished for breach of contract. Since the model abstracts from both asset ownership and specific ex ante investments, standard contract theory would suggest that the parties do not need a contract and should postpone the negotiation of the terms of trade until after the state of the

---

[1] In Fehr and Schmidt (1999) and Bolton and Ockenfels (2000) the fairness reference is defined as an equal split of the surplus among the players in the reference group.

world has been realized. This maximizes flexibility and ensures that trade occurs whenever the gains from trade are positive.

However, in the presence of potentially misaligned reference points, this solution may no longer be optimal. If the parties exhibit a self-serving bias regarding their feelings of entitlement, a flexible arrangement that allows for many possible outcomes not only guarantees trade but also maximizes the potential for misaligned reference points and conflicts. To give an illustrative example, assume that the seller's cost is uniformly distributed between 0 and 120 and the buyer's value is uniformly distributed between 80 and 200. Suppose that ex post the parties observe a realized cost of 10 and a value of 190. Without a contract (or with a contract with maximal flexibility) the buyer would hope for a price of 10, while the seller would hope for a price of 190.[2] This is problematic, because irrespective of the price that the parties choose ex post, at least one of the parties is going to be aggrieved and will reduce his performance accordingly. This problem can easily be fixed if the parties decide to write a rigid ex ante contract which pins down the price from the outset. For example, suppose that the parties have agreed ex ante—under competitive conditions—to fix the price at 100. The advantage of such a contract is that it allows for only one outcome, so that this outcome becomes the reference point for both trading parties. If everybody expects to trade at a price of 100 and trade occurs at a price of 100, there is no discrepancy between the reference points and the realized outcomes and accordingly there is no aggrievement and no performance shading.

Obviously, contractual rigidity also has a downside. Imagine that another state of the world has been realized. For example, take the case in which the seller's cost is 75 and the buyer's value is 85. Assuming that renegotiation is not permitted (the role of renegotiation is discussed later), a rigid contract with a fixed price of 100 does not allow for trade, because the buyer would walk away. This is clearly inefficient as there are positive gains from trade. With a flexible agreement (or no agreement at all) the parties could simply choose a price between 75 and 85 and trade would occur. In this case performance shading would also not be a big problem (at least relative to the previous example), because any realized price would always be relatively close to the reference points of the buyer (75) and the seller (85), so that the aggrievement would be limited.

This implies that there is a trade-off between contractual rigidity and flexibility. Rigid contracts align reference point and avoid aggrievement and performance shading. At the same time rigidity prevents the parties from adjusting the

---

[2] Hart and Moore assume that parties do not hope for outcomes that are unacceptable for the other trading party, that is, in our case the buyer does not hope for a price which is below the seller's cost and the seller does not hope for a price which is above the buyer's value.

terms to the realized state of the world, so that sometimes trade does not occur although positive gains from trade would be available. Flexible contracts guarantee trade, but the multiplicity of outcomes permitted by the contract gives rise to misaligned feelings of entitlement, aggrievement, and shading. Thus, whether a rigid or a flexible contract is optimal depends on the characteristics of the environment.

1.2 Organizational Implications

The payoff uncertainty model outlined in section 1.1 sheds light on the important role that reference points play for contract design and explains why trading parties may write an ex ante contract even in situations in which specific investments are not of importance. However, as governance structures do not play any role, this version of the theory has nothing to say about organizational form. In an extended version of the model Hart and Moore therefore introduce an additional source of uncertainty. This version captures a situation in which the trading parties are not only uncertain about the value and cost, it is also unclear which of several possible versions of the widget should be traded.

Hart and Moore (2008) illustrate that in the presence of contractual reference points, there are constellations in which it is neither optimal to have no contract at all, nor to have a fully rigid contract which fixes both the price and the version of the widget to be traded. Not having a contract can be problematic, because it maximizes flexibility and may trigger lots of shading. Full rigidity is often suboptimal, because it may force the parties to trade versions of the widget that no party desires. In these situations the parties can benefit from writing a contract which fixes the price ex ante and assigns the authority to pick the version of the widget to either the buyer or the seller. But which party should have to right to choose the widget? The answer is simple: the party who cares most about the version of the widget should have the right to choose. This not only ensures that the efficient version of the widget is chosen, it also minimizes the overall level of shading. The extended model yields a theory of the firm in the sense that the model predicts when authority-based employment relations are optimal (buyer authority) and when the parties should rely on an independent contracting agreement (seller authority).

Hart (2009) further extends the theory and reintroduces asset ownership and ex post renegotiation into the model. This version of the theory takes into account that renegotiation in itself may also have important behavioral implications. The idea is that a trading party's attempt to renegotiate the terms of a contract may severely disappoint the other party and lead to much counterproductive behavior. Although ex post renegotiation of contracts is a central element of most theories in the literature on incomplete contracts, the possibility that renegotiation may affect the trading parties' fairness perceptions is typically ignored. However, Hart argues that these psychological aspects of renegotiation have important economic implications. In particular, the credible threat of counterproductive actions has deterrent effects, so that renegotiation is only attractive in extreme states of nature. This creates a self-enforcing range, that is, there is a set of prices for which renegotiation is not attractive. As the self-enforcing range and the temptation to renegotiate depend on asset ownership, the model identifies a new determinant of vertical integration: payoff uncertainty rather than the size of payoffs (as in the transaction cost literature) or the sensitivity of payoffs to investments (as in the property rights literature).

2. Experiments

To test the empirical relevance of the psychological mechanisms underlying the theory of contractual reference points we conducted a series of laboratory experiments (Fehr et al. 2009, 2011, 2015). In all these experiments we implemented a simplified version of Hart and Moore's payoff uncertainty model with voluntary trade (see section III in Hart and Moore 2008).

2.1 Evidence for the Trade-Off between Rigidity and Flexibility

In Fehr et al. (2011) our main condition uses the following experimental environment: a buyer and a seller have the possibility to trade a widget. The buyer's valuation is known (140), but there is ex ante uncertainty about whether the seller's production cost is high (80) or low (20). It is common knowledge though, that the cost is low in 75% of the cases and high in 25% of the cases. Ex post costs are observable but not verifiable, so that state-contingent ex ante contracts are not feasible. Buyers can choose between a rigid contract that determines a single (fixed) price (p^r), and a flexible contract that allows for a range of prices ($[p^l, p^u]$). Flexibility can be helpful, because it allows the price to adjust to the seller's cost ex post. After the buyer has chosen a contract type, a competitive auction determines which seller gets the contract. In the rigid contract the auction determines the fixed price ($p^r \geq 35$); in the flexible contract the auction determines the lower bound of the price range ($p^l \geq 35$). The upper bound of the price range in flexible contracts is exogenously fixed ($p^u = 140$). Ex post trade is possible only if the ex ante contract allows for a price that covers cost. Competition ensures that the price in the rigid contract is sufficiently low so that trade is possible only in the good state, while the flexible contract guarantees trade in both states of the world. If trade occurs the buyer chooses a price from the range determined in the contract, that is, in a rigid contract the price is always equal to the fixed price determined in the auction (p^r), in the flexible contract any price between the lower bound and the upper bound of the price range $([p^l, p^u])$ can be implemented (the price has to guarantee that the seller's payoff is not below the outside option). The seller observes the buyer's price choice and chooses the quality level, which can be either normal (q^n) or low (q^l). The choice of low quality corresponds to performance shading. Choosing low quality is slightly costly to the seller (it increases the seller's cost by 5) and reduces the buyer's payoff drastically (from 140 to 100), that is, performance shading is implemented in the form of costly sabotage. If trade is impossible, the parties realize their outside options $(o = 10)$.

Since shading is costly, the standard self-interest model predicts that sellers should never provide low quality irrespective of the contract chosen by the buyer. Accordingly, buyers should therefore always choose flexible contracts, because a flexible contract guarantees trade in both states, while a rigid contract allows for trade only if the seller's cost are low. The Hart-Moore approach instead contradicts this hypothesis. If contracts constitute reference points, sellers may feel entitled to high prices in flexible contracts and they may engage in counterproductive behavior if they do not get what they hope for. In rigid contracts, in contrast, competition guarantees a low fixed price that should be perceived as acceptable by the sellers. Thus, if the tendency to engage in counterproductive behavior in flexible contracts is strong enough, buyers may prefer the rigid contract, even though it only allows for trade when costs are low.

Figure 34.1 summarizes the results of the main treatment in Fehr et al. (2011). The figure illustrates average auction outcomes, average final prices and the relative frequency of shading for rigid and flexible contracts separately. Our findings are largely in line with the Hart-Moore theory. In particular, we find strong supporting evidence for the empirical relevance of the trade-off between contractual rigidity and flexibility in our set-up.

The figure illustrates that the fixed prices in rigid contracts and the lower bound of the price range in flexible contracts converge to the competitive price of 35 over time. There is no statistically significant difference between auction outcomes across contracts. This implies that in principle, buyers could have chosen the same prices in flexible contracts as in rigid contracts when the seller's cost turn out to be low. However, if contractual reference points are relevant, paying, very low prices might not be optimal, because sellers may feel that they didn't get the price that they deserve and engage in performance shading. In line with this argument we observe that buyers pay on average significantly higher prices in flexible contracts (51) than in rigid contracts (41). Interestingly, however, despite the substantially higher prices in flexible contracts, the shading rate

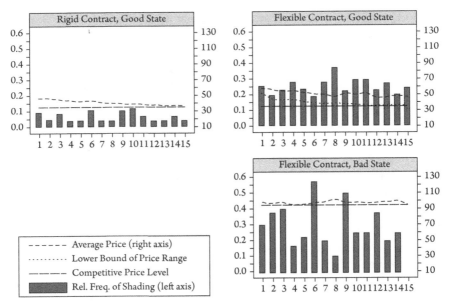

Figure 34.1 Evidence for the Trade-Off between Contractual Rigidity and Flexibility.
Source: Fehr et al. (2011)

is still significantly higher (25%) than in rigid contracts (6%).[3] Thus, when the seller's cost are low, the rigid contract is very attractive. Prices are low and the shading rate is very modest, so that buyer profits (96.8) are much higher than in flexible contracts (78.9). However, the rigid contract has the disadvantage that trade is not feasible if the cost is high. Although the shading rate in flexible contracts is also high in the high-cost state (30%), buyer profits (29.8) are still substantially above the outside option (10).

These results establish that buyers indeed face a trade-off between rigidity and flexibility in the experiment. Since the low-cost state is much more likely (75%) than the high-cost state (25%), rigid contracts are overall significantly more profitable (77.9) than flexible contracts (68.9) in our experiment. Obviously, the result that rigid contracts outperform flexible contracts is highly dependent on the choice of parameters. It would not be difficult to find other parameter constellations that favor the flexible contract. However,

---

[3] One might think that the high shading rate in flexible contracts indicates that buyers fail to maximize their profit, because they should further increase the price to lower the shading rate. This is not true. The buyers' pricing policy is close to optimal. The reason is that the price increases necessary to lower the shading rate to very low levels would be so large, that the cost of increasing the price would be larger than the benefit of the lower shading rate.

the experiment illustrates that the trade-off exists and that there are parameters constellations under which it has consequences for economic choices.[4]

To better understand the psychological underpinnings of the trade-off between rigidity and flexibility we also implemented a version of our experiment set-up in which we reduced the degree of flexibility in the flexible contract. Our main condition compares fully rigid contracts with a fixed price and fully flexible contracts in which any price between the competitively determined lower bound (p^l) and buyer's maximal willingness to pay (upper bound $p^u = 140$) can be chosen. Studying this extreme case is helpful, because it provides us with the best chance to illustrate the trade-off. However, there exist contracts with less flexibility that still guarantee trade. The theory of contractual reference points predicts that reducing flexibility should decrease the shading rate. We tested this hypothesis by comparing our rigid contract with a flexible contract in which the upper bound was fixed at 95 rather than 140. As predicted, lowering the upper bound of the price range significantly reduces shading in both states of the world (the shading rates goes down from 30% to 5% in the high-cost state and down from 25% to 19% in the low-cost state). Outcomes in the rigid contract, in contrast, remain unaffected. These findings confirm that also the comparative statics go in the direction predicted by the theory.

2.2 Competition and the Formation of Reference Points

Our experimental framework also allows us to shed light on the role of competition for the formation of contractual reference points. Hart and Moore (2008) argue that ex ante competition turns contracts into salient reference points, because competition adds objectivity to the term-defining process. To investigate whether the manner in which the terms of an ex ante contract are determined matters for how the trading parties' react to ex post outcomes, we report the result of a third treatment in Fehr et al. (2011). In this treatment we replace the competitive auction with an exogenous price generator. The only difference between this no competition condition and our main treatment is the following: after the buyer has chosen a contract, a computerized random device determines the contract terms and the seller who gets the contract. The random device generates exactly the same distribution of prices as the competitive auction in the main treatment, that is, the only difference between the two conditions is the way the price is determined.

---

[4] Erlei and Reinhold (2012) replicate our experiment. They confirm the trade-off between rigidity and flexibility and show that the advantages of the rigid contract are more pronounced if contracts are exogenously assigned rather than endogenously chosen by the buyers.

As expected, the elimination of the competitive auction increases the frequency of performance shading in rigid contracts. Although the price level remains the same, sellers choose the low quality in 16% of the cases in the no competition condition, while they only do so in 6% of the cases in the main condition. This increase is highly significant. Behavior in flexible contracts, in contrast, is not affected by the change. These results indicate that the way the contract terms are determined is important for the formation of contractual reference points. If the contract terms are exogenously given, the choice of a rigid contract is no longer attractive for buyers, because sellers no longer accept the low fixed prices as justified and respond with performance shading in many instances. Thus, in our no competition treatment the trade-off between contractual rigidity and flexibility is no longer present.[5]

Our experiment demonstrates that the presence of a "fundamental transformation" (i.e., the fact that the parties move from a competitive ex ante market to a situation of bilateral monopoly) turns contracts into reference points. However, in the meantime other authors have demonstrated that contractual reference points can also emerge in the absence of competition. Both Brandts et al. (forthcoming) and Bartling and Schmidt (2015) find that ex ante contracts also importantly shape trading parties' ex post behavior in situations in which the trading relationship is purely bilateral from the outset. The fact that bilaterally negotiated contracts also provide reference points is good news for the theory, because it implies that its scope of applicability goes beyond settings with ex ante competition. However, it seems clear that more research is needed to obtain a more systematic understanding of the conditions under which contractual reference points are likely to emerge.

2.3 Informal Agreements

In (Fehr et al. 2011) we consciously used a very simple framework to test the psychological mechanisms underlying the theory in a clean and controlled way. However, the downside of the simplicity of the set-up is that the experiment neglects important features of real-world trading. One of the most obvious limitations of our first experiment is that it abstracts from the possibility of informal agreements. The theory assumes that states of the world, although not verifiable, are observable. While nonverifiability excludes formal state-contingent contracts, observability implies that the trading parties could, in principle, still reach informal, state-contingent agreements. For example, the parties could agree on a formula that determines price as a function of cost. If the parties succeed in using such informal agreements to manage expectations and align reference points, flexibility may no longer cause performance shading.

---

[5] For further research on the role of competition for the attribution of blame in trading relationships see also our related experiments in Fehr et al. (2009) and Bartling et al. (2015).

In Fehr et al. (2015) one of our two central treatments allows for informal agreements. The experiment builds on the set-up of Fehr et al. (2011), but this time buyers have the opportunity to communicate informally their pricing plans in flexible contracts, that is, they can make nonbinding state-contingent price announcements. If a buyer decides to attach a message to a flexible contract, the price announcements are communicated to sellers before the contract is auctioned off, that is, the seller is informed about the buyer's stated pricing plans when he decides to accept the contract. If informal agreements allow buyers to manage sellers' reference points, one would expect to see that flexible contracts cause less shading, because low price announcements lower sellers' expectations.

Our data show that having the opportunity to attach nonbinding price announcements to flexible contracts indeed reduces the shading rate in both states of the world. In the low-cost state the shading rate decreases from 25% to 13%, in the bad state of the world the shading rate decreases from 30% to 21%. However, the decrease in shading is moderate and does not eliminate the trade-off between rigidity and flexibility. Also when informal agreements are available, low prices still trigger much more shading in flexible contracts than in rigid ones (6%). As a result, rigid contracts yield higher profits for buyers in the low-cost state. This advantage is large enough to offset the disadvantage that rigid contracts do not allow for trade in the high-cost state. Even if informal agreements are available flexible contracts are, on average, no more profitable than rigid contracts. The result that informal agreements do not eliminate the trade-off between rigidity and flexibility is important, especially because the simplicity of our set-up (only two states, symmetric information ex post) gives informal agreements a good chance to be effective.

It is interesting to compare our informal agreements treatment with a recent study by Brandts et al. (forthcoming), which—independently from us—also investigates the effects of communication on contractual reference points. In stark contrast to our experiment they use a setup without ex ante competition. Nevertheless, they find that without communication rigid contracts are superior to flexible contracts. This finding suggests that contracts may also serve as reference points when they are negotiated in a non-competitive manner, although the effects seems weaker than in our competitive setup. When Brandts et al. (forthcoming) allow for the same restricted form of communication as we use in our informal agreement treatment, they find that communication renders flexible contracts more profitable for buyers than rigid contracts. Also in their setup the effects of this form of communication are rather weak, but because the advantage of rigid contracts is small in the absence of communication, the effect is sufficient to destroy the trade-off between rigidity and flexibility. In a third treatment Brandts et al. (forthcoming) introduce two-way, free-form communication over the full duration of the trading phase. They find that this more extensive form of communication substantially reduces conflicts in both types of contracts. As a consequence, flexible contracts clearly dominate rigid ones.

Whether free-form communication would also increase the attractiveness of flexible contracts in a competitive set-up is an interesting and non-trivial question. In a setting in which a buyer faces multiple potential sellers, free-form communication becomes more burdensome as the buyer needs to communicate with many possible trading partners simultaneously before the contract is signed. In addition, competition may introduce incentives for strategic ex-ante communication which may undermine the credibility of promises. I think that this is a very interesting and important avenue for future research. It seems important that we better understand the exact conditions under which communication allows to avoid counterproductive behavior in organizations.

2.4 Renegotiation

Another important real-life feature that our original experiment ignores is renegotiation. The possibility to revise the contract ex post can potentially undermine the theory. To see this, suppose that a buyer and a seller write a rigid contract to align reference points. Assume further that ex post it turns out that the seller's cost is high so that trade will not occur at the ex ante specified price. Obviously, if renegotiation is possible, the parties can change the terms of the contract to avoid this inefficiency. Renegotiation can therefore potentially eliminate the cost of contractual rigidity, because a rigid contract can always be turned into a flexible contract if necessary. However, there are also two potential problems. The first one is quite obvious. If renegotiation is feasible, trading parties may not only initiate a revision of the contract if this is mutually beneficial, but may also try to renegotiate the terms to their advantage in situations in which the original contract would allow for efficient trade. Such opportunistically motivated renegotiations may annoy the trading partner and cause shading. The second potential problem is more subtle. Take again the case in which the original rigid contract allows for trade and so renegotiation is not required. However, one can imagine that the presence of the possibility to renegotiate the contract still influences the parties entitlements. In particular, in the presence of renegotiation opportunities nothing prevents a party from feeling entitled to an outcome outside the initial contract. In the extreme case, the ex ante contract might no longer be a reference point altogether.

To better understand these behavioral elements of renegotiation, the second central treatment that we implement in Fehr et al. (2015) allows for ex post revision of the contract. We implement renegotiation opportunities in a particular form: the buyer has the right unilaterally to replace the existing contract with a new one. Since the seller has no veto, this is actually closer to what lawyers call a "repudiation." We are aware of the fact that this may not be the most relevant form of renegotiation in reality. However, we chose this special type of renegotiation because it provides a powerful stress test for the theory: the easier it is to change a contract, the less likely it is that the contract remains a reference point.

The results of this treatment yield three interesting results. First, our data indicate that contracts continue to be reference points in the presence of renegotiation. If a buyer decides not to renegotiate a rigid contract when the seller's cost is low, this does typically not induce shading from the seller even if the competitively determined fixed price is very low. As a consequence outcomes in nonrenegotiated rigid contracts in the renegotiation treatments are virtually identical to outcomes in rigid contracts of the original experiment. This suggests contractual reference points remain relevant, because sellers do not seem to feel entitled to outcomes outside of the contract.

Second, we also identify circumstances in which a rigid contract that is renegotiated can achieve the benefits of flexibility without incurring its costs. This is the case if the parties have concluded a rigid contract and it turns out that the seller's cost is high. In these situations buyers decide to initiate renegotiation to make trade feasible in about 80% of the cases. These mutually beneficial renegotiations trigger some shading (probably because of misaligned entitlements caused by the newly introduced flexibility). Interestingly, however, outcomes in renegotiated rigid contracts and outcomes in flexible contracts do not differ significantly in the high-cost state. It seems that in this case it is possible to simply turn a rigid contract into a flexible one. Thus, buyers who choose a rigid contract not only benefit from low prices and low shading rates in the low-cost state; contract revision also allows them to realize the same profits as buyers with flexible contracts in the high-cost state.

Finally, we observe that renegotiation is problematic to the extent that it leads buyers to engage in opportunistic renegotiations. Opportunistic renegotiations are situations in which the original contract allows for efficient trade, but the buyer decides to nevertheless change the contract to his own advantage (i.e., he either lowers the fixed price in a rigid contract or decides to pay a price below the lower bound of the price range in a flexible contract). Our evidence reveals that opportunistic renegotiations are perceived as unfair and trigger lots of shading (the shading rate is close to 50% in both types of contracts). This last finding is not only consistent with the theoretical ideas in Hart (2009) but is also in line with the findings of several other experimental studies (see Hoppe and Schmitz 2011; Bartling and Schmidt 2015; Iyer and Schoar 2014).

Our findings from the renegotiation treatment suggest that renegotiation plays a richer and more accentuated role than the existing incomplete contracting literature assumes. In standard models the parties can always do better by committing not to renegotiate. However, in reality we see little evidence indicating that parties go out of their way to protect contracts against renegotiation.

Our study provides an explanation for this. If the parties keep the contract flexible from the outset (to ensure that renegotiation is not necessary), this leads to conflicting feelings of entitlement and ultimately performance shading. The parties can do better by making the contract rigid to fix expectations early on and then renegotiating if needed.

3. Conclusion

While behavioral economics has entered many microeconomic domains over the past two or three decades, the theory of the firm has—until very recently—been one of the few literatures that kept being dominated by standard economic models. Hart and Moore (2008) present a novel approach that is based on the idea that ex ante contracts provide reference points for ex post trade. The big advantage of this novel theory is that it no longer relies on the assumption that ex post trade is perfectly contractible. Unlike in the property rights approach—which is the leading formal theory of the firm in the current literature of the firm—the new theory not only makes predictions regarding the optimal choice of governance structures, but also allows to analyze the internal organization of the firm (see section IV of Hart and Moore 2008 and Hart and Holmström 2010 for first attempts in this direction).

The new theory rests on strong behavioral assumptions, but so far, the data collected in laboratory experiments has been very favorable to the theory. However, much work remains to be done. For example, there are still many open questions regarding the conditions under which contractual reference points emerge (see, e.g., Bartling and Schmidt 2015; Bartling et al. 2015, for recent work on this topic). It is also crucial to explore the extent to which the laboratory result extend to settings outside the laboratory (see, e.g., Iyer and Schoar 2012, 2014 for examples of a field experiments in this context). I am convinced that the importance of the behavioral view of the firm in the literature on organizational economics will further increase in the coming years, and that this new strand of research is bound to reveal further important and useful insights.

References

Babcock, L., and G. Loewenstein. 1997. "Explaining Bargaining Impasse: The Role of Self-Serving Biases." *Journal of Economic Perspectives* 11: 109–26.

Bartling, B., M. Grieder, and C. Zehnder. 2015. "Is Competition Fair? An Experimental Study." Working paper.

Bartling, B., and K. Schmidt. 2015. "Reference Points, Social Norms, and Fairness in Contract Renegotiations." *Journal of the European Economic Association* 13(1): 98–129.

Bolton, G. E. and A. Ockenfels. 2000. "ERC: A Theory of Equity, Reciprocity, and Competition." *American Economic Review* 90: 166–93.

Brandts, J., G. Charness, and M. Ellman. forthcoming. "Let's Talk: How Communication Affects Contract Design." *Journal of the European Economic Association.*

Camerer, C. F. 2003. *Behavioral Game Theory: Experiments in Strategic Interaction.* Princeton, NJ: Princeton University Press.

Cooper, D. J., and J. H. Kagel. Forthcoming. "Other Regarding Preferences: A Selective Survey of Experimental Results." In J. H. Kagel and A. Roth (eds.) *The Handbook of Experimental Economics,* vol. 2.

Erlei, M. and C. Reinhold. 2012. "To Choose or Not to Choose: Contracts, Reference Points, Reciprocity, and Signaling," TUC Working Papers in Economics 0007.

Fehr, E., O. Hart, and C. Zehnder. 2009. "Contracts, Reference Points, and Competition-Behavioral Effects of The Fundamental Transformation." *Journal of the European Economic Association* 7: 561–72.

Fehr, E., O. Hart, and C. Zehnder. 2011. "Contracts as Reference Points—Experimental Evidence." *American Economic Review* 101: 493–525.

Fehr, E., O. Hart, and C. Zehnder. 2015. "How Do Informal Agreements and Revision Shape Contractual Reference Points?" *Journal of the European Economic Association* 13(1): 1–28.

Fehr, E., and K. Schmidt. 2003. "Theories of Fairness and Reciprocity—Evidence and Economic Application." In M. Dewatripont, L. P. Hansen, and S. J. Turnovsky (eds.) *Advances in Economics and Econometrics—8th World Congress, Econometric Society Monographs,* 208–57. Cambridge: Cambridge University Press.

Fehr, E., and K. M. Schmidt. 1999. "A Theory of Fairness, Competition, and Cooperation." *Quarterly Journal of Economics* 114: 817–68.

Grossman, S. J., and O. D. Hart. 1986: "The Costs and Benefits of Ownership: A Theory of Vertical and Lateral Integration." *Journal of Political Economy* 94: 691–719.

Hart, O. 2008. "Economica Coase Lecture: Reference Points and the Theory of the Firm." *Economica* 75: 404–11.

Hart, O. 2009. "Hold-Up, Asset Ownership, and Reference Points." *Quarterly Journal of Economics* 124: 267–300.

Hart, O., and B. Holmstrom. 2010. "A Theory of Firm Scope." *Quarterly Journal of Economics* 125: 483–513.

Hart, O., and J. Moore. 1990. "Property Rights and the Nature of the Firm." *Journal of Political Economy* 98: 1119–58.

Hart, O., and J. Moore. 2008. "Contracts as Reference Points." *Quarterly Journal of Economics* 123: 1–48.

Hoppe, E. I., and P. W. Schmitz. 2011. "Can Contracts Solve the Hold-Up Problem? Experimental Evidence." *Games and Economic Behavior* 73: 186–99.

Iyer, R., and A. Schoar. 2012. "Incomplete Contracting: Evidence from an Audit Study." Working paper.

Iyer, R., and A. Schoar. 2014. "Contract Renegotiation and Fear of Price Gouging." Working paper.

Williamson, O. 1985. *The Economic Institutions of Capitalism.* New York: Free Press.

35

Some Recent Experimental Evidence on Contracts as Reference Points

KLAUS SCHMIDT

I would like to take the opportunity for a short personal note. In 1988, two years after Grossman and Hart (1986) and two years before Hart and Moore (1990), I was a graduate student at London School of Economics when John Moore accepted me as one of his students. This was one of the best things that ever happened to me. He introduced me to the fascinating world of incomplete contracts, mechanism design and implementation, renegotiation and the nature of the firm; my life has become much more interesting ever since.

I didn't know Oliver Hart at the time, but shortly before I finished my dissertation he called me and invited me to visit MIT and teach his course on contract theory. I was very excited but also terrified about this prospect. Fortunately I could take his contract theory course before teaching it myself, and this profoundly shaped my intellectual development. I am deeply grateful to Oliver and John for all I have learned from them.

In these few pages I would like to show you some experimental results that are closely related to Oliver and John's work on "Contracts as Reference Points." In Hart and Moore (2008) they combine contract theory with insights from behavioral economics to explain the trade-off between flexible and rigid contracts and, more generally, why contracting will not always yield ex post efficient outcomes. This new approach is controversial because it departs from the basic rationality assumption imposed by neoclassical economics. However, in Bartling and Schmidt (2015) we show that this departure is necessary for understanding some important phenomena in real-world contracting behavior that cannot be understood by a fully rational model.

Our experiments start out from the Hart and Moore (2008) idea that a contract serves as a reference point, but they look at this hypothesis from the perspective of contract renegotiation. A contract specifies the rights and obligations of the contracting parties. It may turn out that after the state of the world has materialized, the provisions of the contract are inefficient and have to be renegotiated. In this case the contract defines the threat point of the renegotiation game: if the parties do not come to an agreement, then the initial contract will be executed. According to standard contract theory, the only effect of the initial contract is to set the threat point of the renegotiation game. In contrast Hart and Moore (2008) posit that the contract also sets a reference point.

In Bartling and Schmidt (2015) we compare a situation in which an initial contract is renegotiated to a strategically equivalent bargaining situation in which no ex ante contract was written. The experiment is designed such that the threat points and the strategic situations are identical in the two situations. Thus, according to standard contract theory, there should be no difference in observed behavior. We find, however, that if there is an ex ante contract then sellers ask for mark-ups that are 36% lower in the renegotiation game than in the strategically equivalent bargaining game without an initial contract. This is consistent with the idea that contracts serve as reference points, but cannot be explained by standard contract theory.

Let me explain the experiment in some more detail. There ist a buyer and a seller who can trade a good next week. The problem is that the buyer's valuation depends on whether the good is delivered on the right day or on a wrong day. If it is delivered on the right day, then the buyer's valuation is 100. If it is delivered on a wrong day, then his valuation is only 50. The parties have to write a contract specifying a day of delivery before knowing what the right day is. However, they know that they can always renegotiate this contract.

In the experiment the parties know that Wednesday is the right day with 40% probability while each of the other four working days is the right day with 15% probability. Thus, the initial contract specified Wednesday as the day of delivery. If the seller delivers on Wednesday his cost is $c = 20$. If he delivers on some other day his cost $c \in [0, 40]$ with $E(c) = 20$.

In the "contract treatment" the seller offers a price P for delivery of the good on Wednesday to the buyer at date 0. The buyer can either accept or reject this offer. If he rejects the game ends. If he accepts the state of the world materializes at date 1 and the two parties learn what the right day of delivery is. If the right day is Wednesday the contract is executed and the game ends. If Wednesday is the wrong day, the parties learn the right day and the seller's cost of delivery on this day. In this case the seller can make a renegotiation offer at date 2: he can offer to deliver the good on the right day if the buyer pays a mark-up m in addition to the price specified in the initial contract. The good is delivered on the right day only if the buyer accepts the markup. If he does not accept it, the initial contract is executed and the good is delivered on Wednesday.

We compare the renegotiation game of the contract treatment to an identical bargaining game in the "no contract treatment." In both games the seller makes a take-it-or-leave-it offer on how to share the surplus $S = 50 - (20 - c)$. The only difference between the two situations is that there is no initial contract in the no contract treatment. Note that in the contract treatment the threat point of the renegotiation game is given by the price that the parties agreed on in the initial contract: if the buyer does not accept the renegotiation offer, then the initial contract is executed and the parties get $\underline{U}^B = 50 - P$ and $\underline{U}^S = P - 20$. For any buyer-seller pair in the contract treatment we assign these threat points exogenously to a corresponding buyer-seller pair in the no contract treatment.

For all corresponding buyer-seller pairs in the contract and the no contract treatment, the strategies available to both players and the outside options are identical. Thus, the standard model of rational, self-interested behavior predicts that we should observe the same behavior in both treatments. However, we find a large and highly significant treatment effect.

In the contract treatment sellers request a mark-up of 18.8 points on average. In contrast, in the no contract treatment they request 29.5 points! Furthermore, in the contract treatment 20% of the sellers do not request any mark-up, while this fraction drops to less than 9% in the no contract treatment.

There is also a highly significant difference in the acceptance decisions of the buyers. For any given mark-up offer of the seller the buyer is much more likely to reject in the contract treatment than in the no contract treatment. However, because mark-ups are so much lower in the contract treatment, the overall rejection rate is roughly the same.

These results show that the initial contract has an important effect that goes beyond the threat point effect. As predicted by Hart and Moore (2008) it shapes the expectations and feelings of entitlements of the parties. If there is an initial contract, then the price of the initial contract serves as an anchor, and it is difficult to move away from it. This restricts the mark-ups that the seller can charge. In contrast, if there is no initial contract, there is no such restriction and the observed mark-ups look very much like in a standard ultimatum game.

An important open question is whether it matters how the initial contract was formed. Hart and Moore (2008) argue that a contract that was written under more competitive conditions is a more objective measure of what the parties bring to the relationship and therefore a stronger reference point. Fehr, Hart, and Zehnder (2009) find some experimental evidence supporting this hypothesis. Bartling and Schmidt (2015), on the other hand, do not find that competition strengthens the reference point effect.

Our results do not provide a direct test of the Hart and Moore (2008) model. An alternative theory by Herweg and Schmidt (2015) that is based on loss aversion is also consistent with the experimental observations. Additional experiments are necessary to pin down how exactly the initial contract affects the renegotiation behavior. It is clear, however, that the rational self-interest model is not consistent with the data. If we want to understand how real contracts are written and affect behavior, we have to move toward a new behavioral contract theory.

References

Bartling, B. and K. M. Schmidt. 2015. "Reference Points, Social Norms, and Fairness in Contract Renegotiations." *Journal of the European Economic Association* 13(1): 98–129.

Fehr, E., O. Hart, and C. Zehnder. 2015. "How Do Informal Agreements and Revision Shape Contractual Reference Points?" *Journal of the European Economic Association* 13(1): 1–28.

Grossman, S. J. and O. Hart. 1986. "The Costs and Benefits of Ownership: A Theory of Vertical and Lateral Integration." *Journal of Political Economy* 94(4): 691–719.

Hart, O. and J. Moore. 1990. "Property Rights and the Nature of the Firm." *Journal of Political Economy* 98(6): 1119–58.

Hart, O. and J. Moore. 2008. "Contracts as Reference Points." *Quarterly Journal of Economics* 123: 1–48.

Herweg, F. and K. M. Schmidt. 2015. "Loss Aversion and Inefficient Renegotiation." *Review of Economic Studies* 82(1): 297–332.

36

Incomplete Contracting in the Field

ANTOINETTE SCHOAR

Thank you very much for inviting me to this conference. I want to show you some research that I've done jointly with Raj Iyer on trying to test some of these ideas of contract renegotiation in the field rather than in the lab. This is important since as you will see the world imposes constraints on you, which sometimes forces you to not be as close to the theory as you want to, but it gives you other insights. So there is a trade-off.

Obviously Christian Zehnder already set up the ideas nicely (see chapter 34), so I don't have to go through the theory anymore. What we are trying to do is understand where we actually see deviations from ex post efficient renegotiation in real-world negotiation situations. If you think about it, even anecdotally you might have run into situations where it is impossible ex post negotiate things efficiently and aggrievement in the Oliver Hart sense might be one of them, but there might be other dimensions as well. Let me show you what we find and hopefully in the discussion we can go deeper into what we think is going on.

I also want to mention that beyond aggrievement or behavioral concerns about the negotiation parties there might be issues about reputation of the seller of the buyer that play a role here for future transactions or even cultural norms that might not allow for certain types of renegotiations. Obviously I don't need to go into why you need experiments to do this.

Figure 36.1 is a photo of how my lab looks, not as clean and nice as Christian's labs probably look. I will describe the results of two audit studies that we did. Both of them are in India; the first one some of you might have seen is the study we did in the wholesale markets for pens.

These are pen and stationery wholesalers. We hired auditors who are entrepreneurs and sent them into those wholesale stores to negotiate different deals, and we placed wholesale bulk orders for pens. In the first treatment we ordered generic pens that can be sold without any loss even if the buyer reneges

Figure 36.1 Image of typical wholesale market in India

or if the buyer doesn't come back. We had a second treatment with customized pens; we put some printing that is very personal on each pen, and the salvage value of those pens is zero. This modification changes the set-up so that the buyer has a hold-up power ex post or a potential to renege on the seller.

What we wanted to see is how the contractual behavior of buyers and sellers is affected by this change in the bargaining power renegotiation ex post.

Actually I know this is late in the day, so I didn't want to show you many regressions. You can see all the results in the descriptive statistics, and what you see is that if you look at the printed pens, the customized ones, you actually see that in the price that is charged, we don't find a significant difference from the nonprinted pens. The slightly higher price for customized pens is a result of the fact that printing itself costs something.

So there is no mark-up charged for the specialized pens, but where you see all the difference happening is in the up-front percentage that the buyer has to pay, in a way the down payment—here we see the big difference. We do this all carefully with fixed effects for shopper and wholesaler in the regressions.

But if you then take a step back and ask what does this mean? On one hand, it obviously means in this market buyers and sellers take into account the customization of the good, and if it is a custom pen, the up-front payment has to be higher to protect the seller. But this is not all that is going on.

What puzzled us—if you look deeper into what we are finding, and it took some time to actually understand it—is that there actually seems to be much more going on than just customized pens needing more up-front protection. If you look at it, the down payment (or the up-front payment) that the seller makes for the buyer covers only 50% of the cost of the seller.

On top of it we actually find that these two parties spend time negotiating the price and whole deal up front. Now if you think about it in this type of environment—like in India, where there is no enforcement for these types of deals and these types of funds—that's quite bizarre because that doesn't protect the seller against renegotiation, right? I can still renegotiate unless I thought that the value of the buyer will always be so high that I don't need to.

To understand what's going on in this market, we did a survey afterward. What we found, which really stunned us, is that sellers don't seem to be worried so much about renegotiation than they are about flat-out contract breach, which to us is surprising because it seems to say that buyers don't want to engage in renegotiation, but in cases where may have a negative shock, they have no problem breaching the contract.

That might tell us something about the structure of how ex post contracts are enforced or the type of behavior that buyers might display. In particular, it seems to say that there is a lot of apprehension of engaging in renegotiation, maybe because it is socially uncomfortable. I believe what is going on in this market is that the seller is screening out people who might engage in contract breach, and that's why the seller can set the up-front price so low. The seller thus does not have to charge a higher price to screen the buyers, who are not serious about the deal, but they are not necessarily trying to protect themselves against renegotiation.

Of course that implies something about what the seller must be thinking about how buyers behave, either because of norms or some fairness consideration, or maybe the buyer might have concerns about reputation which in this situation I can't tell you about.

Now the second thing we found, which again goes into how people renegotiate, is that when we as the buyers try to renegotiate the price of the generic pens ex post, some of the sellers laughed at us and asked, "What are you doing? I can sell this outside for the normal market price, why should I even start a negotiation with you?" But for the customized pens, they were willing to negotiate and often negotiated to a price below cost. Clearly they understand that they don't have a lower outside option.

What was interesting to us is that there were many calls where there was breakdown in negotiation. On the one hand there were those who said "no way" and hung up on us or didn't even start the renegotiation. On the other hand, we found that a lot of the sellers for whom we had given an up-front payment for the generic pens said to us, "Oh! But I still have some money of yours, why don't you come and get the cash back?" So it's like they were taking the high road, even though we were reneging on our contract.

That is interesting because it tells you that there must be something, a bigger objective, being maximized by the seller than just this one-shot game where it would have been optimal to keep our money. I will give you a really brief summary of a new experiment we did because of those finding. We did a follow-up paper, again in India but this time in the market for tailors. We wanted to set up an experiment where the other side can hold us up.

Here is a situation where the seller can hold us up: we sent a customer into a situation where the customer placed an order for garments to be stitched by a tailor to be picked up 10 days later, and after one day the buyer went back and said "I have an emergency; I really need that garment to be stitched tomorrow, can you do this for me?" They signaled that they are now in an urgent situation. Surprisingly, what we found is that there is almost no renegotiation.

So we have two treatments: we call the first in-between urgency, we come in the middle and we say we have an emergency. What we found is that in about 40% of the cases the tailor said, "Fine, I'll do it for you," but then 60% of the case they declined and said they are too busy. They even offered to give the cloth back to customer.

Now let me show you what we think is really interesting. We did a second treatment where we had the same story I just told you and the buyer says "What if I give you twice the price," so it's the buyer who initiates the renegotiation. What we found is that in 36% of the cases, the tailor accepts. In fact often the tailor says, "I don't need double the price, just give me 50% more." But why is that interesting? The tailor is willing to forgo ex post efficient renegotiation, but they are willing to accept if the buyer offers the higher price. Since this all randomized, it can't be selection or anything like that.

To me that means that it's the seller's concern about not breaking fairness norms or reputation issues that is preventing them from initiating an efficient renegotiation. These types of considerations and maybe worry about agrievement are preventing efficient renegotiation ex post. Obviously there's still a lot to do, and we're going to hear more of what has been done from Klaus Schmidt (see chapter 35).

INDEX

Note: Figures and tables are shown by f and t following the page number.